GHOSTS OF THE ETO

GHOSTS OF THE ETO

AMERICAN TACTICAL DECEPTION UNITS IN THE EUROPEAN THEATER 1944–1945

Jonathan Gawne

CASEMATE

Philadelphia & Oxford

Military Map Symbols

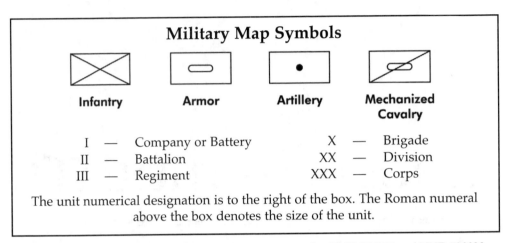

| Infantry | Armor | Artillery | Mechanized Cavalry |

I	—	Company or Battery	X	—	Brigade
II	—	Battalion	XX	—	Division
III	—	Regiment	XXX	—	Corps

The unit numerical designation is to the right of the box. The Roman numeral above the box denotes the size of the unit.

Author's note: All materials declassified under program number NND 735017 and NND 730029.
Photo Credits: Unless otherwise noted all photos are from the U.S. Army.

Published in the United States of America and Great Britain in 2014 by
CASEMATE PUBLISHERS
908 Darby Road, Havertown, PA 19083 &
10 Hythe Bridge Street, Oxford, OX1 2EW

ISBN 978-1-61200-250-7
Digital Edition: ISBN 978-1-93514-992-7

Cataloging-in-publication data is available from the Library of Congress
and the British Library.

10 9 8 7 6 5 4 3 2

Printed and bound in the United States of America.

For a complete list of Casemate titles please contact:

CASEMATE PUBLISHERS (US)
Telephone (610) 853-9131, Fax (610) 853-9146
E-mail: casemate@casematepublishing.com

CASEMATE PUBLISHERS (UK)
Telephone (01865) 241249, Fax (01865) 794449
E-mail: casemate-uk@casematepublishing.co.uk

Table of Contents

Foreword

It is a great pleasure and a distinct honor to provide this contribution to what I consider the finest work yet written on the 23rd Headquarters Special Troops. It documents the story of the first and possibly only army unit organized for tactical deception. This story is a treasure for history and for the future.

What was the 23rd?

Army Material Systems Analysis at Aberdeen Proving Ground once stated: "The 23rd Headquarters was truly an unorthodox unit. Never before had there been such a unit, one developed specifically for tactical deception. During the brief period the unit spent in action, it served with more armies and corps than any other unit. It also perhaps operated over a larger area, serving in France, Belgium, Holland, Luxembourg, and Germany. Rarely, if ever, has there existed a group of so few men which had so great an influence on the outcome of a major military campaign."

Assembling the true story of the 23rd was not easy and required years of painstaking research. The operations of the 23rd were wrapped in secrecy. We used oral orders instead of written ones; the detachments were often fragmented; and even personnel deployed in operations remained uninformed as to the big picture. After reaching Metz, the pace became very hectic. Diaries were prohibited. Over half a century of being classified did not help our memories. At a reunion in Erie, Pennsylvania, in 1997, Congressman Phillip English said, "I can't believe that you men were drafted, served in this unit, were discharged and told to shut up—and you did!"

Because our peacetime army had paid no attention to deception, the CO and staff of the 23rd faced an unknown subject without any help from manuals, guidance, or orders. As West Point officers, drilled in the code of "Duty, honor, country," we had a hard time thinking in terms of deception. After all, our training had been based on trust and integrity. There was no advance understanding of how to deploy the units under the 23rd, although the men were ready and capable. We learned on the job, and we learned from gifted and talented civilian soldiers like Captain Frederick E. Fox, who came from a civilian career in show business. Fox's feeling was, "You old fuddy-duddies stand aside because we are going to be a traveling road show with impersonations and imitations of units, generals, and colonels, even if it violates your dumb army regulations."

The greatest assets of the unit were the intelligent civilian soldiers specially screened for this assignment. Their past careers and interests in art, design, theater, acting, radio, electronics, and other fields provided a valuable and pertinent background for the imitation of real units. Each Army unit (up to and including a 15,000-man division) has a distinct character, personality and atmosphere. We developed the term "special effects" to denote and describe the use of shoulder patches, bumper markings, command post signs, road signs, and other equipment useful to depict a certain unit with its specific atmosphere. The short life of the 23rd (18 months, from 20 Jan. 1944 to Aug. 1945), the secrecy, and the concentrated activity mitigated against providing awards and decorations for the men. It was a command failure that these soldiers did not receive the recognition they deserved for their considerable contributions to our country.

What did we learn from our wartime experiences?

Cover and Deception:

Cover is making the enemy believe that our hostile actions are harmless. Deception is seeking to make the enemy do something, or do nothing, to our advantage.

And the simple thinking for portrayal of a unit:

A. Make the enemy believe that a real unit is in a false LOCATION

B. Make the enemy believe that a real unit has false STRENGTH

C. Gain advantage by our choice of the TIME

The means and methods of deception can be grouped under such headings as visual, communications, sonic, radio, and even smell.

Implementation is the most important and difficult part of any deceptive operation. It also requires the most work. An analogy might be a trapper who wishes to catch a fox. First he must outwit the clever fox! We would like to know each and every means the enemy uses in order to gather information, but we are never certain or sure. We can select a means for passing false information but we must do it in a manner that the enemy will not suspect it is false. The more channels we use to pass this information, the better. An enemy collects bits of information from many sources and collates the bits to produce intelligence.

Deception is called an art of warfare; one that deals with the minds of the enemy. There are no guarantees. We do the best we can with estimates, guesses, hope, luck, evaluations, risks, and just plain ordinary guts. Deception should help to gain victories but it must not hurt. We live in a changing world and what worked before in tactical deception may not work now. A satellite can now read a motor vehicle license plate from space, so we must be ready to outsmart it by turning the license on edge or displaying a false license. For every new means of gathering information there is also a new avenue for passing false information.

Our many years of silence on deception have denigrated this age-old art of warfare. In past ages there was the horse of Troy in 1200 B.C., the battle of Hastings in 1066 A.D., and our own Revolutionary War, in which George Rogers Clark in 1779 opened the northwest territories for the U.S. by deception, preventing the present border of Canada from being south of Chicago.

We need continuous thinking (not silence) on deception. And we need teaching in our service schools and funds for research and development. Let us not repeat the mistakes of the past. We have both the know-how and the knowledge of tactical deception. Let's use it, not lose it.

"Let's Roll."

Clifford G. Simenson,
Colonel USA, Ret.
Wartime S-3, 23rd Special Troops

"Even after the finish of the European war it will be undesirable to publish details of deception practiced on the Germans by the Allies."

—*General A. T. Jones, British Joint Staff Mission*

Top left: Authorized insignia of the Army Experimental Station (AES)
Top right: Proposed, but never authorized or manufactured insignia for the 23rd Special Troops
Bottom: Unauthorized insignia thought to be used by the 23rd Special Troops when reactivated in 1947

Preface

I have learned from writing this book that no matter how much you think you know about a subject, or how much has been written about it, there is always a story left untold. You just have to dig a little deeper. Having spent most of my adult life studying the American Army in World War II, I am currently amazed at how the variety of innovative operations involving the 23rd Special Troops have remained unknown. For more than one reason it is fitting to describe these soldiers—practiced in the art of deception—as "The Ghosts of the ETO."

It was an unusual coincidence that led me to their story. My father had served in the 28th Infantry Regiment in WWII. By chance I ran into Mike Williams who had served in the same unit during the 1960s. In passing, he mentioned that his father had commanded a special unit in WWII that had played recordings off the backs of half-tracks.

Of course I, who had read just about everything ever written on the U.S. Army in WWII, was at first skeptical. All too often I had heard tall tales from families about what a relative had done in the war. But Mike seemed to know what he was talking about and urged me to contact one of his father's former platoon leaders in the 23rd Special Troops, "Big John" Walker. Nervously (and I have to admit that no matter how many times I call veterans I am always nervous) I called John, and upon hearing his story decided there was something there worth pursuing.

John Walker sent me, in turn, to Cliff Simenson—former S-3 of the 23rd—who continues to awe me by casually mentioning such things as how he had worked with legendary men like General Leslie McNair. Simenson also related the story of how he wrote the minority opinion arguing against motorized infantry divisions in 1942, prompting a decision that eventually caused trucks to be pooled at corps level for a more streamlined and effective fighting force.

I happened to be heading to the National Archives to work on a book about the Brittany Campaign, and while there spent my extra time looking for records of the 23rd. Finding some of the unit records, I was amazed at how closely they fit what I had been told conversationally by Simenson and Walker. I decided to investigate further.

A visit to the 2000 reunion of the 23rd Special Troops and the Army Experimental Station (AES) at Watertown, New York, put me in contact with a good number of men from the various deception units. During that reunion we visited their former base of operations at Fort Drum (then Pine Camp). I was privileged to walk around the former AES compound with some of the men who trained there, and later was finally able to meet Cliff Simenson in person as we entered the hangar where they had done all their work on the sonic half-tracks. From Roy Tucker I learned about the 3133rd in Italy, and Laura Lynn Scharer explained her research into the Army Experimental Station.

In talking with the deception vets, many of them told me how they had developed the unit totally from scratch. There were no records of other deception units, no manuals or textbooks to work from. One of the vets remarked that if they had only had access to the history of a similar unit when they were starting, it would have made their lives a lot easier. It seemed I was in the unique position of having the background on the U.S. Army necessary to tell this story, a solid track record in military research, and access to a fair number of veterans from the unit. I promised John Walker and Cliff Simenson I'd write their story, and here it is.

So on one hand, this book should serve as an archive of material on what seems to be the first deception unit in the U.S. Army. With luck, members of today's armed forces will read it and not only develop their own ideas about the use of deception, but become more aware of what might be used against them in time of war. Deception can be a very powerful tool in combat, and it's a lot better to learn from those who have gone before then to try to reinvent the wheel.

The other value of this book is historical. Until now most books on the war have been written without mention of the deception troops at all. I dare say that no one should attempt to write about the ETO in the future without at least being aware of the operations of the 23rd and 3133rd. Some of their operations may have had little effect on the battlefield, but you can no longer fully examine those campaigns without taking into consideration the 23rd's activities. Even if one of their operations did not totally fool the Germans, it may have caused a delay, while more information was gathered, during a critical period.

There are two major events in which the 23rd may well have altered the course of the war. The first was early in the campaign when they diverted German attention to Brittany, allowing Patton's forces to encircle the German Army in France. This is an area in which I hope someone (with the ability to delve into German intelligence reports) investigates further. The second major operation was at the Rhine. The Ninth Army commander, General Simpson, maintained that, thanks to the efforts of the 23rd, American lives were saved. One number given was as many as fifteen thousand lives. That's a lot of men, and a lot of families that did not have to receive that dreaded telegram.

For this book I've spoken to a great many former members of these units (and their wives and children), but would like to acknowledge a few in particular. John Walker and Cliff Simenson played a major role. George Rebh dug some invaluable documents out of a footlocker. George Martin had some wonderful photographs. Also thanks to Gil Seltzer, Bob Conrad, Dick Syracuse, Walter Manser, Roy Tucker for his 3133rd work, and Paul Sarber for information on the still mysterious 3103rd Signal Service Company.

Thanks also to David Farnsworth, Phil Charbonnier, Steve West, Dennis Moore, and Jonathan Lewis for continuous encouragement. The maps are based on those in the Fox history, and John McClain did a wonderful job on them. Special thanks go to Roy Eichhorn, who helped a lot more than he realizes. And most of all I'd like to acknowledge my wife Deirdre, without whose help and understanding this book could not have been done.

After literally hundreds of historians have poured over the records of the war, it still astounds me that the 23rd Special Troops have been overlooked for so long. However, when I wrote a book about D-day I was likewise amazed to find wonderful material that no one else had previously tapped into. It just goes to show that there is a lot that happened during the war that we still don't know.

Although it has taken me many years, I do not consider this volume to be the final story of the 23rd. Too many files are missing from the National Archives, and I have heard too many rumors about undocumented aspects of deception in WWII for all of them to be untrue. I have been told of deception files bearing such names as Operation ARDENNES and Operation OMEGA, which are still classified. I have not been able to confirm some of the stories I have been told by veterans, and due to the nature of the subject I feel such events need hard confirmation such as period paperwork or an unrelated witness, before they can be described.

I hope that with the publication of this book more information will come out of the woodwork in order to help us understand the role of tactical deception in WWII. Anyone with further information is invited to contact me at P.O. Box 2925, Framingham, MA 01703.

A note on unit designations. They follow the pattern of A/603rd indicating Company A of the 603rd Battalion, or 2/28th, indicating the second battalion of the 28th Regiment. Corps are in Roman numerals, divisions in Arabic numerals, and armies are spelled out.

As an unknown historian of the 406th Combat Engineer Company wrote in its unit history, the men I write about here were "Engineers of a democratic nation's great trickery that brought about a speedier, less costly victory over the haughty supermen."

Chapter 1

Military Deception

Deception is possibly the second oldest maneuver in battle. As soon as man learned how to punch, he next learned how to feint and thus deceive his opponent about his intentions. It is not surprising that governments like to keep their means of deception in modern warfare secret, but it is surprising that some of the most unusual deceptions performed in World War II have not only been ignored, but also seemingly forgotten by the army that originally developed them.

Deception in warfare has been practiced throughout history. The most famous example is the Trojan Horse, but the ancient world is filled with other cases. When Hannibal had to cross some mountains he sent a column of oxen through a different pass than the one he planned to use. He tied torches to their horns so that at night they looked like a moving body of men. His enemy moved to defend that pass while Hannibal slipped through the mountains from another direction. The writings of Julius Caesar are filled with examples of deception. In his book *The Gallic Wars*, Caesar instructed his men to build encampments smaller than normal to deceive the enemy about their true numbers. On another occasion, he instructed his men to appear to be tired and worn out, thus purposely drawing an enemy attack.

During the American Revolution, the colonists made frequent use of deception to compensate for their weak numbers and lack of weapons. General Washington allowed phony documents to be captured, constructed decoy installations, and planted information with known enemy agents. Large quantities of supplies were purchased in specific locations to make the British think a Colonial army was massing in that area. Carefully coached deserters fed the British false information on American plans. In the campaign outside Philadelphia, Washington made the British think his 3,000-man army was 40,000 strong. At Boston, he forced the British to withdraw under threat of bombardment, from guns that were seriously short of ammunition.[1]

During the American Civil War, both sides realized they were able to read the other's semaphore signals. On at least a few occasions false signals were sent, designed to be intercepted and read by the enemy. Before the Seven Days battle in 1862, the South planted false information on a deserter sent over to the North. During the Antietam campaign later that year, General McClellan captured the vital Southern documents known as Special Order 191. These described Confederate plans in great detail, but they were not acted upon because the information was thought to be another ruse. At various times, both sides attempted to deceive the enemy with wooden dummy artillery known as "Quaker cannon."[2]

During the First World War, camouflage developed into a high art. Dummy trenches and positions were constructed to fool aerial reconnaissance. Dummy soldiers were created to draw the fire of enemy snipers, thus allowing the snipers to be located. On the oceans, "Q" ships resembling unarmed merchant ships took a toll on German submarines when their hidden guns suddenly opened fire. The letter "Q" thus became a code for a decoy or dummy object. Dummy airstrips would later be known as "Q-strips" and false lighting arrangements as "Q-lights."

One of the better-known deception operations in WWI took place in the Middle East. An intelligence officer appeared to drop a dispatch case containing phony maps and orders. The Turks, upon intercepting messages indicating that the careless officer was to be court-martialed for losing the plans, decided that the documents were real, and thus were misled about the real direction of a British attack.[3]

The story of deception in World War II has, until now, been largely that of strategic deception. The most commonly mentioned operation is FORTITUDE, the Allied plan to deceive the Germans about the location and date of the Allied landing in Normandy. Strategic deception involves attempting to fool the enemy on a grand scale. Tricking the Germans into thinking you will invade Norway or Greece when your real target is France is a strategic deception. Tactical deception concerns events that take place in a more localized area—generally within the same country or within the boundaries of one army or army group. Tactical deceptions in WWII generally involved divisional or regimental sized units, but they could also involve units as large as an entire corps, or down to the level of an individual battalion or company.

Tactical and strategic deceptions also differ in the amount of time involved. Typically, a tactical deception operation will last from a few hours to, at the extreme, a few weeks. The key is to fool the local enemy commander into delaying a decision long enough to effect his final plans. A strategic operation can take place over a matter of months or even years, the object being to compel the enemy into a decision that will in turn take a long time to reverse (such as placing troops in Norway rather than France).

At some point the lines between tactical and strategic deception blur, and many operations contain elements of both. Many deception operations have one name for the overall plan, then many different sub-codenames for each segment. FORTITUDE was actually part of Operation BODYGUARD, the overall plan to conceal preparations for the invasion of France from German eyes. FORTITUDE itself had many components: FORTITUDE NORTH threatened a landing in Norway; FORTITUDE SOUTH pointed to a landing in France; COPPERHEAD involved sending a double of General Montgomery to Gibraltar to draw attention away from England; QUICKSILVER I concerned the imaginary units preparing for D-day; QUICKSILVER II covered the radio deception; QUICKSILVER III the decoy landing craft; QUICKSILVER IV and V the deceptive bombing campaigns; and QUICKSILVER VI the decoy port lights along the southern coast. Operations TROLLEYCAR and TWEEZER dealt with the movements of both imaginary and genuine formations in the UK.

No history of deception in WWII would be complete without mentioning the work of British magician Jasper Maskelyne. He claimed credit for advancing deception by bringing the practice of stage magic to the military. The British emphasis on deception, however, started well before him, in the North African desert when General Wavell established the deception unit "A-Force." According to other memoirs of the period, Maskelyne's contribution to deception was in itself a deception. His principal function in the British Army was developing materials for MI9 to help Allied POWs escape German hands, as well as lecturing on escape and evasion.[4] A popular and semi-fictional account of Maskelyne's wartime effort gives the magician far greater credit for deception than he deserves.[5] His main contribution to deception was that many British officers increased their faith in this unorthodox field of operations only because the well-known, semi-miraculous Maskelyne was supposedly involved in it.

The first British deception unit, "A-Force," was organized in 1940 under the command of Brigadier Dudley Clarke.[6] Outnumbered and out-gunned, the British were desperate to find a way to make their small forces appear more numerous and powerful. The desert is a perfect environment for deception. With so few obstructions, decoy vehicles and dummy installations can be seen for a great distance. A-Force created not only decoy tanks, but also constructed covers for genuine tanks that made them appear to be trucks. These covers were known as "sun shields."

A-Force's Operation BERTRAM was a surprisingly successful attempt to mask General Montgomery's planned build-up before the battle of El Alamein in late 1942. It involved many different forms of deception, including not only decoy tanks, but also dummy pipelines and supply dumps. When Montgomery attacked on 23 October, the Germans were taken completely by surprise, having assumed his attack would come from a different location sometime in November.

One of the more unusual tricks performed in the desert was to disable captured German munitions, then place false notes in them claiming it was the work of anti-German resistance workers in the munitions factories. The munitions were carefully returned to German lines, in hopes that German soldiers would suffer a loss of morale after finding that their supplies had been sabotaged at home. Carefully crafted rumors were disseminated about these sabotaged munitions, and even today it is accepted as fact by many that forced laborers in Germany took the risk of not only sabotaging equipment, but of including notes indicating they had done so.[7]

To coordinate the various deception operations underway around the world, the British formed the London Controlling Section (LCS). The LCS was to make sure that no attempt at deception accidentally conflicted with another deception, or even worse, with a genuine operation. When America entered the war, the British pressed to have the LCS be allowed to govern operations for all the Allies, but the Americans developed their own group to oversee deception. Formed in August 1942, it was initially known as the Joint Security Committee, but the name was later changed to Joint Security Control (JSC).

The duty of the JSC was twofold:

1. Preventing information of military value from falling into the hands of the enemy.
2. Timing the implementation of those portions of cover and deception plans that had to be performed by military and non-military agencies in the United States.

The JSC was composed of three general officers (one each from the army, air force, and navy), each with a colonel (or navy captain) as his assistant. They were allowed to organize their own staff of enlisted men as they felt necessary. Sadly, many of the records of the JSC dealing with deception do not seem to be included in the National Archives, and rumor indicates they may be in the hands of the CIA.

The British were convinced that they should remain the supreme authority on deception, and made a few attempts to bring the JSC underneath their command. At the end of 1943 the British released a report claiming that American deception was poorly organized, whereas the British had everything running smoothly.[8] The ploy did not work, yet while the American and British deception headquarters remained separate entities, they did agree to work closely together.

There were many Allied strategic deceptions during WWII, mostly run by the British, and far more than can be mentioned in this book. A number were used to divert attention from Operation TORCH, the 1942 invasion of North Africa. Operation KENNECOTT pointed to a landing in Greece; Operation SOLO indicated Norway was the target; and Operation OVERTHROW pointed to an invasion of France. The Americans ran Operation SWEATER, which claimed that their troops, actually destined for Africa, were merely being sent to train in Haiti.[9] Operation COCKADE included plans to make the Germans think there were 570,000 Americans in England by August 1943, when in fact there were only 330,000. It also indicated a planned landing in 1943 of British troops in Normandy (STARKEY), in Norway (TINDALL), and of American troops in Brittany (WADHAM). To demonstrate that the Americans were interested in the Brittany region, Operation POUND had the 29th Ranger Battalion raid an island near the port of Brest, with specific instructions to leave behind American equipment for the Germans to find.[10]

Almost every soldier in WWII can recall a time when rumors of his unit shipping out to a cold (or warm) climate were suddenly found to be false. Specialty clothing, supposedly to be used in a cold environment, was rapidly taken back and the unit sailed instead for the tropics. Phrasebooks in Japanese were distributed to troops, who instead set off the following week for Italy. Of course, as veterans will also attest, some of these may have been true military blunders, but the majority were parts of schemes to confuse the enemy as to the final destination of the unit in question.

One of the more famous deception operations of the war has become known as "the man who never was." As part of Operation MINCEMEAT, a dead body was dressed as a British officer, chained to a briefcase containing (bogus) top-secret documents, and dispatched from a submarine to float onto a Spanish beach. The Spanish allowed German intelligence to copy the documents, which indicated that the next Allied invasion would be aimed at Sardinia, not the genuine target of Sicily. The Germans fell for the deception and failed to reinforce Sicily prior to the 1943 invasion.[11]

The Italian front had its own share of deception operations, not all successful. The Germans realized Operation VENDETTA was a deception because there were far too many reports pointing to an upcoming amphibious landing, yet there were not enough landing craft in the Mediterranean to support one. Operation CHETTYFORD attempted to distract the Germans from the Anzio landing, but much of it went unnoticed due to a lack of German aerial reconnaissance. However, decoy tanks and dummy radio traffic did manage to pin down two of Kesselring's best divisions until the Anzio beachhead was established.[12]

There were a number of small feints as the Allies moved up the Italian peninsula. Operation ZEPPELIN tried to make the Germans believe that the American Seventh Army would attack from Italy over to the Dalmatian Coast. This was part of the strategic operation to keep German reserves in France from responding to Operation OVERLORD. Operation NUTON helped pin down German reserves so that the Cassino line could be broken. Operation OTTRINGTON was unusual, consisting of an attempt to portray a badly executed deception and then attack from where the Germans had spotted dummy formations. It was found to be difficult to develop a deception that could be seen through, but not appear as if that was actually what the Allies had intended.[13]

When General Wavell was posted to the Far East, he brought with him the nucleus of a small deception unit. Initially named "D Division," it later became known as "Force 456." This unit sent false information to the Japanese through Chinese sources who were all too eager to sell intelligence to the Japanese. These red herrings were code-named "Purple Whales," and included a phony dispatch case full of secret documents left in a wrecked car. Another time a corpse was dropped behind Japanese lines equipped to appear as an agent with a faulty parachute. The British hoped that the Japanese would assume the agent's identity and send false information by way of his radio, but nothing came of it.[14]

General Slim was able to make good use of tactical deception in his Burma campaign. Operation CLOAK indicated his objective was Mandalay, while he was actually headed for another point seventy miles to the south.[15] However, deception in the Pacific was not as successful as in Europe because the Japanese combat leaders paid little attention to their own intelligence branches. One deceptionist in the Pacific said, "We could get the Japs to swallow the most outrageous and implausible fabrications, but the operational staffs refused to pay the slightest attention to them."[16]

The Americans undertook a few deception operations in the Pacific. These mainly involved hiding the locations of naval or air forces. Operation WEDLOCK in 1944 created a notional force in the northern Pacific that appeared ready to invade the Kurile Islands. This pinned down Japanese troops and equipment in an area the Americans had no intention of attacking.[17] To encourage the Pacific commanders to use deception techniques, the JSC brought teams of three officers (one each from the army, air force, and navy) to the States for a month of training. These teams were then sent back to the major Pacific commands to help spread the concept of deception. Admiral Nimitz, in the Central Pacific, showed enthusiasm for deception and encouraged it. General MacArthur, in the Southern Pacific, did not welcome the outsiders to his command. His headquarters felt they already had a grasp of deception principles and required no outside assistance. Eventually, the JSC team did help develop plans for the invasion of Luzon. The third major command in the Pacific, the CBI (China, Burma, India), did not encourage the deception planners. Part of this was because the region was shared with British forces, who felt they had more experience in such matters and did not want to cooperate with the Americans until near the end of the war.[18]

To beef up British naval strength in the East, an old disarmed battleship, HMS *Centurion*, was visually modified to appear as the new and heavily armed HMS *Anson*, and sent off to an Indian port. Much of British naval deception exaggerated the number of major ships in service, or made vessels under construction appear to be operational by having them send out false radio messages. Operation BIJOU helped keep Japanese subs from patrolling the East African Coast by portraying the aircraft carrier HMS *Indefatigable* cruising the area, months before she had been finished.[19] Near England, the Royal Navy was also able to manipulate the operational areas of the German submarine service with planned leaks about new antisubmarine weapons and phony minefields.[20]

The most important use of strategic deception in WWII was probably Operation FORTITUDE. This was the attempt to deceive the Germans as to the actual location and date of the main invasion of France. One of the key factors in this deception was that the British had managed to take control of most German agents in England. The turned spies then told German intelligence only what the British wanted them to hear, thus painting whatever picture of troop dispositions the British desired. It is generally thought that the British had captured or controlled all German agents in England; however, it is claimed that at least one, codenamed DRUID, remained on the loose and continued to send correct reports to the Germans.[21]

Leaking information through turned enemy agents was known as sending it by "special means." The use of co-opted German agents to convey doctored intelligence to the Wehrmacht was one of the more important aspects of strategic deception in WWII. German reconnaissance aircraft could spot a build-up of troops or a flotilla of landing craft, but when an agent on the ground corroborated the information it simply had to be true. Although this concept of using turned spies to assist in deception operations is best known in conjunction with the "XX Committee" in England, it actually originated with Dudley Clarke's A-Force in North Africa.

The basis of FORTITUDE, normally overlooked by most historians, is that it was constructed on a bogus order of battle begun in 1940 by Dudley Clarke in the desert. Clarke realized that once a military intelligence agency identifies an enemy unit, it would go to great pains to figure out its current location—assuming that established units do not just disappear. Once a unit is thought to exist, only the slightest shred of evidence is needed to convince the enemy as to its current location. Clarke spent the early years of the war carefully building up the background of three dummy British Armies (the Ninth, Tenth, and Twelfth). The Germans became convinced these were genuine units. When they disappeared from known locations, German intelligence became desperate to find where they had gone. A few small hints of a new location (especially where the Germans already thought they were likely to go), and the Germans would readily accept it.

This bogus order of battle was formed by taking a small organization—such as a regional administrative headquarters, training school, or supply depot—and renaming it a battalion, regiment, or brigade. Thus the Mosul Sub-area Command became the 2nd Indian Division. Bogus markings and insignia were used by this inflated unit until its false identity became known in the area. Shifting units and forming new ones helped build up the phony strength. When a unit was confirmed as a corps headquarters, and a few others in the area were found to be corps support elements, the enemy would find it easy to believe that the rest of the corps must be in the region.

The importance of the formation of a bogus order of battle cannot be understated. The turned German spies were important, but without these dummy units firmly established in the minds of the German military, FORTITUDE would have been much harder to pull off. Without a history, developed over a period of time, showing the Allies developing a greater number of units than they actually had, the Germans could not have been as surprised by a large number of men appearing out of nowhere from an unexpected location. The success of the war's most important strategic deception thus relied much on the earlier planning and groundwork laid down by Dudley Clarke. Such other operations as MINCEMEAT would have been much harder to execute had not the Germans thought a far greater Allied force existed than there really was (thanks to the bogus order of battle).

Operation FORTITUDE still remains misunderstood by many historians. Only part of it was to mislead the Germans as to the exact location and time of the Normandy invasion. It did far more. For weeks after D-day, FORTITUDE continued to pin down vitally needed German reinforcements at Calais by making the Germans think another, larger invasion was yet to come in that sector. Had the Germans realized the Normandy invasion was the main effort and thrown everything they had against it, they may well have been able to drive the Allies back into the sea.[22]

Although it is impossible to watch a documentary on D-day without the obligatory shot of inflatable tanks being flipped over, there is no evidence that such decoys were used in FORTITUDE. The British government has at last declassified the final report on the operation,[23] in which the official historian writes, "The only use FORTITUDE made of special equipment was in the employment of dummy landing craft."[24] The only decoys mentioned in the plan were 660 inflatable landing craft (known as "big bobs"), dummy airstrips and aircraft (fifty-six squadrons worth), and "Q-lights" (phony lighting set up along the coast to simulate the nighttime loading of men into landing craft). Rubber dummies would not have been needed when the areas containing the bogus units already had massive supply dumps of equipment and vehicles ready to be shipped to France when needed. It may have been easier in the postwar era to credit the deception to rubber decoys, rather than for the British to explain how they had successfully turned German agents.

Other deception operations tied to the invasion of Normandy were GLIMMER and TAXABLE. These were air and naval operations designed to fool German radar into thinking an invasion fleet was heading for the Calais area. With such operations, deception was entering the electronic age. Operation TITANIC involved the dropping of small burlap dummy parachutists (codenamed "Ruperts" or "Paragons") to confuse the Germans as to the locations of the actual landing zones. A handful of British paratroopers jumped amidst the

The dummy paratroops were dropped from aircraft along with a handful of genuine British troopers with sound playback equipment to add to the atmosphere. Initially a number of such decoy paratroop drops were planned for D-day, but the operation was scaled back to only two such actions. These two drops took place southeast of Insigny and east of La Havre.

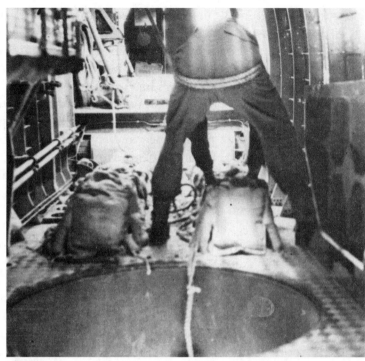

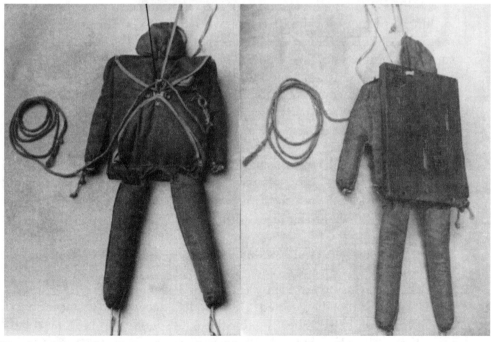

The "Device, Camouflage, Number 15," or "dummy paratroop," was used as part of Operation TITANIC. These small burlap dummies were dropped over Normandy to simulate a paratroop assault and divert German attention from the genuine drop zones. They were also known as "Ruperts" or "Paragons."

dummies to play phonograph recordings of battle noises, while some of the dummies were rigged with small explosive devices to simulate gunfire. TITAN-TIC was scaled back at the last minute to only two drops, each with two parties of five genuine paratroopers and five hundred dummies, but the story of these dummy paratroopers has taken on a life of its own.

No mention of FORTITUDE would be complete without considering a new theory on the subject. There are some indications that the Abwehr, the German military intelligence agency, had a number of anti-Hitler officers within its ranks. Not only does it seem probable that the one-time head of the Abwehr, Admiral Canaris, may have helped the Allies' war effort by providing them useful information, but he may have also distorted German intelligence reports in the Allies' favor. Canaris was dismissed from the Abwehr in February 1944 (and hanged by the Nazis in April 1945), but evidence has come to light that his work may have been carried on by others.[25]

Colonel Alexia Von Roenne of the Abwehr sorted and evaluated all information coming into that agency regarding enemy armies and intentions in Western Europe. He had the key position when it came to issuing reports on what to expect from Allied forces based in England. There is some good evidence that he had discovered the FORTITUDE deception, but reported the inflated troop numbers and locations opposite Calais for an unknown reason. One possibility is that as a loyal but anti-Nazi German he wanted the Allies to land in Europe so they, not the Russians, would get to Berlin first.[26] For whatever reason, he appears to have knowingly passed on the false estimates to his superiors. Von Roenne was eventually arrested during the investigation of the assassination attempt against Hitler in July 1944. On 11 October the colonel was hanged as a co-conspirator. There is a very good possibility that other men in the Abwehr actually saw through the FORTITUDE deception, but chose for political reasons to hide the truth from Hitler and his high command.[27]

On 1 September 1944, a tremendous breach of security occurred when reporter Hanson Baldwin was allowed to publish a two-column article in the *New York Times* mentioning the use of deception in the invasion of France. The members of the JSC were horrified and the British were swift to complain. General A. T. Jones of the British Joint Staff Mission in Washington wrote a scathing letter to the JSC stating, "even after the finish of the European war it will be undesirable to publish details of deception practiced on the Germans by the Allies."[28]

Once the Allies were firmly established in France, the time for strategic deception in Europe had ended. Then tactical deception was needed to defeat the Germans in battle. Shortly after the Allies landed in Normandy, the first operation of the 23rd Special Troops took place. This unit took part in over twenty major operations. It also took part in a number of other less notable missions, many of which are hardly mentioned in the unit files. A propaganda broadcast at St. Malo and a detachment of dummy artillery sent to

Cherbourg, for example, are only casually mentioned in the unit records. Following on the success of the 23rd in Northern Europe, a second sonic deception unit, the 3133rd Signal Service Company, was sent into Italy. It took part in only two operations before the war ended.

With the collapse of Nazi Germany, plans got underway for the deception troops to be redeployed for the invasion of Japan. After all, these deception units had honed their techniques and had proven their usefulness on the battlefield. Men and equipment were sent to the Army Experimental Station at Pine Camp, New York. When Japan surrendered, however, the troops packed up their equipment, sent it off for storage, and went home. Before they left they were told to not talk about their wartime activities for at least fifty years.

Some took this order to heart and took the secret to their graves. Others stayed in the army and pressed for continued research into methods of military deception. They were hampered by the fact that their wartime exploits were still classified, so they could not tell their comrades that not only was tactical deception feasible, but they had been part of an amazing unit that had consistently fooled the Germans during the war. Immediately after WWII, the threat of Soviet Russia grew. It became important to keep deception methods secret in case they someday needed to be used against this new enemy.

There is a massive body of knowledge about WWII in Europe, a small amount on Allied strategic deception, but next to nothing on the tactical deceptions performed by special units under the very noses of the Germans. Some of the records have been declassified, the fifty-year period of silence has come and gone, and the few remaining men of the deception units have started to come forward. There are only a handful of men from these remarkable units alive today, but one of their fondest wishes is that their story be told. Not for their own glory, but because they know firsthand that battlefield deception can save lives.

Chapter 2

Developments in the United States

There is no record of precisely when, or exactly who in the U.S. Army decided a tactical deception unit was needed. The idea probably sprang from reports of British deceptions in the North African desert in 1942. It was hard to ignore that the British had done something unusual. Winston Churchill publicly stated in the House of Commons, "By a marvelous system of camouflage, a complete tactical surprise was achieved in the desert."[1] American military observers investigated what the British were doing along the lines of deception and experimented with similar techniques in Tunisia. A small deception operation allowed the U.S. 1st Armored Division to strike the Germans fifty miles south of Medjez el Bab when the German intelligence service thought the unit was fifteen miles farther to the west.

Operation COCKADE (run by the British) failed to convince the Germans that the Allies would invade France in 1943 because there weren't enough troops in England to support such a claim. As a result of the failure, General Jake Devers, commander of the Headquarters of the American Army in Europe (called ETOUSA at the time), appointed a permanent cover and deception officer for the ETO.[2] Colonel William "Billy" Harris was appointed to this position, and his first task was to issue a report on deception. This was suspiciously close to the time when the British were attempting to take over all deception operations.

Harris's report called for the formation of a deception unit "capable of simulating one corps, consisting of one infantry division and one armored division, by means of prefabricated portable dummies together with the appropriate radio communications."[3] When General Omar Bradley arrived in the European theater to command the First Army (the only American army in England at the time) he discussed the matter with Devers and the theater G-3, General Daniel Noce. As a result of that discussion, a request was made to determine if such dummies were both practical and possible.

The U.S. Army Engineer Board (responsible for selecting and approving engineering equipment), along with the War Department's Joint Security

Control, examined British decoys and went on to develop improved designs. These tests resulted in a proposal for a deception unit in October 1943. With the approval of Generals Devers and Bradley, the production of deception equipment was started and the unit activated. It was at the suggestion of General Devers that the capabilities of the deception unit were expanded so that it could portray one armored and two infantry divisions.[4]

Thus Generals Devers and Bradley along with Colonel Billy Harris appear to have been directly involved in the creation of the deception unit. Generally, it was up to the theater commander as to what types of units should be formed in the United States and sent to him. It must be assumed that a similar deception unit was not sent to other theaters because those commanders must have felt that other types of units were more important to their efforts.

The army's new deception unit was to be formed at Camp Forrest, Tennessee, in early 1944. At this time Camp Forrest was vacant. The 8th Infantry Division had just left for desert training, and it would be another month before the 17th Airborne Division arrived. Camp Forrest had also been home to the Second Army Ranger School, a program designed to train enthusiastic men from various divisions in advanced combat techniques, in hopes that they would bring what they learned back to their units and pass the information on. (Graduates of the school were allowed to wear a red stripe under their division patch bearing the word "Ranger" in white.)

The 23rd Special Troops was activated at Camp Forrest under jurisdiction of the Second Army on 20 January 1944.[5] There is some confusion as to the correct form of the unit's name. The two versions in use were "23rd Headquarters, Special Troops" and "23rd Special Troops." According to the army's official unit register, the correct name for the unit as a whole would be 23rd Special Troops. (For a discussion of the subject see Appendix 1.)

Command of the 23rd was given to Colonel Harry Langdon Reeder. Reeder was an old infantryman, having served with the Maryland National Guard on the Mexican Border in 1916, with the 1st Infantry Division in France in WWI, and later in occupied Germany (where his son Harry L. Reeder Jr. was born) with the 4th Infantry Division. He had been among the first American officers to attend the tank school formed in Paris during WWI. He had most recently commanded the 46th Armored Infantry Regiment—a part of the 5th Armored Division. There is no reason to believe that Reeder was given this assignment due to an inability to command combat troops. Indeed, he may have been chosen with the hope that his personal contacts and extensive experience would help him cope with the army system and gain the cooperation of officers in other units.

Reeder, by all accounts, was very unhappy with his new command. He had spent a long time learning how to lead men in combat but now, when he felt he deserved command of another armored infantry regiment, he was assigned to run a unit that no one really understood. On 20 January 1944,

Colonel Harry L. Reeder was the commander of the 23rd Special Troops. He felt his previous training and experience qualified him for command of an armored infantry battalion, and he was disappointed with this new assignment. Veterans of the unit claim this is the only known photo of him smiling.
PHOTO: WALTER MANSER

Colonel Reeder was authorized fifty-seven enlisted men as a basis to form the 23rd, but he had no real understanding of what they were to do. This was not his fault. No one, not even the War Department offices that had authorized the unit, had any idea what tactical deception was all about. There were no manuals, no plans, no doctrine, nor anyone with experience in such matters. In terms of being issued equipment, the 23rd was given the very high priority rating of A-2-a-0.1.

To his credit, Reeder did his assigned job as best as he was able. Soon, men for his headquarters and the three main component units began to arrive: the 244th Signal Operations Company, Company A of the 293rd Engineer Combat Battalion, and the 603rd Engineer Camouflage Battalion. Later on, in France, they would be joined by a fourth component, the 3132nd Signal Service Company, the sonic deception unit.

Since no one in the American army had ever organized such a unit before, there was no precedent to follow. The War Department gave Reeder a free hand in calling for specific officers and men to help him design his new unit. The initial concept was that the 23rd would need a large staff to develop and plan operations. Along with the regular staff officers assigned to most military units (S1, 2, 3, and 4), the 23rd had three lieutenant colonels as liaison officers (Olen J. Seaman—West Point Class of 1937, John W. Watson, and Edgar W. Schroeder—West Point Class of 1939). Another three lieutenant colonels were on staff to advise on armored matters (James W. Snee—West Point Class of 1934), artillery (John W. Mayo), and antiaircraft (Frederick E. Day—West Point

Class of 1927).[6] Two majors ran the engineer (Frederick D. Vincent) and signal (Charles H. Yocum) sections. This was considered extremely rank heavy for a unit of that size.[7]

When a tentative organizational structure was finally developed, Lieutenant Colonel Merrick H. Truly (the executive officer—West Point Class of 1932), Major Charles H. Yocum (signal officer), and Major David H. Bridges (supply officer) flew to Washington and presented it to the Army Ground Forces for approval. No one in Washington knew anything about deception and so the plan was approved with no changes. The Table of Organization and Equipment for the 23rd Headquarters, Special Troops (T/O&E 60-70-1S) was officially authorized on 4 April 1944. On paper Reeder had twenty-eight officers, one warrant officer, and ninety-two enlisted men under his direct command in headquarters company.

Experienced army officers were in high demand at this time and West Point graduates even more so. Many units in the army were considered lucky to have only one experienced officer that had served before the war. The sheer number of West Point graduates in a unit the size of the 23rd points to the importance assigned to the unit. Even more unusual is that these officers did not try to escape the 23rd for a combat unit (where promotions were faster and one's career could be more easily made).

Perhaps the man most important to the development of the 23rd was Lieutenant Colonel Clifford G. Simenson, the S-3 (operations and training officer). He was a smart officer and one with good connections. Simenson had been sent to the 23rd from the Operations and Training section of the Army Ground Forces (AGF). He was an old army man (West Point class of 1934) and well known in army

Clifford G. Simenson (shown here as the commanding officer of the 14th Infantry Regiment during the Korean War) was the S-3 (training and operations officer) of the 23rd. He was one of the key officers in developing theories and plans for tactical deception in WWII.

circles. At the AGF he had worked directly for General Leslie McNair and had been able to travel all over the country on inspection tours.

Earlier, Simenson had left the Army Ground Forces for parachute training, a move that would probably have led him to the command of a parachute battalion. After his one and only jump, however, he received a phone call from General Riley Ennis ordering him to the 23rd. When Simenson was told of his new position, his initial reaction was, "What did I do wrong now?"[8] He had felt sure he would be given a combat command instead of being sent to some secret unit that no one knew about.

Simenson would eventually leave the 23rd just before the end of the war, but would continue his long career in the army. He would command the 14th Infantry Regiment in Korea. "Commanding an infantry regiment," Simenson claims, "is the best job in the Army."[9] That job was within his grasp during WWII, but he instead remained in the 23rd, playing a critical role in the development of tactical deception.

McNair was powerful enough to get Simenson to any unit he wanted. Allowing such a skilled officer to take a position in deception rather than in a combat unit (the logical choice for an army careerist), may indicate that McNair himself had an interest in deception.

General McNair would later play a starring role in Operation FORTITUDE. General George Patton had initially been selected to play the role of the commanding officer of FUSAG (First U.S. Army Group), a phony unit set up in England to prepare for the main invasion of France at Calais. The Allies needed a general who was highly respected by the Germans to play this role and Patton was the first choice. Once Patton was needed in France to command the Third Army, however, another general was needed to take over the dummy FUSAG in England, thereby keeping German reinforcements pinned at Calais. The new general had to be someone who commanded a high level of respect, and Leslie McNair was the choice. Although McNair was privately crushed that he was not given a combat command on the true invasion front, he did his part to keep the Germans occupied while other, more junior, officers got all the glory for breaking the German lines. Sadly, McNair could not resist a visit to Normandy and was killed when a load of Allied bombs was dropped short during Operation COBRA. General Leslie McNair remains forgotten by most Americans, but was possibly one of the most innovative and unselfish men to serve in WWII.

Simenson admits that in the early days of the 23rd, things were chaotic. No one had any idea of what they were supposed to do, or how they were supposed to do it. He said, "We never got any orders or guidance from above."[10] While the troops were being sorted out on an administrative level, the officers were reading anything related to deception they could get their hands on (there was almost nothing), and working from scratch to develop concepts and plans. Due to the level of secrecy, much of their work was done orally, without written records, so that few documents from this period exist.[11] The most important lesson they were to learn was that pretending to fight is often as tough as actually fighting.

In a stroke of luck, the Army Specialized Training Program (ASTP) was being closed down at that time, and the 23rd received a selection of some of America's brightest young men. ASTP was designed to keep the most intelligent men of draft age in college, under army guidance, until they had finished a specialized program such as engineering or medicine. Men testing high enough on intelligence exams were first sent to basic training to learn how to be a soldier and then they were sent to an accelerated program at a college or university. If they passed, they would be commissioned as officers.

This was a miracle for many bright men who had never thought they would be able to afford a college education. The army was paying them to attend some of the best schools in the country, and as a side benefit was keeping them out of combat. Unfortunately, the drain on manpower was far greater than expected, and in February 1944 the ASTP program was closed down to provide combat replacements. One minute a soldier thought he was going to get a free degree in engineering and become an officer; the next he was being shipped out to a combat unit. Most of the replacements were needed for infantry companies, which was where the majority of the men from ASTP ended up. There is no evidence that the men sent to the 23rd were hand-selected for their intelligence, but many of them had very high IQs. Anyone who could not perform well was swiftly moved out of the unit. Many veterans of the unit felt that the army selected the brightest of them because it was thought that an intelligent man would be better suited to deception work. He would understand the importance of the details and do his best not to give the game away. It turned out to be the right choice because deception work not only requires brains and inventiveness, but artistic and dramatic talents as well.

During the initial formation period, Simenson put the men through some infantry training. With little instruction, the soldiers picked right up on what they were supposed to do and how it was to be done. An average group of men might have had to run through the problems a few times before catching on, but Simenson recalls that the soldiers of the 23rd picked it right up and were able to perform the desired tasks with almost no practice.[12]

Deception has always been linked to camouflage, and the largest element of the 23rd was the 603rd Engineer Camouflage Battalion. This unit was initially commanded by Lieutenant Colonel Otis Fitz. His engineering background was in river-dredging in the New York area and, according to at least one of his officers, Fitz had some trouble functioning in a military environment. At some later date in Europe, probably early 1945, he was transferred out of the 23rd and replaced by his executive officer, Major William "Bill" Hooper.

One of the more famous members of the 603rd Engineers was fashion designer Bill Blass. Shown here outside the 23rd Headquarters in Briey, France, Blass performed the same duties as the rest of the unit and, at the time, was no less or better known than any other man in the battalion.
PHOTO: GEORGE MARTIN

Normally one camouflage battalion was assigned to each field army. The 603rd had been in existence in the Eastern Defense Command and the First Army for two years before it joined the 23rd. One of the things the army did right was realize that the best camoufleurs were men with artistic talent. They understood the theories of color and shadow, which proved to be extremely useful when trying to fool enemy eyes. The 603rd was filled mainly with men with artistic backgrounds from New York and Philadelphia. A number of the battalion's members went on to successful careers in the art world. These included artists Ellsworth Kelly, Arthur Shilstone, and Arthur Singer; set designer George Diestel; commercial artist George Martin; fashion designer Bill Blass; and photographer Art Kane. The flow of artists to the 603rd came partly by word of mouth through the New York Art Student's League and through Professor Rose, who taught an industrial camouflage course at New York University. It was recorded that the unit had an above average IQ of 119.

There was some turnover in the 603rd when it was assigned to deception work. According to at least one veteran of the unit, a number of officers and men were weeded out of the unit before it joined the 23rd. In B/603rd, George Martin recalled that approximately two officers and ten enlisted men left the company at that time. Not all were removed for reasons related to performance.

This comparison photograph was taken during the decoy trials in the desert. Shown at one hundred feet are three ¾-ton weapons carriers. From left to right are the pneumatic decoy, the genuine truck, and the folding decoy. Such decoys were designed to be viewed by reconnaissance planes from a high altitude.

Many of them were separated from the unit due to homosexual or effeminate traits. These were considered a security risk in a secret unit during the 1940s, because it was thought that homosexuals could be more easily blackmailed.

The organization of the 603rd was only slightly altered to fit its new deception mission, and on 4 April 1944, T/O&E 5-95S was authorized for an "Engineer Camouflage Battalion, Special, 23rd Headquarters, Special Troops." It now had twenty-eight officers, two warrant officers, and three hundred and sixty-one enlisted men. It had a Headquarters and Service company (H&S) and four camouflage engineer companies (A, B, C, and D). Each company consisted of a headquarters and four platoons, each with one officer and eleven men.

The 603rd had previously been experimenting with camouflaged and dummy installations on the eastern seaboard. The unit had camouflaged the Martin bomber plant near Baltimore and large railroad guns in Amagansett. There appears to be no special reason why the 603rd was selected for deception work. It may be that it was the camouflage battalion closest at hand. Once assigned to the 23rd, the men learned all about setting up dummy positions and how to use the inflatable decoys. These items were code-named "land targets" in case an enemy agent happened to hear a passing remark about them. The "target" designation was also used to keep the people who made them in the dark about their real purpose. To this day, many of the factory workers probably still think they made lifelike inflatable targets for firing practice.

These decoys were the result of a long series of tests started by the army in 1939 when it was looking for ways to deal with advances in aerial photography. Originally the decoys were duel two-dimensional figures: one silhouette in a light color, and a second in a darker color to simulate the shadow. The movement of the sun caused the stationary shadow to look out of place, so the

The decision to use inflatable pneumatic decoys, over solid folding models, was made after trials of both versions in early 1944. The inflatable decoys proved to be easier to set up in the field. In contrast, a number of small parts needed for the folding models were lost in the darkness.

army elevated the flat cut-out to cast a real shadow on the ground. Finally it was determined that using a three-dimensional decoy was the best method of casting an accurate shadow and fooling the camera.[13]

In February 1944, the Engineer Board tested a number of decoys in the desert.[14] The desert was chosen because it had open spaces with good visibility. The Engineer Board was interested in testing two different types of decoys: a pneumatic (or inflatable) rubber model, and decoys based on a folding metal frame that the General Outdoor Advertising Company was trying to sell to the army.

The metal frame decoys were found to weigh more, were harder to set up in the dark, and became useless if one of the many metal pins that held the unit together was lost. The metal hinges and frames were also prone to breakage. Each type of decoy was erected ten times. The pneumatic decoys suffered only three punctures and one valve failure. The folding decoys suffered from nine hinge and five framework breaks.

The pneumatic decoys, however, were not without problems. The rubber coating stuck to itself when the decoys were rolled up in hot weather. There was also the problem of having to attach the inflatable decoys to the ground so that they were not blown away by the wind. One of the M3 scout car decoys broke free in the wind and was badly punctured by cactuses.

At this time such decoys were used mainly to fool aerial surveillance. Therefore aircraft were used to observe the devices from various heights, and both types of decoys were considered effective when viewed from an altitude of greater than five hundred feet. After all the trials, the pneumatic decoys

This comparison of early decoys for the 105mm howitzer shows the component parts and the assembled decoys. The trials indicated that decoys needed to be as simple as possible, so they could be set up in the dark. Future models did away with as many loose parts as possible.

were ultimately considered superior to the metal framed ones as they were lighter, took less volume in transport, were easier to erect and repair, and were less vulnerable to missing parts.

These decoys are often referred to as "rubber dummies," but they were not inflatable balloons. They consisted of a painted rubberized canvas skin that was held in shape by a series of inflatable tubes four to twelve inches in diameter. The tubes were coated with synthetic rubber to make them airtight. At least some of the decoys were manufactured by the plastics division of the Scranton Lace Company (makers of plastic tablecloths), and the inflatable tubes were made by the Goodyear Rubber company. Later in the war, the army experimented with decoys that had replaceable tubing. That way if the tube that held up the rear deck of a tank decoy sprang a leak, the one leaking tube could be replaced by another, and the decoy did not have to be moved or totally replaced. For the duration of the war, however, the 23rd's decoys had fixed tubing, and if a leak could not be patched on site the entire item had to be deflated and replaced. In a pinch, chewing gum was used to temporarily patch small leaks.

The 603rd would also use their artistic talents for such projects as painting signs, helmet insignia, and even shoulder patches, but their main task was to

Men from the 603rd Engineers are seen erecting a camouflage screen during training. Such screens were designed to conceal an antiaircraft gun, but could be opened up quickly to allow the gun to be brought into action. PHOTO: GEORGE MARTIN

set up and maintain the inflatable decoys and related effects. Almost as important was to erect camouflage netting over the decoys to make them look as though the Americans did not want the Germans to spot them. This was the trick—making a decoy look as though it were poorly camouflaged, and not incongruously sitting out in the open.

These rubber decoys would not look right unless they were placed in properly dug and camouflaged positions. The 603rd was equipped to handle the dummies and paint markings, but they did not have the tools to dig gun positions or construct wooden bunkers. Company A of the 293rd Engineer Combat Battalion, under Captain George Rebh, was chosen to handle the heavy jobs. Along with performing such construction, his engineers served as the primary security force to keep local civilians or curious soldiers from entering the area.

Rebh's company was released from duty with the 293rd Engineers after being selected the best company of that battalion, and was redesignated the 406th Engineer Combat Company, Special.[15] It would be the only numbered combat engineer company to serve in the ETO. The 406th, as combat engineers, had the most combat-related skills of the 23rd. Rebh's unit had been training for the past year and had participated in both desert training and maneuvers in Tennessee. His men took to the new job and he did not have to replace many of them. On 4 April 1944, his new T/O&E (5-17S) was approved as "Engineer Combat Company, 23rd Headquarters, Special Troops" giving him a strength of five officers and one hundred and seventy-one enlisted men. The only major change in organization was the addition of a bulldozer to each engineer platoon (a normal engineer company had only one per company—now Rebh had three). The bulldozers would come in handy as they could not only be used to dig gun emplacements, but also to make treadmarks in the ground simulating tank movement.

The company was also given the equipment of a water point, consisting of a pumping and filtering unit, and a large canvas holding tank. To beef up their defensive capability, light machine guns were replaced by the heavier water-cooled M1917A1 guns. These could fire for an extended period of time because the water in the barrel jacket prevented the barrel from melting. Additional .50-caliber machine guns gave this company a powerful defensive ability. No other similarly sized combat engineer unit had this equipment.

Captain Rebh was a graduate of West Point's class of January 1943. He had graduated twelfth in his class, and traditionally only the best cadets went into the Corps of Engineers. He had been fairly well known at West Point as the captain of the basketball team. Rebh would later be a Rhodes Scholar and go on to a long army career, retiring as a major general. That he was assigned to the 23rd is one more indication that an attempt had been made to find above average officers for the unit.

While training in the desert Rebh had decided that, as combat engineers,

The officers of the 406th Engineer Combat Company (front row left to right): Lt. William Aliapoulous (3rd Platoon), Captain George Rebh (commander), Lt. George Daley (1st Platoon). Second row (left to right): Lt. Ted Kelker (HQ Platoon), Lt. Thomas Robinson (2nd Platoon). PHOTO: GEORGE REBH

his men needed to know not only engineering skills but how to do the job of an infantryman as well. He worked them in infantry tactics during nights and weekends until they reached a fair level of proficiency. Captain Rebh never had any problems with his commanding officer after Colonel Reeder saw his engineers knew how to handle themselves in the field.[16]

To handle signal deception in the 23rd, Reeder was sent the 244th Signal Operations Company under the command of Captain Irwin Vander Heide. He had been the chief switchman at the Santa Monica telephone office when he volunteered as a communications specialist for the army. He had commanded the 244th for almost two years when his unit was assigned to the 23rd in February 1944.

The 244th was a standard signal company that had just finished maneuvers at a desert training site. The senior officers of the 23rd were ruthless in weeding out anyone not up to the high demands they knew would be placed on the men, and roughly 40 percent of the 244th were transferred to other units. Five new officers and one hundred enlisted men were added to the unit to prepare for their new mission of sending phony radio messages.

The signals deception work would be done over radio waves, so initially the company had no capability for wire communications. Once a deception operation was under way, however, wire communications, or hand-delivered messages, would be the only way the entire 23rd could send nondeception messages among its sub-components without being intercepted by the Germans. Another one hundred wire, teletype, and message center personnel were therefore added to the unit, and on 4 April 1944 it was renamed the Signal Company, Special, 23rd Headquarters Special Troops (T/O&E 11-7S). It now had an authorized strength of eleven officers and two hundred and eighty-five enlisted men.

The signal company consisted of a headquarters platoon, a message center platoon, a wire platoon, and four radio platoons. Some confusion exists regarding what the signal company should be called. According to the army, the authority for the 244th's reorganization was received in April 1944 while it was still in the United States. The official record states that the actual unit activation did not take place on paper until 22 June 1944 when the unit was in Warwickshire, England. The activation orders were to be considered retroactive back to the date of constitution, 4 April 1944. That was the date the 244th technically lost its numerical designation and should be called simply the 23rd Signal Company, Special.

The reason for the confusion in dates appears to be due to this signal company being shipped overseas under the name 3109th Signal Company. According to the army, there was no such unit in WWII. But the records of the 23rd show that during its early stay in England the 23rd Signal Company was referred to as the 3109th (during the Thetford maneuvers). While the exact reason for this changing of names has not been uncovered, it seems probable that the 3109th designation was a security measure used to hide the true nature and name of this unit. It alone, of all the subunits in the 23rd, had a designation unusual enough to call attention to itself.

The signal company was authorized a large number of radios: twenty SCR-193s, ten SCR-284s, four SCR-399s (in K-52 trailers), five SCR-506s, ten SCR-508s, and seven SCR-608s.[17] The SCR-399 was a long-range radio with a range of over one hundred miles. The SCR-193 and SCR-506 were medium-range sets with a twenty-five to one-hundred-mile range. The rest were short-range sets with less than twenty-five-mile range. The SCR-608 was designed for artillery observers. With these they could simulate the headquarters of most units from battalion level up to a corps headquarters. They also were allocated sixty-three miles of telephone wire as a basic load.

Another important officer in the 23rd was Lieutenant Frederick Fox. He had been involved in dramatics while at Princeton, traveled extensively, and had tried for a career in the movies before finally going to work for RKO

Radio. He was assigned to the 23rd as a radio traffic analyst, but his flair for the dramatic would make him a driving force in the ability of the 23rd to simulate other units. A number of veterans have indicated that Fox was perhaps the most important officer when it came to developing ways to fool enemy ground agents. Fox liked to refer to the 23rd as the "traveling road show."[18]

At Camp Forrest, the 23rd came up with ideas on how to deceive on the battlefield, tested a number of them, and found out what seemed to work. The engineers practiced camouflage techniques, but it does not appear they had inflatable decoys to work with until they went overseas. Everything was done on a small unit level, and no large exercise was undertaken to put all the parts together. One of the comments made later was that since everyone was as confused as the next man, the rookies sometimes knew as much as the veterans. The main directive given to Colonel Reeder was that the 23rd should be able to simulate an entire corps-sized unit with both radio traffic and decoys. This would involve not only a simulated corps headquarters, but also up to three divisions (both armored and infantry).

There was some concern that Colonel Reeder did not keep the enlisted men as informed as they would have liked. Most of these soldiers were very bright and felt slighted when they were not kept involved in the concept of operations. This tendency of Reeder's was a source of irritation and would later cause some problems with morale.

With the 23rd finally at full strength, and having trained as much as possible under the circumstances, it was time to prepare for movement to Europe. While looking for officers to fill the remaining slots it was discovered that Colonel Reeder's son (Harry L. Reeder Jr.—West Point class of June 1943) had arrived at Camp Forrest to train with the 17th Airborne Division. Reeder was able to request anyone he wanted for his unit (due to the secret nature of the mission no questions were asked) and he had his son transferred under his command as supply and motor transport officer. This was not as odd as it may seem, and similar events happened frequently in the wartime army.[19] Young Reeder appears to have performed his duties well, but his arrival was another situation that irritated some of the men. Still, contemporaries of Harry Jr. indicated he was a very competent officer and well liked.[20] He went on to enjoy a long career in the army in various infantry and airborne units.

40mm antiaircraft gun

M7 self-propelled howitzer

L4 liaison aircraft

2½-ton truck

¼-ton jeep

M3 half-track

one-ton trailer

Inflatable decoys were developed for most of the common equipment in use by the American army. Patterns varied slightly over the course of the war as advances were made to improve their appearance and make them more reliable.

Chapter 3

On to England

On 10 April 1944, a small advance party consisting of Colonel Reeder and six officers flew to England. They hoped to be able to obtain more information on how the German intelligence agencies operated. The primary concerns in the 23rd were the lack of information on German signal intelligence, and on previous attempts to deceive the Germans via radio methods. The feeling was that if they knew what the Germans would look for, and how they would look for it, it would be easier to fool them.

They also needed to document the current operating procedures of American corps and divisions in the UK. Attempts to get this classified information were not well received because all of England was preparing for the forthcoming invasion of Normandy. No one wanted to discuss such matters with unknown officers who might turn out to be army intelligence operatives looking for loose lips—or worse, German agents.

It was in England that the 23rd discovered the term "notional." This was the term used by the British to describe a simulated, or dummy, unit or position. The term had supposedly been adopted in the desert by Dudley Clarke and is still in regular use in the U.S. Army today.[1] The 23rd would find itself involved with notional divisions, regiments, batteries, radio nets, MP platoons, river crossings, and many other simulations before the war was over.

Deception operations for the invasion of France had begun under a "Cover and Deception Group" named "Ops (B)." With the formation of Eisenhower's Supreme Headquarters, Allied Expeditionary Force (SHAEF), Ops (B) continued its deception duties as a combined Anglo-American unit under command of Colonel Noel Wild and his deputy, Lieutenant Colonel Jarvis-Read. Both the British 21st Army Group and the American 12th Army Group reported directly to SHAEF.

General Montgomery's 21st Army Group formed its own deception unit of former A-Force personnel commanded by Colonel David Strangeways, with Lieutenant Colonel Temple as his deputy. General Omar Bradley's 12th Army Group deception unit was commanded by Colonel Billy Harris.[2] It was part of the G-3 (operations) section known as the "Special Plans Branch." Assisting Harris in the Special Plans Branch was another important figure in deception, Major Ralph Ingersoll. The other officers in this section were Lieutenant Colonel Martin Bannister (signal officer), Major Theodore Palik (assistant signal officer), Major Albert Davis (engineer and supply officer) and Captain John Eldridge (intelligence officer). Records of the Special Plans Branch have not yet been located in the 12th Army Group files housed in the National Archives.

Lieutenant Colonel Simenson's West Point background was important when he attempted to get information on deception policy. Colonel Harris (West Point class of 1933) knew Simenson (class of 1934), and Simenson's brother (an Army Air Force officer who was class of 1932).[3] It was probably due to this connection that Simenson was selected for a briefing by Harris and his British counterpart, Colonel Strangeways, on the deception operations surrounding the D-day invasion. Harris felt that someone in the 23rd needed to know what was going on so that the 23rd would not accidentally do something to upset the operation.

Although thrilled to be given such classified information, Simenson would later regret it when another contact in England offered him a position in a combat unit. Although sorely tempted by a combat command, he could no longer allow himself to be put in a position where there was the slightest possibility of being captured by the enemy. Simenson badly wanted to get involved in the real action, but he knew his duty was to protect the information he had been given.

Much of what was known about German radio intelligence techniques came from the capture of the Afrika Korps' 621 Radio Intercept Company and its commander, Captain Alfred Seebohm. This unit had been overrun and captured intact during one of the desert offensives and proved to be a treasure-trove of information about just how good German intelligence was.[4] The German unit listening to radio transmissions in England was Radio Reconnaissance Battalion 13, initially located in Vitre, Brittany.

One of the key finds that came from the desert was a copy of the handbook that German intelligence had issued on British units and their locations.[5] It proved to be remarkably accurate for the first years of the war, and all evidence pointed to it having been compiled through radio intercepts and direction finding. With this knowledge the Allies knew that the Germans would be listening in to their radio calls, and paying careful attention to such factors as number and types of broadcasts, as well as styles of sending. German radio direction-finding equipment was known to be very sensitive, so the location of a sending radio could be located with a fair amount of accuracy. One of the ways German intelligence tracked the movements of an Allied unit was to follow the trail of its broadcasts. For this reason, most units observed radio silence when moving, but it gave the 23rd another card to play.

The 23rd also learned that the German intelligence service had a special organization at its army level responsible for gathering information by sending trained observers across the lines, or by leaving an agent to stay behind when the rest of the army retreated. These agents could be either German soldiers or local civilians who, for whatever reason, wanted to help the German cause.

Radio operators of the 23rd did not help send the deceptive messages needed for Operation FORTITUDE. The American component of that operation was the 3103rd Signal Service Battalion. That unit was tasked with strategic deception operations, although later in the war the 3103rd would be assigned to assist the 23rd with radio deception during the Battle of the Bulge.

Every American unit in the ETO was given a code name as a unique identifier. Instead of putting up signs indicating "2nd Armored Division this way," the unit could post a sign reading "Powerhouse," with an arrow indicating direction. Within divisions, code names were grouped alphabetically, with all attached units in a division having the same first letter (thus all units of the 2nd Armored Division began with the letter "P"). The initial code name assigned to the 23rd while in England was ARIZONA. For an unknown reason, the 23rd's code name was changed in either July or August 1944, about the time the unit was reassigned directly under the 12th Army Group. In what could be considered a total breach of security, the 23rd was given the code name "BLARNEY," an old Irish term meaning a falsehood or a stretch of the truth. Normally in a regimental sized unit, the battalions were sub-named with the additional code of red, white, or blue (for 1st, 2nd, or 3rd Battalion). In the 23rd, the 603rd Engineer Battalion was named BLARNEY RED, the 406th Engineer Company BLARNEY WHITE, the 3132nd Signal Company BLARNEY BLUE, and the 23rd Signal Company BLARNEY ORANGE.[6]

Meanwhile, the rest of the 23rd left Camp Forrest by train on 21 April 1944 and headed for the embarkation area at Camp Kilmer, New Jersey, under the direction of Lieutenant Colonel Frederick Day. After all the usual pre-embarkation inspections, the men were granted an eight-hour leave in New York City. Then, at 2020 on the morning of 3 May, they boarded the transport ship USS *Henry Gibbons*.

The USS *Gibbons* made the crossing in just a little over thirteen days and sailed into Bristol on 15 May. That night, a German air raid hit the port, but no bombs landed near the ship. The troops were met by the advance party at the docks, and after a seven-hour trip by train arrived at their bivouac. This was at Walton Hall in Wellesbourne (near Stratford-on-Avon), an estate owned by the elderly Lady Mordaunt. She wanted to help the war effort and had decided to do so by allowing her grounds to be used by the military. Metal-skinned Nissen huts (known as Quonset huts in the United States) and canvas tents were set up on the immaculate lawns for the enlisted men, while the officers moved into the manor, leaving one wing to Lady Mordaunt. The

Walton Hall in Wellesbourne, England was the first headquarters of the 23rd Special Troops overseas. Officers lived inside the main building, while the men were relegated to tents, Nissen huts and outbuildings. The troops quickly nicknamed the antiquated estate "Moldy Manor."
PHOTO: GEORGE MARTIN

manor was an old Victorian structure and quickly earned the nickname "Moldy Manor."

The 23rd was assigned to the Third Army while in England. The first task of the troops was to collect their unit equipment that was scattered in depots all over southern England. Once vehicles were drawn from the quartermaster, the radiomen began installing their equipment in their trucks, while the others were sent on supply missions to pick up the rest of the material authorized for the 23rd. While the equipment was being sorted out, a group of five officers journeyed to a British installation at Ramsgate to inspect the British inflatable decoys and learn how the British Army managed them. The initial reaction was that the American-produced decoys were not only easier to set up, but far more durable.

To prepare the inflatable decoys, generally called "dummies" by the men, an assembly line was set up on a hill behind Moldy Manor. Each of the rubber decoys was opened up, inspected, and inflated, then left to sit until a carrying crew was available to lug it farther up the hill. At the next stage the decoy, assuming it still held air, was fully inflated again. If it was still airtight it was brought to a painting station where it was stenciled with white stars. The decoys were then carried further up the hill to a holding area, where the inflated unit sat to determine if there were any slow leaks. At any stage a decoy would be sidelined for repairs if it lost air, and a number were eventually found impossible to repair. Those that passed the test were carefully packed in canvas cases labeled with the type of replica it held. Some of the repair material for the decoys was used to make inflatable air mattresses for the officers and men.

Reeder and his staff made an attempt to design a better deception unit.[7] Although never accepted, they proposed a new organization to break up the individual units in the 23rd and shuffle them into groups more suited for deception missions. Instead of assigning a company of 603rd camoufleurs, a platoon of 406th Engineers, one detachment of signalmen, and another from his HQ company, Reeder wanted this mix built into the organization so men would operate in the field under the officers they normally reported to. The most important aspect of this new organization was that it was easy to break down into various subsections.

The staff of the 23rd was considered top-heavy. Reeder felt that a reorganization could trim it down, but he would still need experts in the various branches of service to consult on technical matters. Having all initial planning for operations done at Army Group level would offset a loss of staff officers. One of the key changes he suggested was to get rid of the duplicate administrative and supply functions found in the various subunits. Reeder thought that by creating one specific organization to handle these functions there would be a savings of manpower, with greater overall efficiency.

The engineer camouflage company was to be reorganized into one engineer combat company and three installation companies. Technical advice on camouflage matters would be furnished by a small group of fifty specialists who would serve as the "factory section," where all props for special effects such as signs and painted helmets were made.

The current 23rd Signal Company (Special) organization was considered adequate; however, it was recommended that a second signal company be added to accommodate a greater need for simulated transmissions at a lower echelon. This second company could also be used to portray a second divisional-sized unit. The 3132nd Signal Service Company was to be assigned to the signal battalion alongside the deception radio companies.

At some point in England, Reeder supposedly wrote a letter to the War Department indicating that the 23rd was a waste of men and money, and that he felt the unit should be dissolved. This might have been an attempt to get himself transferred to a combat unit where he felt he really belonged. This information comes from a few veterans who claim they have seen a copy of the letter. However, it was not found in the material held by the National Archives.

From 29 May–3 June 1944, the 23rd held a field exercise in the Thetford maneuver area one hundred and ten miles from Walton Hall.[8] The exercise was broken down into three operations: CABBAGE, CHEESE, and SPAM. CABBAGE ran from 29–30 May and was an attempt to portray the combat commands of a single armored division. About 40 percent of the unit was formed into a simulated armored division HQ and its three combat commands. The unit commanders were allowed to make an initial daylight reconnaissance of the area, then had to position their equipment during the night. These exercises were concerned only with the visual representation of a unit through inflatable dummies and constructed positions. They did not involve signal or sonic aspects of deception. Once the unit was set up in its positions and dummy equipment was in place, aerial reconnaissance was made at noon on the following day to determine how the positions looked from the enemy's point of view.

The 23rd then moved immediately into Operation CHEESE, from 31 May–1 June, where the same procedure was followed. The men attempted to portray another armored division, but this time with an added divisional trains encampment along with the headquarters and combat commands. Afterward SPAM had the 23rd simulate a notional infantry division. The attempt was made to set up positions for an infantry division HQ, three combat teams (simulating the regiments of a division), and an artillery and divisional special troops position. No after-action reports on these exercises have been located, but it appears to have been a worthwhile shakedown for the troops. It was also the first time the men were issued the infamous K-ration. The same group that took part in CABBAGE, CHEESE, and SPAM was to be designated as the advance party of the 23rd in France.

According to most veterans, inflatable decoys were not issued to the 23rd until they arrived in England. This example of a pneumatic decoy Sherman tank shows how the detail in the suspension was painted on. Both the British and the Americans manufactured their own versions of inflatable decoys, but the veterans all claim the American versions were much more realistic and rugged.

In order to simulate the look of an infantry or armored division, small groups of officers traveled to visit various American units in the field. They wanted to get a sense of how such units looked in bivouac, or in a simulated combat zone. At this point the concern was about the overall look of a generic armored division or artillery battalion, and not of a single specific unit.

Of particular interest to the radiomen of the signal company was how various units operated their radio nets. To the trained ear these nets (the network of radio connections made between units) could provide a great deal of information on what the unit was doing. They spent long hours learning the type and amount of traffic sent by various sizes of organizations. Experienced radiomen can identify a specific sender of Morse code by his fist (the style or technique used to tap out the code). Since most radio transmissions above battalion level were sent by Morse rather than voice, the signalmen worked long hours to figure out ways of copying the fists of radio operators in other units.

All too soon, the easy days at Moldy Manor came to an end and groups of the 23rd began to take part in various tasks related to the invasion of Normandy. One group of four NCOs from the 603rd was sent to assist the

602nd Camouflage Battalion with "Q-lighting" on the English coast. "Q-lights" were part of the FORTITUDE deception and simulated the lighting of embarkation areas loading troops. Of course, these were set up in areas opposite Calais where there were no landing craft to load, but at night German reconnaissance aircraft could spot the lights and assume men were working long hours at that location.

The four men left for Normandy with the 602nd to set up similar Q-lights on the French coast. There the lights would signify an area where the unloading of ships was going on late into the night. Hopefully any German air attacks would be directed to those locations and not the actual, blacked out, landing sites. It quickly became apparent that there was too much activity going on along the Normandy coast for the Q-lights to be effective, so the camoufleurs helped to conceal the growing supply dumps in the area. Staff Sergeant Chester Piasecki and Sergeant Tracy Slack were wounded during this operation by falling shrapnel from Allied antiaircraft fire.

The first mission to fall under 23rd control in France was Operation TROUT-FLY.[9] This involved a detachment of thirteen radiomen under the command of Lieutenant Frederick Fox. They took with them three jeeps, three half-ton weapons carriers, and a two-and-a-half-ton truck with trailer. On 22 May they joined a group of one officer, eleven radiomen, and two radio jeeps from the 9th Infantry Division at Winchester and moved on to the marshalling area at Pontllanfraith, Wales. Also attached to TROUTFLY were Captain John Jackson (an intelligence officer from the 9th Division) and Lieutenant Colonel Bannister (a planning officer from the ETOUSA headquarters).

The TROUTFLY detachment was assigned to the 87th Armored Field Artillery Battalion, which, as part of Task Force Howell, had the mission of pushing inland to reinforce the 82nd Airborne Division on D+1. In total, TROUTFLY had three half-ton trucks with an SCR-193 and SCR-608 radio in each, one deuce-and-a-half truck with an SCR-399 radio and PE-95 trailer, two jeeps each with one SCR-610 radio, and three jeeps mounting two SCR-610 radios.

The plan was for them to simulate, by phony radio transmissions, the landing of two 9th Infantry Division combat teams alongside the genuine 4th Infantry Division on Utah Beach. They would try to convince the Germans that the 9th Infantry Division had landed and moved to the area connecting the 82nd Airborne and the 4th Infantry Division sectors. With luck, the German radio intelligence service would think the 9th was in a defensive position, holding an area where the Americans would, in fact, be very weak.

TROUTFLY was to simulate radio links from VII Corps HQ to the simulated 9th Division headquarters, and links from there to simulated combat teams based on the 60th and 39th Infantry Regiments. Those combat teams would simulate their own reconnaissance and artillery nets. Due to a limited number of radios and vehicles, the same equipment would be used for both combat teams—hoping the Germans would be fooled by the differences in operating procedures and code words. All transmissions were to be made in the style of the 9th Division, and to be properly encoded on the M-209 cipher machine or another coding technique known as SLIDEX. Frequencies were assigned that fell within those used by the VII Corps. All elements kept thermite grenades handy to destroy the radio and cipher equipment if German capture was imminent.

The plan called for TROUTFLY to maintain strict radio silence until arriving in the 82nd Airborne area. Then a message would be sent back to VII Corps through 82nd Division channels stating, "In position ready to attack." Nothing would be sent over TROUTFLY channels until a message was received from Colonel Harris at VII Corps HQ on a frequency of 1532 Kc, saying "Execute plan." This was expected to occur on day two after the landing.

As soon as the go-ahead was received, two jeeps would be sent to the vicinity of the 319th and 320th Field Artillery Battalions to portray forward observer units locating firing positions for their guns. Prepared messages would be sent in code, but every coded message would include a special code group indicating it was a dummy message. Another two vehicles would be sent southwest simulating the communication of a reconnaissance officer of the 60th Infantry Regiment. These radios would send not only prepared and coded messages, but also a handful of messages sent in plain language. One suggested message read, "Say Joe, that cover at the place we were talking about is too thin to give concealment." The reply would be, "OK, then take a look at the patch of trees just west of there." Followed by, "OK, and if that's alright I'm coming back in."

To multiply the effect and make it appear that both reconnaissance and forward observers were operating in the region, each vehicle would periodically switch from artillery to reconnaissance frequencies and change roles. The Germans would detect a transmission using a different code sign and frequency coming from the same area, but hopefully think they were two different radios.

The following morning, the simulated 9th Division HQ would come on the air with its powerful SCR-399 and establish a radio link to VII Corps. It would send messages as if it did not yet have a telephone wire laid to it. The reconnaissance parties would continue to report in, and every two hours the artillery units would make a routine transmission of "nothing to report." Traffic from the division HQ to corps was planned to be heavy, and prepared messages included a number of eventualities such as a strong or weak German attack. Phony casualty lists were made up in advance.

In the evening, more reconnaissance parties would be sent out. Radio contact was to be made on schedule, and it was planned to remove some of the SCR-610s from the jeeps and man-pack them off the roads. By this time, field wire should have been laid from division HQ to the regiments and radio traffic on those nets would cease. Reconnaissance parties were to move about during the night reporting in by radio—hopefully tracked by German signals intelligence.

The next day, messages were to be sent to indicate that with daylight a number of things were observed that had not been noticed in the darkness. An example was that an artillery unit might broadcast, "This road has a hump in it we could not see on the map. If you're going to cover everything you have to move over a little." This was to be followed by an argument between two officers as to why the recon parties did not notice the hump before the gun was dug in. Since American Standard Operating Procedure (SOP) required an artillery gun to fire before laying on targets, it was hoped that these messages could be sent from the location of an actual battery already firing missions.

The fifth day plans remark that "anything can have happened, and probably will." Supposedly things should have been fairly static, with transmissions limited to periodic radio checks every two hours. A simulated break in wire communications could be used to develop a burst of radio activity between division and corps until the wire was repaired. The overall situation was to indicate that the 9th was in position and ready to defend against a counterattack.

On the following day it was hoped that the real 9th Division would have landed and would be making its way to its simulated sector. Upon landing, the actual 9th Division would portray itself as the 47th Infantry Regiment—the third unit of the 9th, which had not yet been simulated. With luck the actual 9th would move into the area and take over the dummy radio nets without the Germans suspecting anything. If the 9th had to fight its way inland it was hoped it could still slowly take on the radio nets without warning the Germans that anything odd had gone on. This was important if the Allies wanted to use the same deception routine in the future. Once the actual 9th Division had taken over, TROUTFLY was to make its way back to VII Corps HQ and await further instructions.

At the last moment, the drop zones for the 82nd Airborne were moved closer to Utah Beach and Operation TROUTFLY no longer seemed necessary. Since the detachment was already prepared to make the landing, and space had been allocated to them, General Collins, commander of VII Corps, decided to let them go ashore as planned so that, if necessary, they could act as an emergency signal unit.

When TROUTFLY prepared to embark for France, every man wore a 9th Infantry Division patch and could name the units and officers of the division. All vehicles were given 9th Division markings in case a German spy was watching them load. The men and equipment were placed on board the Liberty ship USS *John S. Mosby*, which in error sailed into the area off Omaha Beach on D+1.

Bad luck continued to follow the *Mosby* as she made for Utah Beach on the evening of 7 June. A nearby ship on her port side was hit by a 500-lb. bomb and sank. A different ship in her convoy hit a mine. In the confusion of the invasion area, Allied ships twice rammed the *Mosby* accidentally. Twice the ship went on submarine alert, and two members of TROUTFLY (from the 9th Division detachment) were wounded by falling flak during an air alert.

TROUTFLY finally began disembarking on D+3 and the entire unit was ashore by the next day. The 9th Division detachment returned to their unit, which was already landing in the same area. General Collins had been right to think it never hurts to have an extra radio unit; the 82nd Airborne had lost roughly 95 percent of its equipment in the D-day jump.

From 10–16 June, TROUTFLY was assigned to the 82nd Airborne as its primary radio unit. One SCR-193 served as the link from the 82nd's headquarters to its rear echelon in England. The other SCR-193s acted as regimental links to division headquarters. The radio jeeps were distributed as needed to provide communications as the 82nd pushed inland.

Finally, on 16 June TROUTFLY was relieved from duty and sent to the First Army HQ near Omaha Beach. There the radiomen helped out with signals intelligence monitoring. On 24 June the men greeted the advance detachment of the remainder of the 23rd Special Troops when it landed in France.

Chapter 4

France and Operation ELEPHANT
1–4 July 1944

Aside from a few small special detachments, the 23rd landed in France in two major groups. The main advance party, consisting of roughly 37 percent of the unit, landed at the end of June. The remainder (known militarily as the "residue") remained in England until shipping space across the Channel could be scheduled.

The first small detachment entered France on 14 June 1944. Lieutenant Colonel Beck, First Lieutenant Bernard Mason, eleven men from D/603rd, and four from the 406th Engineers landed on the airstrip behind Utah Beach.[1] They brought with them a number of inflatable decoy 155mm howitzers. This was an experiment in the use of decoy artillery and, although not well documented, was considered successful. The idea was to test the concept of using inflatable decoys near regular artillery units to divert German counter-battery fire from the real guns. The detachment was sent to France with only their decoys (carried in two trailers on the transport aircraft). They had to scrounge vehicles to tow them once in France.

Passing through Carentan and St. Mere Eglise, the detachment was assigned to the 980th Field Artillery Battalion (VIII Corps). This unit was roughly two miles west of St. Mere Eglise, and engaged in shelling St. Sauvier. On 15 June 1944 the decoy 155mm howitzers were set up about a mile in front of the foremost 980th Battery. Until 23 June the detachment operated as an extra (decoy) battery for the 980th, setting off charges to simulate muzzle flashes at night. They traveled with the artillery unit up to Cherbourg until half the detachment, under Staff Sergeant Herbert Amborski, was split off and assigned to the 981st Field Artillery Battalion. Someone had realized that a typical artillery battery (of four guns) would rarely have more than two visible. Thus for the same manpower and equipment two artillery units could have a deceptive battery to draw enemy fire.

This artillery mission lasted for twenty-eight days. The decoy battery was set up at ten different sites. German artillery shelled some, and once they were attacked by a German aircraft. The corps headquarters was very happy with the results and requested that the rubber decoys be left with the artillery unit for further use.

On 17 June, two liaison officers, Lieutenant Colonel James Snee and Lieutenant Colonel Olen Seaman, flew over to France to select a bivouac area for the 23rd. They also spent some of their time observing the 2nd and 3rd Armored Divisions for peculiarities of the units. Plans were already underway to move an advance party of the 23rd to France in case they were needed in a hurry for a deception operation, and such an operation would most likely have involved one of those armored divisions. This advanced detachment was known as ELEPHANT and the operation to which they would eventually be assigned would be called Operation ELEPHANT. The name ELEPHANT was apparently chosen as it was the first time the unit would see action, and it was an old army saying that "to see the elephant" meant the first time you saw combat.

Colonel Reeder left Moldy Manor on 16 June with the group of thirty-eight officers, one warrant officer, and the three hundred and nineteen enlisted men of ELEPHANT. In the post-D-day confusion they were misdirected and spent two days in a field near Exeter while waiting for permission to move to the embarkation point in Southampton. On 19 June they boarded LST 284 and LST 335 and sailed for France. As a tactical code to identify the vehicles of this detachment, a small white elephant was stenciled on the bumpers.[2]

For an unknown reason, LST 284 dropped out of the convoy and anchored off the Isle of Wight for a few days. The men on board had no complaints, as the weather and food were good and the ship had a supply of movies. While at anchor they could periodically hear the chugging of the German V-1 rocket engines (which sounded to everyone like an old washing machine) and watch them pass overhead.

LST 335 put its share of the men ashore on 24 June, and LST 284 finally followed a few days later. The detachment made their way to the bivouac area and began to prepare for possible missions. On 30 June, Reeder was notified about a last-minute operation involving the 2nd Armored Division.

Operation ELEPHANT used only the advance party part of the 23rd Headquarters. The rest were in transit or on other duty.[3] The mission of ELEPHANT was to cover the 2nd Armored Division when it moved from a reserve position to go into the line. The 2nd Armored Division had been held in reserve, in a position midway between the rear of the U.S. 1st and 2nd Infantry Divisions. It was ordered to move into the front lines to the left of the 1st Division, which placed it on the far left flank of the American lines—next to the British 56th Infantry Brigade on the British right flank. This was an area where the Germans were thought to have many tanks.

Upon receiving orders for ELEPHANT, Lieutenant Colonel Simenson went

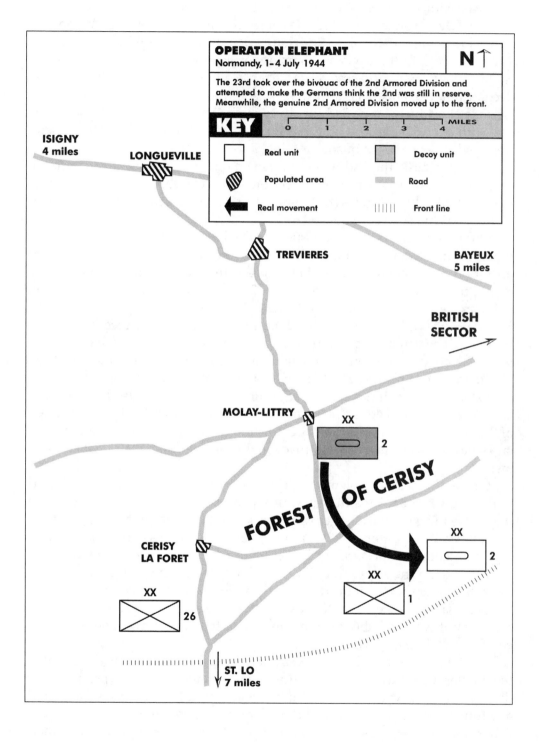

to speak with the operations officer of the 2nd Armored Division, Russell Jenna, a fellow classmate at West Point. According to Simenson, "When told they were going into the line, Russ jumped and asked, 'How did you know?' Then we went to the division commander. I informed the general that we could imitate his radio activities, and replace the camouflage mistakes with decoy dummies and nets, and that he could expect 8–10 hours before the Germans positively identified the division on line. That we would not interfere with any of his troops and that it might help, but not hurt. The General said he had never heard of such a thing."[4]

On 1 July 1944, the 2nd Armored moved out of its reserve position in the Forest de Cerisy. The 23rd was ordered to replace each vehicle with a decoy as the actual vehicles moved out, while the signalmen sent dummy messages on the 2nd Division radio net.

Orders for ELEPHANT were issued at the last minute and were not well thought out. Verbal warning orders were received at 1700 on 30 June; the operation was to begin the next day. A reconnaissance was immediately made of the 2nd Division bivouac area, but the 23rd had been told, for some reason, not to make any commitments to the 2nd Armored and contact was limited.

The actual order to replace the 2nd Armored was finally received at 1015 on 1 July. The actual 2nd Armored began to pull out of its bivouac an hour later. The tanks moved out in daylight and their departure would have been visible to anyone nearby. The tankers, not knowing about the deception plan, left extensive treadmarks in the soft ground that would be visible to any aerial reconnaissance. The Germans must have spotted the daylight movement of the 2nd Armored, as German aircraft strafed one of the tank battalions. The tanks moved over the two main roads in the area with no attempt at concealment.

One of the many problems the 23rd ran into was that when they arrived in the 2nd's bivouac area they first dropped off all the rubber decoys where they were to be emplaced, then went back and began to set them up. At one point it became apparent that four of the rubber Shermans had vanished. This was a potential major security breach and a frantic scramble was made to track down the 2nd Division unit that had been in that bivouac area. Three of the rubber decoys had indeed been taken along by the tank unit and were returned safely to the 23rd. No reason was given as to why they had taken them, but it was probably a simple matter of the tankers packing up all the equipment left in their company area.

The fourth dummy Sherman was not located, and after hours of searching the matter was turned over to the Counter-Intelligence Corps. Had the dummy made its way into German hands it would have severely hampered any future deception operations. The Germans not only would know that the Americans were using such decoys, but could use the example to show their men how to tell a decoy from a genuine tank. As far as the records show, the

Under a camouflage net in Normandy, the 23rd tests decoys in preparation for Operation ELEPHANT. In the foreground some decoys remain packed, while behind them other decoys are being tested to make sure they remain airtight after the trip across the Channel.

missing decoy was never found. It may have been taken home by an unknowing French farmer, or could have been quietly kept by someone in the 2nd Armored (where it could have served as the basis for some stupendous practical jokes).

For ELEPHANT, the 23rd was broken up into three major groups. Captain Oscar Seale commanded the Combat Command A detachment (CCA) simulating the 2/66th and 3/66th Armored Regiments and the 2/41st and 3/41st Armored Infantry Battalions. CCA used one hundred and fourteen decoy vehicles to simulate these units. Lieutenant Colonel Schroeder's Combat Command Reserve (CCR) detachment portrayed the 1/67th Armored Regiment, 1/41st Armored Infantry Battalion, and 2/67th and 3/67th Armored Regiments. Ninety-seven inflatable decoys were set up by his detachment.

The third group, Combat Command B (CCB), under Colonel Mayo, assumed the identity of the 14th and 78th Armored Field Artillery (AFA) Battalions. Mayo had four platoons from the 603rd Engineers to set up one hundred rubber decoys and fifty-eight camouflage nets. They started at 1440 on 1 July and finished at 0600 on 2 July. The 78th AFA Battalion was to be represented with positions of Batteries A, B, C, and the Service Battery, as well as a dummy airstrip for observation aircraft. The 14th AFA Battalion positions included the battalion command post, Batteries A and C, and the Service Battery.

To guard the 78th AFA Battalion area, Mayo had only seven men assigned to four guard posts and an additional three radiomen who could act as either runners or guards. In the 14th AFA Battalion area, there were only six guards and three radiomen. This did not seem to be enough manpower to keep the locals out of the emplacements, and mention was made in the after-action reports that local Frenchmen wandered into the area and discovered dummies were being set up.

This probably refers to an incident where a local French farmer had observed the withdrawal of the guns the night before. Without hearing a new unit move in, he woke to find more weapons in place. Although he spoke no English he wandered over to a group of GIs and asked, "Encore boom-

An artillery spotter aircraft decoy is prepared for use in Normandy. The "49 P" markings indicate it is an aircraft assigned to the 2nd Armored Division. Such liaison aircraft decoys were not effective unless displayed near a decoy landing strip.

boom?" Before the Americans could respond he touched the gun, only to find it was inflated rubber. A smile appeared on his face as he slowly touched his finger to his forehead and said "Ah, boom-boom—ha ha!"[5]

Colonel Mayo strongly suggested that someone who spoke French (preferably a Counter-Intelligence Corps agent) needed to accompany the unit when it first moved into an area of operations. He also felt that decoys should never be set up within two hundred yards of a road. The 23rd intelligence officer, Joseph P. Kelly, wrote of ELEPHANT, "The display of dummy equipment to replace the 2nd Armored Division was made without due regard for security, resulting in disclosure of the use of dummy equipment to numbers of civilians."[6] In the future, more manpower would be used to provide security for the decoy installations.

The sky was overcast and light rain fell throughout the operation. The men quickly found that rain tended to puddle on the flat surfaces of their rubber decoys and gave them a very unnatural appearance. A suggestion was made to cut small drain holes to keep the water from pooling and this seemed to work. Afterwards the crews had to reinforce the holes to make sure they did not continue to rip. Another problem was experienced with the two aircraft decoys. As the air heated up during the day a series of loud reports was heard and one of the aircraft decoys actually burst from the expanding air pressure.

The major problem with the concept of ELEPHANT was that the 23rd was attempting to portray a unit that was moving into the front line only a few miles from its original position. Once troops of the 2nd Armored took their place on the front line the Germans would realize a new unit had moved up. Such a deception could only work for a short period of time, but the 23rd did their best and learned a number of valuable lessons in doing so.

The signal plan for ELEPHANT was simple. The actual 2nd Armored Division had a liaison radio net that essentially placed it in the middle of a triangle. To the front, liaison officers reported back from the 1st and 2nd Infantry Divisions. To the rear, a liaison officer kept in touch from V Corps HQ. These three links were standard procedure for American units, and SCR-506 radios were used for this liaison net.

When the 2nd Armored prepared to shift to the left, it would need to send a liaison officer to the British 56th Infantry Brigade (which would be on the 2nd Armored's new left flank). When the Germans noted that liaison contact had shifted from the 2nd Infantry Division to the 56th they would realize the tanks were on the move, so the plan called for a notional liaison officer to maintain the radio link between the 2nd Armored and the 2nd Infantry Division.

The Germans would only detect a new radio link with a liaison officer of the 56th. Since the original two links were still operational, the Germans would hopefully think that the 2nd was only shifting slightly to its left and

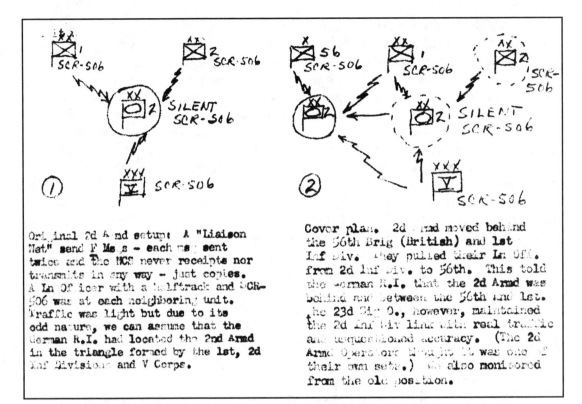

The signal plan for Operation ELEPHANT was explained in the unit records by means of these two drawings. The plan was to use the liaison officers' radio network to fool the Germans into thinking the 2nd Armored Division had just shifted slightly to the left, instead of moving further to the left and up to the front line.

not making a major move. The liaison radio networks carried traffic only to the division HQ. The division did not transmit back a reply unless there was an important reason. This prevented the Germans from tracking the 2nd Armored Division HQ as it moved.

This signal plan would not cover much of the 2nd Armored's movement, but it would hopefully confuse the Germans as to just how much of the 2nd was in motion. By showing the 2nd Armored was still interested in the activities of the 2nd Infantry Division, it allowed the Germans to wonder if only a section of it had moved. There were no comments in the after-action reports regarding the success of the signal plan. Nothing occurred to indicate the Germans had seen through the deception or had been taken in. Like most of ELEPHANT it was looked upon as a learning experience for the unit.

It was realized that a better job could have been done if there had been time to coordinate with the 2nd Armored. No one had cautioned the tankers to be careful about leaving tracks in the ground. Having all tanks in a unit follow the same set of treadmarks when leaving the area could have greatly cut down on visible signs they had moved out. The officers of the 23rd were also very frustrated that they could not have replaced the 2nd Armored in echelons. Theoretically they should have been able to replace one combat command with decoys the first night, while the main bulk of the division stood fast. Then another part of the division could move out and be replaced the next night, and the final elements of the division replaced on the third night.

The 23rd also experienced minor administrative problems common to any unit going into action for the first time. Difficulties in obtaining gas for the vehicles and issuing the correct rations were greater than usual because many of the men normally responsible for such things were still back in England with the residue.

An American L-5 observation aircraft spent thirty minutes over the area at five hundred to nine hundred feet evaluating how the dummy positions looked from the air. The specific problem noted was a distinct lack of activity in the area. It was also decided that the number of decoys and camouflage nets were insufficient for a division-sized unit. Although the full 23rd was supposed to be able to portray a corps-sized unit (three divisions), this operation showed that such a massive undertaking was not feasible at the authorized strength. The feeling was that at best the 23rd should only attempt to portray elements of two divisions.

Suggestions from the aerial observation were: to obtain salvaged shelter halves so they could be set up near the dummies; that white cloth be hung to simulate washing; that all men in the area should spend as much time in the open as possible; and that genuine vehicles should park partially under cover so they were still visible—but not obviously so.

Another area of concern was that the men were doing too good a job in camouflaging their decoys. The men had to make some errors (known as "camouflage mistakes") in their work to allow the Germans to spot what was supposedly hidden. If everything was properly camouflaged the enemy would never even notice the simulated unit. As a rule of thumb it was decided that one third of the mistakes should be minor ones, one third medium, and the final third would be severe, or very poor camouflage jobs. When simulating a headquarters unit it was decided that twice as many camouflage mistakes should be made than with a frontline combat unit.

A major problem discovered was that there were no antiaircraft weapons in the area. This alone might tip off a German aircraft that something was not right, if they were able to observe a supposed American unit without receiving any fire from the ground. The suggestion was made that to really fool the Germans, a token amount of antiaircraft fire needed to be present. It was also suggested that the camouflage netting should have the burlap garnish stripes thinned out by 50 percent to give aircraft a better chance of spotting an equipment silhouette underneath.

Colonel Reeder and a visiting British officer observe how a hand-cranked blower is used to inflate a tank barrel. Although many jokes were made about it, a partially inflated barrel was a sure giveaway to enemy agents that something was amiss.

The American compressor blower unit used for the inflation of the pneumatic decoys.

From an equipment standpoint, the inflatable half-track decoys did not look right. Officers decided that when viewed from the front they were totally incorrect and urged they not be used in future operations. A more important equipment problem was with the air compressors used to inflate the decoys. Some of the compressors refused to work after having been knocked about in transport. It was decided that all compressors needed to be run for a short period each day to ensure they were always ready for action.

Another major problem was how the men and equipment were loaded for transport to the operational area. Most of the equipment had been loaded in England long before the operation was planned. The numbers and types of equipment loaded had been an estimate of what might be needed. This led to problems locating the necessary equipment amidst the trucks. Most of the officers agreed that in future operations the trucks should carry only as much equipment in the first load as to allow for all of the assigned men in their detachments to be transported to the final destination first. This way all the men could begin work while the trucks were sent back to pick up the remainder of the equipment at the 23rd bivouac.

There was no real evidence that the Germans ever noticed the dummy positions of ELEPHANT. The 2nd Armored Division reported on 3 July that there had been no indication yet that the Germans had identified their unit as having moved from their original position. Later on, German maps were captured that indicated the 2nd Armored was still in the original bivouac area. Even so, the Germans had probably realized the 2nd had moved up once they spotted the armored infantry and artillery on the front lines and the information on this had probably not yet filtered down to all frontline units.

Four men from the 406th Engineers were accidentally left behind at their guard post in Chantpie. They were strafed by a German aircraft, and later claimed to be the only members of the ELEPHANT detachment to have "come to grips with the Hun on the problem."[7]

ELEPHANT quietly ended on 3 July when the 3rd Armored Division moved into the area. The chance to have the 3rd Armored tanks replace the dummies was missed, as no one had thought that far ahead and planned for a coordinated relief. But it was an idea not missed by the 23rd officers and they hoped that in the future they would be able to work with the actual units to end an operation in such a way.

★ ★ ★

The remainder of the 23rd, technically known as the "residue" but referred to by the joking code name GARBAGE, left Walton Hall on 8 July 1944 and headed for the embarkation port of Falmouth. Before leaving, all old demolition materials, including foreign mines used for practice, were taken to a safe location and detonated by First Sergeant Toth. The resulting explosion was so great that windows in Moldy Manor, as well as many in the nearby town of Wellesbourne, were shattered. The locals wondered if a buzz bomb had landed in the area and the local airport sent up planes to search for what had caused the explosion. Lieutenant Colonel Truly's final combat advice to the men was "to dig deep and don't forget to change your drawers."[8]

By this time, cross-Channel transportation had been improved and the entire GARBAGE detachment was able to reach Normandy on the same boat without incident. By coincidence, it was the USS *John Mosby*, which had carried the men of TROUTFLY to Utah Beach. At 2200 on 21 July, the 23rd Residue landed on Omaha Beach and proceeded to Mandeville. At this time the 23rd HQ was relieved from Third Army control and placed under General Bradley's First Army.

At this point in the war the German Luftwaffe was fading away, and the 23rd was now sure that their principal audience would no longer be aerial reconnaissance. Enemy agents (both stay-behind Germans and local Frenchmen) would attempt to compensate for the enemy's lack of aircraft. There would still be a few German flights watching the Americans (each night a German plane nicknamed "Bedcheck Charlie" flew over the American lines at dusk), but the deception troops now needed to be able to look and act like the unit they were supposed to portray, both to aerial observation and at a very close range.

A far greater emphasis was going to have to be placed on simulating the distinctive characteristics of the units they replaced. This included insignia and vehicle markings, road and Command Post (CP) signs, how the uniforms were worn, and how the Military Police (MPs) were positioned around the division area. As soon as ELEPHANT had ended it was decided that the 23rd had to gather the needed intelligence on American units whenever possible, even if it was never used. Once the information on a specific unit was in the files it could be made instantly available if another last-minute operation was ordered.

The term for reproducing these specific aspects of a unit was "special effects," and covered everything from painting the correct bumper markings on vehicles and installing signage to manning dummy MP posts. The problem was that although the army did most things in a similar way, many units had their own peculiarities. Some painted tactical markings on their vehicles but most did not. Some MPs had painted helmets while others wore netting. The 23rd reasoned that if they could note the peculiarities of certain units, then so could the Germans.

The process of collecting detailed information on units was not without incident. George Martin recalled that two men from B/603rd were up on a ladder carefully measuring a unit's sign so they could duplicate it exactly. A colonel who was unfamiliar with the 23rd pulled up in his jeep and demanded to know what the men were doing. Whether it was sheer annoyance or a genuine concern for secrecy is unknown, but rather than give the real reason the men replied, "We are measuring signs, sir." This was too much for the colonel. He threw his helmet to the ground and started spluttering with an artistic use of profanity that there was a war on and what idiot would tie soldiers up with something as stupid as measuring signs. The soldiers then continued on with their task.

The result of the investigation into friendly units was a series of information sheets on each U.S. division. They were quickly dubbed "poop sheets." They detailed such things as unit code names, markings, how they wore their uniforms, and how signs were painted. During the war, officers were sent out between operations to keep the information up to date and, at times, were flown back to England to report on new formations preparing to land in France. Unfortunately, only a handful of these poop sheets, those used for Operation BRITTANY, have survived in the unit records.[9]

Enlisted men were encouraged to go with the officers to help gather information and see what frontline units really looked like. This was where having former ASTP men paid off because they were able to quickly realize objectives and help the unit achieve its goals. Lieutenant Fox, the 23rd radio traffic analyst, seems to have been the driving force in pushing for a drastic increase in special effects and the creation of what was now called the "atmosphere" of a type of unit in the locale.

At one point, Lieutenant Fox went to Lieutenant Colonel Simenson with plans for someone to portray a general officer with stars on his uniform and a jeep marked with general's insignia. In the army, impersonating a general officer is not taken lightly and Simenson grimly informed the enthusiastic lieutenant that such an impersonation was not only highly improper but a court-martial offense. After listening to the argument that they were already breaking many regulations by impersonating other units, and how they could not perform their duties if they were forced to stick to the rules, Simenson finally broke out into a laugh. He told Fox that the matter had already been discussed at headquarters and approved, but that he could not resist playing a small joke on the impassioned young officer.[10]

The 23rd signalmen made their own reconnaissance of American units, visiting various signal outfits to observe how they operated. They also eavesdropped on friendly radio transmissions to see how the different radio nets functioned. It was only by knowing the type, number, and distinctive style of a division's or corps' transmissions that they could take over a radio net without alerting the German signal intelligence service. This kind of radio deception is very difficult, but the operators of the 23rd were very good at it and practiced continually.

On 11 July 1944, the following memo was issued in the 23rd. The draft copy of it appears to have been written by Lieutenant Fox, but the final version was put out over Colonel Reeder's name, showing he agreed with the contents. This memo more than any other report shows where the 23rd was lacking. It is a concise summary of the transition the 23rd needed to make, from a strict regulation army unit to a group that could play the game of battlefield deception:[11]

23rd Headquarters, Special Troops
APO #655

11 July 1944.

The attitude of the 23rd HQs towards their mission is lopsided. There is too much MILITARY (WDs, ARs, FOs, etc.*) and not enough SHOWMANSHIP. The 603rd Engineer, on the other hand, contains too much ARTISTRY and not enough G.I. TACTICS. The successful practice of military deception by the 23rd HQs requires the proper amount of both SHOWMANSHIP AND ARMY PROCEDURE.

Like it or not, the 23rd HQ must consider itself a traveling road show ready at a moment's notice to present:

THE SECOND ARMORED DIVISION—by Brooks
THE NINTH INFANTRY DIVISION— by Eddy
THE SEVENTH CORPS—   by Collins

The presentations must be done with the greatest accuracy and attention to detail. They will include the proper scenery, props, costumes, principals, extras, dialogue, and sound effects. We must remember that we are playing to a very critical and attentive radio, ground, and aerial audience. They must all be convinced.

May we recount some past examples of the 23rd's failure to play its role thoroughly—due either to its servile obedience to the ARs or its lack of appreciation of the fine art of the theater:

1. SHOULDER PATCHES & BUMPER MARKINGS: This comes under the heading of costumes and their importance cannot be underestimated (see G-2 Estimate #8, 3 July 44 FUSA), the 23rd HQ argued against these on the grounds;

    a. They weren't necessary (obviously false—see G-2).
    b. They took too long (It takes time to bring up ammunition, but the artillery can't shoot without it. Patches and markings are just as much ammunition to a deception unit as 105mm shells are to the field artillery. Besides, not over three-dozen patches will be worn by the officers and selected enlisted men. These can be sewn on in seven minutes. The bumper markings, of course, take longer

---

* War Department Bulletins, Army Regulations, Field Orders

but a definite team can be given this job. (Bumpers must be reconnoitered just like signal, armored, artillery, etc.)

c. Against regulations and army practice. You're not allowed to wear a patch unless you belong to the unit. (If that follows we should not be allowed to replace steel tanks with rubber tanks. It wouldn't be right.)

d. The unit you are impersonating will steal your men and vehicles. (The unit which we are impersonating should be advised of our business.)

2. "Get the installation in, then lie down and take it easy. All you got to do is blow up the tanks and then you can go to sleep," said one colonel to a group of 603rd Camoufleurs. This is very bad "theater." The colonel forgot that we were in the show business and thought he was actually dealing with real tanks and tankers. In reality only part of the job is done when the dummy tanks are in position. They merely represent the "scenery"—the PLAY must go on until the 23rd is released to return to its base camp. They must repair their "tank," hang out washing, go looking for cider, and generally mill around in typical GI fashion.

One of the big indications of armor is demand and movement of gasoline. The radio traffic should include requisitions for gas. The 603rd trucks should make normal runs to the gas dumps and various depots. The EM must also be completely familiar with their roles and be able to answer simple questions about the unit's organization, history, and key officers.

3. The presence of a general officer's jeep with its scarlet license plate is an essential. Nothing gives away the location of an important unit quicker than a silver-starred jeep. This suggestion was dismissed because it was contrary to ARs. (Is not the whole idea of "impersonation" contrary to ARs? Remember we are in the theater business. Impersonation is our racket. If we can't do a complete job we might as well give up. You can't portray a woman if bosoms are forbidden.)

A G-2 of considerable experience with the 9th Division lists the seven following sources of battlefield intelligence. The 23rd HQ should be available to present the enemy with information through all of these sources.

1. Documents (Our installations could be included in some front-line division or corps overlays).
2. Civilians (Shoulder patches, bumper markings, etc.). We also have French linguists who could spread prepared rumors while seeking wine. ETOUSA hints that it will send agents through the lines with stories. We recommended that NO civilians be allowed to come near any dummy equipment. Some Frenchmen were amazed and delighted with our dummy tanks in the Forest de

Cerisy. They have certainly spread this delicious gossip far by now. (Wouldn't it be wise for the unit, which we are replacing, to tighten up on their security so that the changeover to our strict regulations would not seem so strange and abrupt to the civilians).

3. Prisoners of war (Have we considered clothing a front battalion of a neighboring division with our patches? They don't have to be told why. Some patrols will naturally be captured.)

4. Aerial (We have prepared for this.)

5. Adjacent units (We can tell neighboring divisions about our story and be included in their SOIs overlays and FOs. Information about us, therefore will come not only from us, but from other units.)

6. German recon and patrols (We doubt whether we will ever be close enough to the front line for the enemy to probe our defenses with active patrols.)

7. Radio (We have prepared for this.)

We make the following recommendations:

1. Road signs, sentry posts, bumper markings, and the host of small details which betray the presence of a unit should be reconnoitered and duplicated with special teams of the 23rd. (Inactive periods such as the one which we are enjoying now could well be used in preparing signs.)

2. EM of the 603rd should accompany officers on every possible trip in order to familiarize themselves with tactical dispositions and the "atmosphere" of fighting units. (Chosen men from the 603rd might well occupy the rear jeep seat on all staff officer trips.) The EM of the 603rd are exceptionally intelligent artisans, but are woefully unfamiliar with military units in the field. Radio operators of the Signal Company have already accompanied the Signal Officers and will continue to do so.

3. All personnel should study the histories and orders of battle of FUSA units. We want our officers and men to get the theater attitude. We want them to realize that they may be called upon to "play" any division or corps in France. This will make the deceptive mission of the 23rd much more clear, stimulating, and capable of performance.

On 3 August, the 23rd moved to Fremondre, and a few days later was placed under direct command of General Bradley's 12th Army Group, where it would remain for the remainder of the war. The 23rd would henceforth report directly to the Special Plans Branch, G-3 Section (Operations), 12th Army Group. The official shoulder patch of the unit was now the red, white, and blue "top" insignia of the 12th Army Group. Although rarely worn, there

John Walker started out as the supply officer for the 3132nd. When one of the sonic platoon leaders suddenly left the unit, just before Brittany, there was no time to train a replacement. Walker knew how the unit and equipment worked, so he both commanded a platoon and continued to serve as supply officer for the unit until the end of the war.

were enough nameless administration units assigned to the 12th Army Group to allow the 23rd to keep its anonymity. The 12th Army Group was formed in France when the Third Army, under General George Patton, arrived. General Bradley was moved from command of the First Army (taken over by General Courtney Hodges) to oversee both field armies from the 12th Army Group.

The 12th Army Group commanded all American units in Northern Europe, so when orders for a deception were issued, the individual corps and division commanders would have to follow orders and assist the operations. One of the first things Reeder made sure of was that if he requested something odd from the quartermasters, such as division shoulder patches for a number of different units, they should be issued quickly and with no questions asked.

When the 23rd had been organized it had been assumed that its own officers would do all deception-related planning. This turned out not to be the case, as the staff of the Special Plans Branch took over the task of looking for potential deception operations and making sure they did not conflict with any other activity. Heading up the Special Plans Branch was Colonel Billy Harris, the former head of American deception operations in England.

On 7 August the Special Plans Branch thought they had found a good opportunity to use deception. They ordered Colonel Reeder to begin preparing for an operation to take place in the First Canadian Army Sector. This would involve the simulation of the 7th Armored and 80th Infantry Divisions, as well as a yet unnamed corps headquarters. Reeder and his staff quickly began to prepare for such an event, but the situation changed and word came down that the proposed operation was cancelled.

Meanwhile the rest of the unit settled down to life in Normandy, sampling the local calvados. The camouflage troops soon learned they could bluff their way past MPs by claiming they were searching for blue paint (a color not normally stocked by the quartermasters). The radio operators were assigned to SIAM (Signals Intelligence and Monitoring) duty for the 12th Army Group. This not only helped monitor the Allied airways for possible security risks but provided valuable experience in how different types of combat radio networks operated.

While the unit was in Normandy, one of the highly trained platoon leaders of the 3132nd went off sick to a hospital. He did not return and there was some concern over filling his slot. But Lieutenant John Walker, the supply officer, had learned the job well enough to take over running the platoon. Due to the secrecy of the unit there was no replacement for his former job, so he had to fulfill the duties of both jobs for the rest of the war.

Also while in Normandy, a small incident occurred that made many of the men feel more at ease fighting the Germans. For years they had been subjected to propaganda and news reports about the superhuman qualities of the German soldier. Now they came across a German command post that had been hastily evacuated. Scattered around were documents and, when someone translated them, they found they were handwritten reports on daily troop strength—how many men wounded, sick, or AWOL. This was the same type of paperwork done in the U.S. Army known as morning reports. Upon hearing this, one of the enlisted men exclaimed, "They can't be supermen! They have to fill out morning reports the same as us!" Not only that, but the Germans wrote their reports by hand, evidently not having typewriters such as the Americans possessed. To some men of the 23rd, the myth of German superiority was shattered by the discovery of their mundane, bureaucratic paperwork.[12]

Chapter 5

Sonic Deception

The 23rd Special Troops were trained in the conventional deception techniques of the time: false radio signals, decoys, and camouflage. But once in France the 23rd would be joined by a new kind of deception unit, one that would attempt to deceive the enemy through sound. The development of this new type of unit was separate from the rest of the 23rd and started in the early days of the war.

The science of recording and playback was still in its infancy during WWII. Recording equipment was large and cumbersome. Loudspeakers had limited range and did not reproduce recordings with the accuracy to which we are accustomed today. The British first attempted sonic deception in the desert when they used an Egyptian film company to record sounds and play them back over propaganda loudspeakers.[1] Early in the war, the task of using sound as a deceptive measure was assigned to the National Research Defense Committee (NRDC), an American group that organized scientists, universities, and laboratories to focus the best scientific talent on areas of interest to the war effort.

The idea of sonic deception was first studied in February 1942 at the Stevens Institute of Technology in Hoboken, New Jersey. The overall field was assigned the project number "17" by the NRDC.[2] Working with AT&T Bell Laboratories, a number of experts in the field of acoustics and sound reproduction investigated if sonic deception was feasible. Two of the key scientists involved were Hallowell Davis, M.D., a professor of physiology at Harvard Medical School and Harold Burris-Meyer, who had developed the theatrical stereo system for the Walt Disney film "Fantasia." An experimental station for sonic deception was set up where the army tested coastal artillery at Fort Hancock, Sandy Hook, New Jersey in 1942.

NRDC Project 17.3-1 tested the physiological and psychological effects of sound on men in combat. With the recent advances in recording and playback technology, sonic deception appeared to be a worthwhile area to research.

Five hundred-watt loudspeakers designed for announcements on the noisy flight decks of aircraft carriers were obtained from the navy. Commercial sound-effects records were purchased as a source of various types of acoustic material. Not only was the plan to test equipment for playback, but also to study the transmission of sound over long distances. At that point no one had done any serious research into how sound traveled.

The navy was particularly interested in the use of sonic deception to assist in amphibious landing operations. Two fishing boats in military service (YP-254 and YP-257) were loaned by the navy to carry out testing at sea. Also the Walgreen family (of drugstore fame) had loaned the Army Transport Service their yacht *Dixonia* to assist the war effort (it was heartily welcomed as an additional test vessel because it was extremely comfortable and luxuriously fitted out).

Testing commenced with the 500-watt loudspeakers and a lighter weight, but higher fidelity, 25-watt sound system. The smaller system was soon found to have too short of a range and work quickly focused on the larger speakers. Portable phonographs were used to play the recordings, with the obvious problem of keeping the needle in the groove on rough water. The playback units were given the code name "water heaters," and soon the command to start the playback became "heat 'em up."

The problem of a needle skipping during an operation would have stopped the project, had it not been for the recent development of magnetic wire recording. Magnetic recording tape had not yet been invented, but Bell Labs was able to record and playback an audio signal onto a thin metal wire using a magnetic field. The wire recorder used a stainless steel wire .0006 inch in diameter moving at five feet per second. A two-mile spool, housed in a magazine, would run for thirty minutes. Two playback units were included in each system so that the recorded program could be extended as long as needed by switching from one playback unit to another as each magazine ran out. Since the thin wire did break on occasion, the solution was to tie a knot in it and hold a match underneath to form a temporary joint.

The first real test of sonic deception took place on 27 October 1942. The war game had been scheduled for the previous night, but had been postponed due to a storm. A three-mile stretch of beach at Sandy Hook was to be defended by a force of three hundred men. Another three-hundred-man landing force, in six LCTs (Landing Craft Tank), would attempt to establish a beachhead. Assisting the landing force would be the two YP boats, the *Dixonia*, three airplanes to drop flares, and another six planes to lay a smoke screen.

The night of the 27th had bright moonlight and a strong offshore breeze that blew the smoke screen out to sea. At the southern end of the beach, an initial feint was launched with the three sound boats. The commander of the beach defenses sent his reserve forces to reinforce the southern sector. A second feint was launched against the south, this time joined by one of the LCTs.

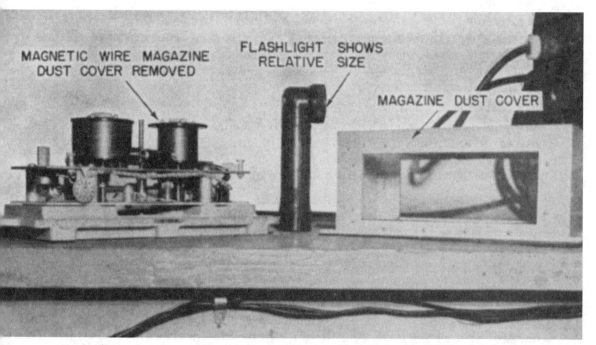

MAGNETIC WIRE MAGAZINE
DUST COVER REMOVED

FLASHLIGHT SHOWS
RELATIVE SIZE

MAGAZINE DUST COVER

Each playback unit contained two magazines so the playback could be faded from one to the other for constant playback. Note the gearing mechanism to the right, used to raise the speaker in this trial vehicle. This design was improved for the half-tracks, then further refined for the M-10's of the 3133rd.

The stainless steel wire used to record the magnetic signal was mounted in a magazine for quick loading. Each magazine could record thirty minutes of sound. If the wire broke, the men were taught to tie a knot in the wire and hold a match underneath to fuse the two pieces.

The defending officer stripped his men from the north and central sectors and rushed them to the south. The remaining five LCTs landed in the north with no opposition and were on the beach for eighteen minutes before the defenders arrived. This was enough proof for the navy that they should develop a waterborne sonic deception unit.

Key to the navy's interest in deception was the famous actor and wartime navy lieutenant, Douglas Fairbanks Jr.[3] He had been assigned as a naval observer to the British group involved with deception, and had returned to the United States to promote its use. He lobbied long and hard with the navy to create a special naval deception unit, and was finally rewarded when such a group, named the Beach Jumpers, was formed on 15 May 1943 at Camp Bradford, Virginia.[4]

Command of Beach Jumper (BJ) unit number one was given to Captain Anthony L. Rorschach. Fairbanks was made the training officer and continued to play a major role in navy deception for the rest of the war. The name Beach Jumper had an unusual origin. Burris-Meyer, who had been commissioned a navy lieutenant commander, was once asked what the goal of the unit was. He replied, "to scare the 'Be-Jesus' out of the enemy." After that comment the men began to evaluate the effectiveness of their trials by what they called "the BJ factor." When it came time to name the navy deception units, the letters "BJ" were turned into "Beach Jumpers," which seemed to be a more respectable use of the initials.[5]

The navy's theory for sonic deception was to mount the "heaters" on small, fast boats and play back sounds of a fleet preparing to land troops under cover of a smoke screen. They also experimented with various other devices such as chaff-firing rockets that would confuse radar systems, and "gooney-birds." These were half dummy soldiers weighted to float upright in the water. When tossed overboard it was hoped they would look like soldiers wading in the surf. Other key elements of BJ equipment were radar jamming and spoofing devices, which could blind enemy radar or make a few small boats appear as a large invasion fleet on German radar screens.

Eventually the Beach Jumper School was moved to the outer banks of North Carolina for security reasons. Beach Jumpers were used as a diversion one hundred miles west of the actual landing beaches during the invasion of Sicily in 1943. It was deemed a success since the Germans were confused as to the actual landing spot and did not commit their reserve forces until the Allies had established a firm beachhead.

The naval Beach Jumper units 1, 3, and 5 took part in Mediterranean operations, including the Salerno landings in September 1943. They also played a major role in convincing the German garrison on the island of Ventotene to surrender. BJ unit 4 took part in a number of small operations in the Adriatic Sea. The culmination of BJ activity in Europe was during the invasion of southern France in 1944, under command of Douglas Fairbanks. His deception task force took part in two major diversions to either side of the actual landings. The BJs did not take part in the Normandy invasion, as the British were in charge of the overall deception plans for that operation and did not feel they were needed.

Later, the BJ units in the Pacific were more concerned with the growing field of radar deception and jamming. They took part in broadcasting false radio signals to deceive the Japanese as to the composition and location of the Allied fleets. The last BJ operation of the war helped General MacArthur make his famous return to the Philippines by drawing off Japanese defenses. Lieutenant Commander Burris-Meyer eventually operated a facility where he trained officers in the theory and practice of strategic and tactical deception. Operating under control of the JSC, it was code-named the "Young Ladies Seminary."[6]

When the navy moved its deception operations to Camp Bradford, the army took over the facilities at Fort Hancock, organizing it as the Army Experimental Station (AES) on 4 June 1943. Control of the facility was initially under the Army Ground Forces, but passed in January 1944 to the Chief of the Signal Corps. All activities that took place at the AES were classified as "secret." Command of the AES was given to a very interesting officer, Colonel Hilton Howell Railey.

Colonel Hilton H. Railey was the visionary commander of the Army Experimental Station. Beloved and respected by all, he more than any other individual deserves credit for the sonic deception program in WWII.
PHOTO: DICK SYRACUSE

Railey had a very unusual past. He was an intensely charismatic man and had started off as a journalist, but when WWI broke out he found himself developing a class on venereal disease for American soldiers. He was commissioned in the U.S. Army and spent the war at various camps, providing what must have been the first sexual education many of the troops had ever had. After the war he went to cover the fighting in Poland as a journalist and, in an odd series of events, ended up on the Polish Army General Staff.[7]

Railey then moved into the new field of public relations and found himself involved in such diverse activities as raising money to salvage the *Lusitania* and helping to fund Admiral Byrd's Antarctic expedition. He was the primary public relations man who helped make Amelia Earhart a household name. When WWII broke out, he helped the army survey the opinions of its soldiers. That project resulted in the "Why We Fight" series of films used to educate American troops. Returning to the army as a colonel, Railey seemed the perfect man for the job of developing deception. The theatrical nature of deception greatly appealed to him and he used his many contacts in New York to further the cause. It was Railey who had convinced the Walgreen family to loan their yacht to the army for the duration of the war. Everyone who worked with him recalled that he was truly a larger than life character. His uniforms were tailored for him in New York City, and he periodically cooked exotic dishes for his officers.

Railey was convinced that deception could play a major role in the war. Most officers at the time, however, thought of the field as somehow underhanded and not a fair way to fight. Most of the senior officers had no concept of the technical nature of sonic deception or, for that matter, even the recent breakthroughs in recording. At one point Railey had hooked his telephone line up to a wire recorder as an experiment. When he was called by a general he informed the officer that "this line is being recorded." The general had never heard of such a thing and remarked, "What the hell does that mean?"[8]

Fort Hancock was not the best location to test out sound transmission. There was a lot of activity in the area and the background noise hindered accurate measurement. Railey looked around for another location for the AES and found a perfect site at Pine Camp, New York. Pine Camp, now known as Fort Drum, was located in upper New York State. It was quiet, had Lake Ontario nearby for testing on water, and both open and wooded areas for testing on land. The Wheeler-Sack airstrip could be used to bring in necessary men and equipment, while the hangar was perfect for working on secret equipment, or vehicles, in all types of weather.

In February 1944 the AES officially moved to Pine Camp. Railey took over a small complex of buildings off to one side of the camp. (Today those buildings house the 10th Mountain Division Light Fighters School.) A barbed wire fence was erected around the complex and all traffic in and out was carefully monitored. Secrecy was paramount; if the enemy knew that Americans were working on sonic deception they would be prepared for it.

Colonel Railey wrote, "Real security can only be attained in the long run through confusion. False speculation concerning the mission of this station has been encouraged and, on occasions, initiated."[9] Personnel were encouraged to fuel the imagination of anyone who questioned the mission of the AES. To this day, local residents are still convinced that top-secret work on the atomic bomb was performed in the AES compound. Adding to the security problem was a group of Italian POWs housed at Pine Camp. Although never allowed near the facility, there was concern that one of them would find out that the AES was working on sonic deception and somehow inform Axis intelligence.

Given Colonel Railey's concern with security, it is odd that he designed a distinctive insignia for the men of the AES. A small silver shield was produced bearing the image of a devil thumbing his nose. This pin, roughly half the size

Exact meteorological information was vital to determine how loud to broadcast the sound. Of particular importance was measuring the temperature and wind direction, both at and above ground level. This jeep was used at Pine Camp to take such measurments, but in Europe the same equipment was carried on a ¾-ton truck.

of a standard U.S. Army metal insignia, was worn on the left side of the garrison cap. Railey issued written orders to his men stating that they were to thumb their noses at anyone, officers included, pressing them for information on what was going on in the AES compound. This badge was worn by the staff of the AES, as well as by the 3132nd, and the later organized 3133rd Signal Service Company. It became known as the "big deal insignia" (stemming from others asking what was the big deal about all the secrecy). Later in the war, the AES newspaper would be called "The Big Deal."

The AES was primarily concerned with sonic deception, but took on other related projects. One of the more unusual was based on the German idea of mounting sirens on their dive-bombers to add to the fear of men being attacked. Since an eerie noise was made when you blew across the mouth of an empty bottle, someone had the bright idea of dropping empty beer bottles out of an aircraft to scare men on the ground. When tested, the bottles made no sound, but the men chosen as targets did find they became afraid of being hit by one of the falling bottles.[10]

Other sonic devices were tested at Pine Camp. An entire range of combat noise simulators was developed under the overall code name of CHARLES. MR. CHARLES was a .30-caliber machine-gun simulator; MRS. CHARLES sounded like rifle fire; and CHARLES JR. mimicked the sound of a 60mm mortar. CANARY made the noise of a vehicle motor, and SIREN the sound of a tracked vehicle. No records were located to indicate if any of these projects were continued past the testing stage. Railey and the AES must have caused quite a stir on the post, or as one anonymous veteran later claimed, "Never in the history of military organizations have so few caused so much trouble to so many."

On 27 January 1944, the JSC issued an order that sonic vehicles should never be used for anything other than the reproduction of tactical sounds for deception work. The feeling was that if the sonic cars were used for other purposes, such as propaganda broadcasts, it might make the enemy aware of the ability of the playback equipment and compromise future deceptive operations. Although the members of the JSC voted unanimously against nondeceptive uses, the officers of the 3132nd would later find themselves ordered to take part in propaganda missions.

To increase the security of the sonic troops, the JSC also ordered (in February 1944) that all references to the terms "sonic" and "deception" were to be eliminated from all published material or tables. Instead the term "special" was to be added to the end of the unit designation as an indication they were something different. From that point on neither tables of organization, orders for men to report to the unit, passes, nor any other form of printed material would make a reference to sonic deception.

The main focus of the AES was the formation of the first U.S. Army sonic deception unit: the 3132nd Signal Service Company. Officially organized on 1 March 1944 under the command of Major Florian, the 3132nd was composed

Colonel Railey (in front row with dark uniform) was photographed at Pine Camp along with the men of the 3132nd Signal Service Company before they shipped out for Europe. This was the first, but not the last, sonic deception unit organized by the U.S. Army. PHOTO: WALTER MANSER

of three main elements: a headquarters platoon, three sonic platoons, and a chemical platoon.

The headquarters platoon consisted of the necessary supply, communications, and mess sections, and a technical and maintenance section (T&M). The T&M section was in charge of the library of recorded sounds, mixing the recordings onto the wire magazines, and maintaining all the sonic equipment. Two enlisted weathermen were allocated to the T&M section to take the readings essential to figuring out how loud the broadcasts should be played. The weathermen were obtained from the Army Air Force, where there was a surplus of men trained in that skill.

The three sonic platoons each had five "sonic cars" (M3A1 half-tracks mounting playback and loudspeaker equipment) and a standard half-track as a command vehicle. The half-tracks were altered to carry the sound equipment by adding new steel cabinets, shockproof mountings, a speaker-lifting structure and swivel head, rectangular gas tanks, mounting shelves, and a modified canvas top. These modifications cost $1,000 per vehicle, and every effort was made to finish them by 1 April 1944.

Once the modified half-tracks arrived at Pine Camp, the men began to install all the necessary sound playback equipment. The large speakers were mounted onto an armature that could be cranked into an upright position. This was not an easy task, and the complicated system of gears was soon dubbed the "coffee grinder."

When the speakers were cranked into an upright position they pointed to the rear of the half-track. They were designed that way so that if attacked by the enemy the sonic cars would be positioned to immediately withdraw, by driving away without having to turn around. When not in use, the speakers were lowered into the half-track bed. With the canvas covering in place there was no way to tell the sonic cars apart from the thousands of other half-tracks being used by the army.

To prevent the sonic gear from falling into the hands of the enemy, each half-track was rigged for emergency demolition. Captain Walter A. Ford, a demolition expert from the Engineer Board, arrived in May, "in order to insure the proper installation of demolition devices in certain combat vehicles."[11] He decided that to totally destroy the vehicle and its equipment, two separate containers of explosives were needed. Each held eight blocks of demolition chain M-1 and one block of demolition M-2. Both were connected by explosive detonation cord and could be triggered by an M2 waterproof fuse lighter. The igniter was located under the driver's seat and, once pulled, only eighteen inches of blasting fuse had to burn before the charges would go off. This was roughly a fifteen second delay.

Spares of the special mounting equipment were kept in the unit supply trucks so, in a pinch, broken equipment could be replaced, or a command half-track could be converted in the field to sonic use. There had been enough difficulty in obtaining the necessary equipment in the States. An adequate stock of replacements was mandatory if the unit expected to be able to operate in a combat zone.

The chemical platoon was to provide smoke screens to cover the activities of the sonic platoons. However, it rapidly became apparent that such a smoke producing unit was not really needed in the 3132nd, but a reconnaissance and security platoon was. The 4th Platoon Leader, Lieutenant Dick Syracuse, was told to turn his smoke platoon into a tough commando-like security platoon able to perform whatever task was necessary. He was told his primary mission was to make sure that, no matter what happened, none of the sonic cars would ever fall into enemy hands. His 4th platoon was eventually named the "special operations platoon."

Lieutenant Syracuse was one of the more interesting men in the 3132nd. He had been a chemical engineering student before the war, and had earned an infantry commission in ROTC. He later remarked that one of the only smart things the army ever did was utilize that experience by transferring him to the Chemical Warfare Corps.[12] He was given command of an all-black chemical company in the Deep South and set about training them in their job of creating smoke screens. At this time, white officers commanded most black

The speaker assembly mounted in the sonic half-tracks was raised to an upright position by means of a cranking assembly known as the "coffee grinder." The sonic equipment could be totally hidden beneath a canvas cover when not in use so that no one would realize the vehicle was anything but a typical half-track. Raising the speaker was a tough task to perform at night in a total blackout.

An aircraft hangar at Pine Camp was used to house all the sonic vehicles. This allowed them to be hidden from prying eyes, as well as to be worked on around the clock without regard to darkness or weather conditions. Note the man with the Army Air Force patch on his uniform: he is one of the weathermen acquired from the Air Force to take meteorological readings. Photographs of the sonic equipment were strictly prohibited, and not one of the veterans had any in their collections. These were found in various, formerly classified, military files.

Lieutenant Syracuse's 4th Platoon, seen here during an inspection (above), and during training (left) had its mission changed from being a smoke-screen unit to the security unit for the sonic vehicles. Their orders were that under no circumstances were any of the sonic half-tracks to be allowed to fall into enemy hands.
PHOTO: DICK SYRACUSE

units and many of those officers not only looked down upon their black soldiers, but also felt that such an assignment was beneath their dignity. Syracuse, being from the Bronx, did not care about the color of a man's skin, but only how well he could do his job.

Syracuse soon ran into an unsympathetic commander who resented his treatment of the black troops. Lieutenant Syracuse respected his men for what they could do and they responded by giving him the best company in the unit. During a unit readiness test, his was the only company to qualify for overseas movement. This was not the way to make friends in his unit, and his commander had him transferred after a minor incident. As an unassigned chemical officer, he ended up being selected for the 3132nd Signal Service Company.

As a chemical officer, Lieutenant Syracuse had to rely on his own imagination to train his men for their new reconnaissance and security role. He had them constantly on the move and his cries of "hubba hubba" (meaning "hurry up") were continually heard in the AES encampment. He developed a signature technique for keeping his men alert at all times. At random intervals he would suddenly strike his chest with his right fist and cry out "Jab!" To show they were alert his men also struck their chests and cried out "Jab!" The sound of this training became commonplace in the AES area and it was only a matter of time before Syracuse acquired the nickname "Hubba Hubba Jab Jab."

Most of the enlisted men in the 3132nd came from disbanded ASTP programs and were extremely bright. This came in handy because they were organizing the very first unit of its type in the U.S. Army. Fifty-six percent of the officers initially selected for the unit washed out for various reasons. Colonel Railey replaced anyone he felt was not the very best for the 3132nd. Major Florian was one of those transferred out (according to rumor, due to a disagreement with Colonel Reeder). He was replaced by Major Charlie Williams, who went on to command the 3132nd until the end of the war.

The technical staff of the 3132nd was trained in how to record sounds, mix them onto the wire magazines, and determine the volume at which the recordings should be played for maximum effectiveness. The sonic platoons learned how to maintain their vehicles, set up the speakers and play back a recorded program. One of the key elements of a sonic deception was the "playing in" and "playing out" of a unit. To play a unit in meant to start with silence and gradually increase the volume of activity. The sounds of approaching vehicles or a column would grow until they moved into a simulated bivouac or assembly area. Conversely, playing a unit out involved starting with the sounds of the engines starting up, then simulating the unit moving out and away from the assembly area. It was important to always try and play a non-existent unit out. If the enemy heard them move up, then later found nothing there, it might tip them off that the Allies were using sound to deceive them.

Major Charlie Williams commanded the 3132nd throughout its time overseas. His position as C.O. (Commanding Officer) was phonetically known as "Charlie Oboe," which became his unofficial nickname in the unit.
PHOTO: WALTER MANSER

The 3132nd was supplied with a library of recordings to meet most of its potential needs. If recordings of a specialized nature were needed, the technical section could make their own recordings in the field. The basic capability of the 3132nd was that it was able to reproduce the sounds of up to three battalions of light, medium, or mixed tanks, field artillery or self-propelled artillery. These could be made to sound as if they were moving along a road, or entering or leaving an assembly area. Truck columns of any size could be simulated.

They could also reproduce the sounds of an engineer battalion constructing fortifications, roads, or a light or heavy bridge. Once the bridge was built, recordings of any type of unit moving across it were available. Activity at railheads (trains, trucks loading, etc.) could also be simulated.

It was always known that one day the 23rd and the 3132nd would operate together, but there had been minimal contact between the two units. A few officers of the 3132nd did travel to Camp Forrest to brief the 23rd on sonic deception, but it appears that the 23rd had little understanding of what the 3132nd could do until they began working together. There does not seem to have been much effort to attempt to let the units train together before they were sent overseas.

On 6 May 1944, the chief signal officer of the army, Major General Harry Ingles, inspected the AES and the 3132nd. Colonel Railey felt under a great deal of pressure to demonstrate everything the unit could do in a very short amount of time, but the program was rushed through so that Ingles could catch a train back to Washington. Everything went reasonably well, with the exception of a miscalculation of sound transmission during the nighttime operation.

A few days later, on 11 May, the 3132nd was inspected to see if it was ready for overseas movement. This was the final step before shipping out. Minor deficiencies in paperwork were fixed and on 30 May 1944, the 3132nd left for Europe. The sonic vehicles were shipped separately. Due to their secret nature, a detachment from the unit was sent with the vehicles as a 24-hour armed guard. The sonic unit arrived in England on 11 June and assumed the code name HEATER.

At the request of Colonel Railey, the 3132nd was allowed an extended period of training in England. They did not leave for France until 8 August.

The sonic half-tracks of the 3132nd are lined up for inspection on the runway at Pine Camp. Each three-man crew stands before their vehicle while one of many visiting dignitaries observes how they operate. A large part of Colonel Railey's job was convincing the army that sonic deception would be useful to the war effort.
PHOTO: WALTER MANSER

Some time was spent training at Tidworth, and an observer at a 12 July 1944 demonstration on the Salisbury Plain remarked, "The exercise was successful from a technical standpoint, but proved that the unit lacked sufficient field training. This was especially true from a standpoint of night operations since some of the elements of the company became lost and delayed the exercise for several hours."[13]

Observers in England had some concern for the ruggedness of the sound equipment. Major Williams sent a memo to Colonel Railey later in July 1944 warning him that the 12th Army Group Special Plans Branch felt the sound equipment had "too much laboratory and not enough practical field G.I. characteristics."[14] This was probably due to a tendency for some of the speaker cones to blow when there was a sudden rise in volume. Williams went on to express his concern about how his unit might be used: "Matters are very confused and in fact many of the people using the tools and planning their future uses don't seem to want to read the instructions that come with them. Preconceived ideas seem to be in fashion."

As soon as the 3132nd arrived in England there was talk of using the unit for propaganda broadcasts, although this had been expressly forbidden by the JSC. Complaints made to ETOUSA resulted in a promise that the unit would only be committed in accordance with its primary mission. Yet it would only be a matter of weeks after landing in France that the 3132nd would be sent on a propaganda mission.

A remarkably fast Channel crossing allowed the 3132nd to finally meet up with the rest of the 23rd HQ at Le Fremondre (north of Coutances) on 9 August. Sixty-three days after the D-day landing, the 23rd HQ, Special Troops was finally all in one place. In hindsight it might have been a good idea to have trained both the 23rd and the 3132nd at the same camp in the United States, or allowed for joint training in England. It also seems that at least some of the staff above the 23rd should have been more closely involved with the development of the unit for which they were to plan operations. However, the timetable of war never waits for a perfect plan, and eventually everyone would work well together.

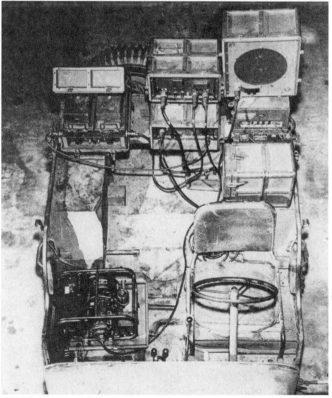

The AES attempted to mount a small sonic system in a jeep, but it was found to be impractical due to the low output and amount of extra equipment needed. In this version the entire passenger seat is taken up with a small power generator. The twin wire magazines are seen in left rear corner.

Chapter 6

Operation BRITTANY
9–12 August 1944

With ELEPHANT completed and the men adjusting to life in the field, the 23rd Special Troops was ready for a new assignment. The Allies held the Normandy coastline and had captured the port of Cherbourg. The next objective of the American Army was to drive west to liberate the port of Brest and to prepare the area around Quiberon Bay for the development of an artificial port.[1]

In early August, the Special Plans Branch at 12th Army Group requested that the 23rd develop four different operations to simulate reinforcements arriving in Brittany. One plan would have two columns of simulated troops move to the port of Brest. The second would move only one column to Brest, but also portray the landing of a division on the north shore of Brittany, which would then move to Brest. The third plan was to feign the arrival of a new division along the Normandy beaches, then move it to Periers, and on to Brest. The fourth proposal was to include all of the above.

Plans were drawn up for the approval of 12th Army Group, taking into account what had been learned through its short time in France and from other intelligence sources. To update the entire unit on what was now known of the German intelligence services, the 23rd S-2 (intelligence officer), Major Joseph P. Kelly, issued a lengthy memorandum on 8 August 1944.[2]

S-2 Estimate—Capabilities of German Intelligence Agencies

1.   a. This estimate is based upon information obtained from G-2 weekly and periodic reports of FUSA: intelligence notes, Weekly Intelligence Summary and Martian Reports from SHAEF; Air Intelligence Summaries from USSAF; Daily Summary of Events from ETOUSA and other information obtained from various other sources of military and intelligence in the UK.

---

b. The conclusions drawn concerning the capabilities of certain German intelligence agencies are based on factual information contained in the above reports and estimates made by the above mentioned intelligence agencies.

2.   a. The German Air Force is capable of:

> (1) High altitude photo reconnaissance carried out by single fighter type planes on a very limited scale and of value chiefly for locating large permanent or semi-permanent installations.
> (2) Low altitude fighter reconnaissance, either visual or photographic, on a very limited scale in forward combat areas and of value chiefly for spotting movements of motor and/or armored formations.
> (3) Visual reconnaissance at night by fighter or fighter-bomber type aircraft, of value in locating firing batteries of artillery, forward landing strips and large supply installations. These types of reconnaissance planes employ flares to illuminate their targets, which are then bombed and strafed. Flares have also been used in forward areas to spot night movements of troops, particularly armored formations.
> (4) GAF aerial reconnaissance has been rendered almost completely ineffective by allied air superiority and heavy AAA protection and is carried out only on a very limited scale under great difficulties. There is confirming evidence that the German Air Force has used captured Allied aircraft and cameras for reconnaissance purposes.

b. German radio intelligence is capable of intercepting all radio traffic down to and including frontline battalions. Radio intercept platoons are an organic part of each German signal battalion and are always active. Both fixed and mobile direction finding stations are used extensively. Reliable information has been obtained confirming the activities and excellent results obtained by German radio intelligence in this theater. POWs from a German signal battalion claim to have broken the British codes used by air support nets in ten minutes. Each radio intercept platoon includes an interpreter section and possibly cryptographic personnel.

c. German artillery observation battalions are capable of locating firing batteries by flash or sound ranging, but the mass of artillery employed by our forces has largely nullified their effectiveness to date. At least one observation battalion was employed on the First Army front by the German *LXXXIV Corps*. The following method of employment was noted on the American First Army front: reconnaissance planes would fly over suspected battery locations at night and spot the batteries by the flash of the guns. The planes would then drop flares over the battery positions and the location would be obtained by flash ranging devices.

d. German ground agents are capable of identifying all units of the American forces, locating all military installations and observing all troop movements. Agents have been extensively employed by Germany in the current Neptune Operation. Most of those apprehended have been Frenchmen in the employ of the Germans. Definite evidence has been secured proving that women have also been used for this purpose. French civilians are present in all operational areas and have access to the above listed information, which may be transmitted to agents either deliberately or misintentionally.

3. **Conclusions**

a. In operations undertaken to deceive enemy intelligence agencies, the relative importance of deceptive measures are in the following order: radio deception, deceptive measures against ground agents, visual deception against aerial reconnaissance.

b. Radio deception is of exceptional importance because of the widespread activities of the enemy radio intelligence and the apparent importance of radio intelligence to the enemy. It is conceivable that situations might present themselves whereby desired deception could be achieved by radio alone. This would probably be effective only on a small scale and for a relatively short period of time.

c. Deceptive measures against enemy ground agents are important in that they would, if successful, confirm in part the false information broadcast by radio deception. These measures should include the use of appropriate shoulder patches, bumper markings, road signs, Command Post signs, MPs, typical road traffic, sonic deception, etc., coupled with proper security measures to prevent disclosure of operational equipment to civilians. Failure to use deceptive measures against ground agents would undoubtedly result in the early failure of any deceptive operation.

d. Visual deception against enemy air reconnaissance, both visual and photographic, is necessary to present a deceptive picture complete in all details. However, due to the present limitation of GAF reconnaissance, the excellent cover available and the existing tracked and littered fields, this part of the deceptive scheme does not necessarily have to be highly detailed to achieve its purpose. As a general rule, nothing but heavy and bulky equipment need be indicated since anything else could easily be concealed from air observation. Except in areas where existing traffic is heavy, some movement along roads toward the operational area would have to be indicated to deceive

> both aerial observation and ground agents. The extent of this deceptive traffic would depend upon the type of operation, road net available and weather. Sonic deception at night would be particularly valuable to indicate heavy traffic in any given area.
>
> Joseph P. Kelly
> Major, Infantry
> S-2

Before the proposed operation could be approved, the situation was drastically altered. The original plan had called for General Patton's Third Army to break through the German lines and sweep out to Brittany. There the Americans would construct a massive port at Quiberon Bay to supply the drive to the German border. However, Patton had broken through the German line with such force that the bulk of the German Army in France was in retreat. The Third Army was now focused on swinging around to the south in an attempt to surround the German forces.

The 23rd was ordered to conduct an operation to "create an impression that the United States Army was weakening its forces in front of the main battle position and turning to clear the Brittany peninsula prior to a major push in Normandy."[3] Although no documentary evidence has been located to indicate the actual concept behind the plan, it would appear that the 23rd was to make the Germans think the real American objective was still Brittany and not the encirclement of their army. If the Germans felt the pressure on them was being reduced, perhaps they would not withdraw from their positions as quickly and more of their troops could be caught in the pocket. What other reason could there be for pulling combat units out of the front lines and diverting them to the west?

One of the code names given to the plan to pin the German Army in place was "Tactical Operation B." Not only was the 23rd involved in this plan, but also the turned German agents in England, who sent messages to the Abwehr indicating that the front lines were being weakened to send troops to Brittany.[4] It is debatable if some of these preparations were intended to draw the Germans into a counterattack (such as the one they made at Mortain), which would pin down and destroy their last remaining mobile reserves in the Normandy area. The timing was a bit late if that was the Allied intention. What is interesting is that the name "Tactical Operation B" bears a striking similarity to the SHAEF deception group named "Ops (B)."

Part of "Tactical Operation B" was Operation BRITTANY, and it would be the first time the 23rd attempted to spread what was termed "atmosphere." This was the look and feel of a military unit in the area. Whenever possible, men were encouraged to wander the area wearing their (phony) division patches. They were encouraged to talk to the locals and spread word of the

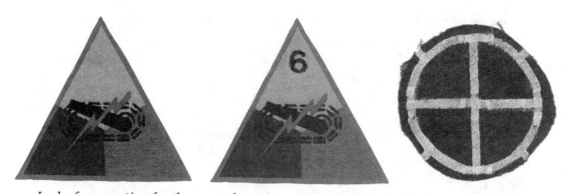

Lack of cooperation for the secret deception missions meant the 23rd was not able to obtain issue shoulder patches from the quartermasters. The artists of the 23rd were forced to hand paint the insignia on scraps of old shelter halves for the first few missions. These are original examples of insignia from (left to right) the 2nd Armored Division, the 6th Armored Division and the 35th Infantry Division used in Operations ELEPHANT, BRITTANY, *and* BETTEMBOURG.

imminent arrival of their division. Normally, soldiers are warned not to give civilians such information, but it was commonplace to drop a few tidbits of gossip when bartering for some eggs or calvados.

Operation BRITTANY took the form of four separate columns, each assuming the guise of a different division heading west. Each of the four columns was given a code name taken from the phonetic alphabet: MIKE, NAN, PETER, and OBOE. Lieutenant Colonel Day went on ahead to the Brest area and set up an SCR-399 radio to simulate an advance party of the 35th Infantry Division. Captain Edward Cowardin was sent to Lorient with an SCR-506 as an advance party of the 80th and 90th Infantry Divisions. The proposed illusion would have the units heading west, communicating with the advance party near the ports. Each column left Sartilly on 10 August and headed for the genuine location of the unit they were portraying. They then turned west along an arranged route.

The 23rd was able to obtain only a handful of each division's shoulder patches. The artists of the 603rd were called to create reasonable substitutes on salvaged canvas at a moment's notice. PETER had only six genuine patches and one hundred and twenty-four painted ones. NAN used seventy-five painted patches and thirty-eight genuine ones. These numbers were still not enough as men had to move the patch from jacket to shirt as the weather grew warmer.

Stencils for bumper markings were also created so the vehicles could be properly marked when they reached their initial assembly point. A few of the trucks had their markings painted on from the start, but were kept covered by canvas bumper covers until the time was right to reveal the markings. This was found to work well and was suggested for future operations.

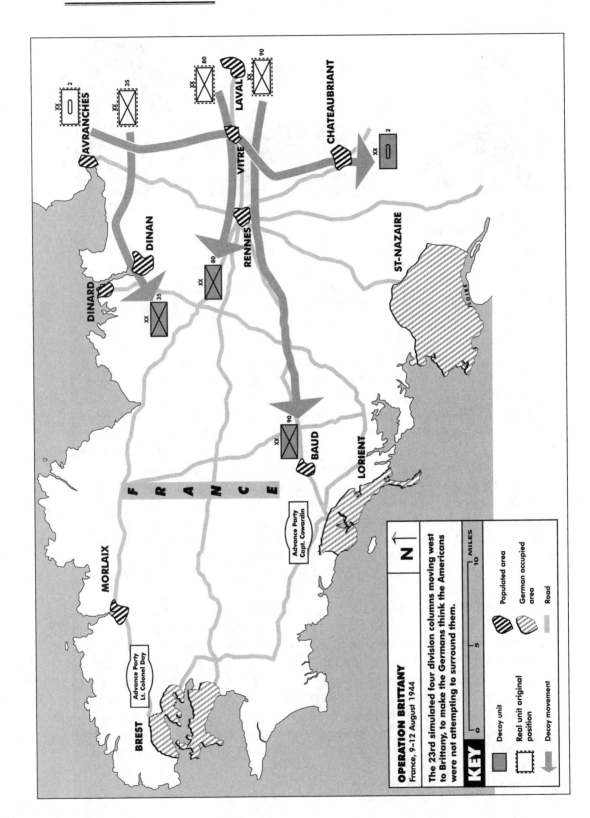

OPERATION BRITTANY
France, 9–12 August 1944

The 23rd simulated four division columns moving west to Brittany, to make the Germans think the Americans were not attempting to surround them.

KEY

Decoy unit

Real unit original position

Decoy movement

Populated area

German occupied area

Road

N

MILES
0   5   10

Task Force MIKE with seventeen vehicles, under command of Colonel Mayo, simulated a combat team from the 35th Infantry Division (the 314th Infantry Regiment plus an attached 105mm artillery battalion). MIKE started their march from St. Hilaire and moved on to Dinan. Germans were known to ambush convoys in the area beyond Dinan, so Colonel Mayo decided to wait there until he could join up with an armed guard.

MIKE sent only four radio messages and received seven on the first day. Radio conditions were so bad it took over two hours to send the first message, then another hour and forty-eight minutes for the second. The assumption was that the Germans were broadcasting on the same frequency to jam it. Most of the messages sent indicated only that the unit had crossed a specific phase line. Colonel Mayo went on ahead to the VIII Corps HQ to request an armed guard for his convoy, but was directed to the 6th Armored Division to try and join one of their supply convoys. He was unable to find anyone heading to Brest that he could join up with, and upon reporting this back to Reeder was ordered to stay in place and continue to transmit. The radio frequencies were continually jammed until the operation was finally called off.

Colonel Mayo was later quite upset that he had been given a mission of traveling one hundred and sixty-six miles through enemy infested territory (referred to as "Indian territory" by the army) without anyone arranging for an armed escort. Also frustrating was that VIII Corps had not been notified of their operation and refused to help them get to Brest. On the plus side, he did feel that a forty-six-mile journey west, transmitting periodically, would be enough for the Germans to note a unit headed in that direction. The stopping of his convoy would have probably been explained by the massive traffic congestion happening in the area.

Task Force NAN was commanded by Captain Seale. It simulated the movement of a combat team of the 80th Infantry Division (318th Infantry Regiment plus an attached 105mm artillery battalion and an element of the 80th Signal Company) to Brest. Leaving Sartilly, NAN moved to an assembly area at Laval. There they were to head to Brest along the route Rennes–Rostrenen–Landernau.

Captain Cowardin, acting as a divisional advance party, was ordered to proceed no further than the vicinity of St. Meen if he was not able to find a combat unit to travel with through "Indian territory." His small party would have made a tempting target for any German soldiers.

NAN traveled an average of ten miles an hour. At 1400 on the first day (10 August) a bicycle-riding Frenchman reported two German snipers in the area. Captain Seale sent out two dismounted patrols to investigate, but found nothing. That evening, NAN moved into a bivouac near Pace and a third of the men were sent into the villages of Pace and St. Gilles to spread the word that the 80th Infantry Division would be moving up. The next day, soldiers dressed as 80th Division MPs were sent into Rennes. That morning two officers from the genuine 80th Division appeared at the bivouac area looking for their unit. They had been told elements of the 80th were in the area. These officers were quietly told to forget everything they had seen and were pointed in the right direction.

Captain Seale and Pfc. Charles Gorman fitted themselves out as 80th Division MPs and went into Rennes spreading word that their division would soon arrive. Seale discussed the matter with the Americans already in Rennes, while Gorman, who spoke French, freely talked to the city's inhabitants. After they returned to camp, two parties raided local French farms suspected of harboring German soldiers, but none were found.

That night German air activity in the area was heavier than usual and the radio channels being used by the Americans were jammed. The next day Captain Seale and Pfc. Gorman returned to Rennes to again spread word of the imminent arrival of the 80th Division. Dressed as MPs they found the best method was to enter a bar, loudly announce that it was now off limits and that the GIs should finish their drinks and leave. While waiting for the other Americans to finish their drinks they had a chance to join them in a comradely fashion and spread their gossip.[5]

A messenger arrived at 1205 with orders to end the operation, and everyone removed all 80th patches and bumper markings. The men left the bivouac area at ten minute intervals to avoid calling attention to themselves. They rendezvoused about four miles away, and returned to the 23rd encampment.

Task Force OBOE, under command of Lieutenant Colonel Schroeder, simulated a combat team of the 90th Infantry Division (plus one attached 155mm artillery battalion) en route to Lorient. On 10 August OBOE transformed into a unit of the 90th Division (put on patches, MP helmets, and removed bumper covers) and moved from Le Mans to Rennes. They received a small amount of sniper fire along the route but took no casualties. American MPs along the way were able to offer little in the way of directions or information on the conditions ahead. Schroeder was concerned that he had not been issued a map of the area, and warned the men that they were going to be moving into potentially dangerous territory and to be on the alert.

By 11 August OBOE had still not been able to achieve radio contact with Captain Cowardin at Lorient due to intense German jamming, but continued to send periodic situation reports of its progress, the same as a genuine unit would do. The column left Rennes at 0430, but was forced to halt for two hours due to an extremely thick fog. The going was slow until they reached Ploermel, where a few members of the French Forces of the Interior (FFI) joined the column. Radio communications were restored that morning and a number of messages were sent. They bivouacked that night on a hill near Baud and could see scattered Germans filtering to the south in the valley below them. Periodic firefights occurred between the Germans and parties of the FFI.

On 12 August OBOE made contact with elements of the 4th Armored Division, from whom they received supplies of food, water, and gas. Patrols were sent out in the daylight to scout the area, attempting to simulate advance patrols of the 90th Division. Staff Sergeant Wendell Tuttle led combat patrols to clear the area of German stragglers. He would later be awarded a Bronze Star for his efforts on these patrols.

Even though Tuttle did not find them, there were a number of Germans moving through the area. The local FFI claimed to have taken over a hundred casualties during nighttime actions. The French seemed greatly encouraged to know a larger unit of the American Army was on the way. To prevent there being any bad feelings, Lieutenant Colonel Schroeder informed them that they were on a special mission and were unable to assist, but that eventually another American unit would arrive to help clear the area.

Worried that he had been out of contact too long, Schroeder sent a small patrol off in a jeep to try and contact the 23rd Headquarters. Sergeant Martin Cogan and his detachment were able to make their way to Rennes, without a map, where by pure luck they spotted Major Hooper who was out looking for the missing column.[6]

On the morning of 13 August, a message was received that Operation BRITTANY had ended. Task Force OBOE had traveled six hundred and two miles, much of it through unsecured territory. OBOE was considered to be a success since the Germans had attempted to jam their radio transmissions and then had suddenly stopped, obviously listening in to figure out who this unit was and where it was going.

Task Force PETER, commanded by Lieutenant Colonel James Snee, simulated a tank battalion, an armored infantry battalion, and an armored field artillery battalion of the 2nd Armored Division on its way to Lorient. PETER left Sartilly at 0600 on 10 August with only one map of the region, and headed to an area just to the north of Chateaubriant. The column moved into a bivouac area in a wooded area just south of Martigne. Rubber decoys were put into position by 1800 and three men dressed as 2nd Armored Division MPs were sent into Martigne.[7] They spread rumors of a convoy of infantry that would soon pass by, while accepting drinks of wine and champagne offered by the mayor's daughter. When they returned to the bivouac to tell of their adventure there was no shortage of volunteers for similar duty.

Everyone not otherwise occupied was told to roam the area, spreading "atmosphere." A few of the trucks were driven around the area allowing bystanders to see the bumper markings, but they were back by 2300. That night a few German aircraft did pass overhead and it seemed that two circled, indicating an interest in the area.

Of the four columns, only PETER set up an encampment with inflatable decoys. Company C of the 603rd was responsible for setting up the fifty-four decoys, thirty-two camouflage nets, and thirty-five shelter halves (out of one hundred and thirty-seven decoys and sixty camouflage nets brought along). Seven of the inflatable decoys had to be patched and another five were so badly damaged that they had to be replaced. Locals were kept away from the decoys by being told the fields in which they sat were mined.

The next day a group of simulated MPs from PETER were sent into Chateaubriant, while other men from the task force were told to go bathing in local streams. The same group eventually ended up swimming in a few different locations to make it appear that there were more men in the area.

The locals throughout the area were delighted to talk to the Americans, and full of information on small groups of Germans hiding out in the woods. Five German POWs were handed over to PETER by the FFI. One of them was a German Army mechanic. He was amazed at the quality of the American vehicles, but once he saw the food the American soldiers were fed he declared he wanted to renounce his German citizenship and join the American Army!

In both Martigne and Chateaubriant, one overly curious Frenchman was provided information on the size and composition of the notional 2nd Armored. The other locals warned the Americans not to talk to him, as that individual had been very friendly with the Germans and might be working with them. On 11 August a French messenger arrived requesting help for his forces at Nantes. He was driven to the local FFI commander in Chateaubriant who had been expecting him. Later that night a number of German aircraft circled the bivouac, but did not drop any flares.

At midnight on 11 August the orders came to end the operation. The orders actually told them to "fade," which was the term indicating they should quietly fade the simulated unit into the background and disappear. Patches were removed, dummies stored away, and bumper markings removed. The now anonymous elements of PETER moved off in small groups heading for a rendezvous point south of Vitre.

One small detachment of PETER remained behind in 2nd Armored markings. The vehicles leaving made lots of noise, so those remaining behind told any civilians in the area the unit had moved on to Lorient, and not to worry because any vehicles they saw headed north were moving back to bring up more supplies. The same information was disseminated in Martigne and Chateaubriant. Once the engineers reached a quiet area, all markings were removed and they headed back to the 23rd camp.

With the return of PETER to the 23rd encampment, Operation BRITTANY had ended. The most positive result was the enemy's jamming of their radio frequencies. Evaluation of the jamming indicated it was probably directed at the deception units for the following reasons: the jamming was spread over a fifty kilocycle band that centered on the deception frequencies; the jamming started when they transmitted and ended when they stopped; there were no other ground units using that radio band (only long established Air Force units); and no other jamming had been detected on that frequency before.

The signal company felt that jamming was like the inflatable decoys being strafed or shelled—a sure sign the Germans had taken the bait and thought it was a real unit. A decision was made to construct four mobile radio direction finders so that in the future they could track the source of any such jamming.

Most of the officers involved had many suggestions to improve the unit's efficiency in the future. There were supply problems, such as obtaining enough shoulder patches and maps beforehand (PETER had only one map of the area they were to travel). Obviously there was still some difficulty in getting the necessary cooperation from higher headquarters. The signal officer had trouble getting assigned frequencies, call signs, and authentication codes. It was suggested that no task forces such as these should ever be sent out without a case of pigeons for emergency communications, due to the possibility of losing contact because of enemy jamming or radio malfunction.

Everyone felt they had turned in a good performance, but that far greater coordination and planning were needed. Many of the men had not been briefed on the correct names of senior officers in the unit they were portraying. The "atmosphere" could have been improved among the simulated armored units by issuing men the distinctive jacket, with knit collar and cuffs, that tank crews traditionally wore. Soon afterward, a third of the men were issued with both the desirable tankers' jackets and the one-piece herringbone twill overalls used by vehicle crews and mechanics.

Major Kelly was particularly upset at being sent off in a jeep to contact OBOE, having been given only a vague location of the unit. After searching the area around Rennes for OBOE, Kelly finally returned to the 23rd only to discover he had been given the wrong map coordinates. Kelly subsequently wrote a two-page memo, stating, "the practice of dispatching officers on missions with incomplete information is extremely wasteful of manpower and actually causes far more delay than if they had waited for more definite instructions."[8]

It is very difficult to assess the effectiveness of this operation. There are tantalizing clues that it may have slowed the German withdrawal from the Falaise Pocket, where the bulk of the German forces from the Normandy front were destroyed. The 23rd's own report states, "German troops delayed withdrawal in the Normandy pocket sufficiently for five (5) U.S. divisions to drive in behind them."[9] The 23rd, however, did not claim credit for delaying the Germans. In the army's official history of the campaign it is mentioned that an order arrived from Hitler on 14 August "alluding to what seemed to the Germans to be a change in the direction of the XV Corps' thrust from north to the west."[10]

The history of the 406th Engineers, written during the war, states, "Although no enemy documents were captured to show that the Wehrmacht believed U.S. forces were being diverted from Normandy to the clearance of Brittany, the German did what the American Army commanders wanted him to do—keep his troops in the Falaise Pocket until the trap was sprung."[11]

Now that the principal commanders on both sides have passed away, there is no way to determine how much the deception affected the battle. While there is some evidence the deception troops were noticed, this does not necessarily mean the German commanders altered their plans on account of them.

The next best thing to an admission that the Germans were in fact fooled would be if the deceptive information made it into German intelligence summaries. Most behind-the-lines intelligence was gathered and processed by the German military at the Army Group level. Thus, if the Germans took the bait, the movement of the false units might show up on Army Group B's intelligence summaries.

After WWII, the Americans captured many German records. Eventually the originals were returned to Germany after being microfilmed and copies placed in the National Archives. Sadly, many of the records relating to the German withdrawal from the Falaise Pocket appear to have been lost. There are numerous gaps in the records, which frustratingly always seem to be on key dates. Additionally, the microfilming was not always of the finest quality (government contracting) and some sections are blurred or otherwise unreadable.

A number of situational maps of the Western front do exist and these were examined for any indication of the false movements.[12] The records covering the period of Operation BRITTANY are missing key dates, possibly due to the confusing and rapid retreat of the German forces during this period. Given that there should have been a time lag between locating the unit and preparing the maps, the dates during and after the operation were examined. No confirming evidence in these files was found to prove the Germans were fooled, although there were a number of question marks in locations traversed by the deception columns, which might indicate reports of American troops being spotted.

In any event, due to the missing records, the poor quality of the microfilm, and the author's admittedly imperfect background with fifty-five-year-old German intelligence styles and nomenclature, this may be a fruitful avenue of research for an expert in German intelligence methods with access to the original records. (Hopefully this book will stir interest in the question.)

Operation BRITTANY may also be connected to one of the most controversial events in the ETO. On 13 August 1944, General Bradley ordered the XV Corps to stop their advance at Argentan, on the southern flank of the German pocket. To quote Martin Blumenson, an official army historian, "Why General Bradley made his decision and whether he was correct are questions that have stirred discussion ever since WWII."[13] Had Bradley allowed General Wade H. Haislip to continue his advance north, the XV Corps might have been able to surround the German Seventh and Fifth Panzer Armies.

The XV Corps had reached its last approved objective near Argentan on 12 August. Bradley immediately sent word that the XV Corps was to stand fast and not continue the attack.[14] Bradley later claimed he was worried about a head-on encounter between British and American forces attacking toward one another. Skeptics have pointed out this could have easily been solved by close coordination and carefully selected landmarks. Bradley also claimed he preferred the XV Corps to form a solid shoulder rather than risk being overrun as the German forces became desperate to break out of their encirclement. Bradley worried that a possible nineteen trapped German divisions would trample the thinly held American line.[15] The result was that even though an estimated fifty thousand Germans were captured in the pocket and another ten thousand were killed, up to forty thousand Germans escaped the trap and were able to bolster defenses on the German border.[16] (The staggering amount of vehicles and equipment lost by the withdrawing forces, however, proved difficult to replace.)

What is curious is that two of the units simulated by the 23rd (the 80th and 90th Infantry Divisions) were lead elements of the XV Corps. If the halting of the XV Corps was tied into the deception operation, it would make sense to stop the attack of these divisions that were supposedly heading to the west. It is also interesting that two of the chosen divisions were the very ones being sent to the far flank, and would have posed the most danger to the German forces.

There is no hard evidence that Operation BRITTANY was actually connected to the halting of the XV Corps, or successful in delaying the German withdrawal from the Falaise Pocket. The principal officers have passed away and the records of the 12th Army Group Special Plans Branch cannot be located. There is, however, enough circumstantial evidence to warrant further investigation into the matter. Normally there is no one reason why things are done in war; decisions tend to be made for a number of reasons. It may be that one of those reasons involved a classified deception operation that senior officers did not feel comfortable mentioning in their postwar memoirs.

Chapter 7

Operation BREST
20–27 August 1944

The first time the 23rd utilized all four types of deception (decoys, signal, sonic, and atmosphere) was during the three-part operation at the port of Brest. This city at the tip of the Brittany peninsula was besieged by the American 2nd, 8th, and 29th Infantry Divisions. It was heavily defended by German General Bernard Ramcke and his 2nd Paratroop Division. The importance of Brest was not so much for its port facilities (which were expected to be demolished by the Germans), but to clear the region of coastal artillery so that components of an artificial port could be towed around the Brittany peninsula to Quiberon Bay.[1]

In view of the breakout of Allied forces into central France, the need for such a port was dwindling because it was thought that the rest of the Atlantic ports would soon be in Allied hands. But with supply lines to the east already stretched to their limit, it made sense to shift some units west to eliminate the German stronghold at Brest, particularly because Ramcke's men had already sallied out of the city on a daring raid to rescue a number of their men who had been captured by the French. There was concern that other, larger raids against the American supply lines might be attempted.

The 6th Armored Division had driven across the Brittany peninsula to surround Brest, but as soon as the infantry units arrived, the 6th was sent farther south to surround other ports. American tank strength at Brest was weak, but the VIII Corps' commander felt the best avenue of attack was to push down directly from the north, in the sector of the 8th Infantry Division. The 23rd was called upon to try to shift German antitank weapons and reserves to the flanking 2nd and 29th Divisions sectors.[2]

A recon party under Colonel Snee was sent to Brest to look over the area and make note of the composition and visual characteristics of the 6th Armored Division. On 20 August a selected portion of the 23rd left the main

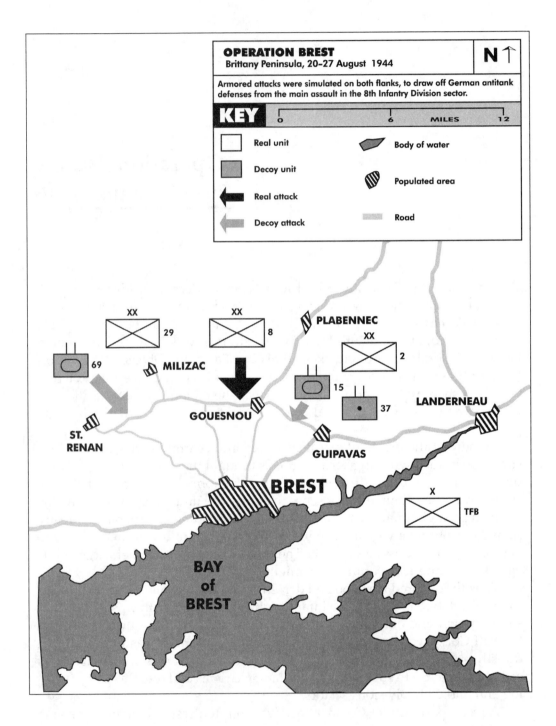

camp at Le Fremondre and headed west. They arrived at a bivouac area near Lesneven on the night of 21 August. Once in Brittany, this detachment of the 23rd was under command of Colonel Snee. He divided the troops into three Task Forces: X, Y, and Z. Task Forces X and Z were both to simulate tank forces, while Y would portray an artillery unit.

Task Force X was under the command of Captain Oscar Seale and consisted of four platoons of camouflage engineers, one sonic platoon, one platoon of combat engineers, and attached medics and signalmen. On 23 August 1944, Task Force X reconnoitered its assigned area in the 9th Infantry Regiment sector (2nd Infantry Division). That evening, after a thorough briefing, the men moved to the chosen area and began to set up their decoys (fifty-three in total). Company D of the 709th Tank Battalion (M3 light tanks attached to the 2nd Division) arrived to add some genuine tanks to the operation. The plan was to take the single company of tanks and make it appear to be the entire 15th Tank Battalion of the 6th Armored Division. The genuine 15th had moved from the area a few days before and was now operating to the south at Lorient. A full briefing on the plan was made to the 9th Infantry Regiment, and later that night officers from the 2nd Division headquarters arrived to inspect the setup.

The signalmen assigned to Task Force X set up an SCR-506 radio and prepared to send messages to the 2nd Division, simulating an attached tank battalion. The 2nd Division signal officer proved very helpful, providing assigned frequencies and call signs. The company radio of D/709th was to maintain radio silence unless the unit actually had to go into action.

While reconnoitering the area, some of the 23rd men found a grisly scene. Fifteen American half-tracks were lined up along a hedgerow, all burnt out. They inquired about them and were told that early in the siege a group of Germans had infiltrated through the front line under cover of a heavy fog and had destroyed them with bazookas. It was a grim reminder that security had to be in place even in rear areas.[3]

Captain Seale directed a tank from the 709th around the bivouac area to make treadmarks in the ground. At 2230 the sonic program was started, bringing up three companies of medium tanks. This started with the sound of one tank approaching and eventually built up to the noise of an entire company. The recording of the first company moving up ran for thirty minutes, followed by a thirty-minute silence. The second tank company was played in, followed by a ten-minute break, then another thirty-minute recording for the final company to move in.

Captain Bill Paden, the assistant operations officer of the 2nd Infantry Division, was sent to observe the deception. He reported, "Sound effects throughout the entire operation were extremely realistic, being actual recordings of a medium tank battalion approaching and being placed in an assembly area. There was no distortion, and the equipment used was such that the

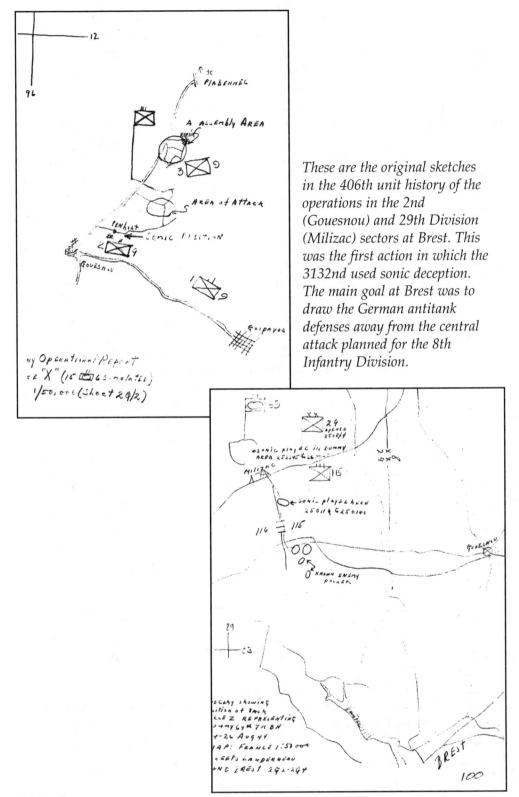

These are the original sketches in the 406th unit history of the operations in the 2nd (Gouesnou) and 29th Division (Milizac) sectors at Brest. This was the first action in which the 3132nd used sonic deception. The main goal at Brest was to draw the German antitank defenses away from the central attack planned for the 8th Infantry Division.

usual indications of mechanical reproductions of sound were entirely absent. Careful consideration was given to details such as normal intervals between tanks for night driving, normal rate of speed, intervals between companies, etc. Sounds such as shifting of gears, tread noises, cracking of brush and voices of guides leading tanks into final positions could be clearly distinguished. Realism was consistent at varying distances from source of the sound."[4]

The following afternoon, a party from 12th Army Group Special Plans Branch toured the decoy encampment. Major Ingersoll began taking photographs of the area and was stopped, because he had no permission to do so. Major Rushton eventually ordered Captain Seale to give written authorization to Ingersol to continue his photography. Needless to say, there was some friction between the 23rd officers in charge of the task force and the more senior officers from 12th Army Group who appeared to be hindering operations.

Of the decoy bivouac, Captain Paden remarked, "In general, the observer was very favorably impressed by the operation, particularly concerning the attention paid to detail and the apparent results. It is my opinion that any interested observer within a two-and-a-half-mile radius would have been convinced that a large number of armored vehicles were being assembled, that impression of heavy motor movement would have been revived at much greater distances, and that daylight investigation from a distance of 200 yards from the dummy positions would have apparently verified the presence of the tank battalion."[5]

Colonel Billy Harris (from 12th Army Group) ordered Major Williams of the 3132nd to move his sonic cars as far forward as possible for the second night. This created some confusion, as it was not the location previously decided upon. The commander of the 9th Infantry Regiment was unhappy, since they had moved up to only two hundred yards from known enemy positions. Eventually Lieutenant Colonel Higgins, the local battalion commander (2/9th Infantry), gave his approval and everything was straightened out. From 2245 to just after midnight, the sonic cars played sounds of three tank companies moving up for an attack.

Seale made sure that every company commander in the area, as well as every American gun position, knew his vehicles were going to be traveling up route N788 and then be returning after dark. He did not want a trigger-happy GI to mistake his men for the enemy. The sonic platoon played their program of recordings and returned without incident to the rear by 0100 on 25 August.

Orders arrived that day for all but the sonic units to fade out and return to the 23rd bivouac at Lesneven. The sonic platoon was to play the tanks moving out after dark. At 1300 the VIII Corps' attack started and German artillery fell in the area for the next few hours. At 2300 the sonic cars played a thirty-minute program in the forward area. After a ten-minute gap they played another thirty-minute program in the rear area. After that the remainder of Task Force X closed up and returned to the bivouac.

The men of the 23rd found this knocked out M8 assault gun at Brest. It appeared to have taken a direct hit from a mortar shell into the open topped turret. Sights like this reminded them that they were really moving up into dangerous territory.
PHOTO: GEORGE MARTIN.

The commander of VIII Corps, General Troy Middleton, had ordered an attack all along the line for 1300 on 25 August. Many veterans of the 23rd were later told that their actions at Brest had drawn German antitank weapons to the very area of a genuine American tank attack. The rumor in the 23rd was that the American tanks were devastated in the attack because of the attention drawn to the area by the sonic programs.

The records of the 709th Tank Battalion were examined to see if this claim was true. The 709th was an independent tank battalion that had been broken up into separate companies, all assigned to different divisions outside Brest. Company D, the light tank company with M3 Stuart tanks, was attached to the 2nd Infantry Division. This company, under command of Captain John J. Cochrane, was in support for the 25 August assault.

The 2nd Platoon, with five tanks, supported the attack of the 1/9th Infantry. One tank bogged down in the soft ground before the attack. The platoon leader's tank also became stuck when it fell into a German emplacement.

The remaining three tanks moved forward and were knocked out within fifteen minutes. One of these tanks was overturned and the crew was trapped inside. They could hear German soldiers tapping on their tank as a German machine-gun crew took a position next to the Stuart. The trapped men stayed silent for two days, until they finally heard American voices nearby. The crew was finally rescued unharmed.

Both the 1st and 3rd Platoons were attached to 2/9th Infantry (the area where the deception had taken place). Three of the five tanks in the 3rd Platoon bogged down near a stream before they started, but the other two were able to assist in the attack. Four of the five tanks in the 1st Platoon bogged down, but the platoon leader was able to advance. His tank, however, was eventually hit by German fire three times and destroyed. On the following day, the 1st Platoon attempted to advance, ran into a minefield, and lost all four remaining tanks.

There is no way of knowing if this outcome was better or worse than if the deception had not occurred. The location of the simulated tank attack had been chosen in conjunction with Captain Cochrane (D/709th) as the best place in the sector for an armored attack. Cochrane's company had also been involved in the deception, but recorded no concern over his attacking in the same location. The Germans may well have moved reinforcements and anti-tank weapons to the 9th Infantry sector as a result of the Task Force X deception. However, the loss of only four out of fifteen light tanks from D/709th provides no firm evidence of an increased German defense.

These casualties of D/709th did, however, prove a very important lesson in deception work. From that point on, the 23rd was very concerned about making sure they were not drawing attention to a point where there was the possibility a real attack would occur.

One amusing incident took place on the first night of the operation. Captain Rebh wanted to observe the sonic operations, so he had his driver, T/5 Milton Feldman, drive his jeep as close to the front lines as possible. Feldman become somewhat nervous, being left alone in the dark, and began to talk to some nearby riflemen. He asked so many questions they became suspicious of him and he became the first man of the 406th Engineers to be taken prisoner—by the American Army! He was brought before the local infantry commander, but due to the secrecy of the mission refused to answer questions about why he was in the area. Feldman was passed onto the 9th Infantry Regiment Intelligence Section, who finally located someone in the 23rd who would vouch for him.[6]

At the same time as Seale's Task Force X was operating in the 2nd Division sector, Task Force Z had moved to the 29th Division sector on the far-right flank of the American lines. This group, under command of Lieutenant Colonel Simenson, was given the mission of turning Company A of the 709th Tank Battalion into a notional 69th Tank Battalion of the 6th Armored

Division. This was to take place near the town of Milizac. Captain Thomas C. Perry was in command of A/709th, a medium-tank company (consisting of M4 Sherman tanks).

Lieutenant Colonel Simenson was given four platoons of engineers, one sonic platoon, part of the sonic security platoon, and signal and medical detachments for a total of ten officers and one hundred and forty-nine men. Not only would he try to simulate the 69th Tank Battalion with decoys and sonic means, but also report to the 29th Headquarters with the simulated tank battalion radio (SCR-506).

On the afternoon of 24 August, one real tank arrived, painted with markings from the 69th Tank Battalion, and was used to make tracks in the selected bivouac area. The area had been picked that morning in consultation with the commander of A/709th. At 2200 the decoy bundles were dropped off in their selected locations and guards were posted to keep out any unauthorized personnel. Meanwhile, a reconnaissance of the forward area was made to decide where to locate the sonic cars. The threat of enemy patrols was great so two squads of combat engineers were used as security.

Due to a lack of German aerial reconnaissance in the region, the decision was made to emplace the decoys so they could also be seen from the ground. They were located on the southern slope of an incline eight hundred to one thousand yards from a ridge overlooking the position. Around dusk, at 2100, the remaining genuine tanks of D/709th moved into the area. All were properly painted in 69th Tank Battalion markings. The notional radio link with the 29th Division was established and the rubber decoys were erected. Care was taken to conceal the lower sections of the exposed tank decoys because the area around the decoys' suspension and bogey wheels would not hold up to close observation.

Twelve decoy medium tanks were erected per company along with a detachment of six light tank decoys. Two decoy jeeps and two 2½-ton trucks were added per company. Red colored aerial recognition panels were placed on every vehicle and camouflage nets were set up.

By 0100 on 25 August, the sonic cars had moved up and played a program of tanks moving into position. After the first company was played in, a radio message was sent to 29th Division HQ stating that the first company of the battalion had closed into its assembly area. When the sonic program ended, a radio message was sent indicating the battalion was in position. The pre-planned message read: "Entire battalion closed into its area by ___ [actual time]. Vehicle casualties: one medium tank, three light tanks. Personnel casualties two men, no officers."[7]

The sonic program was originally planned to start at 2245. A chance meeting, however, between Simenson and an adjacent infantry company commander revealed that a local attack had been planned for 2300. Had the deception gone as planned it would have put the Germans on alert fifteen minutes before the infantry attack. This showed that careful liaison was needed not only with the units in the immediate area, but also with the adjoining ones.

The erection of the decoys was particularly difficult in the dark due to constant rain. There were many leaky valves and rubber tubes. In the Company C area, only two of twelve tanks were standing by morning. Most were put back into shape, but three could not be repaired and had to be removed. The jeep decoys were removed at daylight when it became clear they did not look real enough for ground observation.

To help create the proper atmosphere, a detail of camoufleurs was sent to A/709th to mark the tanks and brief the crewmen. Vehicles were also dispatched to nearby towns with 6th Armored Division markings and patches. Smokey fires were lit, pup tents set up, and laundry hung out in the bivouac area. The men neither observed enemy aircraft nor received any German artillery fire. Over thirty soldiers were needed to guard the dummy bivouac. The most trouble came from locals who traditionally pastured their cows in those fields and who did not feel that the war should change their habits.

Once the dummy bivouac was installed, Lieutenant Colonel Simenson and Captain Perry went up into the church steeple in Milizac to examine the position. Perry was very enthusiastic about the display. He claimed that even through his binoculars he could not tell the difference between his real tanks and the decoys. The genuine tanks of A/709th were carefully positioned closest to the road so they would be the first ones seen by anyone passing by.

During the daylight hours of 25 August, the men all worked very hard to create the appearance of a bustling tank battalion bivouac. This continued until dark when the decoys were packed up, the 6th Armored Division patches taken off, and unit markings removed from the genuine tanks. At 2345 the sonic cars played out the three tank companies, and at 0600 on 26 August, the simulated battalion radio checked out of the 29th radio network. The deception troops faded from the area in small groups, followed by the single company of genuine tanks (now re-marked as A/709th). The operation officially ended at 1000 on 26 August.

While operating near Milizac, some 406th men noticed an infantryman wandering by carrying a bottle of liquor. By following his path they found that the Milizac rectory had a massive supply of alcohol in its cellar. They returned with a jeep and, although some members of the FFI were already loading most of it into their own truck, the 406th jeep was soon loaded up with all it could hold. The supply was later passed around to everyone in the company.

Task Forces X and Z had been given missions to portray tank units while Task Force Y was sent to the 2nd Division sector for a different type of mission. Lieutenant Colonel Mayo was assigned two platoons of camoufleurs, a squad of combat engineers, and a wire team. The fifty-six-man task force attempted to draw German artillery fire away from the 37th Field Artillery

Battalion by the use of flash devices simulating the muzzle blast of 105mm howitzers. If the Germans were fooled by the dummy flashes, the guns of the 37th should have been able to support the upcoming attack without suffering counter-battery fire.

Three notional artillery battery positions were laid out on Hill 103, roughly twelve hundred meters in front of the genuine 37th Artillery Battalion. No decoys were used, just wires run to the flash simulators spaced as if they were real 105mm howitzers. Telephone lines were run to the Fire Direction Center (FDC) of the 37th Artillery for coordination. An officer stationed at the 37th FDC synchronized the flashes with the genuine fire of the guns to the rear.

The attack in the 2nd Division sector was scheduled for the afternoon of 25 August. The previous two nights, Task Force Y had set off its simulated gun flashes in conjunction with the actual artillery fire of the 37th guns located behind them. The combat engineer squad provided security for the troops reloading the simulators.

The simulators were spent 105mm howitzer shell casings, which confined and shaped the blast of the simulation charge to give the effect of something coming from a tube. Various sized charges were tried, with the best results obtained from half a pint of black powder. On the first night, the heating-element–type igniter posed some problems, with an unexpected delay of three to ten seconds depending upon the humidity and strength of the battery. On the second night, a very fine copper wire was improvised for an igniter with good results.

The Germans were known to be rationing their remaining ammunition stocks, so no counter-battery fire was expected until a ground attack was actually in progress. As expected, thirty minutes after the attack began on 25 August, the Germans shelled the dummy artillery positions. The focus of their fire appeared to be two hundred to four hundred meters southwest of the simulated Battery A position. The Germans shelled the area again the following day at 0900 with single rounds roughly three to five minutes apart. This time the rounds landed both over and short of the simulated battery. Colonel Mayo, an artillery officer, felt sure that they had been targeted by one of the large German coastal guns situated around the port of Brest, as the craters were six to ten feet across.

Although the only firing battery in the area was the 37th, located twelve hundred meters to the north, that unit was not fired upon by German artillery. Mayo reported, "We definitely drew enemy fire. The heavy flashes we made; shortage of appropriate enemy weapons or ammunition; lack of other located and definite Allied targets to shoot at—all may account for the type of fire delivered near our position."[8]

This was a very positive result for the simulated artillery flash devices. Colonel Mayo strongly recommended that they be authorized for artillery groups to help draw counter-battery fire away from genuine firing batteries. Task Force Y closed up and returned to the Lesneven bivouac on 26 August.

Colonel Cyrus H. Searcy, chief of staff of VIII Corps, submitted a report on the deceptions in which he stated, "Visual effects were thorough and complete for both enemy air observation and/or enemy agents or patrols."[9] About the sonic deception, he claimed, "The sound remained consistent with distance involved, and individual noises were distinguishable at approximately 2-1/2 miles. 2nd Division Engineers, located over a mile away, having no knowledge of the operation, were firmly convinced that tanks were assembled in their vicinity."[10] He also reported that German POWs taken shortly afterwards in the 29th sector reported such rumors as: the 6th Armored Division was opposing them; there were many tanks about to attack them; and that more than one armored division was ready to attack. Colonel Furst, commander of the German coastal artillery battery at Le Conquet, stated after his capture that he was certain the 6th Armored was there since he had heard tanks in his area.

As to the artillery deception, Colonel Searcy felt the enemy fire on the area of the notional field artillery battalion indicated tangible results of their operations. Thanks to the deception, the 37th Field Artillery Battalion, which had been doing the actual firing, drew no counter-battery fire. In conclusion Searcy wrote, "the work of these units is complete, thorough, and correct to the smallest detail, and it is believed that units of this type are of considerable value and usefulness to the Army."[11]

Once all elements of the three task forces had returned to the Lesneven bivouac, they headed back east to the main 23rd camp on 27 August. On the way, a grenade fell off a man's cartridge belt and hit the floor of the truck. The impact knocked the handle off and ignited the fuse. Private Irving Mayer of the 406th noticed it smoking on the truck floor, grabbed it and threw it out of the truck. The resulting explosion drove everyone to cover, but after the story came out, Mayer was congratulated for his fast thinking.[12] The column arrived at Le Fremondre during the evening of 28 August, concluding Operation BREST.

The question of how successful this operation was is hard to answer. They may have helped draw defenses off to the flanks, but Ramcke would still hold out a lot longer than expected. He did not finally surrender his troops until mid-September. Part of the reason was that the terrain surrounding Brest had been developed for defense over many years. In addition, Ramcke had a very dedicated and professional force of soldiers under his command. On the American side, Middleton had been urged to move slowly and try to keep casualties to a minimum. The 25 August attack did not break the German lines, but was the start of the assault that eventually drove the Germans back to their final defenses at the city wall.

Only two of the sonic platoons were used at Brest. The third had been diverted to St. Malo, another besieged port in Brittany. St. Malo was being defended by the Germans to the last man. After the German commander finally surrendered the heavily fortified medieval citadel on 15 August, one more troublesome German position continued to hold out.

Four thousand yards off the coast was the heavily fortified island of Cezembre. Seven heavy coastal artillery guns controlled the approaches to all beaches and minor ports in the region. The Americans desperately wanted to capture this island so they could land supplies. Cezembre was constantly under air attack, but the island commander refused to surrender. A sonic platoon from the 3132nd was sent to St. Malo to broadcast propaganda messages to the island garrison. The garrison finally surrendered on 2 September after the troops had run out of drinking water. Little mention is made of this mission in 23rd files and not much is known about it.

The main criticism of Operation BREST was that the task force officers had received too many conflicting orders from Reeder at the 23rd and from the 12th Army Group staff. The officers involved felt that having the 12th Army Group staff show up in the middle of a mission and contradict them affected everyone's morale. It had become apparent that the original plan to have the 23rd's staff develop operational ideas had been superceded. From then on it would be Colonel Harris at the Special Plans Branch of 12th Army Group that would sell the idea of a deception operation to a corps or army commander, and then direct the 23rd to where they were needed. This removal of the top level of planning from the staff of the 23rd must have irritated Colonel Reeder, but he made no mention of it.

Another problem was that the officers in the 23rd felt that, as the only unit of its type in the army, the 23rd was being treated as irreplaceable. The deception troops were thus kept far from the front lines. The suggestion was made that if another similar unit was developed, perhaps the senior officers might not feel they had to keep the 23rd so far from any danger.

Chapter 8

Operation BETTEMBOURG
15–22 September 1944

The elements of the 23rd that did not participate in Operation BREST moved east into France. The 23rd was the first Allied unit to arrive in the town of Tonce and became subject to the kind of welcome only newly liberated Frenchmen can provide. Feasts, speeches, and a parade were all part of the festivities (Major Kelly obtained a few bottles of Cointreau and transformed these into "Sidecars," using a recipe of one-third Cointreau, one-third Cognac, and one-third lemon powder. Previously, the men had tossed away the lemonade powder packets found in their K-rations, but now they became a valuable commodity.)

The Third Army proposed a deception plan, known as TROYES, that would involve the 23rd in a simulated build-up on the right flank of Patton's Third Army. This would involve simulating the 6th Armored Division and a combat team of the 83rd Infantry Division in the area around Bar-sur-Seine. At this time, Patton was racing east toward the German border. He had little strength on his southern flank and there was a good possibility of a German attack from that direction. Patton later claimed that he hadn't been worried about his flanks, and had used air cover to watch for any German assaults. He also had a string of organized FFI units spread along his southern flank ready to sound the alarm if a German column showed up.

Reeder was concerned about taking on such a task without any combat units at hand, and requested that he be loaned at least a few tanks. He requested them chiefly to make treadmarks in the ground, but also for defense against a possible German attack. Planning for TROYES was called off when it became apparent the Germans to the south were in full retreat and no longer a threat.[1]

Another proposed operation during this period was DIJON. This involved the simulation of an armored unit and elements of the 35th Infantry Division just north of Sens, France. They would portray a notional advance towards

Dijon to link up with the American Seventh Army heading north from the invasion of southern France. Plans for DIJON were ready on 30 August 1944, but the operation was scrapped when it was realized that the German forces in France were in headlong retreat. Colonel Maddox, the G-3 of Third Army, canceled DIJON because he felt it was too risky; however, it was a very useful planning exercise in that it helped explore the capabilities of the 23rd.

While waiting for new orders, the 23rd was bivouacked in a field outside Mauny. A large store of German liquor was discovered and the unit acquired an estimated five hundred and twenty cases. The result was that the bivouac area became known as "Cognac Hill." Colonel Simenson later discovered his driver had filled their five-gallon water can with cognac. The 23rd was next moved to St. Germain, near Paris. The 406th was billeted in the Maison d'Education de la Legion d'Honneur. This was a school Napoleon had built for the daughters of soldiers who had died on the battlefield. The rest of the 23rd was housed at the French military base of Camp des Loges. Paris was alternately put on- and off-limits for the troops, but many seemed to find one reason or another for a visit to the legendary city.

At this time Lieutenant Colonel Simenson became concerned about the information—or lack of it—provided to the unit when asked to plan a deception operation. He wrote the following memo on 5 September 1944.

It is my belief that any deception plan should contain the following necessary basic information, which should come to us from higher headquarters.

1. OBJECTIVE: What reaction is desired from the enemy? For example, 'The objective is to prevent the Germans from moving their reserve armor from the west to the east flank during the period 3–6 September 1944.'

2. MISSION: Mission to 23rd Headquarters, Special troops. Example, 'replace combat elements 4th Armored Division at once until further notice.'

3. TROOPS:
a. What troops are to be represented? At this particular time it is necessary to consider each battalion.

b. The following factors should be considered in selection of troops:
    1. Possibility of real units going on radio silence.
    2. Tactical position and probable employment of real units.
    3. Disappearance of real unit by radio silence, removal of bumper markings, shoulder patches, CP signs, and activity where fifth columnists can report.[2]

On the road east into France, this photograph shows half-tracks of the 3132nd. With the canvas covers in place there was nothing to indicate that these were anything other than typical half-tracks. PHOTO: WALTER MANSER

Operation BETTEMBOURG was a purely defensive operation that took place in southern Luxembourg.[3] At the time, the XX Corps was located just west of Metz. Two infantry divisions were attacking Metz from the south, with a single division (the 90th Infantry) to the west. To the north of Metz, a seventy-mile line was held only by a thin screen from the 3rd Cavalry Group. The deception was to simulate the 6th Armored Division (which was only now starting to move east from Lorient) moving up to fill in that gap. It was hoped the operation would prevent the Germans from trying to attack through the weakly held area. A secondary objective was to draw off some of the German forces defending Metz against the XX Corps.

The 23rd was expected to keep up the deception for only sixty hours, until the 83rd Infantry Division could be brought up to plug the gap. CCB of the 6th Armored had already reached the front at Nancy. The Germans were very good at identifying units once they entered the front lines, so the 23rd was limited to portraying only the 6th Division Headquarters, CCA, and CCR.

Roughly half of the 23rd was involved in the operation, the rest of the troops remained behind in St. Germain in case they were needed for another mission. A total of forty-eight officers, six hundred and eighty-two enlisted men, and one hundred and seventy-four vehicles from the 23rd were assisted by a platoon of light tanks from the 43rd Cavalry Squadron. At 0900 on 14 September the 23rd was notified of the pending mission. Their column left St. Germain that afternoon and arrived at Bettembourg (two hundred and seven miles away) at 1600 the next day. Two light liaison aircraft were obtained to fly the officers in ahead of the men, but they were grounded by bad weather.

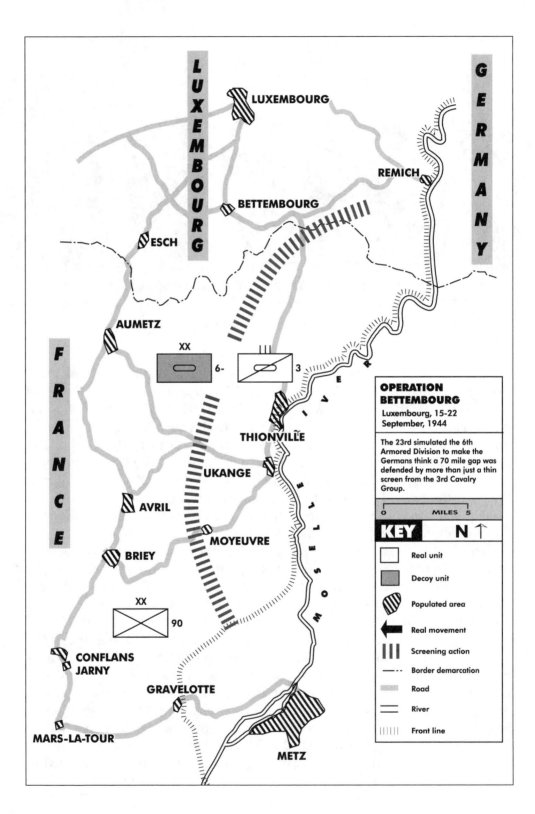

LUXEMBOURG

GERMANY

FRANCE

LUXEMBOURG

REMICH

BETTEMBOURG

ESCH

AUMETZ

XX
6-

III
3

THIONVILLE

UKANGE

AVRIL

MOYEUVRE

BRIEY

XX
90

CONFLANS
JARNY

GRAVELOTTE

MARS-LA-TOUR

METZ

MOSELLE RIVER

OPERATION BETTEMBOURG
Luxembourg, 15-22 September, 1944

The 23rd simulated the 6th Armored Division to make the Germans think a 70 mile gap was defended by more than just a thin screen from the 3rd Cavalry Group.

0   MILES   5

KEY   N ↑

Real unit

Decoy unit

Populated area

Real movement

Screening action

Border demarcation

Road

River

Front line

The troops were broken down into three main groups. The 23rd Headquarters was to simulate the division headquarters of the 6th Armored, with men from the 406th Engineers serving as 6th Armored MPs. Lieutenant Colonel Schroeder was given a company and a half from the 603rd, a detachment of signalmen, and a platoon from the 406th to simulate Combat Command B.[4] Captain Seale had a similar sized detachment to simulate CCR.[5] The 3132nd was kept near the division headquarters until needed.

Due to bad weather and the lack of German aircraft, the decision was made to use only a handful of inflatable decoys. The operational area was so close to the German border that it was felt the danger of ground agents spotting the decoys would be greater than the possibility they would be noticed by aerial reconnaissance. The emphasis for BETTEMBOURG would be on signal deception, sonic deception, and "special effects."

For the first time, 23rd signal officers received good cooperation from their counterparts in the XX Corps and at Third Army headquarters. Information on frequencies, call signs, cryptographic systems, and authenticators were provided without any problem. The 3rd Cavalry Group, which was responsible for defending that stretch of the line, provided whatever assistance was requested. The 3rd used their own code to send quick messages called the "3rd Cavalry Brevity Code." They quickly provided information on how this operated (which was also filed away for future reference in case the 23rd ever needed to simulate the 3rd Cavalry).

On the night of 15 September, the notional 6th Armored Division radio began to operate. The division's SCR-399 HQ radio could not make contact with the XX Corps due to atmospheric conditions, but CCA and CCR began reporting their arrival by radio in the new bivouac area. The next day the division link was established and a liaison net was opened connecting to the XX Corps Command Post, 90th Infantry Division, and 3rd Cavalry Group. By 16 September there were nine operating radio sets simulating the 6th Armored. Five of them were clustered in the 6th Armored bivouac area so that German radio direction finders would notice a division-sized cluster of transmissions at that location.

On 18 September, the liaison network was expanded to include CCA of the 5th Armored (the flanking unit to the north). After allowing for the time it would normally take to run telephone wire between the 6th Armored and XX Corps, radio traffic over that link was stopped, simulating the transfer of communications to land lines. Actual wire connections (sixty miles worth) were run to all involved units, and one 23rd wire team captured two German soldiers while doing so. The liaison net continued to transmit periodic reports and radio checks until 22 September when radio silence was ordered.

Simulating such a network was not an easy task. One of the most important aspects of signal intelligence is the number and timing of transmissions. A good signal interpreter can tell a lot about what a unit is doing just by watching the number of radio transmissions, even if he cannot understand what is being said. The signalmen had studied the transmissions of different units, and their carefully planned simulation of a division radio net required only seventy messages be sent during the entire operation. This was the correct amount to simulate that specific size of the unit during that type of operation.

Much of the success of the signals operation was due to the cooperation the 23rd received from the local units and the XX Corps. The notional 6th Armored HQ radio received as many radio messages as did the other genuine divisions of the corps. By having the radios of the 23rd enter an already established network, the illusion of a new unit moving into the area was more realistic than if it had started operating its own network without any of the standard connections to adjacent units. One major mistake was noted, however, when a message was accidentally sent on 16 September signed "23rd Hq Sp Trs Ln O" (liaison officer).[6]

The main command post for the operation was the notional 6th Armored Division HQ at Baschager. Each of the two combat commands were sent to their assigned locations and were given instructions on how much traffic they should have in their area. The headquarters was in charge of keeping vehicles moving around Baschager, as well as along the supposed division Main Supply Route (MSR). During WWII a division's MSR was an important route, which was always supposed to be well-marked and patrolled.

Signs were painted and posted along the routes indicating the presence of BAMBOO (the code name for the 6th Armored Division), as well as the locations of the CCA (BACON) and CCR (BACK) command posts. Military police were sent out to patrol the area, and men were stationed at road intersections to guide any subsequent vehicles to their proper destination. Everything that a normal division does when moving into a new location was simulated as accurately as possible.

The main water point for the men was placed in view of Bettembourg. The first day there were only enough trips to collect water as necessary for the actual number of men involved in the operation. After that the traffic to the water point was increased fourfold to simulate drawing water for the number of men supposedly in the area.

To increase the amount of traffic in the region, each vehicle was driven about the area, then returned back to its camp to have the crew and bumper markings changed. A jeep that had driven around in the morning with only a driver and the markings of a tank battalion, would be seen later that day with three men in it and bearing the bumper markings of an artillery unit. Two men were placed at the rear of each truck, just visible behind the canvas flap. Anyone seeing them would assume the rest of the truck, concealed by a canvas top, was filled with men.

Five light tanks from the 1st Platoon, Company F, 43rd Cavalry, under command of Lieutenant Wadeton, were assigned to add a touch of armor to

"Eileen Marie" was the command jeep of Major John Williams in the 3132nd. Note the wire cutter welded to the front bumper (to snap wires stretched across the road) and the lack of unit markings on the bumper. In the background is one of the sonic half-tracks.

the atmosphere. The first day they were sent to the two combat command bivouacs to tear up the ground with their tank treads. Later the tanks were formed into convoys, along with half-tracks from the 3132nd, and sent out along routes through the region so the locals would actually see tanks moving around.

Allied air power controlled the skies, so most vehicles prominently displayed an aerial recognition panel to prevent being strafed by their own planes. This was a fluorescent colored marker panel which could be changed from red to yellow, depending upon the correct color for the day. All vehicles, both real and decoy, had a red aerial recognition panel tied to their top.

Roughly half of the men involved in the operation wore patches of the 6th Armored. In a combat unit it was unusual for every man to wear such insignia due to the rapid turnover of men and uniforms. A handful of the distinctive leather crash helmets worn by tank crewmen were spread throughout the various units as additional "atmosphere." Many of the men already had been issued the jacket and overalls worn by armored vehicle crews. At intervals, soldiers were trucked into Luxembourg City on 6th Armored marked vehicles, so they could take a shower at the city's bath house.

The three bulldozers from the 406th Engineers were quietly brought together, placed on their trailers, and formed into a convoy heading through Bettembourg as if they were part of a larger unit. A wrecked jeep was hitched to a 10-ton wrecker and towed through Esch. A column of half-tracks and jeeps with .30-caliber machine guns was formed and driven into Bettembourg. The officer in charge, pretending to be a 6th Armored staff officer, then publicly asked a soldier for the route to the division area. A crowd of roughly fifteen civilians watched as he was given directions, and then listened to a conversation about a treadway bridge company that was expected to arrive that night.

While this column was in transit, the men noticed an unmarked sedan pull to a halt on the opposite side of the road. A civilian got out and was seen to be writing in a notebook as they passed. Two civilians in Esch were noticed photographing vehicles from the front, possibly to catch the bumper markings. Such incidents were not stopped, but quietly reported back to headquarters as an indication that they were being watched.

Captain Seale's CCR arrived in its assigned area late on 15 September. The region was quickly reconnoitered by Captain Bob Hiller and Lieutenant Syracuse from the sonic company. At 0300, the 3132nd arrived and an hour later began to play a sonic program of the three notional tank battalions moving into the bivouac. Each battalion program lasted for twenty minutes separated by a ten-minute interval. It was a dark and moonless night, and according to reports the sonic deception was considered very effective.

As dawn broke, multiple fires were lit in the bivouac area and necessary tents and equipment were installed. That morning the light tanks arrived and were stenciled with markings of the 6th Armored. Such genuine tanks were mandatory if the 23rd was to portray an armored unit. The camoufleurs had brought with them enough decoys to simulate two tank battalions and an armored infantry battalion. Due to the danger of enemy agents, only eleven decoys were set up on the first night (eight M4 tanks, two 2½-ton trucks, and one jeep). A handful of M7 (a fully tracked, self-propelled 105mm artillery piece) decoys were also set up in the notional artillery battalion bivouac, but taken down the next night so inquisitive civilians would not discover they were only dummies.

In the late afternoon, a third of the men assigned to CCR were sent into Bettembourg to create atmosphere. Most wore 6th Armored Division patches and all had been briefed on the history and principal officers of that unit. Word was soon received that a civilian in town was spotted apparently copying down bumper markings and counting the numbers of vehicles, as well as asking slightly more questions than usual. Curiously, he seemed to not only know that the 6th Armored had recently left Lorient, but also appeared to know the names of a few of the 6th's unit commanders.

By now the officers of the 23rd had decided that the few decoys they had installed put the operation at risk. If even one enemy agent was able to sneak through the guards and find out they were fake, the plan would be given away. All decoys were taken down and the main focus shifted to special effects and atmosphere.

The morning of 17 September started with morning campfires and the posting of road guides. The bivouac areas were heavily guarded so it was a good guess that enemy agents would try to obtain their information from unsuspecting GIs. Groups of 23rd men were sent to church in the local villages. Half-tracks were sent out by the 23rd HQ with 6th Armored markings and driven throughout the area. One of the drivers noticed that most people seemed to look first at the bumper markings, then up at the crew. Half of the men were sent out in the morning, then returned to take over guard duties while the other half were sent into the town during the afternoon.

Captain Seale later wrote in his after-action report that, "The men did go into cafes to drink beer while in town. Even though ordered not to do so, it was the normal thing for all men to do. I was never able, while in town, to catch anyone in my command drinking, but I am sure some drinking was done."[7]

Things began to heat up that afternoon as German activity increased along the front. The German 36th Infantry Division had moved up to the front on

One of the more curious decoys developed by the army was the inflatable rubber soldier. These were not widely used. A soldier seen in the same location in more than one set of aerial photographs might arouse suspicion. They were utilized on occasion in locations where it made sense for a man to appear for long periods of time.

117

the right of the enemy 19th Division at Wormeldange. A German patrol was spotted roughly two miles to the south. Orders were issued that evening to evacuate the area at once if there was any indication that a German attack was in progress and there was any danger of them breaking through the cavalry screen.

Although the operation was only supposed to last for sixty hours, the 83rd Division was delayed, causing the deception to be continued until a genuine unit could arrive in the area. Due to the increase in German activity, the 3rd Cavalry Group reinforced the area with two assault gun troops and a tank company. One of the cavalry outposts spotted and fired upon a suspicious group of men in a wooded area on the afternoon of 20 September. They were only five hundred yards from the CCR headquarters. Then shots were fired by an unknown party at the water point.

Security was beefed up all around, including a machine-gun post at the water point and combat patrols around the bivouac area. Captain Rebh mounted machine guns on his trucks, removed the canvas covers, and set off along the roads behind the front lines in a cavalry-style mounted patrol. For a brief period of time, near the town of Mondrof, their route took them right along the front lines in view of the Germans.

Orders were received on 20 September that the operation would definitely end in two more days. The light tanks on loan from the 3rd Cavalry were recalled to help defend the sector, but the deception troops continued their illusion. Finally, at 1730 on 22 September, the men of CCR were all packed up and the vehicles began to move out. The vehicles left individually at ten-minute intervals and within a few hours the area was deserted.

Lieutenant Colonel Schroeder's CCA had a similar schedule during the operation. They moved into their assigned bivouac area during the night of 15/16 September and immediately erected twelve rubber M4 tank decoys. Two sonic platoons "played in" the unit to the area with sounds of the three armored units moving up. The decoys were left in place until the following night, when they were removed before enemy agents could spot them. A great deal of effort was placed on creating "atmosphere" in the area since local civilian traffic was heavy, and some civilians were seen taking notes of what they saw in the area.

At one point a jeep with genuine 6th Armored Division officers drove into the bivouac area. They had mistakenly been directed to the region and had followed the posted signs to what they thought was their unit. As usual the men were quietly informed they had stumbled onto a secret operation, told to not mention it, and quietly pointed in the right direction. After a program of special effects, performed along the same lines as CCR, the men of CCA packed up and were "played out" of their bivouac by two sonic platoons on the night of 21 September.

Lieutenant Colonel Simenson later remarked that up until this operation the 23rd was still in a learning period. Only with Operation BETTEMBOURG did things come together and the unit begin to operate as it should.[8] One of the main lessons learned was that in earlier operations the 23rd should not have split up, but instead should have used its entire strength. This would have made it easier to appear as a larger unit, and also prevented the problems associated with having the administrative staff over two hundred miles away. It was also now thought that successful operations were only possible over a short period of time. Trying to stretch them to over a week greatly increased the danger of compromise. It did not help the deception that a photo of a 6th Armored Division soldier appeared in *Stars and Stripes* with the text mentioning that his unit was in a different sector.

The results of BETTEMBOURG appeared to be good. There was a drastic increase in aggressive German patrol activity opposite the deception troops. This was normally seen when the Germans were trying to identify a new unit in the front lines. German reinforcements consisting of at least two infantry divisions (one of them the 36th Infantry Division) were also discovered moving in opposite the 23rd's positions. This was considered to have taken some pressure off the American XX Corps attacking to the south. The primary goal of preventing a German breakthrough was accomplished, and though the Germans may not have contemplated such an attack, it is also possible that the 23rd played a major role in making them fail to realize the opportunity.

Chapter 9

Operation WILTZ
4–10 October 1944

During Operation BETTEMBOURG, the troops of the 23rd who had not been involved had moved to Verdun, then to Luxembourg City. Those participating in the operation joined them there on 25 September 1944. The staff first moved into the spacious mansion that had formerly housed the German Legation, but were bumped out of it by a higher-ranking officer. They were then moved to the well-furnished house of the former Italian Legation. They hired a local woman as a cook, along with two maids, and a man to keep the furnace going. The 3132nd was housed in the Hollerich School and the rest of the unit was billeted in a large seminary (with Nazi-oriented murals on the walls). The 406th and 603rd Battalions and the 23rd Signal Company were housed in the Preistar seminary, which had previously been used as a German barracks.

A week later there was another opportunity for the 23rd. The 5th Armored Division was being shifted from Luxembourg north to Belgium. Operation WILTZ was proposed to make the Germans think that the 5th Armored was being held in place, while it was really driving sixty miles to the north.[1] To hide the fact that the 5th was moving would have required a total "blackout" of the unit. This means no visible bumper markings, shoulder patches, signs, or radio transmissions. The 5th would only be allowed to move at night and in small groups. Unfortunately, this was not possible because the division had to be moved quickly. The large armored columns would congest the roads heading north and be very visible. The 23rd decided to let the Germans know the 5th was moving north, but make them think it was only moving a short distance.

Operation WILTZ would involve no decoys and only a small amount of sonic deception. The main emphasis would be on signal deception and "special effects." From a signals aspect, WILTZ was a large step forward. It would

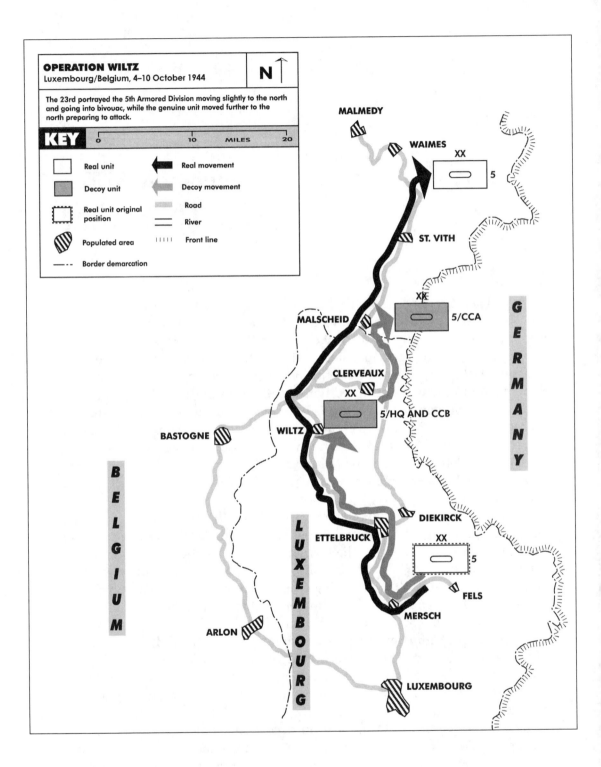

OPERATION WILTZ
Luxembourg/Belgium, 4–10 October 1944

N↑

The 23rd portrayed the 5th Armored Division moving slightly to the north and going into bivouac, while the genuine unit moved further to the north preparing to attack.

KEY

0   10   MILES   20

☐ Real unit
▨ Decoy unit
⬚ Real unit original position
🛡 Populated area
–··– Border demarcation

➤ Real movement
➤ Decoy movement
▬ Road
══ River
ⅠⅠⅠⅠ Front line

MALMEDY

WAIMES

XX
5

ST. VITH

MALSCHEID

XX
5/CCA

GERMANY

CLERVEAUX

XX
5/HQ AND CCB

BASTOGNE

WILTZ

BELGIUM

DIEKIRCK

ETTELBRUCK

XX
5

FELS

MERSCH

LUXEMBOURG

ARLON

LUXEMBOURG

involve seventeen radio stations operating in an area of over one thousand square miles.

The men of the 23rd Signal Company had enough time to meet up with their counterparts in the 5th Armored and take over operations on those networks before the division began moving out. The BLARNEY operators began to infiltrate the network by slowly taking over the duties of the regular crews and substituting BLARNEY radios. Hopefully, the slow change would not be noticeable to any Germans monitoring the airwaves. By the time the 5th Armored was ready to move, every radio net in operation was under BLARNEY control. (The genuine ones were under radio silence.) This required the absolute cooperation of the units involved and was considered the best way to fool the enemy radio-monitoring stations.

Radio teams were also sent to the V Corps HQ and 83rd Infantry Division to take over the radio networks connecting to the 5th Armored. On 4 October, the entire V Corps went on radio silence. This was to prevent an accidental transmission that might have given away the troop movement. To continue the normal amount of division-to-corps traffic, radio teams were also dispatched to the 4th and 28th Infantry Divisions to keep a carefully controlled, but simulated, radio link operating. To complete the picture, an SCR-605 was sent to VIII Corps to simulate a temporary S-4 radio link, commonly found while units were changing corps.

Every radio link exchanged the normal radio checks, but few actual messages were sent. As examples: on 6 October the 5th Armored HQ sent two messages to its quartermaster unit and received one. The same day they also sent four messages to CCA and received six. The next day the same link sent two messages and received none. All messages were sent in Morse code and properly encoded in the appropriate cipher system. If the Germans had broken the code they would have read a message that fit perfectly with the situation that was being portrayed.

The 23rd divided into three main groups to simulate the 5th Armored Headquarters, as well as its CCA and CCB.[2] The 5th Armored Division Trains and CCR had already moved out the day before, so no attempt was made to simulate them. On the afternoon of 4 October 1944, the notional division headquarters moved to an assembly area near Fels, immediately next to the genuine 5th Armored HQ. The next morning the genuine 5th Armored HQ moved out in daylight with all bumper markings obscured. Although the tankers had been ordered to remove all identifying insignia, a number of 5th Armored patches were still being worn.

There were still not enough genuine 5th Armored patches for the men, so roughly half the six hundred and fifty shoulder patches needed were painted by the 603rd Special Effects Section (SES). There was also a shortage of the red and yellow aerial recognition markers. Instead of allowing vehicles to go without (as few did in real life) they cut the fabric markers in half. The same

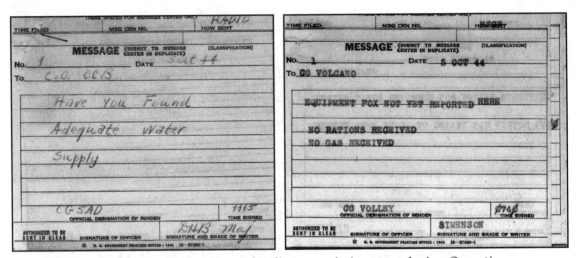

These original message forms record radio transmissions sent during Operation WILTZ. They show the typical type of message that would be sent by any unit. "CO Volcano" and "CO Volley" refer to the commanding officers of the 5th Armored Division and Combat Command A. These messages were sent by Cliff Simenson and David H. Bridges. Later in the war, the 23rd would assume the Germans knew the genuine officers' names and use them in dummy transmissions.

water point used by the genuine 5th Armored was kept busy with the same number of trips as had occurred before the move.

The notional CCA, under the command of Lieutenant Colonel Simenson, consisted of thirteen officers and two hundred and forty-seven enlisted men.[3] Their column consisted of twelve jeeps, twenty half-ton trucks, twenty-one deuce-and-a-half trucks, and nine half-tracks. At various times, two genuine 5th Armored tank platoons (of four M4 Sherman tanks under Lieutenant Jonasch and five M3 Stuart tanks under Lieutenant Potts) were attached to help add to the atmosphere and create treadmarks.

Simenson's "CCA" column departed from Luxembourg on the morning of 4 October. They moved into the Malscheid assembly area at 1600. This was north of the genuine CCA bivouac, but along their proposed route of march. The idea was to make the Germans think the CCA convoy had stopped at that location and not traveled any farther. The detachment was broken down to simulate two battalions (34th Tank and 46th Armored Infantry) as well as CCA HQ. The vehicles were carefully positioned around the outskirts of a heavily wooded area to give the impression that more vehicles and men were hidden in the trees. Signs to all applicable units were posted, warming fires built, and MPs posted.

On 7 October, the 3132nd played a sonic program of tanks moving around, as well as some bridge building sounds and general camp sounds from 1930 to 2100. Convoys were sent out to the surrounding area at intervals, all marked as vehicles from the 5th Armored. When the genuine tanks on loan from the 5th were present, they were always parked in highly visible places. There was a delay in obtaining the SCR-506 radio that was to send messages for CCA. It finally arrived on 9 October when the signal program of deceptive messages began.

Two MPs in a jeep were sent to the police station of a local town to ask for help retrieving a lost vehicle. They told the police that if the vehicle was found (actually none had been lost) it was to be returned to the 5th Armored Division at their (notional) bivouac. Men were allowed to visit local farms and towns, and a number of volunteers attended services in Wiltz on Sunday. Most displayed 5th Armored Division patches on their uniforms. To help the men play their roles, all officers of the 23rd had been given a short history of the 5th Armored and its principal commanders, with instructions to pass this information down to all enlisted men.

While the notional 5th Armored was patrolling the area, two German soldiers, apparently looking for a way to surrender, were captured by 1st Sergeant Jerry Glucken of A/603rd. They had to be quickly moved to a nearby POW processing point before they might discover there were only a handful of troops in the area. Because the 5th Armored had passed along the same road, a number of officers from the genuine unit followed the dummy signs into the notional encampment and had to be directed to their actual unit.

The notional CCB, under Lieutenant Colonel Schroeder, moved to Moesdorf next to the genuine CCB.[4] It was a poor location for a deception because the area was an open field with good visibility. Unlike the CCA bivouac, there were no woods to hide in. The genuine CCB moved north on the morning of 5 October. Its large and noisy convoys were clearly visible during this daylight move.

It became rapidly apparent that the local population could not have missed the movement of the genuine CCB, and in the present situation no attempt at deception was feasible. Therefore Colonel Reeder ordered the notional CCB to move to a more concealed bivouac, along the route of march the genuine 5th Armored had taken. On the afternoon of 5 October, Lieutenant Colonel Schroeder headed north with his men and set up a simulated CCB encampment northwest of Wiltz, near Derenback.

On the following day, the notional 5th Armored HQ also moved to the Derenback location, creating a larger cluster of simulated radio transmissions, road signage, and atmosphere to attract the attention of the Germans. On 7 October, the tank platoon attached to CCB switched places with the one at CCA. This change of vehicles helped to create the illusion of more armor in the area. On 8 October, the men were allowed to listen to a radio broadcast of a World's Series baseball game at 2030.

WILTZ ended at midnight on 8 October. All the radios were slowly

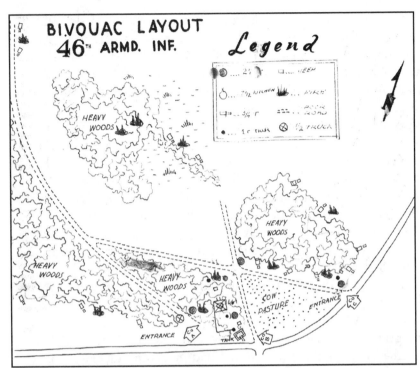

This drawing of the decoy 5th Armored Infantry bivouac set up for Operation WILTZ was done by an artist from the 603rd Engineers. It shows how vehicles and campfires were clustered around the outskirts of the woods to make it appear there were more hidden away just out of sight. A genuine tank placed at the entrance to the command post helped complete the illusion.

By the side of the road these vehicles, and men warming themselves over a fire, play a convincing role as 5th Armored Division soldiers during Operation WILTZ. The jeep is marked as belonging to the headquarters company of the 22nd Armored Engineers.

removed from the airwaves. The next morning the 23rd (now stripped of 5th Armored markings and patches) left their camps at fifteen-minute intervals to return to Luxembourg, infiltrating in small groups so as to not attract attention.

Afterward, the officers noted a few errors in how the vehicles had been marked. A 4-ton truck from 23rd HQ had been given a bumper marking starting with a "5-X" (division headquarters) when the table of organization for an armored division authorized no such vehicle. One of the CCB vehicles had D Battery markings from an armored field artillery battalion. The problem was that there was no D Battery in such a unit. These may seem like mild errors, but it showed that more care had to be taken so that nothing done in future operations would arouse suspicion. The after-action reports from WILTZ contain many of the same complaints noted in previous operations. More equipment, such as tankers' leather crash helmets and Thompson submachine guns (typically seen in armored units), were requested to hang from vehicles while on patrol.

The 23rd had not expected to run into men from the genuine unit so often. During WILTZ, a soldier from the 5th Armored Engineer unit wandered by and noticed the 23rd vehicles stenciled with his own unit designation. He asked one of the MPs what was going on, as he did not recognize anyone from his unit. Not knowing what to tell the man, he was sent from private to sergeant to lieutenant, and finally to the headquarters where he was told these men and their equipment were being prepared as replacements, because his unit was expected to be shortly wiped out in an attack. The speechless man was then directed back to his genuine unit.[5] This was not the only 5th Armored Division man who was baffled by the notional unit.

To keep the tank crews that assisted in the operation from talking about what they had done, they were first told they were being used on a dangerous mission. They were then told to forget everything they saw or heard, and were threatened with a general court-martial should they talk about it.[6] This impressed the men enough that they developed a high respect for the 23rd troops and, as far as anyone knew, kept quiet about it.

It would have been terribly hard for Operation WILTZ to be a complete success. Most of the reasons were out of the hands of the 23rd. The failure of the genuine 5th Armored to be able to move at night, and in small groups, made it impossible to conceal that some type of movement was going on. The 5th also neglected to remove all their shoulder patches and bumper markings, which instantly revealed their true identity. The pending attack of the 5th Armored never happened so there was no way to know if the Germans had been fooled.

Given the situation, the officers of the 23rd did the best they could. They realized they could not create the impression of a stationary 5th Armored and so tried to simulate a shorter move. The visibility of the initial bivouac of CCB could have proved highly embarrassing, had not the order been given to shift to a more appropriate location. It was better to try and fool the Germans halfway than give the whole show away by sticking to a plan that had rapidly become obsolete.

Lieutenant Colonel Schroeder later wrote, "At best, I believe the results of this operation were to possibly confuse the enemy as to the exact location of all elements of CCB 5th Armored Division. Therefore I consider the results unsatisfactory. Had not headquarters ordered my command to the second position, the efforts of CCB would have been hopeless."[7]

Chapter 10

Artillery, Operation VASELINE, and Propaganda

While the bulk of the 23rd was involved in Operation WILTZ, a task force of six officers and seventy-one enlisted men (mostly from B/603rd) took part in an experiment involving the simulation of artillery fire from 2–9 October 1944.[1] This task force was under command of Captain Cowardin, the assistant artillery officer for the 23rd.

The initial plan called for the testing of simulated artillery flashes to determine if they were useful in confusing German counter-battery fire. Three XX Corps artillery units (the 204th and 739th Field Artillery Battalions and the 195th Field Artillery Group) were to each construct a dummy artillery position near Rezonville equipped with captured German guns.

Cowardin's task force headed off with their vehicles bearing the bumper markings of the 204th FA Battalion. When they arrived at the designated artillery units they found that someone had misunderstood the abilities of the deception troops. Enemy artillery positions were located (by both sides) through both flash and sound ranging. The deception troops were only able to simulate the flash portion, and had expected to be positioned close enough to a genuine artillery position so they could time their flashes to the firing of the real guns.

The selected positions were too far away from the corps artillery units and were under direct enemy observation. The 195th Field Artillery Group position was under direct fire from German guns and could not be used. The position selected for the notional 204th gun sites were seven miles from the actual guns (too far for the flash simulators). There was also not enough telephone wire available to connect the units together to coordinate the flashes with the genuine firing. At that time the decision was made to construct only one dummy artillery position at the 739th site and set off flashes in coordination with the 90th Infantry Division's 334th Field Artillery Battalion. The task force quickly altered their bumper markings to indicate vehicles of the 739th Field Artillery Battalion (in case enemy agents were lurking nearby).

On 4 October, Captain Cowardin was notified that his unit should move up to the planned location, a few thousand meters from Fort Driant, but that the 334th (which was needed for synchronized flashes) would not move forward until Fort Driant had been captured. This would delay the operation until those guns were in position. The dummy artillery site was finally prepared about midway between Rezonville and Vionville. One bulldozer had been brought along to help dig out the gun positions, but they hit solid rock only three to four feet below the surface. Topping off the problems was that it rained all day on 5 October, and Cowardin was informed that the promised captured German artillery pieces were no longer available.

The selected site was in view of the German lines on the high ground to the west of Metz. As soon as possible, the men dug their own reinforced shelters and covered them with abandoned artillery shell boxes in preparation for the expected German artillery fire. On the night of 5 October, the 334th fired four volleys from a nearby position, with the flash devices coordinated by the telephone system. The artillerymen felt that the flash duration was too long, the color too red, and the positions too close together for such open ground, but on the whole felt it put on a very good show.

The next morning it was discovered that some of their telephone wires had been cut and a few of the batteries used to trigger the flash devices had been stolen. The immediate fears were of a German patrol, but the problem was soon traced to an antitank position nearby that had been out scrounging in the night. The Germans shelled the nearby town of Vionville at approximately 1700. Eight American volleys with simulators were fired between 2030 and 2300 on the night of 6 October with no response from the Germans. The glare of the flash devices temporarily blinded the men reloading them, which slowed down the operation. All night the Germans shelled the Vionville area, but no shells landed directly on the notional battery area.

On 7 October, the word was passed down that the Germans seemed to be short of artillery ammunition and were probably saving their remaining rounds for an expected infantry attack. Again at 2030, more American volleys were fired with simulated flashes. This time they were coordinated with the ad hoc "D battery." Normally there is no D Battery in an artillery unit, but this one consisted of captured German 105mm guns that had been turned on their former owners. The artillerymen felt it was better to use up the captured German ammunition and to save their own stocks for when they were needed. By the time the firing had ended at 2300, fifteen volleys had been fired. To help conceal the less than perfect timing, the genuine guns would fire two volleys: the first with all guns simultaneously, the second as soon as individual guns were ready. This made the second volley a bit irregular and concealed any delay in the flash simulators.

After four quick firings of the simulators, a fifteen-minute cooling period was needed. After the tenth firing, the wire heating elements began breaking down, requiring replacement. Finally, the storage batteries used to trigger the simulators began running low and causing misfires. On the night of 7 October the simulators were again put into action, but the crews found they could not reload and be ready to fire as quickly as the real guns. Firing ceased at 2300, but the Germans fired a few rounds in the vicinity of the nearby airfield, possibly indicating continued interest in the area.

Sunday 8 October was relatively quiet, but that evening one stray German shell detonated high in the air over the flash simulator positions. At nightfall the best remaining batteries were selected and gathered together for one simulated battery, which fired their last five volleys between 2100 and 2300.

The 23rd task force finally broke camp and left the area on the morning of 9 October. All bumper markings were removed and the vehicles infiltrated back to Luxembourg. The conclusion drawn from the exercise was that "phantom artillery," as the flash devices were being called, was worthwhile, but needed more work. Although the dummy flashes did not draw enemy fire (possibly due to the Germans' lack of ammunition), the participating artillery officers felt the idea showed great promise.

The suggestion was made that an artillery unit, more familiar with the appearance of a real flash, should be involved in developing a better and more robust flash simulator. Such an improved simulator would be useful for creating the impression of a larger amount of artillery in an area, drawing enemy counter-battery fire away from genuine gun positions, forcing enemy guns to reveal their positions, and to make the enemy waste ammunition.

The flash simulators were supposed to draw German fire, which made it a dangerous job. Genuine artillery batteries normally did their best not to attract enemy attention, which explains the following comment in the official report: "None of the units we had to work with had any idea of how we work, and after they found out, all were glad to pass us on to some other unit."[2]

★ ★ ★

Before Operation WILTZ had ended, Lieutenant Colonel Schroeder was notified about another potential mission for the 23rd. Operation VASELINE would involve only the sonic company.[3] Schroeder and Major Mike Williams of the 3132nd immediately headed off north to Kalterherberg, near Montshau, to meet with local officers. The mission was to portray, through sonic means, the assembly of a mass of tanks preparing for an attack through Hofen. The sonic program would take place at night; meanwhile the genuine 5th Armored would be moving to a location to the south, so as to be in place for an attack the following morning.

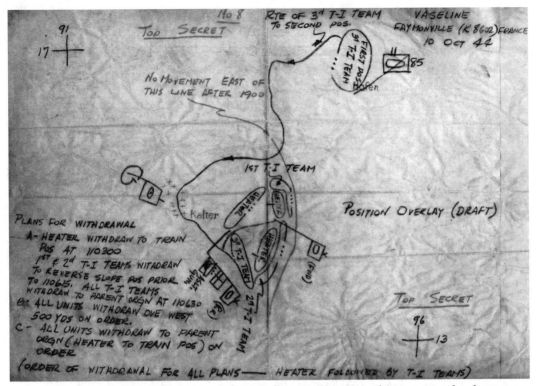

One of the few records of the aborted Operation VASELINE *is this map overlay kept by Dick Syracuse as a souvenir. It was supposed to take place around Faymonville, France on the night of 10 October 1944. "HEATER" refers to the 3132nd sonic vehicles and the "T.I. Teams" stand for "tank-infantry teams."*

To provide security for the operation, a company of Sherman tanks, a company of armored infantry, and a battery of self-propelled artillery were to be attached to the sonic platoons. Each sonic platoon would have its own tank-infantry screen in front of it to prevent any German patrol from discovering the sounds were coming from speakers.

The chosen area for the deception was well within the observation and range of German artillery, and it was expected that as soon as the sonic platoons began playing their program the Germans would begin to shell the suspected assembly area.

VASELINE should have taken place on the night of 10 October, but the genuine attack was delayed. For the next few days the men assigned to VASELINE waited for word that the attack was on, but each time it was delayed for one reason or another. Eventually it was decided that the main 5th Armored attack would take place in another location and VASELINE was scrapped.

Lieutenant Colonel Schroeder felt that the operation would have been successful, since he had been given a clear-cut mission with no ambiguity about the desired objective. The exact planning, time, and method of operating was left to the decision of the task force commander. Schroeder cited adequate time for planning and reconnaissance, complete cooperation from the 5th Armored Division, reasonable ground security, and good staff officers as reasons he thought it would have succeeded. He finished by saying, "I believe the plan was tactically sound. I know it was thoroughly understood by every private soldier under my command."[4]

★ ★ ★

The following weeks in October were a quiet time for the 23rd. The relaxed atmosphere in Luxembourg City ended when General Bradley's 12th Army Group Forward CP moved in, bringing with it a large number of high-ranking officers. The Germans must have discovered this, as the city was subjected to intermittent shelling from a large caliber railroad gun. The influx of high-ranking officers and periodic shelling made life in the formerly relaxed city slightly more tense.

From 20–24 October a sonic detachment from the 3132nd was sent to the 83rd Infantry Division sector on a propaganda mission.[5] One officer and three men, along with a lightweight sound system mounted on a truck (not one of the sonic-equipped half-tracks), reported to the 329th Infantry Regiment headquarters. A 329th intelligence officer wrote a propaganda speech in German, and directed the detachment to the 2nd Battalion area near Herborn. At 1900 on 20 October, the speech was broadcast over the loudspeakers.

The next day, a new propaganda speech was written containing current news of the war. Most of the speech was in German, but it was known that some Yugoslavs were working for the Germans in the area so parts were in the Yugoslavian language. This time the broadcast was from the 3rd Battalion sector near Echternach.

No broadcasts were made the next day, but on 23 October a propaganda speech in Polish was broadcast in the afternoon, about three kilometers from Betzdorf. The sonic detachment returned to Luxembourg that night, only to be called back for one more broadcast on 24 October. This was to be in German, broadcast near Oberdonven. When the equipment was set up for a midafternoon session, however, the system would not work. Although the detachment attempted to fix it on the spot, they were unable to do so and the detachment returned to Luxembourg. No reason was noted as to why such a mission was attempted, even though the 23rd's participation in propaganda was technically against the orders of both the JSC and ETOUSA.

About a month later, on 23 November, another detachment from the 3132nd was sent out on a similar propaganda mission in the 83rd Division sector. Again they used a portable lightweight speaker carried on a truck.

Lieutenant Leonard Davis and four enlisted men arrived at the 3rd Battalion command post of the 329th Infantry Regiment near Herborn, Luxembourg.

The following day at 1000, a planned ten-minute propaganda broadcast was cut short when the volume was turned to maximum and six speaker cones blew out. The detachment returned to Luxembourg City, made repairs, and returned to Herborn in time to successfully broadcast the planned speech at 1630. These speeches were read live over a microphone, as the small detachment had no way of making a recording.

Again on 25 November, a ten-minute speech was played at 1000. Afterwards the sonic car was moved fifty yards closer to the front lines and another broadcast was made. Within six minutes, the Germans fired three artillery rounds at them. The artillery shells landed roughly sixty yards from the microphone. Although no one was hurt, the amplified sound of the explosion was enough to blow four speaker cones. These were quickly repaired with the help of a radio repairman from the 3rd Battalion CP. Later that day, at 1535, a third speech was sent over to German lines. This one was limited to five and a half minutes to prevent German shelling.

On 26 November, two more speeches were made. The first came at 1035, lasting five minutes, and the second was at 1502, lasting seven minutes. The following day, a Psychological and Propaganda Warfare (PPW) unit arrived, and the sonic detachment stood by observing their broadcast on official PPW equipment. This crew set up the PPW speaker roughly four hundred yards in front of their microphone position. Three minutes after the broadcast had begun, German shells landed roughly seventy-five yards away from the speaker. The detachment returned to Luxembourg City on the afternoon of 27 November.

Based upon what he had seen, Lieutenant Davis concluded that the Germans could locate a single speaker to within one hundred yards in three to five minutes. To a request for information on the value of the second mission, Lieutenant Colonel Desertels (S-2 of the 83rd Division) replied, "Some good was accomplished," but he furnished no specifics.[6]

The 3132nd crews learned from the experience of being shelled, and checked the sonic car equipment to make sure it would not be ruined from the amplified sound of a close artillery blast. Although the sonic car equipment was far more durable, it was decided to obtain long microphone cables in case they were necessary for a future operation.

Reeder questioned why his men had been called upon for this mission, "If PPW is available to the 83rd, why use our apparatus?"[7] Upon investigation, Lieutenant Colonel Simenson discovered that the 83rd Division had had difficulty obtaining assistance from a PPW unit due to their equipment not working. When the PPW unit was available and functioning it was called for first.

One troubling fact was that the PPW units were now beginning to mount their broadcast systems on half-tracks instead of the standard PPW trucks. The PPW units wanted the greater mobility of the half-track, which would allow them to move off road. They also appreciated the armored sides, which gave more protection against shelling than a thin walled truck. Major Williams hoped that this new development would not tip off the Germans that sonic equipment was being mounted on half-tracks, which might lead to identifying his own half-tracks as a sonic unit.

During this period, the men of the 23rd created their own entertainment with a show they called the "Blarney Breakdown." Shortly afterward, Marlene Dietrich performed on their stage with her USO show. As a German national, Dietrich took a great risk by performing in Europe. Had she been captured, she would have been tried for treason by the German government.

About this time, one of the officers of the 603rd Engineers, Lieutenant Gilbert Seltzer, was sent off on a special mission to Patton's Third Army headquarters. General Patton had requested that a camouflage officer conduct a survey of how well his headquarters was following proper camouflage procedure. Though this type of camouflage audit was commonly done by the standard camouflage battalions, it was highly unusual for the specialized 603rd. It was the only mission of its type that Seltzer recalled.

Seltzer visited Patton's headquarters and found its camouflage discipline terrible. Washing was hung out, attracting attention from aerial surveillance; vehicles were not parked under netting; nor were any precautions taken to keep tire tracks to a minimum. Worst of all was Patton himself. The general insisted on traveling in a well-marked vehicle with what some might consider an ostentatious display, including his trademark lacquered helmet liner and pistols. There could be no doubt that everyone in the vicinity knew that Patton was in the area.

Seltzer bravely wrote up his critical report and submitted it through channels, wondering if it would get him in trouble. Eventually he heard back that Patton felt it was a well-conducted survey and an excellent report. General Patton may not have altered his own habits, but in this case he appreciated an honest opinion about his command.[8]

Chapter 11

Operation DALLAS
2–10 November 1944

In early November 1944, the 23rd Special Troops were involved in three over-lapping operations: DALLAS, ELSENBORN, and CASANOVA. This stretched the abil-ities of the 23rd to the limit as the unit had to execute three unrelated opera-tions in different locations simultaneously.

Operation DALLAS was a small artillery show.[1] The main focus was to help the XX Corps artillery move into a new supporting position for the 90th Infantry Division's assault on Metz. From 2–10 November, a deception detachment maintained a large display of decoys and flash devices in the XX Corps area around Jarny while the genuine guns moved to new locations.

Intelligence officers know that it takes time to move and set up artillery positions, so tracking the movement of artillery units can often indicate the location of the next offensive. If DALLAS was to be effective, the first the Germans would know of the new artillery positions would be when the guns of XX Corps opened fire in support of the 90th Division's attack.

As the artillery officer of the 23rd, Lieutenant Colonel Mayo was put in command of DALLAS. He took with him one hundred and ninety-five men and thirty-six decoy artillery pieces, as well as camouflage netting and flash sim-ulators. XX Corps artillery supplied him with an additional five hundred men and twelve genuine artillery pieces. This detachment was to replace twenty-two hundred and thirty men and forty-eight artillery pieces. DALLAS involved only decoys, flash simulators, and special effects. No radio or sonic deception was involved.

Each of the genuine artillery battalions (204th, 736th, 949th, and 733rd) left one battery behind in their original positions. They had been given clear instructions to cooperate with the deception troops so there were no problems in that area. Telephone lines and switchboards were left in position to handle incoming calls. Two separate notional artillery groups would be portrayed by the 23rd as part of this operation.

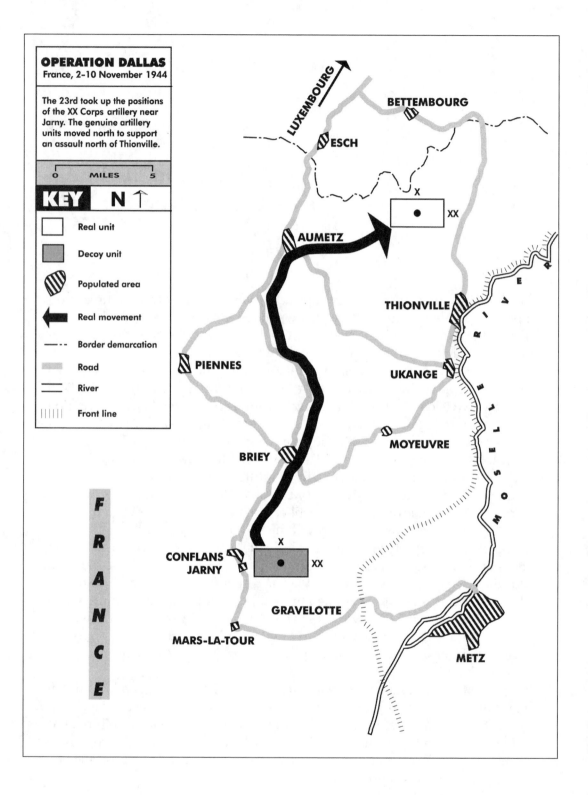

OPERATION DALLAS
France, 2–10 November 1944

The 23rd took up the positions of the XX Corps artillery near Jarny. The genuine artillery units moved north to support an assault north of Thionville.

0   MILES   5

KEY   N ↑

☐   Real unit

▨   Decoy unit

▨   Populated area

◀   Real movement

–·–·   Border demarcation

──   Road

──   River

|||||| Front line

LUXEMBOURG

BETTEMBOURG

ESCH

AUMETZ

THIONVILLE

PIENNES

UKANGE

MOYEUVRE

BRIEY

MOSELLE RIVER

CONFLANS JARNY

GRAVELOTTE

MARS-LA-TOUR

METZ

FRANCE

Captain Cowardin was put in charge of the first notional unit. This was the 193rd Artillery Group, consisting of the 949th Field Artillery Battalion near Batilly and the 204th Field Artillery Battalion on the edge of the Bois de Marziers (both to be simulated primarily by men from the B/603rd Engineers).

On 3 November, the detachment moved to an assembly area near Vionville, stenciled on the proper vehicle markings, and sewed on XX Corps patches. Their movement into the area was coordinated to mix with the movement of the genuine C/204th through the area. At first the deception troops took over the newly vacated positions of batteries A & B/949th, while the genuine C/204th occupied the former C/949th positions. The B/603rd headquarters detachment occupied the area of the 949th Headquarters Battery. At dusk, rubber decoy guns were installed under camouflage netting and flash simulator units were dug in to their front. The deception troops were slightly dismayed to find that many of their camouflage nets were beginning to rot after having been stored too long in a damp environment.

Throughout the operation, the genuine artillery units' observation aircraft kept up their same patterns of flight. The light aircraft maintained their landing strips and acted as though nothing had changed, until the end of the operation when they moved to rejoin their units in the new location.

On 4 November, two of the 603rd platoons shifted locations to take over the now vacated positions of B&C/204th. They moved their gun decoys in under the camouflage nets left in place for them by the former occupants. The genuine A/204th remained in place. Each night a fire was lit at each notional gun position, as a genuine unit would do to keep the gun crews warm. The weather was turning cold and after the first day everyone's boots were soaked through and remained so until the end of the operation. Galoshes were requested, but the limited supply held in the ETO was being issued to the frontline troops.

One of the keys to replacing the genuine artillery units was to maintain the regular pattern of harassing fire. The genuine batteries kept to a typical firing schedule. In addition, from 5–8 November, a number of simulated volleys were fired by setting off the flash simulators. A/949th fired seven volleys (four rounds in each), C/204th five volleys, B/204th six volleys, and B/949th eight volleys. This was not a large number, but just enough to keep up the normal rate of fire for such units in a quiet sector.

The report on the operation stated: "The pattern of real shooting and flash shooting was varied in such a away that it was impossible to tell just what was being fired. Our own observers, including the writer, were unable to tell just what happened when a change in timing of the firing was made at the last moment."[2]

On the morning of 9 November, everything was taken down in the 949th Battalion area and the troops infiltrated at five-minute intervals back to Luxembourg City. The next day, the 204th Battalion area was closed down and the men returned to Luxembourg.

From a distance this inflatable 155mm gun decoy looks like the genuine article. As part of Operation DALLAS the decoy gun was set up at night while the genuine artillery piece was moved to a new location. The emplacement, scattered debris, and camouflage netting add to the realism.

Up close it is obviously an inflatable decoy, but the shadow pattern created by the burlap garnish in the camouflage net helps to hide any flaws. The decoys were never designed to fool anyone at close range, but were very effective at deceiving aerial reconnaissance and observers at a distance.

The second notional artillery group taking part in this operation, under Captain Joseph Sidwell, consisted of the three batteries from the 733rd Field Artillery Battalion and one gun battery and the headquarters battery of the 736th Field Artillery Battalion.

On the night of 2 November, two batteries of the genuine 949th moved out under cover of darkness and were replaced by decoys. On 3 November, the genuine 733rd and 736th moved out at night and were also replaced by decoys. The remaining genuine battery of the 949th fired battalion volleys, in keeping with a schedule of harassing fire, which was enlarged with flashes from the decoy positions to simulate a battery volley.

A system of guard posts was set up to keep unwanted visitors out of the area. Each unit had two guard posts in the battery firing position. One soldier manned each during the day and two soldiers manned each post at night. Two additional guard posts were on a similar schedule covering the battery headquarters position. During the day each inflatable decoy had one man with it at all times to make sure the dummy gun maintained air pressure.

The 155mm gun decoy is shown here in both deflated and inflated states. The long barrel of this weapon posed a particular problem in remaining upright when inflated.

141

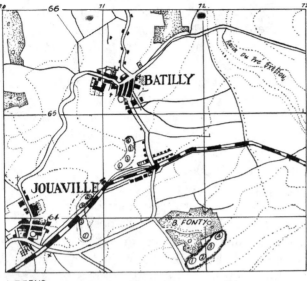

The 204th Field Artillery Battalion positions near Jouaville consisted of the genuine Battery A guns—next to the Bois Fonty—and two decoy batteries dug in along the road. The decoy guns were moved into the positions of the genuine Batteries A and B guns once they withdrew.

LEGEND

⊡⊡⊡⊡ "B" BTRY 209 E - 3ʀᴅ. PLT. CO. "B"
①②③④ "C" BTRY 204 F - 2ɴᴅ PLT. CO. "B"
⊡⊡⊡⊡ "A" BTRY 204 F -

The 949th Field Artillery Battalion was set up along the Bois de Maizieres. The genuine C Battery guns remained in a central position, while the men of Company B, 603rd Engineers replaced the genuine A and B Battery guns with inflatable decoys.

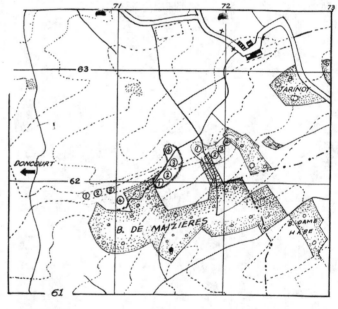

LEGEND

①②③④ "A" BTRY. 949 F - 1ST. PLT. CO. "B"
①②③④ "B" BTRY. 949 F - 4TH. PLT. CO. "B"
①②③④ "C" BTRY. 949 F.

This is the decoy Number 2 gun (105mm howitzer) of Battery A, 949th Field Artillery Battalion set up and manned by men from the 1st Platoon of Company B, 603rd Engineers. This position is third from the right of the battery line. Note the portable air compressor used to inflate the decoy.

This is the decoy Number 2 gun (105mm howitzer) of Battery B, 949th Field Artillery Battalion set up and manned by men from the 4th Platoon of Company B, 603rd Engineers. This position is second from the left along the battalion line north of the Bois De Maizieres.

143

One of the main problems with this operation was that the wind had a terrific effect on the decoys. It caused swaying and bending of the thin-walled fake artillery pieces. The men tried weighing them down with sandbags and also tried tying them down, but the motion could not be prevented. They also had trouble with the fabric at the muzzle end. It bent in with a wrinkled edge that destroyed the appearance of a steel cannon barrel. This was fixed by packing mud on the inside to push it out to a normal shape.

On 4 November, the genuine B/204th moved to a new position between the notional 733rd and 736th areas. The new location was chosen so the guns could fire with the flash of either unit, thus adding to the confusion of how many guns were firing. The remaining 204th gun pits were set up with decoys. The 736th and 949th continued their harassing fires, which were made to appear as battalion volleys. On 5 November, the guns were involved in a "serenade." This was an artillery tactic whereby all guns in a specific area fire simultaneously.

On 8 November, a German aircraft (tentatively identified as a Focke Wulf 190) circled the battalion area. This was considered a good sign, as it indicated the Germans were interested enough in the area to conduct an aerial reconnaissance. The simulated battery fire continued until 9 November when the notional 736th and 949th were pulled out. The following day, the remaining genuine artillery left the area to rejoin their original units. What remained of the 23rd also departed, after quietly removing all bumper markings and insignia.

There was, however, no feeling among the men that they had managed to fool the Germans, although there was also no indication they had failed. The comments on the operation were that more men were needed so that the engineers did not have to handle both the decoys and flash simulators, as well as guard duty. A platoon of engineers from the 406th would have made their job far easier.[3]

The main complaint of the men was in regards to the blasting caps used to set off the flash charges. They had been issued British manufactured caps that had only a short wire lead. Numerous problems were blamed on these caps and it was recommended that not only should the American version, with longer wire leads, be used in the future, but that the simulator should always be rigged with two caps in case one failed.

The other lesson learned was that the men of the 603rd may have been camouflage engineers, but they had not received as much training in explosives as the standard combat engineer. There were some problems with handling the explosive materials and in setting up a system to make sure every man had vacated the artillery simulator position before triggering the flashes. The officers felt that more classes on explosives would be a good idea before another such mission was attempted.

Chapter 12

Operation ELSENBORN
3–12 November 1944

During the month of October, the Allied Army was at a standstill along the German border. One place where the Americans were taking a great number of casualties was the wooded and hilly area known as the Hurtgen Forest. There the 9th Infantry Division was slowly moving forward against strong German defenses. To get his army moving again—across the Roer River into Germany—General Bradley proposed Operation QUEEN to clear the plain between the Roer and Wurm Rivers. This called for the largest amount of air support for any ground operation in WWII. Part of his plan to press forward into Germany involved a fresh division suddenly making an appearance in the Hurtgen Forest for a surprise attack.

In late October, the V Corps discussed the idea of the 23rd notionally keeping a division in a rest camp, while the actual division was secretly moved into the front lines. This would be known as Operation ELSENBORN, named after Camp Elsenborn, a military barracks area one and a half miles southwest of the town of Elsenborn, used as a rest center for units pulled off the front line.[1]

The V Corps was convinced there were enemy agents operating in the Elsenborn area keeping an eye on troop movements. Just across the front lines to the east were three German divisions and their corps headquarters. This caused the Americans to feel certain that there would be some German radio interception units in the immediate area.

The 28th Infantry Division, resting up in Camp Elsenborn, was scheduled to replace the 9th Infantry Division in the Hurtgen Forest on 1 November. That left no time for the 28th Division to be used in setting up a deception operation. Plans were then made to set the stage for ELSENBORN with the arrival of the battered 9th Infantry Division in the rest camp, and to make the main focus of the operation the simulation of the next unit to move into the camp. This would be the 4th Infantry Division, which was occupying the front lines just to the west of Elsenborn.

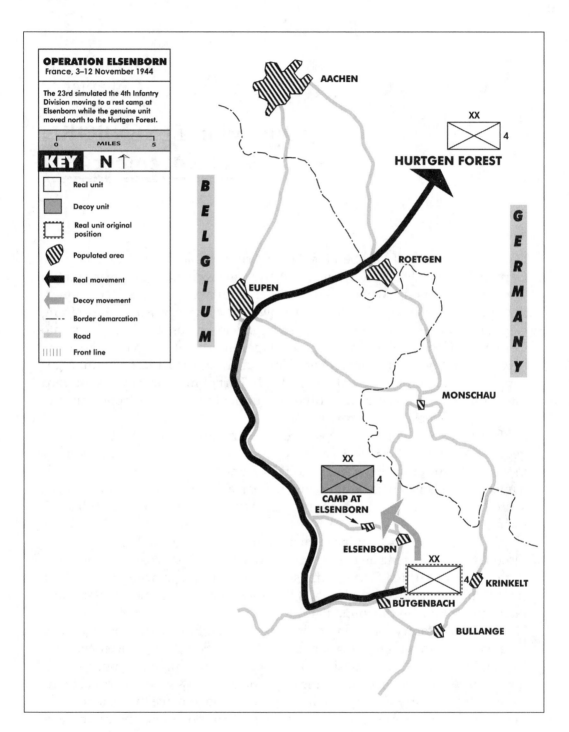

OPERATION ELSENBORN
France, 3–12 November 1944

The 23rd simulated the 4th Infantry Division moving to a rest camp at Elsenborn while the genuine unit moved north to the Hurtgen Forest.

0 — MILES — 5

KEY N ↑

- ☐ Real unit
- ▨ Decoy unit
- ⬚ Real unit original position
- ◩ Populated area
- ◀ Real movement
- ◀ Decoy movement
- –·–· Border demarcation
- ▬ Road
- ||||| Front line

AACHEN

XX 4

HURTGEN FOREST

BELGIUM

GERMANY

ROETGEN

EUPEN

MONSCHAU

XX 4

CAMP AT ELSENBORN

ELSENBORN

XX 4

KRINKELT

BÜTGENBACH

BULLANGE

The 4th was to be replaced in the front lines by the 99th Infantry Division. While the 4th was being simulated in the rest camp, it would secretly be shifted roughly thirty miles north, where it would hopefully make a surprise appearance in the Hurtgen Forest. The deception operation was to last no longer than four days, by which time the Germans would have discovered the real location of the 4th.

The 23rd was involved in two other missions during this same time (CASANOVA and DALLAS), so only a third of the deception unit was available to take part in ELSENBORN. Due to the multiple operations, no decoys or sonic troops would participate in ELSENBORN, only radio deception and special effects. Task Force ELSENBORN, under command of Lieutenant Colonel Edgar W. Schroeder, consisted of thirty-six officers, four hundred and thirty-one enlisted men, and one hundred and eight vehicles. Due to the heavy demand for radio operators in this mission, one hundred and ninety-three of the men were from the 23rd Signal Company. On 3 November 1944, Task Force ELSENBORN headed to the camp to prepare for the operation.

One of the problems for ELSENBORN was that the 23rd had previously only simulated units in the field. They had no information on how a division appeared in a barracks area. To prepare for the operation they sent out teams to reconnoiter the 9th Division once it had been pulled out of the line. Careful notes were taken on such items as signage, distribution of military policemen, local patrols, and water distribution points. Other teams were sent to the 4th Infantry Division to make sure the poop sheets for that unit were up to date.

One of the other problems with this operation was that while in a rest camp a unit's radios were normally silent. This meant that either the 23rd would have to forgo one of its greatest tricks, or else come up with a reason for radios to transmit while in camp. Thus the signalmen of the 9th Division had expected a chance to rest and clean up, but instead were presented with an order mandating a daily test of all CW radio sets and operators.

Going out over the name of William C. Westmoreland, chief of staff of the 9th Infantry Division (and later commander of U.S. forces in Viet Nam), was the order for a radio operation test:

1. Commencing at 1400 on _____ October 1944 the following messages (enciphered by means of the M-209 Converter) will be transmitted on your _____ net. The net control station will divide the traffic as equally as possible among the subordinate stations.
2. All stations will turn in their logs and files covering these transmissions to the Division Signal Officer.[2]

What followed was a list of sixteen messages ranging from (message #1) "Patrols third Bn have taken seven enemy prisoners," to (message # 16) "Activity slight. Baker and Charlie reported nothing and Able reported only slight patrol action. Dog Company had some trouble in their sector but OK now."[3]

What this did was set the stage for the Germans to see that American divisions in a rest area might be called upon to test their equipment and operators' competency with transmissions and cipher machines. When the 9th moved out, the Germans would not suspect anything when 4th Division radios began sending the same type of test messages. It was even possible that a German agent might hear some grumbling from signalmen who had to give up some of their free time to take part in some ridiculous radio test.

With the stage set for radio transmissions from a rest camp, the signal experts of the 23rd had to begin preparations for the next phase. They had to assume the guise of the 4th Infantry Division radio net so that the Germans would have no question about the authenticity of the notional radio network operating in Camp Elsenborn. The radio experts of the 23rd were dispatched to the 4th Division at Bullange to observe the idiosyncrasies of their transmissions.

On 27 October 1944, ten radio teams from the 23rd arrived at the 4th Infantry Division. Message center personnel of the 23rd were instructed by their counterparts in the 4th Division on how they actually wrote up messages to be sent. The 23rd radiomen took notes on the style of the 4th Division radio operators. The division had a distinctive way of using the SLIDEX code, and the 4th Reconnaissance Troop message center had their own TPC (Troop Prearranged Code). Records indicate that the 4th Division gave their full cooperation and understood that a successful deception operation could save the lives of their men.

One of the findings was that each message center of the division had its own style of partially encoding their messages. The division headquarters habitually left a few words in clear (not encoded) while the staff of the 8th Infantry Regiment coded every word. The signalmen also discovered that the 8th Infantry Regiment operators dragged out an "R" to indicate a message received. Division artillery always repeated the all-clear text words in their SLIDEX messages, and the transmissions of the 4th Recon Troop were slow and methodical in style. To ensure that this style remained consistent throughout the operation, the actual 4th Division message center personnel coded the proficiency test messages in advance. Once they were familiar with the 4th Division operations, the 23rd signalmen slowly took over operation of the division's radios and began to handle the actual transmissions of the 4th Division while still in the front lines.

On 5 November, the 4th Division's radio net was operated by 23rd signalmen only. At 0100 on 6 November, the division was ordered to observe radio silence, as it normally would during a move. The 23rd signalmen moved to Camp Elsenborn and set up their radios to prepare for the notional radio proficiency test. The genuine 4th Division radio operators were instructed to only listen in to their assigned frequencies in case of an emergency call. Under no circumstances were they to transmit unless they received a message classified as urgent.

The radio deception teams at Camp Elsenborn briefed the rest of their comrades on what they had learned about the 4th Division's style of operation from 6 to 8 November. From 8 until 11 November, the notional 4th Division radio net in Camp Elsenborn transmitted the prepared messages of the radio test. All radios were physically dispersed throughout the camp area in a pattern similar to that used previously by the 9th Division. Transmissions were made using the 4th Division's SOI (Signal Operation Instructions), authenticators, and frequencies.

To simulate the division, twenty-two radio sets and over one hundred operators were used. Special care was taken to make sure that each operator transmitted only on a specific radio. This was to prevent the Germans from identifying an individual by his "fist" and discovering him transmitting from two different units. Each radio transmission was monitored both by an officer and the man who was to send on that radio the next day.

Major Yocum, the 23rd signal officer, was so pleased that he wrote, "It is recommended that this operation be used as a guide in the future, both for BLARNEY and for the units with which we operate. The time allowed for planning and coordinating, the cooperation given by all headquarters involved, were the best encountered so far."[4]

The one element of the 4th Division not simulated on the radio net was the 12th Infantry Regimental Combat Team. By the time the preparations were under way, the 28th Infantry Division had taken such a beating in the Hurtgen Forest that the 12th was sent across the corps border to help out. This infantry regiment, plus attached artillery, engineer, and medical troops, was desperately needed to bolster the line in the Hurtgen. Sending this part of the 4th Division ahead to the battle may have helped the situation temporarily, but in the long run it may have compromised the entire deception operation.

The special effects aspect of the mission called for close cooperation with the 4th Division. 4th Division patches were sewn on 85 percent of the deception troops' uniforms, and vehicles were marked with correct 4th Division bumper markings. Starting on 6 November, the men put on raincoats to conceal the patches and covered over the bumper markings as they drove singly to the 4th Division area. Everyone was given a briefing on the history and commanding officers of the 4th Infantry Division so the men could play their parts.

Over the next few days, the deception troops would work closely with the genuine 4th Division in a series of moves to make any enemy agent think the 4th was being pulled back to Camp Elsenborn. The 4th Division made sure that during the upcoming move every bumper marking, helmet insignia, and shoulder patch was hidden. To assist in the shift north, the 4th Division was to use the code name RED WING. Combat elements were to move only at night, while the support units were to move during the day in a strictly controlled fashion. Some groups would travel in a standard column while others would move individually with roughly two-minute intervals between them.

Men assigned as road guides, to be left at key junctions along the route to direct traffic, were ordered to put a four-inch cross of one-inch white tape on their helmets for increased visibility. At night, traffic was directed by using a flashlight with half of the lens covered by a blue filter and half by a red filter.

Signs directing the way were to bear no relation to what was normally used by the 4th Division. A new system of signage was created, based on a cross with a symbol in one of the four quadrants. A mark in the upper right quadrant indicated the route for the 8th Regiment, the lower left quadrant for the 22nd Regiment, and all other troops used a specific letter in the upper left quadrant. (M was for the division command post, J for the 70th Tank Battalion, B for the 4th Medical Battalion, and so on.)

While preparing for the mission, the 23rd troops discovered that trying to hide their bumper markings with mud was not practical. This tended to smear the fresh paint. The solution was to use canvas bumper covers to hide the markings. The men, however, then discovered that wet roads caused the tape used to hold the covers in place to loosen and fall off. Finally the men learned to use wire or string to tie the covers in place until the time came to remove them.

On 6 November, a detachment of deception troops in fifteen vehicles infiltrated into the 4th Division Command Post area. There they assumed the guise of the 4th Division headquarters. While a great show was made of the newly formed 4th Division convoy heading to Elsenborn, the genuine vehicles of the divisional headquarters made their way via a circuitous route north to an assembly area behind the Hurtgen Forest.

The following day, another group of fifteen vehicles quietly entered the 8th Infantry Regiment area and took on the appearance of a convoy from that unit. They headed back to Camp Elsenborn while the genuine 8th, with their identity concealed, headed north. On 8 November, twenty-three vehicles assumed the guise of a convoy containing troops from the 22nd Regiment, 44th Field Artillery Battalion, plus the 4th Engineers, and made the journey to their assigned area in Camp Elsenborn. They shared the road with another convoy of eight vehicles playing the role of the 4th Quartermaster Company. The move was marred only by a road accident that demolished one of the message center vehicles. No one was hurt, but an appropriate show was made to make sure anyone watching could see that the wrecked vehicle was from the 4th Division.

One of the 4th Division men making the secretive journey north was Lieutenant George Wilson from the 22nd Infantry Regiment. As he recalled, "Long after darkness on about November 10, 1944, the 4th Division leapfrogged some thirty miles further north along the German–Belgian border. This was to be a highly secret maneuver, so elaborate that pains were taken to erase all signs of our identity. Divisional and regimental numbers were blocked out on all vehicles, and the green, four-leafed ivy shoulder patches, of which we were so proud, were removed from our uniforms. . . . Our blacked-out trucks took long confusing detours to the rear to mislead enemy agents."[5]

Once the notional convoys arrived at Camp Elsenborn, they were directed to the area of the camp where they were to set up a display of the unit at rest. On the night of 9 November it began snowing, which added an extra element of difficulty to the operation. Just driving vehicles around the area became increasingly difficult as the military tires were designed for off-road use and provided little traction on a slippery road. Chains had to be put on to increase traction, and the men hoped that the noise made by the chains added a new element of reality to their show.

Once the notional convoys had arrived in the camp they were directed to set up operations in their assigned buildings. Signs and sentries were posted in a manner similar to what the 9th Division had used during their stay there. Roving patrols of MPs moved about the camp and surrounding area. Signs bearing the name CACTUS (the code name of the 4th Division) were prominently displayed around the same building where the 9th had based its headquarters.

Military police posts were stationed in neighboring towns and manned night and day. Two jeeps marked as 4th Division MP vehicles were used to bring food to the posts and patrol the area. Water points continued to operate in the manner used by the 9th Division, but with 4th Division–marked personnel. Anyone observing their actions would see water being drawn for a full division, less the one combat team.

Vehicles were sent out in a pattern based on that previously observed. On the recommendation of the 4th Division, these movements were made by trucks marked according to individual regiments and battalions, since the quartermaster trucks of the genuine 4th Division were badly in need of maintenance. Messenger vehicles, wire patrols, and mail trucks made their rounds so as to conform to the normal practices of the 4th Division. Other trucks made runs to the garbage disposal point, shower point, and ration depot.

This did not always entail a large number of vehicles. On 10 November, the special effects section noted that the following vehicles were sent outside the camp: at 1000 one 2½-ton truck to the water point, 1000 one jeep sent to Malmedy, 1100 one truck sent to the ration depot, 1350 two trucks sent to nearby towns, and at 1500 one truck sent to the garbage disposal point. From 1300 to 1600 vehicles drove about the camp area to lay new tracks in the snow. This was done in the late afternoon so they would be ready for any German aircraft making a twilight reconnaissance run.

The snow posed an additional problem because an enemy agent could see from the tracks that only a few vehicles had actually passed by. Trucks were sent out specifically to increase the number of tracks in the snow. This would not only deceive an agent watching the roads, but also any German observation aircraft looking for activity in the area. A regimental headquarters was set up in the town of Elsenborn, properly marked as a 4th Division unit.

Most of the local population had been evacuated from the area before the operation, and the snow and cold weather kept the remaining few indoors most of the time. However, a number of American soldiers looking to visit friends in the 4th Division turned up at the notional divisional HQ, and a handful of men from the genuine 4th trying to find their unit ended up at the camp, totally confused by the familiar signs but the unfamiliar faces.

The display of a division at rest was slowly built up over three days as the new notional convoys arrived. Left out of the display were all the elements that had gone with the 12th Regiment to the Hurtgen. It would not do to try and simulate a unit that was already fighting in the front lines.

There was some confusion on 10 November when an advance party of the 9th Infantry Division arrived at the camp to prepare for their division's move back. The camp could not house two divisions at once, so the return of the 9th would indicate that it had all been a deception. Calm heads prevailed, and it was eventually decided that the 23rd would shift their activities and signs to another area of the camp while the 9th prepared to move in.

Finally, at 1800 on 11 November, the word was received that the operation would end the following day and the 9th Division would once again take over the camp. All visual aspects of the 4th Division were slowly dismantled that night. Starting at 1000 the following morning, the now unmarked vehicles of the 23rd began infiltrating out of the camp, at three-minute intervals, heading back to Luxembourg City.

The radio aspect of the deception had gone off without any problems. It had been carefully planned out, so everyone knew exactly what he was supposed to do. To keep the radio aspects of the deception from standing out, the next unit to arrive at the camp, the 99th Infantry Division, was also requested to transmit radio proficiency test messages. This would also allow the Americans to use the same ruse of a radio test in a rest camp for any future operations without drawing attention to it.

Overall, the staff at the V Corps and 12th Army Group were happy with the operation. It was claimed in the 23rd's records that a German intelligence document was captured shortly afterward indicating that the 4th was still in Camp Elsenborn.[6] George Wilson, of the 22nd Infantry Regiment, however, recalled that the 4th Division had been welcomed to the Hurtgen Forest by Axis Sally, the German radio propaganda broadcaster, when they entered the area.[7] This could indicate the operation was a failure, but also could have been only hearsay information obtained from other troops, or, more likely, a reference to the 12th Infantry Regiment that had previously been fighting in the forest. Thus a well-performed deception might have been ruined by the necessity to send part of the division on ahead. There is little use in trying to hide the movement of a unit if part of it has already been sent on ahead.

One of the lessons learned was that the 23rd could pull off appearing as a division in an enclosed rest area, but the officers realized that they could not have pulled off the same deception if the division had been bivouacked in a less controlled or more open area, due to the lack of men and vehicles. Nevertheless, everyone was very happy with the cooperation they had gotten at every level. The 4th Division's quartermasters had happily handed over a supply of divisional patches when asked, and the 23rd's signalmen had no trouble obtaining any information they requested.

This time, the problem of men looking for their friends had been anticipated. Anyone who came to the notional 4th Division area looking for someone was told that, while most of the division was in the camp, that specific unit was located elsewhere. This worked, with the exception of one time when a soldier came looking for his brother in the 4th MP Platoon. Since he was asking men dressed as 4th Division MPs, they could not claim the unit was elsewhere. At first they replied, "Never heard of him." "Why, he's your cook, you must know him," argued the brother. The quick thinking MP replied, "Oh, you must mean 'stinky.' I didn't recognize the name. Sure I know him. He just moved out with a bunch that went north."[8] On another occasion, a 23rd man replied that the reason he did not know many others in his unit was that he had been wounded in the infantry and had just arrived as a replacement.

Chapter 13

Operation CASANOVA
4–9 November 1944

Operation CASANOVA was an attempt to help the 90th Infantry Division cross the Moselle River by drawing off enemy troops to a dummy crossing site.[1] Initial reports called the operation UKANGE, after the town where the notional crossing was to take place (just north of Metz). Officially, in the after-action reports, it is named CASANOVA after the code name for the 377th Infantry Regiment (95th Division) that took part in the operation. The deception troops assigned to CASANOVA were given the code name CHEESE to avoid confusion with two 23rd detachments involved with other operations during the same period. Lieutenant Colonel Simenson was put in command of CHEESE, which consisted of fifteen officers, two hundred and sixty-five enlisted men, and sixty-four vehicles (forty-two of which were from the sonic company). The Ukange area was under enemy observation, and whenever a reconnaissance party from CHEESE went down to inspect the riverbank, they drew German mortar fire.

This was to be a classic deception operation. The special effects men of the 23rd were to help a standard infantry battalion appear to be a full regiment from another division, while the sonic troops were to fool the Germans into thinking a major crossing was taking place. If all went according to plan, the Germans would be surprised to find the regiment they thought was crossing at Ukange actually making their river crossing miles to the north. With luck, German reinforcements would be diverted to the deception site and thus make the crossing easier for the real assault.

At a 3 November staff meeting in Ukange, the decision was made that the entire operation was to be under command of the 1/377th Infantry Regiment. This battalion was the one that would be impersonating the 359th Infantry Regiment and making the minor river crossing. The genuine 359th (90th Infantry Division) was roughly eleven miles away, preparing to cross the Moselle in conjunction with the 10th Armored Division. The orders for the diversion had apparently come from the XX Corps, to which both divisions were assigned.

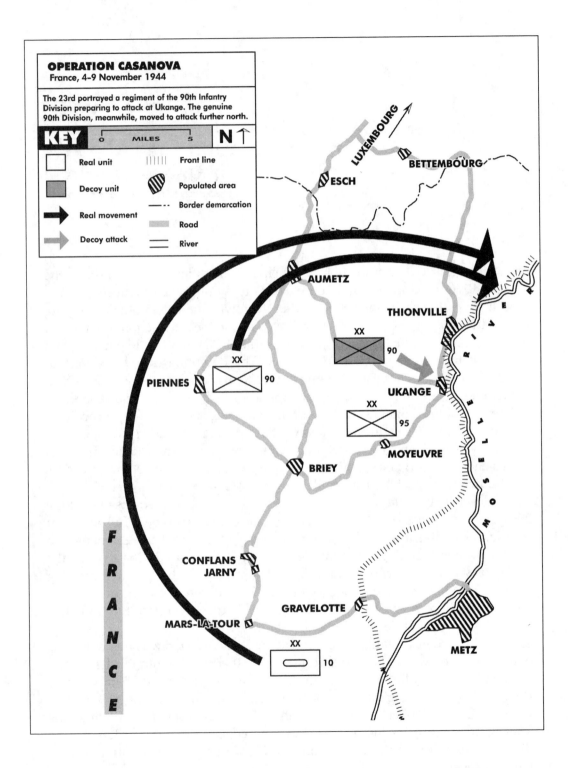

OPERATION CASANOVA
France, 4–9 November 1944

The 23rd portrayed a regiment of the 90th Infantry
Division preparing to attack at Ukange. The genuine
90th Division, meanwhile, moved to attack further north.

KEY

Real unit	Front line
Decoy unit	Populated area
Real movement	Border demarcation
Decoy attack	Road
	River

The plan called for the men of the 1/377th to put on shoulder patches of the 90th Division and mark their vehicles as the 359th. On the day of the notional crossing, assault boats were to be moved into the assembly area near the river. A bulldozer from the 406th Engineers was moved up to simulate preparations for building a bridge. At 2100 a single rifle company from the 377th was to cross the river in the boats, move inland four hundred yards, and dig in. The hope was to capture the town of Bertrange, which would allow them to control the highway between Metz and Thionville, thus providing a secure right flank for the 90th Division's attack on Metz.

That night, the sonic cars of the 3132nd would play a carefully constructed program of bridge building sounds. This included unloading trucks, hammering, and the sound of outboard motors and bulldozers. The plan for what was to follow is not clear. The operation was changed at the last moment and the records make it hard to determine what was in the original plan and what was a change. It appears the original plan was to cross the one company, dig in, and hold the bridgehead to draw off German troops, while the 90th Division crossed to the north and swept down to surround Metz.

The CHEESE detachment arrived in their bivouac area near Morlange (five miles southwest of Thionville) at 1130 on 4 November. The special effects part of the operation began on 7 November and proceeded with no problems until 0800 on 8 November, the day of the initial notional crossing. At that time, Lieutenant Colonel Decker of the 1/377th notified Lieutenant Colonel Simenson that the operation had changed. The commander of the 95th Division, General Twaddle, had decided he was going to make a larger genuine crossing at Ukange. He did not want a deception operation calling attention to the very spot he wanted to cross his division.

It has been suggested that the change was made without consultation with the XX Corps, thus potentially exposing the 90th Division assault to a stronger defense than necessary. It is also possible that Twaddle was only following orders from corps or army level, though there is no evidence to indicate where the change originated. In fact, the later German counterattack against the 90th's crossing was directed at the sector held by the genuine 359th Infantry Regiment.

The 95th Division did have an alternate crossing site a mile to the north, which they could have used, thus leaving the deception plan intact. However, General Twaddle felt it had no cover for men moving up to the riverbank, and he claimed no smoke was available to cover the assault. Twaddle ordered that a genuine treadway bridge be built on the notional crossing site to allow him to move more men into the bridgehead.

Because of the change, the only participation of the 23rd was to mark their vehicles as belonging to the 359th, put up 359th signage, and post suitably attired MPs in the area. They sent out convoys in the area with 90th Division markings, but the main element of CASANOVA was the river crossing. Its cancellation was a letdown for the men. Simulating a river crossing had been one of the things they had trained for, and their first chance to prove they could do it had been canceled. Although disappointed by the cancellation of their sonic mission, the officers of the 3132nd felt it had been good practice in planning and organizing for such an event.

After the cancellation of the notional crossing, Twaddle's newly planned river crossing ran into a number of problems. On the night of 8 November, a group of combat engineers crossed the Moselle in assault boats and opened a gap in the German minefield and barbed wire defenses. At 2100 the 1/377th crossed the river without finding any German outposts and moved into their positions on the far bank. Eventually the Germans responded with heavy artillery fire and stopped the attempt to put up the treadway bridge. By 9 November, a second rifle company and heavy weapons platoon had been sent across the river, which was now well covered by German machine-gun fire.

The real problems with the crossing began on 9 November when the river started to rise. By nightfall, the Moselle was swollen with such a strong current that boats could not safely cross it. The troops trapped on the far shore were kept supplied by airdrops from artillery observation planes until another crossing could be made three days later. Curiously, this second crossing was accomplished through deception, without the help of the 23rd. It involved combat engineers loudly running outboard motors some distance south of the actual crossing site to draw off the German defenders.[2]

The deception troops of the 23rd had no knowledge of what happened after the initial crossing, because on the morning of 9 November CHEESE packed up and moved back to the 23rd's home base in Luxembourg City. Both the 90th and 95th made their river crossings, but what remained of Operation CASANOVA was not considered to have been very helpful. The after-action report remarks that, "the enemy, according to POWs, were surprised by the 90th US Infantry Division's crossing of the Moselle river, but fought doggedly, primarily with small arms."[3]

Many of the 23rd men were under fire during this operation. Sergeant Anthony Sauro's squad from the 406th Engineers was detailed to repair a bridge on the Budange to Ukange road. The work had to be done at night because it was under observation by the Germans. It took two hours of work in pouring rain and under constant artillery harassing fire to complete the job. Other men brought a bulldozer into Ukange as part of the atmosphere, and were continually shelled for the next two days. As one of the men, Private Brassfield, later remarked about the shelling, "That was the time when ah re-e-eally got religion."[4]

One incident during CASANOVA shows how seriously the men took their jobs. As mentioned in the 406th unit history, Private Creerar, in the course of his traffic direction duties, was approached by Major General Twaddle of the 95th Infantry Division, who questioned him about his identity. "You're from the 95th aren't you?" said the general. "No sir, I'm from the 90th," replied this well-trained 406th man. "I know better, soldier. You're not from the real 90th," insisted the general. "I don't know what you're talking about, sir. Of course I'm from the 90th. Don't you see my patch?" But the general didn't let him off that easy. He asked him for the names of various officers in the division, only to receive satisfactory replies. Try as he might, he wasn't able to make Private Creerar change his story. In fact, Creerar thought the general drove off looking a little confused. Not long afterward, however, Lieutenant Colonel Simenson drove up to the outpost and reported that General Twaddle was highly pleased with Private Creerar's conduct.[5]

Perhaps the most important lesson of CASANOVA concerned command of a deception operation. Based upon CASANOVA, George Rebh, commander of the 406th Engineer Combat Company, wrote the following memo posing the interesting question of "Who Commands?"

Subject: Who commands?
To: Commanding Officer, 23rd Headquarters Special Troops

The role played by the 23rd Headquarters Special Troops in the operation 'CASANOVA' at Ukange France 3–9 November 1944, was a minor one. However, in spite of the relative unimportant casting the operation proved to be very worthwhile. First it aroused, and then in light of subsequent events, proceeded to answer a very significant question: In a deception operation which involves a far greater proportion of real divisional troops than it does personnel from 23rd Hq Special Troops (the Army Group's deceptive unit) who should command the undertaking? Shall the overall commander be an officer from the real troops or shall he be provided by 23rd Hq Special Troops?

At the Command Post 377th Infantry 031000 November 1944, Commanding Officer 377th Infantry agreed that Detachment 23rd Hq Special Troops would operate as if attached to 1st Battalion, 377th Infantry and would receive orders through commanding officer, 1st Battalion, 377th Infantry.

At 080800 November 1944 at CP 1st Battalion 377th Infantry, Lieutenant Colonel Decker informed Lieutenant Colonel Simenson that plans had been changed so that a real treadway was to be constructed.

At 1730 at the 95th Infantry Division CP, there was a conference of the following:
Commanding General 95th Infantry Division, Major General Twaddle
Commanding Officer 377th Infantry, Colonel Gaillard
G-3 95th Infantry Division, Lieutenant Colonel McCrary
95th Division Engineer, Lieutenant Colonel Crawther
23rd HQ Special Troops, Lieutenant Colonel Simenson

As a result of this conference, the Commanding General, 95th Infantry Division, through his divisional engineer, decided that *NO* sonic

---

operation was to take place that night since, firstly, a real bridge was being built at the site; secondly, the alternate place about a mile further to the north lacked cover from protecting infantry, with no smoke available; and thirdly, he did not desire to employ sounds prior to building the actual bridge.

I wish to add that during the meeting of 031000 November 1944 at CP 377th Infantry the original plan provided for but one rifle company to cross the Moselle River. It was on this assumption that the preliminary subordinate plans were made. But this was changed on D-1, the afternoon of 7 November 1944, to having the entire battalion attack.

Having the commander of the real troops in charge of the operation insures one definite advantage, namely that of cooperation. The division would do its utmost to assist its officer in command of the operation because of the responsibility involved. The officers, the staffs, and the men have previously worked together. They know each other. Whereas, if an "outsider" were to assume command of the operation there would exist undoubtedly at first a certain reluctance, hesitancy to be of utmost service, to do any more than required.

With the command channels still intact, control also would be affected to a higher degree. However, other than cooperation and control there are not readily apparent other advantages which cannot be more easily or better exploited with the operation commanded by a 23rd Hq Sp Trs officer.

Why then should the operation be commanded by 23rd Hq Sp Trs? What are the advantages?

We shall begin by adapting a negative approach—why not use the commander of the real troops? Firstly, there are few officers erudite in the art of deception. Deception constitutes but a meager portion of the curriculum in our training. In our service schools it is merely mentioned 'in passing.' We hear of Alexander and the deception by which he was able to cross the Hydaspes. We read of how Napoleon fooled Beaulieu in his crossing of the Po River and of how Maude gained initial surprise through deception in his crossing of the Tigris. But its employment in present warfare just hasn't been taught. It isn't available—mainly because we are only now writing its doctrine now on the battlefields of this theatre. In training, the closest we get to deception is our camouflage instruction, which rarely exceeds the draping of one or two fishnets and the construction of a few flat tops. Usually a dummy gun or vehicle is attempted, but rarely more than once. This is the extent of the deception education of most of our officers. Summarizing then, our commanders do not, through no fault of their own, know the possibilities of, the extent of, the intricacy of, or the capabilities of deception.

Assuming that some commanders were vaguely familiar with deception, this is still insufficient. At the time of the inauguration and birth of the 23rd Hq Special Troops back in the United States, many of the underlying principals and points of doctrine which were stressed and thought to be basic and fundamental have either been relegated to a niche of relative unimportance or have fallen by the wayside altogether. Then again many phases and aspects that were not even conceived in the U.S. have developed and now assume a greater part of our endeavor and attention in this theatre.

The classic example of the former being the disappearance of the enemy aircraft upon which we at one time, too heavily, depended, and of the latter the extensive measures necessary to satisfy ground agents— shoulder patches, bumper markings, MPs, etc. Besides, the employment of deception is an art requiring exactness and attention to minute details, the importance of which is often not realized nor properly evaluated.

During the Ukange operation there were a few details which went by unnoticed. After the 1st Battalion, 377th Infantry had changed to the 359th Infantry of the 90th Infantry Division there were in the 1st Battalion bivouac area and in Ukange still many men wearing 95th Division shoulder patches. Likewise a few of the vehicles in the area still possessed their 95th Division bumper markings. Also to substantiate the story that the 359th Infantry Regiment had replaced the 1st Battalion, 377th Infantry the vehicles parked deep in the woods, out of observation from the road, should have been moved to positions easily visible from the road thus painting the picture that more vehicles had moved into the area during the night. Knowledge of the relative importance of these details along with those allied to signal procedure and the visual display to deceive enemy agents has been gained principally through the actual employment of the 23rd Hq Special Troops in the combat zone. Hence few officers aside from those closely associated with the 23rd Hq Special Troops could possess adequate, up to date, battle-tried knowledge of deception.

Probably the most important consideration is that there are too few officers who are cognizant of or even familiar with the capabilities or possibilities of the 23rd Hq Special Troops. How large of a unit can be simulated? What difficulties are entailed? How close to the true picture can it be reproduced? What outside props and help are required? What is the 'Heater' unit?

The 23rd Hq Special Troops is truly an unorthodox unit—both in organization and equipment. Without close affiliation with the unit a stranger could not possibly surmise the unlimited and almost unbelievable capabilities of this Headquarters. The 'Heater' unit alone borders on fantasy. Hence operated by an inexperienced officer the fullest advantage of this organization could not possibly be exploited nor utilized.

Now for the sake of this discussion just let us suppose that the outsider is thoroughly tutored in deception and that he is thoroughly acquainted with the abilities of the 23rd Hq Special Troops. Does it seem plausible that he would knowingly utilize this deception unit to create and build up a large scale and false picture, attract all possible attention, and then send his own troops into this highly advertised attack? Considering human nature I doubt it seriously. The avenue of escape is to slight the employment of the deception unit. This I believe would be the result since it is the 'small picture,' rather than the 'large picture,' which concerns this commander more deeply. These attacking troops would be his casualties.

Another point which though not decisive in nature but which should be considered is that the overall commander seldom has sufficient time to accomplish the necessary preliminaries for both the real and fake picture. The commander of troops should be making his personal reconnaissance of the terrain. Coordinating artillery and supporting fires, contacting adjacent commanders, and formulating his attack plan without having to worry about proper bivouac areas, signal procedure, and the road traffic of the simulated unit. Time consumed on the latter could be more advantageously spent on rounding out the realities of the operation.

Now aside from the above mentioned negative aspects, there are positive reasons to be considered as to why the 23rd Hq Special Troops should command a combined operation.

Firstly, being an Army Group unit the 23rd Hq Special Troops is in a position to view its operations from the standpoint of the so-called 'big picture.' Its interests are: 'what effect will this operation have on other divisions, corps and armies?' Will it aid these other units in their impending struggles? Will small sacrifices of men and material in this section insure thousands of other troops an easier battle somewhere else along the front? With this large scale outlook the 23rd Hq Special Troops is able to operate with less regard to the realities of the practically certain casualties involved in employing deception in a river crossing or in the building up of a large task force followed by contact with the enemy.

Secondly, the deception officer is in a position to participate in the planning during the early stages and to receive the corps and army order hot off the presses. The latter allowing the maximum time to be devoted to the operation since the time consumed for the orders to pass down the chain of command is eliminated. Being in on the early planning practically does away with last minute changes. In the Ukange operation it was not decided until the afternoon of D-1 that the entire battalion was to cross the river. This change served to complicate the plans within the battalion. Likewise the site for the 'fake' bridge changed to become that of the real bridge at 1730 on D-day, three and one half hours before H-hour. When construction of the bridge started at 2300 the site was shelled thoroughly. As a result the bridge could not be built during that night or the following day. These difficulties and failure could have been averted with the proper, early planning.

Lastly, the 23rd Hq Special Troops officers are capable of accurately portraying virtually any type of unit or organization of our army engaged at the front—be it infantry, armor, field artillery, antiaircraft, engineer, quartermaster, or ordnance. There are few officers with divisions who could be released for such an operation who are so well versed.

Truly, deception entails a little more than just changing shoulder patches. It requires special equipment, special personnel, and most importantly, leaders who are not only thoroughly acquainted with this equipment and personnel, but who also possess the technique of employing the same in this theatre.

Thus it is my recommendation that if a deception operation is planned and it is important enough to employ all or even a portion of the 23rd Hq Special Troops, that certainly the commanding officer of the project should be of the 23rd Hq Special Troops.

The above comments are in no way meant to be all-inclusive. In many cases they are broad statements without substantial proof. But possibly these comments will stimulate others to research and write on the subject of the 23rd Hq Special Troops, from which may evolve a more efficient, productive, method of handling and using this novel and at times fantastic, but indeed practical organization.[6]

Lieutenant Colonel Simenson forwarded the memo to Colonel Reeder with the note, "The attached paper is an excellent and interesting paper of much work by Captain Rebh. I do not concur with Captain Rebh that 23rd Hq Sp Trs should command deceptive operations such as Ukange because I believe:

a. Deception troops are supporting troops.

b. Control should be with the commander receiving the benefit."[7]

In a handwritten reply, Colonel Reeder noted,

"Many good points. However Ukange is hardly a fair example. There appeared to be a lack of understanding on the part of lower units in regard to plans of the corps and army commanders. Also failure of those commanders to see that their orders were promptly promulgated, understood, and executed. There was a natural desire to gain a cheap advantage with unseasoned troops. In my opinion, it would have been better for you to have acted as an assistant G-3 of the corps, in addition to your command of our troops. Your advice as to means to be employed by both real and deception troops, as well as coordination of the two could have been procured by necessary orders from the corps commander—the proper source of orders in this case. You could also have checked our compliance with such orders and insured best results from combination of real and deceptive means. This is not in any way a slap at you. Merely my idea of a workable solution to this and other problems. In many cases, I believe Rebh's idea is sound. Please let Rebh see this."[8]

While there is no evidence as to why or at what level the changes to CASANOVA were made, it seems possible they were made by a division commander not wanting to risk his men for a deception operation he did not fully believe in. The question of who commands in such a situation may have planted the seed in Colonel Reeder's mind that perhaps the 23rd needed to be commanded by a brigadier general. That would not only give him the general's star he desired, but also allow him a chance to command troops in actual, instead of notional, battle.

Chapter 14

Operation KOBLENZ and the Bulge
6–15 December 1944

KOBLENZ is considered by many to be one of the more embarrassing operations of the war.[1] The 23rd attempted to draw German attention to the dullest sector of the line, which happened to be in the path of the massive German attack that would become known as the Battle of the Bulge.

On 15 November 1944, the 12th Army Group directed the 23rd to prepare a deception plan to pin down German troops in the VIII Corps region. The goal was to force the Germans to keep their troop levels in this quiet sector at their present strength, thus preventing these units from being used to reinforce other sectors of the front. With luck, they might even decide to pull badly needed reinforcements from other areas to defend against the perceived American threat. The Germans were using the sector to break in green troops before moving them to hotter combat areas. By making it seem a major attack was brewing, it would also deny the Germans their ability to use this quiet region for training their new units.

The 12th Army Group reasoned that the terrain of the Moselle River corridor was the only reasonable area for an attack in the VIII Corps zone. This area had been relatively static and quiet for the past two months. The Moselle corridor was heavily defended immediately to the west of Trier, with lighter defenses and blockhouses in the mountainous regions to the north and south. The notional American plan was to prepare for an attack to capture Koblenz and the Moselle corridor—first to split the German forces on this side of the Rhine River, and second to capture the rocket launching sites in the vicinity of Trier.

The American IXth Tactical Air Command was to show an increasing interest in the Koblenz region (through surveillance, bombing, and patrolling). Bridges over the Moselle River between Trier and Koblenz were to be bombed in an attempt to isolate the area. The ground effort was to position the troops to indicate a double envelopment of Trier. This would involve shift-

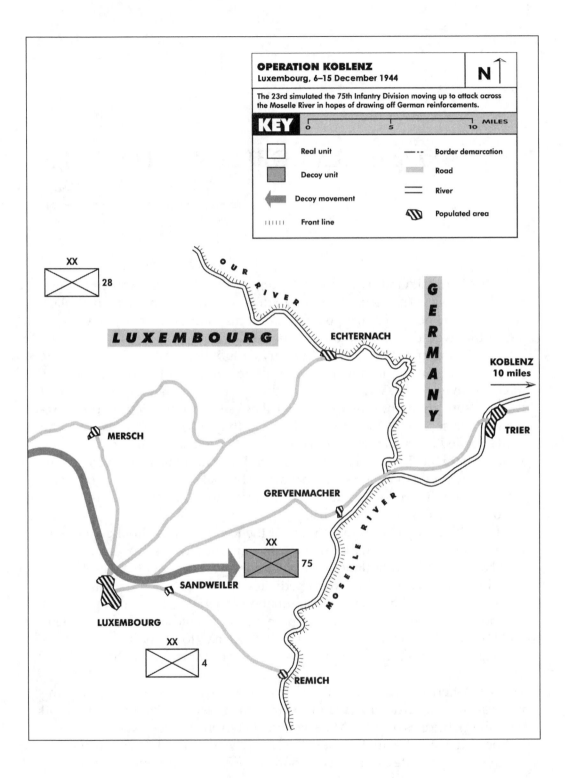

ing corps support units into positions situated to sustain such an attack, and to simulate the arrival of more troops.

The initial plan was submitted a few days later under the code name BAR-BECUE. A slightly revised version was returned to the 23rd on 18 November 1944 under the new name Operation TRIER. TRIER was to be a two-stage operation. The idea was to continue postponing the forthcoming attack to fool the Germans as long as possible. Eventually the notional attack would be officially canceled, so the Germans might never suspect they had been duped.

The entire VIII Corps was to be the focus of the deception plan. The 23rd was to act as the supervisory group coordinating the deception activities. The genuine units of the corps would be situated as if they were preparing for the attack, and the 23rd would develop a notional infantry division to make the threat appear larger. To ensure that the operation had the correct appearance, the VIII Corps staff actually drew up attack plans for pressing into the Moselle River corridor.

There was discussion about actually publishing a field order for the attack, but it was felt this would end up causing more confusion, as it contradicted the current orders for defending the sector. After further discussion it was decided to only issue letters of instruction, telling the various units what actual tasks they were to perform in order to paint the desired picture. This way no one would misunderstand the actual situation.

To ensure proper coordination at the corps level, Lieutenant Colonel Simenson was attached to the VIII Corps Headquarters in Bastogne from 30 November until 17 December as an assistant operations officer and representative of the 23rd. At some point the VIII Corps HQ began referring to the deception plan as Operation KOBLENZ and the name stuck. The VIII Corps chief of staff, Colonel Stanton, spent a great deal of time making sure that everyone cooperated with the plan.

General Middleton himself was concerned about the security of the operation. He allowed the operation to proceed only after strict counterintelligence measures were drawn up. Only the absolute minimum number of personnel would be allowed to know that the operation was a deception and that the 23rd was involved. All material concerning the deception would be classified TOP SECRET. Communications about the operation would be carefully handled through liaison officers and not over phones or through standard message centers. He also requested that the 23rd "put into effect proper counterintelligence measures, and safeguards to insure against compromise of their own activities in the operation, and to preclude the enemy gaining information of their presence and type of organization."[2]

The initial plans for KOBLENZ called for two phases. Phase one would begin on 26 November when the First Army would issue a letter of instruction to prepare for an attack in the Trier area. From 27 November to 2 December there would be increased aerial reconnaissance and bombing of the area. From 2–5

December, frontline units would be instructed to begin selecting assembly areas, and frontline staffs would begin making a limited reconnaissance of the attack sectors. From 5–8 December, there would be a build-up in reconnaissance in the areas of attack. Genuine units would be moved to the assembly areas during the day, and notional units moved into other locations during the night. There would also be a slight increase in artillery fire.

From 8–15 December, there would be a slowdown of activity, indicating the attack had been postponed. Phase two would commence on 15 December with another increase in reconnaissance and aerial activity. From 22–26 December, things would quiet down, but running from 27–29 December there would be a sudden and heavy increase in the amount of artillery fire and aerial reconnaissance, centered on a new proposed attack in the Diekirck area to the north. Ground reconnaissance would also intensify, as would any other indication that a major attack was imminent. Then, if all went as planned, the operation would end on 30 December. The notional units would fade away and the area would revert to being a quiet sector once again.

The choice for the notional division kept changing as selected divisions were sent into the front lines. The original choice had been the 9th Infantry Division, but that was soon changed to the 78th, and then 106th Infantry Divisions. As each was sent into the front lines, and thus probably identified by the Germans, a new division had to be selected. Finally the decision was made to pick the 75th Infantry Division, which had only recently arrived in England. Lieutenant Colonel Truly from the 23rd visited the 75th in England to develop a set of poop sheets on the unit characteristics. He was also supposed to ensure that the genuine 75th landed in France without showing any patches or markings. Due to the late nature of the selection of the unit, this mission was delayed and he was not able to get back to Luxembourg with a supply of 75th patches and the unit history until after the operation had begun.

There was some concern that the Diekirck area had such terrible terrain that no one would believe that an attack would be planned there. While this was being discussed, the 23rd decided that because the genuine 75th Division would be arriving in the area about that time, they would then assume the identity of the 76th Infantry Division, which was due to follow the 75th to the continent.

A corps artillery component of seven field artillery battalions, two field artillery group headquarters, and a field observation battery were simulated by a detachment from the VIII Corps artillery (fifty-two officers, four hundred and seventy-nine men, and one hundred vehicles). The VIII Corps artillery intelligence officer, Lieutenant Colonel Vanek, was put in charge of this mission to set up notional positions for these units.

A maintenance detachment was assigned to the 23rd to take care of all the vehicles. This had been requested so that the 23rd, while portraying the 75th Division, could get their vehicles serviced without having to answer any awkward questions. Four ambulances were also attached to the 23rd, and all of these additional personnel were briefed on the mission and issued 75th Division shoulder patches.

Time frames kept shifting and it would not be until 7 December that KOBLENZ would actually begin. Starting on that day, the notional 75th would begin moving into the region. From December 9–13 there would be an increase in aerial reconnaissance and bombing. This would coincide with an increase in ground activity, which would escalate up to a minor feigned attack by the 28th Infantry Division on 13 December. That would end phase one, and the notional 75th would fade from sight until the genuine 75th Division arrived two weeks later in northwest Belgium.

The men of the 23rd began the operation in an assembly area west of Arlon, Belgium. The information and patches had not yet arrived from England, so bumper markings were stenciled in the strict official manner. Everyone was briefed that this was a new division just arrived on the continent, so they were to act as if they were "brand new green troops."[3]

Since Truly was delayed in returning from his trip to England to collect information and shoulder patches from the genuine 75th Division, the men were instructed to mention, "The old man won't allow us to wear patches for security reasons." As soon as the patches showed up they were issued to the men in the most conspicuous positions. Eventually only about 40 percent of the troops wore patches. There is no mention in the unit records if this was due to the shortage of them, or if that was the approximate percentage observed being worn by the genuine unit. Lieutenant Colonel Truly also provided the following short history of the division the 23rd was to represent:

"The 75th Infantry Division was organized at Fort Leonard Wood, MO, 13 April 1943. They went through normal training there until the Louisiana maneuvers in March–April–May 1944. After that the division moved to Camp Breckenridge, KY. and stayed there from June until September 1944, when the division came to South Wales. It started arriving there October 20 and closed the latter part of November having come over on 29 different vessels landing in 9 different ports. It was spread over South Wales, the Headquarters being at Tenby. It embarked early in December for the continent, being staged through the Le Havre–Rouen area, then to its present location. It was organized under the December 4 T/O and General Paul was the first division commander but was circumceded by General Pricket after four months."[4]

A notional list of 75th Infantry Division (DIAMOND) officers was circulated, which listed the real names of the most senior officers (such as the unit commanders), but added in as executive officers and assistants were the names of the forty-two officers from the 23rd. Reeder was made division chief of staff. His son, Harry Jr., was made the traffic control officer. Lieutenant Colonel Mayo (the artilleryman) was named the executive officer of the division artillery. Lieutenant Colonels Truly, Schroeder, and Seale were named the executive officers of the 289th, 290th and 291st Infantry Regiments. Lieutenant Colonel Day played the dual roles of division inspector general and commander of the division special troops.

Other officers were named to posts in the notional division: for example, Lieutenant Walter Manser was named the assistant ordnance officer, Lieutenant George Daley the provost marshall, Lieutenant Syracuse the assistant chemical officer, Captain Rebh the assistant engineer officer, Captain Vander Heide the commander of the 575th Signal Company, and Captain Hiller the commander of the 75th Recon Troop. Assigning specific roles, and including them on the notional directory of division officers, allowed the men to better play these roles and helped the signalmen in constructing more believable messages. Under orders from VIII Corps for the operation, these men were to wear appropriate rank and branch of service insignia.

The signal plan for KOBLENZ was to start with the movement of the notional 75th into the area. An examination of the radio traffic already in the VIII Corps area showed little activity. This was because the front had been relatively stable for two months and telephone wire had been laid for most communications. Thus it was decided to keep the 75th radio transmissions to a minimum to blend in with the current scene. A total of five radio nets were simulated, with the most active being the one referred to as the traffic control chain net. This was a network of five SCR-193s and one SCR-399 that stretched from Sedan to Sandweiler. Over a period of three days, this network transmitted messages coordinating the progress of the notional 75th along its route of march.

This traffic control chain net began transmitting on 9 December in the afternoon. Only a few messages were sent each day and they referred to the movements of the various 75th elements. Times were set not for the message to be sent, but for the radio team to begin encoding the messages using SLIDEX. Thus the messages would be sent on a slightly random time frame depending upon how fast the radio teams were at coding. The message would be transmitted as soon as it had been encoded. Certain words were underlined, indicating that they were to be sent in the clear.

As an example, the first position in Sedan began coding the message "291 CT head passed thru Sedan" at 1435 on 11 December. Later that day, at 1550, they would start on the message, "291 CT tail passed thru Sedan. Division *now* cleared completely *except* ordnance vehicles *at* Reims."[5]

Messages would be passed along the six-point network from west to east (Sedan–Bouillon–Tintigny–Arlon–Mersch–Sandweiler) which would allow the Germans to track the flow of a message, even if they were not able to decode it. The Sandweiler station was the high-powered SCR-399 simulating the division headquarters. This radio would send two messages to corps headquarters during the movement period (coded by SIGABA) indicating the division command post had opened (1405, 8 December), and that all division elements had arrived (2135, 11 December). The radio picture the Germans would detect was that of some kind of movement ending at Sandweiler.

The notional radio networks would be set up once the troops had supposedly moved into position. The corps command net operated between VIII Corps at Bastogne and the 75th Division headquarters' SCR-399. This corps command net was kept active during the entire operation by frequent radio checks. A division command net ran between an SCR-193 at division headquarters and the SCR-193s of the 289th, 290th, and 291st Infantry Regiments and the division artillery post at Ernster. This network was patterned on that of the neighboring 4th Infantry Division.

Another radio network was called the VIII Corps Artillery Officers Net and connected VIII Corps Artillery HQ at Beho with their forward command post at Graulinster and three notional artillery units: the 30th and 220th Artillery Groups and the 202nd Artillery Observation Battalion. These units were actually real artillery units from the VIII Corps operating under assumed identities. They transmitted on this radio net through 23rd operated radios. The radios of the genuine artillery units had been left behind in their original locations, transmitting as if nothing had changed. This was how the VIII Corps artillery support was made to grow from nine to twelve artillery units. The decision to add an air support network was to be made later, depending upon the situation. Investigation showed that the corps air support network was very quiet, so no attempt was made to open up a station on it for the 75th.

The false artillery network started on 7 December when the BLARNEY radio teams moved to the corps artillery headquarters to examine their practices. On 10 December, the radio teams moved south with the fictitious units, and from 13–14 December handled all the normal radio traffic. On 15 December, the BLARNEY radio teams were replaced by the genuine artillery radio operators, and the units reverted to their original designations.

One problem in the radio networks was that the assigned frequencies were very crowded with other units. No alternate frequencies were provided, forcing the BLARNEY operators to remain on the 2528 KC band. This was not just a minor inconvenience for the signalmen; it also meant the Germans would have a harder time sorting out the transmissions from other stations.

The 23rd signalmen were also active in laying and maintaining one hundred and eight miles of telephone line connecting thirty-three phones. Their wire patrols were constantly checking the lines for breaks in the guise of signal troops from the 75th Division. This activity only added to the appearance of a division in the area.

On 7 December, Lieutenant Colonel Schroeder arrived in the 4th Division sector under the guise of the 75th Division billeting officer. He arranged to have the notional 75th Division housed in areas east and northeast of Luxembourg. On the same day the notional regimental commanders began to reconnoiter their assigned areas in preparation for bringing in their troops.

As the notional units were moved along the route of march by means of radio transmissions, the men of the 23rd began to enter their assigned bivouac areas and began a display of the newly arrived 75th Division. As the units moved up, the sonic troops played sounds of columns moving to create the impression that many more vehicles than had been seen in the daylight were involved. Infantry divisions did not have enough transportation to move the entire unit at once by vehicles, so it made sense that an attached truck company would make a trip to the bivouac area at night, drop off the men, then return to the rear.

The 23rd had been broken up into separate groups to simulate the 289th Combat Team,[6] 290th Combat Team,[7] 291st Combat Team,[8] and the 75th Headquarters element.[9] A detachment of the 23rd Signal Company posed as the 575th Signal Company. They moved into their assigned billeting area and began setting up signage, marking command posts, visitor parking areas, and traffic directions.

From 0600 to 1800 each day, the men worked at giving their impression of a typical GI unit. When they were not sent out on road patrols or convoys, they visited the local population spreading tales of their unit. Requests were made to find translators to help debrief any civilians who might have knowledge of the German defenses in the area of the proposed attack. As a highlight to the operation, Colonel Reeder donned general's stars and visited each command post on 11 December playing the role of General Pickett.

A handful of the rubber decoys were installed under camouflage netting to simulate the guns of the artillery units. The three 105mm artillery battalions were considered part of the combat teams. Lieutenant Colonel Mayo was given the task of simulating the 75th Division Artillery HQ and the 730th Artillery Battalion (155mm howitzers). He was given a detachment from the 23rd and four hundred and seventy-five men and eighty-two vehicles from the genuine 730th Field Artillery Battalion. They set up a bivouac in the vicinity of Ernster and advertised themselves with such standard items as shoulder patches and signage. In addition, Mayo had the local mayor issue a proclamation forbidding any civilian from entering their camp.

The 3132nd played the roles of the 775th Ordnance, 75th Quartermasters, and 75th Recon Troop billeted around Rodenbourg. When night fell the sonic cars made their way to specific locations to play a program of more vehicles moving up. The local population may not have seen that many trucks during the day, but at night they got an earful of them moving around. On 9 December the sounds of truck convoys were played from 2200 to midnight in

These two military policemen manning a 75th Infantry Division dismount point are men from the 23rd Special Troops adding atmosphere to Operation KOBLENZ. The helmet markings and signs were painted by the 603rd Engineers and were based upon detailed notes about how the genuine unit operated.

the Rodenbourg area. The next night an hour and a half of truck convoy sounds were played in the area around CT 290.

On 11 December, word arrived that it was too wet for sonic work, and that night's program at CT 291 was canceled. The reason it was canceled though was not actually due to the weather, but because there were too many civilians in the area. Sixteen civilians had broken curfew and were being held at local checkpoints. It was too much to risk that a civilian might realize they were hearing, but not seeing, the trucks.

The 406th Engineer Combat Company was to simulate not only the 75th Division's engineer unit, but also the 75th MP Platoon. The MP platoon was considered one of the most visible aspects of a division, so it was one of the only notional units to have a full compliment of men (one officer and thirty-three men). The 1st Platoon, under command of Lieutenant Daley, set up MP posts at the divisional command post and important crossroads in the area. Jeeps marked as 75th Military Police patrolled the area. The MPs manned various guard posts and patrolled the area, making sure the nighttime curfew was followed.

The notional 275th Engineer companies performed the visible duties of a real divisional engineer battalion. They maintained a water point at Hostert, hauled coal and gravel, and made minor repairs to the roads. The dump trucks and bulldozers of the 406th were particularly helpful in creating the picture of a division engineer unit.

Later, Captain Rebh would comment that his engineers were too spread out for him to be able to coordinate their activities. He suggested that in the future the separate engineer platoons (portraying companies) should be put under the command of the notional infantry regiments, with his headquarters acting as a consultant on what engineering duties they should be performing.

Starting on 11 December, the notional unit commanders began reconnaissance of the forward areas in preparation for an attack. This attack would involve a river crossing, so Captain Rebh made arrangements to borrow assault boats from the local 4th Engineer Battalion.

On 13 December, he sent four trucks to Osweiler to simulate the movement of footbridge equipment up to an assembly point. On the return trip the trucks passed by the 4th Engineers where they picked up two trailers loaded with eighteen assault boats. That afternoon, a notional 275th Engineer Battalion convoy consisting of Captain Rebh in his jeep, two trucks with assault boat trailers, and a dump truck left for the Osweiler assembly area. Once darkness fell, the assault boats were returned to the 4th Division, with grateful thanks for the loan.

On 12 December, Lieutenant Colonel Fitz (603rd) and Captain Rebh (406th) went on a reconnaissance of the forward area near Girsterklaus with a handful of men in two jeeps. They found a place to leave their vehicles behind a building, and then started down to the riverbank on foot. As soon as they entered the tree line on the slope leading to the river, they were caught in a hail of small-arms fire, some of it from their rear. A German patrol had crossed the river, probably to try and take prisoners. Everyone in the 23rd had been strongly cautioned about not being taken prisoner, so this was a serious problem. A firefight ensued for about fifteen minutes until they could withdraw under the covering fire of Sergeant Duckworth. Thankfully, no one was hurt, but three Germans were seen and Duckworth claimed to have hit one of them.[10]

The 70th Tank Battalion provided a platoon of Sherman tanks to add to the display. On 13 December, the tanks were twice moved along roads near Herborn that were visible to the Germans. These tanks not only provided a visual presence of armor, but left tracks for any German reconnaissance the following morning.

Meanwhile, the 3132nd had reconnoitered the area and prepared for a sonic program to be broadcast. From 1800–1900 on 13 December, a program of three battalions of medium tanks moving up was played. After the program, the 3132nd packed up and infiltrated back to their billeting area.

On 14 December, the operation was coming to an end and the various units began to pack up and filter back to Luxembourg. This was to be disguised as a shift to the north by the 75th Division, after the planned attack had been called off. To indicate northern movement on 13–14 December, the notional division radio net reported units moving through Arlon and Libramont. The plan was for the notional 75th to be shifted north where the genuine unit would shortly appear. If the Germans had noticed anything suspicious, the appearance of the actual 75th Division in the expected area would allay all their doubts. It was important to try and conceal the fact that a deception had taken place, so the same tricks could continue to be used.

On the return back to base, Captain Rebh's jeep fell victim to the danger of driving at night under blackout regulations. His jeep missed a turn in the road and ran off a small cliff. The driver, T/5 Feldman, was not hurt, but Captain Rebh spent a few days in the hospital with minor injuries while the jeep's smashed windshield was replaced.

The effectiveness of KOBLENZ is hard to measure. Any benefit of pinning down German troops was nullified by the fact that the Germans were massing their units across the line for a major attack. There were some suggestions that the Germans had fallen for the notional 75th Division. A German POW captured by the 4th Infantry Division stated that he thought he had been captured by the 75th Division.[11] One 23rd man reported that 4th Division troops were upset at getting no support from the notional 75th, which they thought was in reserve. A few days after the attack, a 4th Division soldier waiting for treatment in an evacuation hospital was heard to say, "I'd like to get my hands on those elusive bastards of the 75th."[12] According to the 406th history, the 4th Division continued to feel that the 75th, which had never really been in the area, had run out on them in the first days of the Bulge.[13]

The official army history of the Battle of the Bulge claims that German agents in France reported that the only two uncommitted American divisions were the 82nd and 101st Airborne.[14] The notional 75th apparently made the German situation maps as a question mark indicating a possible unidentified unit. However, according to the U.S. Army evaluation, the Germans had decided by 15 December (the day KOBLENZ ended) that there was no new division along the VIII Corps front. Curiously, the same source mentions that the Germans had identified the 75th Infantry Division in the Roer Sector, at a time when the genuine division had just arrived on the French coast at La Havre and Rouen.[15] Thus the Germans must have picked up the identity of the notional 75th from the deception operation.

One additional division was not enough to get the Germans to call off their largest attack on the western front. Had there been no planned offensive it might well have pulled German reinforcements to the area. There is also another aspect of KOBLENZ that needs to be explored. A theory exists that the American senior commanders knew of the German offensive and allowed it to take place, thus sucking the German Army into a position where it could be cut off and destroyed. Keeping in mind, however, that orders for Operation

KOBLENZ came from 12th Army Group, it is curious that one of the most secret units in the ETO would be put into a situation where it was known an attack was about to take place. Not only might this have compromised the deception unit, but it also put the men and their equipment in a position where they might easily have been captured.

KOBLENZ was valuable in teaching lessons in how to manage a deception. Key to the plan was the high level of assistance and coordination received from the VIII Corps. Instead of pushing the deception aside as a minor irritation, General Middleton's staff worked very hard to provide whatever help they could. As to the question of keeping the operation a secret from all but the few senior commanders, Lieutenant Colonel Simenson wrote, "Commanders in whose areas deceptive troops operate must be informed of at least a portion of the operation. Too much secrecy on deceptive operations will confuse our own troops more than the enemy."[16]

The radio phase of the operation brought out the suggestion that the notional division could have been moved across France from the ports by means of radio traffic. Another signal unit could handle that task and then turn the notional communications over to the 23rd when it had supposedly reached the front. This would provide an even greater history for the unit, which hopefully the Germans could not ignore. It was also noticed that the 23rd's radio operators were a bit rusty from weeks of no practice. They had grown stale without any real sending or receiving to do. A suggestion was made to obtain a practice frequency that the men could take turns using when not involved in a mission.

KOBLENZ II was scheduled to start on 21 December. It was essentially the same type of mission, only slightly to the north and utilizing the 76th Infantry Division as the notional unit (scheduled to arrive in that area in roughly five weeks). There was concern about the two areas being so close to one another. It was pointed out that the men had gone out of their way to identify themselves to the locals as being in a specific unit, and it might pose a problem if they suddenly appeared a short distance away in a new unit. This problem was still being discussed when the Germans attacked.

The second phase was officially canceled on 20 December, but after the Germans attacked through the Ardennes on 16 December there was little doubt in anyone's mind that phase II would not happen. When the Germans attacked, the deception troops were immediately ordered back to Luxembourg City. Lieutenant Colonel Simenson was still in Bastogne at VIII Corps Headquarters. He and his driver were told to leave the city as rapidly as possible. They decided it was prudent to evacuate at once, rather than cross the town to pick up their jeep's trailer. Simenson later regretted losing four good bottles of cognac stored in his baggage, but was glad they had gotten out before the Germans surrounded the town.

The official chronology of the 23rd has the following entry for 16

December: "German counterattack launched. Organization alerted, documents and records placed in vehicles under guard for immediate departure. Guard doubled. Squads organized, machine gun nests set up for defense of sector surrounding billets of 23rd Hq & Hq Co, and 3132nd Signal Service Company. Drills accomplished both day and night. Attacked by air. 23rd Hq & Hq Company gunners posted on roof of billet fired at enemy planes during the entire night."[17] The rubber decoys were prepared for burning should the Germans arrive. Captain Fox's comment on the incident was: "What the official report leaves out is the enthusiasm with which those guns were fired. It was the first and last time they were to have shot at the enemy."[18]

With the front line in chaos, most of the American troops moved west trying to either reorganize or find a place to defend. Luxembourg City became crowded with thousands of troops, and the 23rd was shifted further west to Doncourt, France. Colonel Reeder and his headquarters remained in Luxembourg City in the former Italian Legation.

The word quickly spread among American troops that the Germans had dropped men dressed in GI uniforms behind the lines. Countless checkpoints were set up to weed out any possible Germans. The easiest way was to question GIs on such American trivia as, "Who won the World Series?" or "Who writes the newspaper column 'My Day'?" Woe to any soldier who did not know that the capital of New York State was Albany. With every soldier suspicious, it was not a good time for the 23rd to portray a different unit.

One small incident deserves mention. Colonel Railey of the Army Experimental Station was making an inspection tour of the 3132nd at this time. He was well known to the men of the sonic unit, but not to the rest of the 23rd, which had trained at Camp Forrest. Men on guard stopped him outside the 23rd headquarters. His story sounded suspicious and they were sure they had caught a German spy attempting to steal the secrets of American deception. He started asking for them to call an officer from the 3132nd to vouch for him. They asked if he knew Lieutenant Dick Syracuse. Railey replied that he knew him very well and asked if they would please bring him over to testify to his identity. Syracuse was summoned and, in a moment of inspiration, took one look at Railey and said, "Never seen this guy before in my life." He waited a moment until the shock registered on Railey's face, then quickly broke into a grin and cleared up the confusion.[19]

Chapter 15

Operation KODAK
22–23 December 1944

With the German Ardennes offensive in full swing, the American Army was put on the defensive. The first few moves to recover the initiative would become known as the "period of piecemeal reaction."[1] In an effort to try anything to drive back the Germans, the 23rd was hastily given a job.

The 23rd had been withdrawn from Luxembourg City, out of the path of the German advance. While en route to their new location at Doncourt, the 23rd Signal Company was alerted for this new mission. Operation KODAK was a last-minute plan to confuse German radio intelligence as to the location of the 80th Infantry Division and 4th Armored Division.[2] The plan was to reveal two separate locations for the units (real and notional) and give the Germans a "double exposure" (hence the operation's name) of the American situation.

KODAK was to be a short twenty-four-hour operation involving only radio transmissions. The genuine 4th Armored Division was preparing to drive north to relieve Bastogne. The 80th Division was preparing to attack from a location due north of Luxembourg. The notional positions for these units were to be southeast of the genuine units (80th Infantry at Lorentzweiler; 4th Armored at Gosseldingen).

The plan was to present the picture of these divisions being held in reserve, ready for a renewed German attack. The notional transmissions were to start at 1000 on 22 December, and cease when the genuine units were to break radio silence and attack.

The signalmen set up twenty-nine radios in their assigned locations. They were guarded by a security detail of one hundred men from the 406th Engineers. Unfortunately, the technical details of frequencies, call signs, and cryptographic information were late getting to them and KODAK was delayed from going on the air until 1310 on 22 December.

With no preparation time, the messages were created and enciphered on

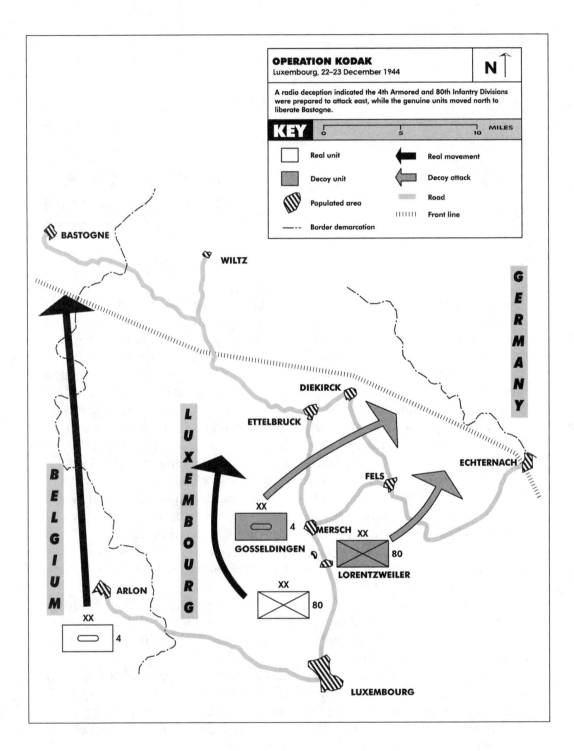

OPERATION KODAK
Luxembourg, 22–23 December 1944

A radio deception indicated the 4th Armored and 80th Infantry Divisions were prepared to attack east, while the genuine units moved north to liberate Bastogne.

N

KEY

Real unit		Real movement
Decoy unit		Decoy attack
Populated area		Road
		Front line
Border demarcation		

location by each detachment. The III Corps radio net (under which the genuine units were serving) did not recognize the notional 80th Division transmissions, because the 23rd men had been given an older series of authentication signs that were known to have been compromised during the German offensive. The notional command post continued to transmit, but the genuine corps command post refused to acknowledge the messages.

In a list of messages sent, a curious notation in the notional 317th Infantry Regiment logs mentions that the "Colonel Fisher and Major Craig skit" had been sent at 0750 on 23 December. No mention is made of what this skit was, but it was probably a pre-written confrontation between the officers designed to draw attention to the broadcast in such a way that the Germans would think it was an argument between two overworked officers.

The background information furnished to the signalmen was that "both the 80th and 4th Armored Divisions have been placed in position northeast of Luxembourg with the mission of counterattacking an expected enemy attack in the vicinity Echternach. The troops have arrived on the position 21–22 December after a long hard march and are in a state of low morale. Frightened by the Germans, they do not know the situation, and are confused and panicky. They are tired, irritable, cranky, and show jangled nerves in their conversation. See separate sheets for units and commanders, etc."[3]

During this period of the battle, it was not unusual for units to be given such hasty and poorly organized missions. General McBride, commander of the genuine 80th Infantry Division, received the order to make his 22 December attack only the afternoon before.[4]

In looking back on the possible effectiveness of the operation, the records noted that having duplicates of the same unit on the air must have tipped off the Germans that radio deception was being used. Had they not already realized the Americans were using this technique, it would have now been given away. The signalmen also felt that the use of their FM radios was of doubtful value in KODAK due to the unfavorable terrain, distance from the German intercept stations, and the abnormal amount of radio traffic in the area.

At best, this operation might have caused some confusion in the German lines for a brief moment. However, by the time the notional units might have been identified, the genuine 4th and 80th Divisions would have begun their attack. An undocumented mention is made in the army's official history of the Battle of Bulge that, "The enemy traced the 80th Infantry Division into Luxembourg, but on 22 December believed it was reinforcing 'remnants' of the 4th Infantry in a purely defensive role."[5] This might indicate the notional 80th was picked up under the cover story, but without further information it remains inconclusive.

After KODAK, the entire 23rd was shifted to billets in an old French military barracks at Verdun. Verdun had been the scene of horrendous slaughter

Tech.4 George Martin, the 603rd Battalion photographer, is seen here having just received a package from home containing "Mrs. Gray's Vegetable Noodle Soup." As the only official photographer of the deception unit, Martin was eventually moved up to the 23rd Headquarters to docu-ment their operations. Sadly, many of his official photographs cannot be located in the unit files. PHOTO: GEORGE MARTIN

during WWI, and as Lieutenant Fox put it, "Verdun is a depressing city filled with a million ghosts of other unhappy soldiers. That makes it much too crowded."[6]

The assigned barracks was dirty and very drafty in the cold winter weath-er. Rats scuttled about and devoured a number of food packages sent from home. Between continued training sessions, the men were assigned guard duty at First Army Headquarters, also located in Verdun. According to Lieutenant Fox, the time spent in Verdun was very disheartening, given that it included both Christmas and New Year's Eve. He later wrote, "It is hard to celebrate in dreary, cold, unlighted barracks. Especially when neither liquor, victory, home, nor girls are available."[7]

Although the unit was under strict censorship, there was a group of wives back in the United States that was kept well informed of the location of their husbands in the 23rd. George Martin of the 603rd Engineers had devised a code he used to send hidden messages in his letters home. He would ask in the letter if his wife had heard from a specific person, and the phone number of that person (known to both of them) was the key to the code.

Martin kept his wife Betty well informed as to the location of the unit, but it was Betty who added the real touch of creativity. She regularly got together with a group of other wives from the unit, and used a Ouija Board to ask for information on their husbands. When she had news, the board would answer. When her information was confirmed, sometimes weeks or months later, the other wives would marvel at the accuracy of Betty and her Ouija Board.

The artists of the 603rd Engineers designed a number of different Christmas cards for men of the 23rd to send home in 1944. This selection from various artists was kept by the 3132nd Technical and Maintenance Officer, Walter Manser.

Christmas.......when men unite in thoughts of peace and dreams of home.

Headquarters
Twelfth Army Group

184

Chapter 16

Operation METZ-I
28–31 December 1944

The American Army took a beating when the Germans attacked through the Ardennes in December 1944. Gradually, however, the Allies stopped the enemy advance and began to push the Germans back. The fighting was made even tougher by the poor weather and the lack of suitable winter clothing. In the scramble to gain any advantage, 12th Army Group issued orders for one final deception mission of the year.

METZ-I was designed to cover the movement of the 87th Infantry Division on its way to Reims.[1] It was a simple plan, involving men from the 23rd portraying the unit and a radio component. For an undocumented reason, the radio component was not to be handled by the 23rd Signal Company but by a sister unit, the 3103rd Signal Service Battalion. It may have been that the 23rd's signalmen were just finishing up Operation KODAK and command did not want to move them right into another mission without any time to rest or prepare; or it might have been that someone wanted to give the 3103rd a chance to practice working on a deception mission. In any event, the 3103rd was based in the immediate area and, according to 3103rd veteran Paul Sarber, was idle at the time.[2]

The 3103rd was the American Signal Corps unit in the ETO concerned with strategic deception. Prior to D-day they had been involved in transmitting dummy messages from England. Records of the unit are missing from the National Archives and may still be hidden in some classified files. From what has been discovered about the 3103rd, it appears that they were concerned with longer-range transmissions. While the 23rd was generally concerned with radio signals from division down to regiment, the 3103rd was able to portray division through corps and up to army level.

The 3103rd had arrived in England in January 1944. After a lot of training and practice sending radio messages, they went on to play a major role in

Operation FORTITUDE SOUTH. The men were split up into small groups to simulate the various notional units supposedly waiting to invade at Calais. They did not, as some would later claim, wear insignia of phantom or ghost divisions. For their efforts in this operation, the 3103rd was awarded a Meritorious Unit Citation.

The British counterpart to the 3103rd was the 5th Wireless Group. They operated in a different manner. In place of the small, scattered groups of trained operators, the British had a device that played back previously recorded messages. These were broadcast on a radio system that allowed one specially equipped truck to transmit six different signals (simulating a divisional-sized unit).[3]

At the end of August 1944, the 3103rd moved to France and was billeted first in Verdun, then moved to Longwy, Belgium, in November. In Belgium, the 3103rd did not at first take part in any deception missions. A veteran of the unit recalled that the men were given various make-work tasks such as learning how to climb telephone poles to repair phone lines and conducting surveys of Allied radio networks.

After the start of the German attack in the Ardennes, Paul Sarber's detachment of the 3103rd was ordered to perform a hasty deception mission, transmitting on SCR-284s from Sierk, just north of Metz on the Moselle River. This appears to have been part of the radio deception work for Operation METZ-I. For a few days they sent dummy radio transmissions, until small-arms fire was heard down the road. The unit hastily evacuated and fled to Reims.

Instead of starting up another deception mission, Sarber was assigned to help guard a bridge, alongside a contingent of French volunteers. The other men in his detachment were given similar assignments. With the new year, the 3103rd was broken up into small detachments and sent out to perform various radio-related functions. Sarber's group was assigned to the 127th Signal Radio Intelligence Company, Ninth Army in Holland. There they monitored enemy radio nets until the end of the war.

Command of the METZ-I detachment of the 23rd Special Troops was given to Captain Oscar Seale. He had one hundred and fifty-seven men and forty-two vehicles of the 23rd at his disposal. Orders were received at noon on 28 December 1944 for him to take Companies B and C of the 603rd and the 4th Platoon of the 3132nd (Lieutenant Syracuse's security platoon).

Preparations for the move were started immediately, but the companies of the 603rd were still in Doncourt on their way to Verdun. Seale had to leave for Metz and hope the 603rd was not too delayed. It was not until 1615 that B&C/603rd finally arrived in Verdun, only to be turned around and sent to Metz (which was only sixty-five kilometers from where they had been that morning). To top off Seale's frustration, he had to pick up supplies for the mission and was given incorrect directions, delaying him even further.

Finally Captain Seale headed to Gravelotte, where he was met by

This message was sent to start Operation METZ-I, *under command of the assistant armored officer, Captain Oscar M. Seale. Colonel Reeder signed this as commander of* BLARNEY (*the code name for the 23rd Special Troops*). HEATER *refers to the code name of the 3132nd Signal Service Company.*

THESE SPACES FOR MESSAGE CENTER ONLY

TIME FILED   MSG CEN NO.

MESSAGE (SUBMIT TO MESSAGE CENTER IN DUPLICATE)

No. 1   DATE 28

To CO BLARNEY REAR

SECRET

PREPARE TASK FORCE CONSISTING OF TWO COMPANIES : FOURTH PL HEATER UNDER COMMAND CAPT SEALE FOR MOVEMENT FROM YOUR CP BY 281200. MOVE WILL BE WITHOUT MARKINGS. TAKE SPECIAL EFFECTS & MATERIALS FOR ADDITIONAL SIGNS TO BE MADE AT DESTINATION. TF WILL MOVE ON GRAVELOTTE (U7559)SO AS TO ENABLE TF CMDR TO MEET LT COL SNEE AT CHURCH IN GRAVELOTT AT 281600. FURTHER ORDERS AT THAT POINT. FINAL DESTINATION METZ TO SIMULATE 87 DIV.

CO BLARNEY   1000
OFFICIAL DESIGNATION OF SENDER   TIME SIGNED

AUTHORIZED TO BE SENT IN CLEAR   SIGNATURE OF OFFICER   R Reeder Col. SIGNATURE AND GRADE OF WRITER

☆ U. S. GOVERNMENT PRINTING OFFICE : 1942 16—27886-1

Lieutenant Colonel Snee and Lieutenant Harker of the 3103rd. Snee approved the final instructions to "put on shoulder patches, bumper markings, directions signs, but no CP signs, and proceed by other special effects to show the 87th Division in the city of Metz."[4]

By 2030 the entire detachment had arrived in Metz and had set up shop in the Caserne de Genie. At 2135 the final briefing to the men was made, shoulder patches distributed, and orders were issued to paint bumper markings so they would be visible at first light. It was not uncommon for a normal unit to have to remove and repaint bumper markings whenever it was shifted to a new area, so the painting did not have to take place in total secrecy.

The next day, a total of fifty signs indicating the directions to the various units of the 87th Division were posted. No actual command post locations were marked and therefore no MPs were needed to guard those locations. It was hoped that signage alone, indicating the direction for a specific CP, would be noted by enemy agents. This also cut back on the manpower demands to staff a command post. Captain Seale visited the town mayor with a request for billets for eleven hundred men. Eventually some of this space would be used for a future move of the rest of the 23rd to Metz.

Little mention is made of the activities of the 3103rd, but it was entered into the unit log that at 1430 bumper markings were painted on the vehicles of that unit. This confirms that at least some of the 3103rd was present in Metz.

At 0415 on 30 December, Captain Seale was woken to take a phone call from the personnel office of the Third Army. They wanted to know why the G-1 periodic report for the 87th Division had been submitted incorrectly. Captain Seale, claiming to be the assistant S-1, explained that the division was currently split up and asked that the caller contact Lieutenant Colonel Watson of the operations office in the Third Army headquarters, as he would be able to explain what part of the division was currently in the city.

Apparently Watson was able to adequately explain the confusion, as the officer never called back to follow up. Complaints were also made to the detachment by a signal officer of the 10th Armored Division who wanted to know why his unit had to provide telephone switchboard support for another division. He was put off with an explanation that the 87th Division was just moving into the area and he would not be inconvenienced for much longer.

The day continued with the usual special effects displays of men with unit insignia moving about the area, establishing a water point, and trucks carrying men to a shower point. Starting at 1115, elements of the detachment began to move out of the city to a quiet location where patches and markings could be removed. At 1140 the order to close down the operation arrived from Colonel Reeder. All posted signs were recovered and all remaining troops headed back to Verdun on the morning of 31 December. The roads were terribly slick and driving was difficult, but there were no accidents and by 1150 everyone had reported back. Within a week, the 23rd would make the drive back to Metz for a second time.

Operation METZ-I *ended on 30 December 1944 with this final order sent to Captain Seale at 1205. All such classified messages of the 23rd were declassified in the 1990s under authority NND735017 and NND730029.*

No other mention of the 3103rd's activities was made in the records of the 23rd. It can only be assumed that they put on a notional radio show simulating the 87th Division in Metz. Captain Seale was happy with the results of the operation as he saw them, because he was confident that both civilians and military personnel thought that a large segment of the 87th was in Metz. A number of officers and men looking for friends in the 87th had stopped by to inquire about the locations of the various units supposedly in the city. Needless to say, many were probably confused, as they had followed the posted signs but never seemed to actually locate the unit's position.

There was some concern about the value of the operation, since it had been discovered that the genuine 87th was making its move without having removed patches and bumper markings. Thus the best Americans could hope for was some confusion among the Germans until they sorted out where the 87th really was.

Chapter 17

Operation METZ-II
6–9 January 1945

Following on the heels of METZ-I was a similar operation, METZ-II, centered on the same location.[1] The 90th Infantry Division was then holding the Saar line east of Thionville in the XX Corps sector. Patton wanted to pull this veteran unit out of the line and use it to replace the 26th Infantry Division in a renewed attack elsewhere to push back the Germans.

The 94th Infantry Division was supposed to be moved up to replace the 90th in the front line, but it had been delayed on its journey from guarding the Germans trapped in the Brittany ports of Lorient and St. Nazaire. The delay of the 94th left the sector very weak and open to a German attack. The 23rd was to simulate the 90th Division moving into a reserve position behind the lines until the 94th could arrive. The genuine 90th Division was meanwhile being shifted to a new location. Third Army intelligence believed that enemy agents were particularly active in the city of Metz, so it was decided to bring the notional 90th Division to a reserve position in Metz.

Due to some initial confusion, the first elements of the 90th Division pulled out with all unit markings visible. Even worse, one of the infantry regiments had used its real unit number on road signs. When this was noticed, a quick message was sent to the 90th's commanding officer to make sure that all visible markings were immediately removed.

The men of the 23rd were given quite specific instructions on how to portray the 90th. Eighty percent of all men were to have the division insignia stenciled on their helmets. All men would wear the division patch (with at least half of them being the style with a rounded lower edge). It was forbidden for anyone to wear the combat jacket and pants normally worn by tank crews, but camouflage scarves made from parachute material were permitted. It was also allowed for captured German material to be displayed on the vehicles, which might reinforce the notion that this was a veteran unit.

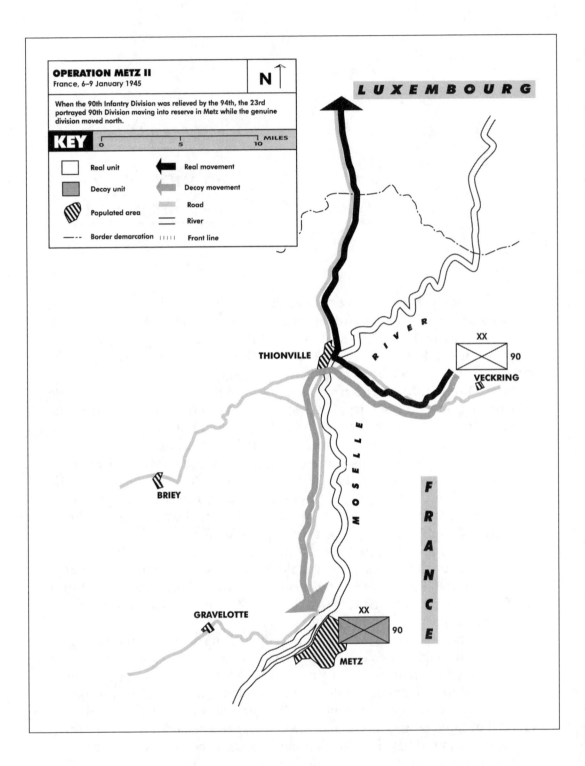

OPERATION METZ II
France, 6–9 January 1945

When the 90th Infantry Division was relieved by the 94th, the 23rd portrayed 90th Division moving into reserve in Metz while the genuine division moved north.

KEY

Real unit	Real movement
Decoy unit	Decoy movement
Populated area	Road
	River
Border demarcation	Front line

LUXEMBOURG

THIONVILLE

RIVER

XX 90

VECKRING

MOSELLE

BRIEY

FRANCE

GRAVELOTTE

XX 90

METZ

Artists of the 603rd Engineers paint the military police markings of the 90th Infantry Division on this jeep for Operation METZ-II. The sudden cold posed a problem as the paint was hard to work with in the freezing weather.

The 23rd Headquarters Company would portray the 90th Division Headquarters. A/603rd under Lieutenant Colonel Truly would simulate the 357th Combat Team;[2] B/603rd under Lieutenant Colonel Schroeder represented the 358th Combat Team;[3] C/603rd under Captain Seale took on the role of the 359th Combat Team;[4] and D/603rd (less one platoon) under Captain Sidwell played the 345th Field Artillery Battalion. All would have a detachment of signalmen to keep up the radio network.

The 603rd Headquarters, under command of Lieutenant Colonel Mayo, would portray the 90th Division Artillery Headquarters. The notional 90th Division Special Troops would be commanded by Major Hooper. The 90th Signal Company was portrayed by the remainder of the 23rd Signal Company; the 406th Engineers took on the role of the 315th Engineer Battalion; and the remaining elements of the 90th Division (ordnance, recon, quartermaster, 712th Tank Battalion, 773rd Tank Destroyer Battalion, and the 537th AAA Battalion) were portrayed by the 3132nd in their half-tracks.

The 23rd was to move to the 90th Division bivouac area by infiltration, in small groups of vehicles over two different routes, before the 90th departed. They were to set up camp and take over the operating radio networks.

Hopefully this would create the image that the 90th was still in its original position. Unfortunately, the 357th Infantry Regiment had pulled out early, before the notional radio communications could be set up. Due to this mishap, no radio broadcasts were made to simulate the 357th, but the rest of the 90th Division had radio transmissions continue from their original locations for roughly a day after the genuine unit had pulled out.

The genuine elements of the 90th began pulling out of their bivouac on 6 January and the last vehicle left at noon on 7 January. The deception troops maintained the picture on the ground that the 90th was still in place for twelve to twenty-four hours, and then headed in convoy to their new billets in Metz. Once on the road, the notional 90th assumed radio silence, which is what a division would normally do when on the move. The radios would not be used for the rest of the operation.

Strict mail security was also imposed. Everyone was cautioned not to leave any mail lying about where someone might see it was not addressed to a soldier in the 90th Division. The orders were for all envelopes, packages, or parts of letters bearing an address to be collected by a mail clerk, or sergeant, and burned.

The weather at this point was very bad. It was cold and the roads were slippery with snow. Once the notional convoys entered Metz, they were driven on a lengthy route through the town to give the vehicles as much visibility as possible. Upon arriving in their assigned locations, the men were allowed to circulate in their immediate area, but were told to be tight-lipped about their unit. This was a different method of operation, but to an enemy agent the shoulder patches, bumper markings, and helmet insignia would be a giveaway.

The men were forbidden to associate with civilians except on business. They were also prohibited from entering cafes and restaurants except on official business, and drinking alcoholic beverages in public was totally prohibited. The special effects show in Metz only lasted from 8 January until the afternoon of the following day, when the operation ended.

One incident that occurred in Metz may have taken place during this operation (or possibly during METZ-I a week earlier). Men from the 23rd were cleaning out a building of discarded material left by the previous occupants. There are various descriptions of the incident, but according to Lieutenant Dick Syracuse (who was ten yards away) it was an explosion in a cast-iron stove. The day was fiercely cold, and the men were trying to light a fire in the stove. One report indicated they were using the remains of straw mattresses (which were quite literally lousy). It is believed that the previous occupants of the building, a German military unit, had booby-trapped the stove with an explosive device. They may have just left a grenade inside so it would detonate the next time a fire was lit.

In the resulting explosion, T/5 Chester Pellicioni of the 1st Platoon,

3132nd, was killed, another man hit in the arm, and at least one man knocked down with no injuries. An official report on this incident has not been located. It was common knowledge, however, throughout the 23rd. If it was indeed a booby trap, Pellicioni should have been awarded a purple heart, but his name does not appear on the list of 23rd men given that award.

The overall tone of the records from METZ-II can be summed up by a quote from Lieutenant Colonel Mayo's after-action report: "No conclusions, no comments."[5] The 12th Army Group, however, was very pleased with the results and ordered another similar operation immediately. METZ-III called for the 23rd to assume the identity of the 94th Division and hold it in place while the genuine unit moved to replace the 26th Division elsewhere on the line. The 23rd radio operators had just started to infiltrate into the 94th radio networks when the operation was called off. By this time the situation was well in hand and there was no longer a fear that the Germans might attempt another attack in a thinly held section of the line.

There is one curious note found on a handwritten document in the METZ-II files. In a list of radio operations covering the movements of the 90th, 26th, and 94th Divisions, there is an entry indicating that the 3103rd Signal Battalion was to simulate the radio network of the 90th Division while it moved to relieve the 26th Division. This might have been only a preliminary planning memo, as 3103rd veteran Paul Sarber recalled only one deception mission in the Belgium area. It might, however, be a clue to the planned further use of part of the 3103rd for tactical deception. Until the unit records of the 3103rd are located, their exact role in tactical deception will not be known.

Chapter 18

Operation L'EGLISE
10–13 January 1945

The 4th Armored Division was being moved from the VIII Corps sector to a new location in Luxembourg. The objective of Operation L'EGLISE was to cover this movement by making it appear as if the 4th was moving into VIII Corps reserve near Neufchateau.[1] The orders for this operation were received on 10 January, and immediately the 23rd signal officer went to the 4th Armored headquarters to make arrangements to take over the radio nets.

The VIII Corps assigned an area to the 23rd in which to portray the notional 4th Armored Division in reserve. The region already had a number of tank units moving about (the 6th, 10th, and 11th Armored Divisions) so it was decided that no sonic or rubber decoys were needed. Only spoof radio and special effects would be used.

On the night of 10–11 January, the 23rd headed out to an assembly point near Hanay La Neuve, Belgium. Beginning at 0900 on 11 January, the various detachments infiltrated into the designated areas. Lieutenant Colonel Schroeder was in command of the notional CCA centered at Offlang,[2] Captain Seale was in command of CCB at Les Bulles,[3] and Lieutenant Colonel Truly had command of CCR at Hanay La Vielle.[4] Playing the role of the 4th Armored MP Platoon was the 1st Platoon of the 406th Engineer Company, with the help of a detachment of three jeeps and drivers from the 3132nd Signal Service Company.

The 23rd Headquarters Company, along with the headquarters of the 603rd Engineers, played the part of the 4th Armored Headquarters based in L'Eglise, hence the name of the operation. A lack of manpower and vehicles prevented this element from portraying the 4th Armored Division Command Post very well. The weather was extremely cold and outdoor traffic was at a minimum.

The detachments were scheduled to arrive at their final destinations at a time consistent with when the genuine units had pulled out of their starting

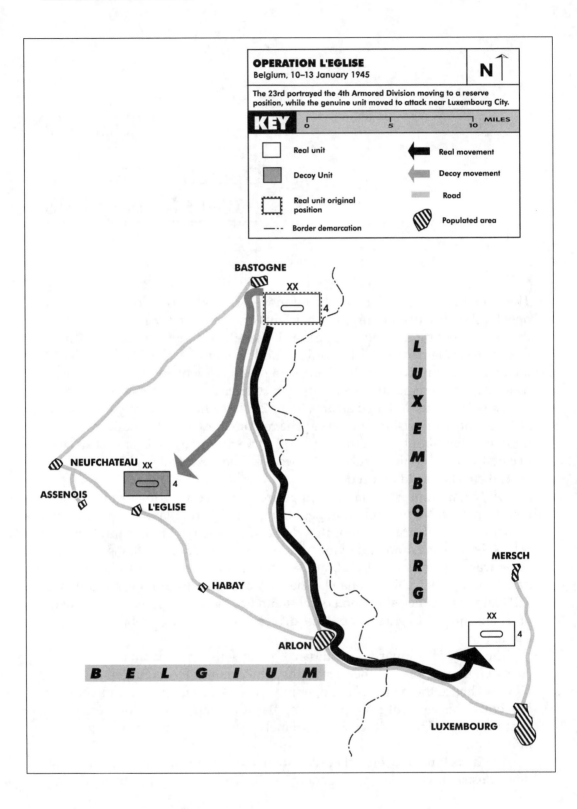

locations. The genuine 4th Armored traveled blacked out in both radio trans-missions and unit insignia (signs, patches, and vehicle markings). For the 23rd it was a typical show involving bumper markings, shoulder patches, and posted signs. The notional MP platoon patrolled the region with painted hel-mets, MP armbands, and MP-marked jeeps.

On the night of 10–11 January, the assistant signal officer plus five other officers went to the VIII Corps headquarters in Assenois to coordinate the radio plan at that end. At the same time, a detachment of signalmen, with four SCR-399s, four SCR-193s, and ten SCR-506s, were dispatched to the genuine 4th Armored units. Fog, icy roads, and driving with only tiny blackout lights slowed everyone down. The signalmen did not arrive at the 4th Armored until 0230.

The final signal plan was completed at 0600, and the officers left the VIII Corps to bring the orders to their men. The assistant signal officer of the 23rd Signal Company remained at VIII Corps as a liaison and to ensure that no one was confused by the notional traffic.

The first notional radio went on the air at 1150 on 11 January. By the end of the day, eighteen notional radios were being operated. The 23rd opened up a notional 4th Armored HQ radio before the genuine unit pulled out, calling

Atmosphere for Operation L'EGLISE was added by these men from the 23rd portraying military police from the 4th Armored Division. The jeep and helmet markings were based upon observations made of the genuine 4th Armored. Even the style of stencil matched what the genuine unit used on their vehicles.

itself OLYMPIC FORWARD (the forward command post of OLYMPIC, the code name for the 4th Armored Division). The first day's traffic was relatively heavy to coincide with the notional movement to the reserve area, but then lessened on the following two days.

The 4th Armored normally operated its combat command network on SCR-506 radios, of which the 23rd did not have enough to simulate all stations. The SCR-506s were formed into roving teams that transmitted in the CCA assembly area, then moved back and forth to the CCB area to try to keep up the appearance of different radio stations. Different frequencies and operators were used for the different locations. The radio traffic was written by two different officers so the style of messages would vary slightly, but consistently, depending upon which command was transmitting.

On 12 January, the liaison network was planned to open up with links to the neighboring 101st and 17th Airborne Divisions. These links were never established, at the direction of the VIII Corps, because the 101st signal officer reported that every time they began to transmit the Germans shelled them. The liaison radios were set up and ready to transmit, but they maintained radio silence during the entire operation.

All traffic in the division and combat commands was written by the respective notional commanders. The 23rd Signal Company message center prepared bogus messages for the notional coded traffic. SIGABA was used for messages to corps, M-209 was used on the G-4 link, and the 25th Reconnaissance Troop used SLIDEX. On the final day of the operation (13 January), only a few messages were sent and the radios went silent by noon.

The notional division headquarters had been billeted in the house of a known collaborator, but not much out of the ordinary had taken place to indicate if the Germans had been fooled. At one point during this mission, Gilbert Seltzer and a driver were traveling along a road in full 4th Armored Division markings. A command car overtook them and pulled them over. The genuine 4th Armored officer bawled them out, saying that their orders specifically stated that no 4th Division markings were to be seen on any vehicles. On the suspicion they might be German spies, the 23rd men were disarmed and an armed guard was placed in their jeep. While Seltzer was trying to figure out how to get out of this mess, the officer in the command car realized what was going on and suddenly stopped, pulled Seltzer aside, and quietly said, "You are one lucky guy—there are only four officers in the 4th who know of this operation and I'm one of them!" He then sent Seltzer, driver, and jeep on their way.[5]

Operation L'EGLISE ended at noon on 13 January and the majority of the 23rd infiltrated back to their new home base at Briey, France. The planning and staff officers of the 23rd remained billeted in the building of the former Italian Legation in Luxembourg City so that they could remain close to higher headquarters.

At Briey, the Caserne Guard Mobile was assigned as the new billet for the 23rd troops. They would keep this building as their new home base until April. Problems were immediately discovered with the heating and plumbing systems. The local water commissioner demanded a payment of two dozen bars of chocolate, a case of soap, and six loaves of white bread before he would help. The men decided not to pay the bribe, so the plumbing system remained erratic through their entire stay.

Chapter 19

Operation FLAXWEILER
17–18 January 1945

FLAXWEILER was a strictly sonic operation for the 23rd, taking place on one day only.[1] The basic idea was to draw German attention away from a genuine attack by the XII Corps at Diekirck, nineteen miles to the north, by simulating a river crossing at Flaxweiler. The XII Corps had been holding the southern shoulder of the German Ardennes offensive. It had been essentially stable since 26 December, but an attack had been in the planning stage since 2 January.

The information for the mission arrived at the 23rd on the afternoon of 17 January, the day of the mission. The 23rd was to play a sonic program of tanks moving along the road next to the Moselle River during the night of 17–18 January. The troops involved were the 3132nd Signal Service Company and the 1st platoon of the 406th Engineer Company. They left their billet at Briey at 1600 and arrived at the target location just before midnight.

The sonic operation took place along the Niederndorf to Lenningen road at a point halfway between the two villages. This was roughly fifteen hundred yards from the Moselle River. The German front line was on the east bank of the river, and it was hoped the enemy would report the build-up of armor opposite them and draw attention to this spot.

The sonic operation plan ran from 0025 to 0500 on 18 January. It consisted of twenty minutes of tank column sounds, followed by five minutes of silence. Interspersed would be two one-hour periods of intermittent individual tank movement (0125 to 0225 and 0405 to 0500).

In this operation, the 23rd was only assisting in a deception actually performed by the 2nd Cavalry Group. This genuine unit had been involved in a series of tasks to provide a visual impression of a unit preparing for a river crossing. The orders given to the various task forces of the 2nd Cavalry Group were:

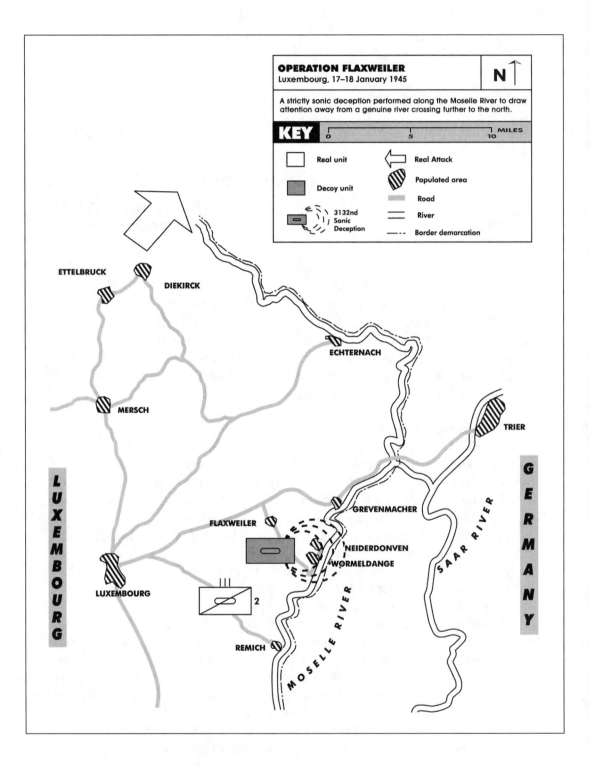

Task Force Reed—night of 17–18 January increase patrolling—demonstrate by increasing activity to simulate preparations for attack and river crossings. Protect south flank of Corps along Moselle River.

Combat Team Costello—Within zone and particular area Wormeldange and Ahn have evident movement that enemy can observe. 2–3 man parties with field glasses obviously reconnoitering river. Before dark move at least one platoon of tanks to Gostigen. Immediately after dark until midnight run tanks over road Gostigen to Ehnen, send one combat patrol to Helingen during night and one recon of small arms and mortars simulating a river crossing. Tank destroyers in direct firing positions will fire on any desirable target. Alert reserve troop.

Combat Team Hargis—Within zone and particular area Greveldange and Ehnen have evident movement enemy can observe. 2–3 man parties with field glasses obviously reconnoitering river. Push a patrol across at Wehr. Force of at least a reinforced platoon will cross Moselle River at Palzem and seize town and if enemy resistance is light, force will remain in town. TD's in direct firing positions will fire on any desirable target.

Task Force Reserve—Alert one company of engineers for movement.

Artillery—255 Field Artillery Battalion—H-30 artillery perpetration on Wincheringen, Helfant, Brastwald woods. H-15 smoke screen area directly in front of Ehnen. Time on Target barrage on Palzem as directed by CT Hargis. Time on Target barrage on Relingen as directed by CT Costello.

Engineers—4–5 trucks with bridge building material and boats will be run over road Canach, Oberwormeldange-Gostingen, Beyren and back to Canach to create an impression that a river crossing is intended at Ehnen or vicinity.[2]

For the first time, the 23rd was in a strictly supporting role during a deception operation. No records indicate where the plan for the operation originated. The orders for the 3132nd to assist were issued at the very last minute, which is a good indication that the 23rd was not involved in the planning of FLAXWEILER. The last minute performance was a good example of how quickly the 3132nd could put their prerecorded library of sounds to work.

It appears that the idea for the diversionary river crossing may have come from XII Corps, and the 23rd was added in at the last moment when someone realized that the sounds of a large number of tanks might help draw attention from the genuine crossing further to the north. The only obvious result of the operation was a definite increase in German artillery firing. This indicated that at least some attention had been drawn, as ammunition was in short supply and the Germans could not afford to waste it.

To the north, the genuine crossings along the Our and Sure Rivers took place on 18 January. In this area the American artillery had been silent, and ordered not to fire registration or preparation barrages. The 5th Infantry Division crossed the river with hardly any resistance. At one spot, the 10th Infantry Regiment loaded into their assault boats on the snow-covered banks and rode them down the bank into the river as toboggans. At other locations, the men crossed on footbridges that had been quietly positioned during the night. German artillery did not respond to the attack for three hours; then sporadic shelling began. The attack was considered highly successful and by nightfall a two-mile deep bridgehead had been established.[3]

During this operation, Colonel Reeder visited the 3132nd and noticed that someone had brought along a mattress in their half-track. Further inspection showed that many of the sonic crews had found room in their vehicles for mattresses, pillows, and other items of luxury not normally found on the battlefield. Infuriated, Reeder moved down the line of vehicles tossing anything not regulation out into the snow.[4]

Operation STEINSEL
27–29 January 1945

At the end of a cold and snowy January, the 23rd was given a mission to cover a secret move of the 4th Infantry Division. Operation STEINSEL was proposed at the last minute, so it was decided that only spoof radio would be used to create the notional unit.[1]

The 4th Infantry Division was to move out of its current XII Corps position in the Diekirck-Echternach line for a move north. There the 4th would be attached to the VIII Corps in order to make a surprise attack in the Houffalize area. The 23rd was to provide a radio picture of the 4th Division moving slightly behind the lines into a reserve position, but staying in the XII Corps area.

It was hoped that other movements in the area would help cover the move of the genuine 4th Division. Four other divisions were being shifted at the same time and in the same area. The 80th Infantry Division had been brought in to replace the 4th, and the 76th Infantry Division had just replaced the 87th. The 26th Infantry Division was being sent from the III Corps to replace the 95th Infantry Division in the XX Corps. The 95th was being sent north to a reserve position in the VIII Corps. The remainder of the 23rd would be covering this move of the 95th under Operation LANDONVILLERS (29 January–2 February). All divisions were to make their moves blacked out (no unit markings or patches showing). With so many other units moving about the region, the hope was that the 4th would disappear into the vast welter of activity on the ground.

Only a small detachment was assigned to STEINSEL. Frederick Fox, now promoted to captain, commanded the mission. He had four officers, seventy-two enlisted men, and twenty-two vehicles to work with. The radiomen of the 23rd Signal Company had worked with the 4th Division previously and so had some background to the unit. To capitalize on their prior work, the signalmen were placed with the units they had previously worked with during

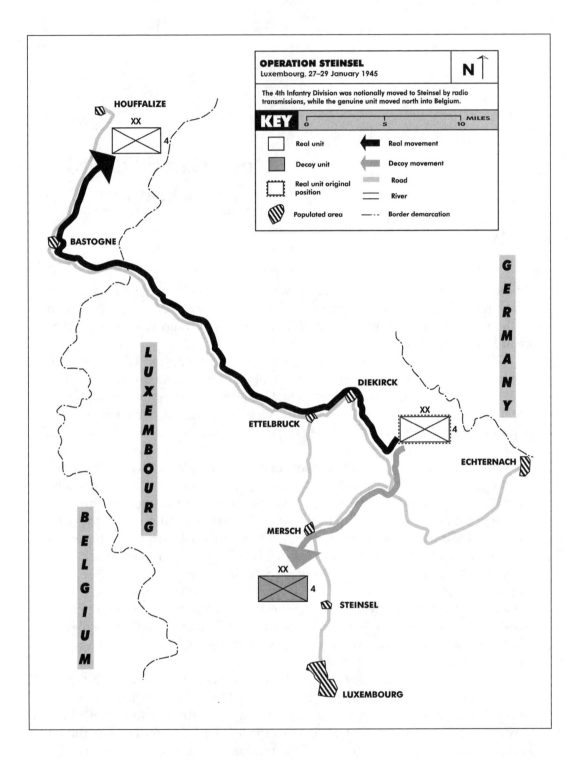

OPERATION STEINSEL
Luxembourg, 27–29 January 1945

The 4th Infantry Division was notionally moved to Steinsel by radio transmissions, while the genuine unit moved north into Belgium.

KEY

□ Real unit	← Real movement
▦ Decoy unit	← Decoy movement
⬚ Real unit original position	Road
▨ Populated area	River
	Border demarcation

This original document from the Operation STEINSEL after-action report illustrates some of the planning that went into a radio deception. Here eighteen different radio networks were used for this one operation alone. The number of messages sent, and routine call ups made (far right), is quite low, but accurately reflects the amount of radio traffic for a unit in this situation.

Net	BLARNEY Radio Started Sending as CACTUS Units in Old Position	CACTUS Units Withdrew	BLARNEY Held Units in Old Position	BLARNEY Started Sending as CACTUS in New Position	BLARNEY Faded Out	Msgs	Call-ups
XII CORPS COMD	261400	280600	/	281000	291045		15
XII CORPS SP PUR			/				
NCS	(New net)	280600	/	271025	291245		37
4th Inf				271145	290920		13
5th Inf			Did not attempt to hold CACTUS	281530	281600		
76th Inf				271200	291200		10
80th Inf							
CORPS ARTY COMD	271630	280703	in old position	281100	291030	Sent 6 Recd 4	23
CORPS ARTY SERENADE	261830	280600	/	281100	291015		11
DIV COMD			/				
NCS	252300	280800	/	281100	291020		28
8th Inf	261805	271500	/	271700	291100		6
12th Inf	261245	270900	/	271250	290954		17
22nd Inf	261310	280900	/	281130	291130		6
4th Engr	261745	280800	/	281124	291135		28
CG			/	271030	271440		2
22nd REGT COMD*	261343	280900	/				
NCS			/	281246	291150	Sent 3 Recd 2	44
1st Bn				281318	291040		8
2nd Bn			/	281245	291137	Sent 1 Recd 1	9
3rd Bn			/	281300	281700	Sent 1 Recd 1	9
Sv			/	281311	291146	Recd 1	19

* This was the only regimental command net in existence. The 8th and 12th were silent. BLARNEY SCR-284's were not taken out to battalions because they were in the process of being withdrawn.

Operation ELSENBORN. When the signalmen entered the 4th Division mess they were greeted with a cry of "Here come those sons-o-bitches that helped us into the Hurtgen Forest!"[2]

At 0880 on 25 January, three officers from the deception troops visited XII Corps, 4th Division, and its regimental headquarters to begin organizing the operation. A few hours later, eighteen of the radios that were to take over the division's net were set to begin infiltrating the genuine division network. After two days of the deception teams slowly taking over transmission duties, then gradually switching from the genuine 4th to the 23rd radio sets, the 4th Division began to pull out.

As each genuine unit of the 4th left the lines, the 23rd's radios began transmitting in the notional reserve area. All notional radios were in position and operating by 1130 on 28 January. This radio activity was maintained until 1150 on 29 January when the genuine 4th Infantry Division attacked, and thus could no longer be concealed.

In the notional division, the only battalion-to-regimental transmissions were in the 22nd Infantry Regiment. The battalion networks of the other two regiments (8th and 12th Infantry) remained silent. There was no definite statement why; however, there was some indication in the records that there had been trouble getting enough of the SCR-284 radios in use at that level.

One of the more helpful radio nets used by the notional unit was that of the XII Corps artillery. Traffic on this network was sent according to a strict timetable and followed a very stereotyped pattern. The information was sent in the weak SLIDEX code. Everyone thought that the Germans would certainly keep a close eye on this network, since the information was particularly useful.

The artillery net traffic used only one call sign per day. The 4th Division used the number "6" as a suffix, and reports were always sent in at 0700, 1100, 1500, 1900, and 2300. Reports could always be added if the situation changed, but those five periodic reports had to be sent each day.

An example found in the unit records was, "T1A 806502 830500 861514 T1B 800510 857525 T2 19F MVG T3 Light resistance." T1A stood for the coordinates of the front line. T1B was the probable front line coordinated in four hours. T2 was the disposition of friendly artillery units in the area. T3 concerned enemy activity in the region. The ideal picture for the notional 4th was to indicate that everything was stable, so the 23rd radios sent mainly "NCH" (no change) and "NKN" (unknown) for positions, but under T2 they sent the notional positions of the 4th Division artillery battalions.

The radio aspect of STEINSEL was becoming fairly standard by now, but there had been some compromise by the genuine 4th Division. They had not followed directions, and the divisional advance party moved north with a full display of shoulder patches and bumper markings. A few other 4th Division convoys were spotted moving north with bumper markings intact. It must have been very disillusioning for the deception troops to plan such an operation, only to have the men (who stood to gain an easier time on the battlefield as a result) not cooperate.

Operation LANDONVILLERS
28 January–2 February 1945

Operation LANDONVILLERS was similar to Operation METZ-II and took place in roughly the same location.[1] The 23rd was to cover the movement of the 95th Infantry Division, which was being shifted from the XX Corps to the XII Corps sector. The 26th Infantry Division had been transferred from the III Corps to replace the 95th Division in the front lines. The 95th was moved into an VIII Corps reserve position on 28–29 January. It was then to move under a blackout of unit markings and radio transmissions to its new location.

To conceal this movement, the 23rd was to create a picture of the 95th holding its initial position for twelve to twenty-four hours after the genuine unit had left, and was then to bring the notional unit to a reserve position east of Metz. This would be accomplished using only spoof radio and special effects.

The 95th Division Headquarters was portrayed by the 23rd Headquarters Company under command of Colonel Reeder. This group, along with every other section of the 23rd playing part of the 95th, had its own detachment from the signal company to transmit on the divisional radio net.

The notional Combat Team 377,[2] commanded by Major Thomas Raggio, was composed of A/603rd, the 1st Platoon of D/603rd, the 3rd Platoon of the 406th Engineers, and a signal detachment. Lieutenant Colonel Schroeder commanded the notional Combat Team 378,[3] which was composed of B/603rd, the 2nd Platoon of the 406th, and a signal detachment. Combat Team 379[4] under Captain Seale was composed of C/603rd, the 3rd Platoon of D/603rd, and a signal detachment.

Captain Sidwell commanded the notional division artillery headquarters with D/603rd (less four platoons). He was also in charge of one platoon from D/603rd portraying the 360th Medium Field Artillery Battalion.

The other notional 95th Division units included Major Hooper and the 23rd Battalion HQ portraying the 95th Division Special Troops Headquarters.

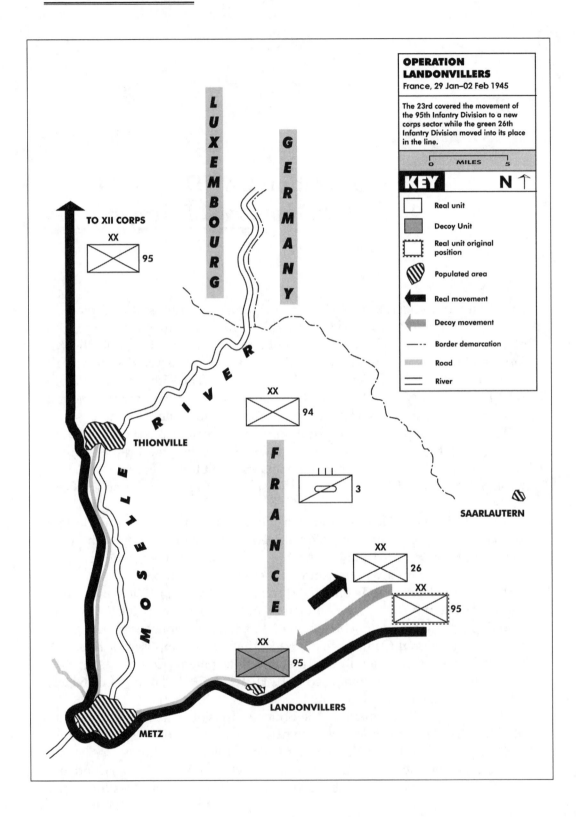

OPERATION LANDONVILLERS

France, 29 Jan–02 Feb 1945

The 23rd covered the movement of the 95th Infantry Division to a new corps sector while the green 26th Infantry Division moved into its place in the line.

MILES 0 — 5

KEY N ↑

- ☐ Real unit
- ▨ Decoy Unit
- ⬚ Real unit original position
- ◩ Populated area
- ◀ Real movement
- ◀ Decoy movement
- –·– Border demarcation
- ▤ Road
- ══ River

TO XII CORPS

XX 95

LUXEMBOURG

GERMANY

MOSELLE RIVER

THIONVILLE

FRANCE

XX 94

⚋⚋⚋ 3

SAARLAUTERN

XX 26

XX 95

XX 95

LANDONVILLERS

METZ

This notional headquarters of the 95th Infantry Division was set up in the town of Landonvillers itself as part of Operation LANDONVILLERS. *Note that an entirely new style of wire cutter has been added to this jeep to conform to those found in the genuine 95th Division.*

In addition, the 3rd Platoon of the 3132nd played the 95th Recon Troop; the H&S Company of the 603rd portrayed the 95th Quartermaster Company; and the 1st platoon of the 406th Engineers represented the 95th Division MP Platoon. The remainder of the 406th took on the role of the 320th Engineer Battalion. The half-tracks of the 3132nd were used to simulate the 795th Ordnance Company, 567th AAA Battalion, 607th Tank Destroyer Battalion, and the 778th Tank Battalion. The medical detachments from the 23rd were used to portray the 320th Medical Battalion.

All vehicles participating in the operation received a coat of whitewash as snow camouflage (as did the genuine 95th vehicles). The proper bumper markings were put on all vehicles before leaving the base camp. They were covered up with burlap or cardboard until arrival in the 95th's sector. This was not an unusual sight, as most units were required to remove, or cover, their markings when changing position.

According to the information gathered on the 95th Infantry Division, shoulder patches, but no helmet markings, were worn. Captured German equipment could be displayed, if available, to indicate that the unit had pre-

Although illustrating a 95th Division MP, this photo may have been taken outside of Operation LANDONVILLERS *as an illustration of how the unit could operate. It took skill to portray military policemen when having to work alongside the genuine article from other units. The men of Lieutenant Ted Daley's 1st Platoon, 406th Engineers, were normally given this task and became quite expert at impersonating MPs.*

viously been in combat. The uniform was specified as combat jackets and pants (a dark green cotton uniform generally referred to as the model 1943), which could be worn with a camouflage scarf made from a piece of parachute. Gas masks were to be issued to all men before they moved out.

Very specific instructions were issued for the use of air recognition panels. These were to be placed perpendicular to the long axis of the vehicle. Only one out of five vehicles in a convoy would be displayed. If fewer than eight vehicles were on the road only one panel would be shown. From 25–28 January the yellow side would be used, then from 29 January–4 February it would change to yellow in combination with red. These panels did not stop a German aircraft from strafing a 23rd column on 29 January. One jeep was hit, but not seriously damaged.

The men were cautioned about drinking in public, and were carefully instructed to burn all letters or other papers that might give away their true unit identity.

Eight radios from the 23rd arrived at the 95th Division at 1100 on 27 January. The 23rd signalmen took over the 95th radio nets, then after a specific period of time (twelve to twenty-four hours) began moving them to the new notional reserve position. Little traffic was sent, but scheduled radio checks were made at 0100, 0900, 1500, and 1900 each day. Adding to the radio traffic was the genuine 5th Ranger Battalion that had been attached to the 95th Division while it held a section of the front line. The 5th Rangers were left in place, and their genuine radio continued to report in through the notional 95th network until the end of the operation.

After a few days of portraying the 95th Division, the participating men began to filter back to the 23rd's base camp. Four different routes were authorized for the return convoys, and the men were instructed to travel in groups of no more than ten vehicles. By 1603 on 3 February, all units had checked back in at headquarters and the operation officially ended.

This type of operation was becoming standard for the 23rd. The final report indicated that the degree of success was unknown. While "efforts had been made to impress the local inhabitants of the presence of the simulated unit, no definite statements of observations by natives were obtained."[5]

	REAL UNIT DEPARTED	HELD IN PLACE BY RADIO	FIRST RADIO CHECK NEW LOCATION	100% SPECIAL EFFECTS BY	REMARKS
CT 377 RAGGIO	280700	290900	291500	300800	Partial Special Effects shown on 29 Jan.
CT 378 SCHROEDER	292300	300900	301500	310800	Partial Special Effects on arrival in area 301125 Jan.
CT 379 MAYO	290600	300100	300900	300800	
DIV HQS	291200	300100	300900	300800	Cmd control passes 95th Div to 26th 292400.
FWD ECH DIV HQS			291500 to 300100		This radio net opened the Div Advance CP.
DIV SP TRS	291200			300800	
795th ORD	291100				
SIG	290800			300800	
QM	292300				
320 ENGR BN	291200			300800	
MP PLAT				300800	
320 MEDICAL BN	292300			300800	
DIV ARTY	291200	300100	300900	310800	Partial Special Effects on arrival in area 301245 Jan.
360 FA BN (M)	291200			310800	
95th RCN TRP	290730			300800	

TOP SECRET

3 February 1945

TIME SCHEDULE OF OPERATION

CONFIDENTIAL SECRET RESTRICTED

REGRADED ORDER SEC ARMY BY TAG PER OK 419

NOTE: Radio checks were made daily at 0100; 0900; 1500; and 1900.

ALL OPERATION CEASED NIGHT OF 1-2 FEB 45.

TOP SECRET

This was the schedule for Operation LANDONVILLERS. *It provides the time the genuine units would pull out, how long the decoy radio transmissions would hold them in place, when the decoy transmissions would begin transmitting in the new position, and when the 23rd special effects and atmosphere would begin to complete the picture. The first two digits are the date, followed by the 2400 hour military time.*

215

Operation WHIPSAW
1–4 February 1945

Operation WHIPSAW was a two-part effort on the southern front of Patton's Third Army.[1] The name stemmed from the concept of drawing attention to one place, then suddenly whipping it away to a second location (neither of which was going to be the location of a genuine attack). The overall plan was to indicate a build-up of troops threatening the line from Grevenmacher to Saarlautern (today known as Saarlouis). The first half of the operation was purely sonic; the other half was to build up notional artillery units through the use of rubber decoys. No spoof radio or special effects were used.

The sonic half of the operation was under the command of Lieutenant Colonel Schroeder. He was assigned eight officers and one hundred and eighteen enlisted men for the task of simulating, by sonic means, three tank battalions moving in along the Moselle River. The first location for the sonic program was near the town of Grevenmacher and the second was at Wormeldange. This was in the same area where Operation FLAXWEILER had taken place. The 3132nd troops (with the 2nd Platoon of the 406th Engineers for security) left their base at Briey on the morning of 1 February. They arrived in the operational area at noon, and at 1300, two separate reconnaissance parties went to locate the best positions for the sonic cars. The first group, composed of Lieutenant Colonel Schroeder, Major Williams, Lieutenant Syracuse, and Lieutenant Fasnacht, looked over the Grevenmacher area, while Captain Hiller, Lieutenant Robinson, and Lieutenant Walker reconnoitered around Wormeldange.

When these parties returned, the final plans were drawn up. The security elements moved out first at 1700 to make sure no German patrols had moved into the planned area of operation. Roughly thirty minutes later, the sonic cars followed and were put into position. The sonic program of the notional tank battalions (three at each location) began playing at 2000. The program ended

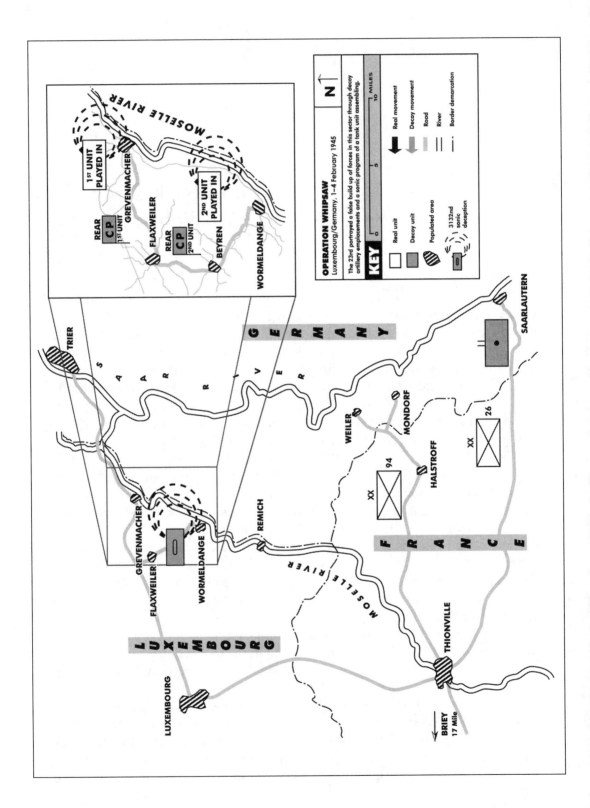

by 0300 on the morning of 2 February. The first group finished by 0200 and withdrew back to its bivouac near Flaxweiler.

The second group finished its program at 0115 and arrived at their bivouac near Beyren by 0200. The next morning, Lieutenant Colonel Schroeder and Lieutenant Syracuse returned to Luxembourg to receive further instructions. They were back by the afternoon to brief the men as to that night's operation. The two groups once again left for their operational area about 1700 (security elements leading the way), and the second night's programs began playing between 1930 and 2000. This time the recordings painted the picture of three tank battalions adjusting their positions and establishing outposts. The idea was to convince the Germans on the opposite bank that an armored unit had moved up and was preparing to cross the river at those points.

To help create this impression, the 2nd Cavalry Group was assigned the task of adding to the local activity by shifting its tanks about in visible locations, displaying bridge building equipment, and increasing its patrolling. Another technique to draw attention was to have the local artillery units begin to increase the number of targets they fired registration salvos on. To a trained artilleryman this would indicate not only that an attack was coming, but also where the enemy thought they would need to support it with artillery fire.

At one point the 2nd Cavalry Group sent three assault boats across the river to patrol the opposite bank. The boats could not reach the far shore due to the strong current, but this action attracted the attention of the German defenders. Through both days the cavalry units also began increasing the amount of traffic in the area so it would appear to German observers that something was going on.

The activity obviously stirred up interest as an "exceedingly large number"[2] of German flares were sent up both nights. There was also a noticeable increase in German mortar and artillery fire directed at the region. Most important was that German planes were spotted conducting reconnaissance flights over the area. Four unidentified aircraft were spotted flying at six thousand feet around 2000 on the night of 3–4 February over the area where the tank sounds had been played. A check with the local antiaircraft unit (the 119th AAA Gun Battalion) confirmed that the radar operators were sure these were German aircraft (although they were too far away to fire on the aircraft).

It would be unusual for the Germans to risk their limited number of aircraft in a reconnaissance of an area that they were not concerned about. Lieutenant Colonel Schroeder took this as a good indication they had attracted attention and that the Germans wanted to confirm that the tank units were in the area. Schroeder suggested that in a future operation they should display rubber decoys to give the Germans something to see. At 0930 on 3 February, the troops involved in this sonic mission packed up and returned to Briey.

The second phase of WHIPSAW was the emplacement of notional artillery units. Lieutenant Colonel Mayo, along with most of the 603rd and 406th Engineers, left Briey on the morning of 3 February. They arrived at Saarlautern by noon and set up two battalions worth of artillery decoys underneath camouflage netting as soon as it became dark. Vehicles were driven around the area so that an adequate number of tire tracks were left in the snow for the simulated units.

The decoy guns were left in position from 0100 on 4 February until nightfall the next day. Then the engineers packed up and returned to Briey. Originally the plans for WHIPSAW called for a continuation of the sonic display and the emplacement of an additional two artillery battalions near Saarlautern on 5 February. The 12th Army Group canceled these plans with no reasons given.

The deception was helped by the fact that genuine artillery units had previously used these positions. This was important because the ground was frozen and new emplacements could not have been dug in the allotted time. Unlike the sonic mission, no German aircraft were observed in the area. Lieutenant Colonel Mayo had been given no indication the Germans were even aware of his efforts. He suggested that in future operations of this type one genuine gun be assigned to each notional artillery battalion. That gun could fire registration missions to draw enemy attention to the fact a new artillery unit had moved into the area.

Unlike an infantry or tank unit that could move into an area and attack almost immediately, an artillery unit takes time to set up. This is why a good indication of a pending attack is to observe artillery units moving into a new area. Artillery can set up their guns and prepare to fire by working only from maps, but they are far more accurate if a few rounds are fired to register their guns (to double-check all calculations and map work by checking the relationship between where a round is targeted and where it actually hits). Such registration fire is a key indication that a new unit has moved into the region and so is normally concealed among intermittent shelling by other artillery units already in the area.

Operation MERZIG
13–14 February 1945

MERZIG was a small, sonic-only operation designed to pin down the German 11th Panzer Division.[1] This German unit had been located somewhere in the vicinity of Remich and Merzig, but was believed to be withdrawing from the area. The Allies felt this was a place where the 11th Panzer Division could not do much harm, so they wanted to pin the German tanks in place to keep them from being used to shore up weaker parts of the line elsewhere. The 23rd was to simulate the massing of tanks in the XX Corps sector near Merzig by playing a sonic recording of tanks during two consecutive nights.

Lieutenant Colonel Schroeder was put in command of a detachment consisting of the 3132nd and the 2nd Platoon of the 406th Engineers. These units left Briey on the afternoon of 13 February and arrived at their forward bivouac area near Halstroff that evening. They set up a command post alongside that of A Troop, 43rd Cavalry Squadron. The area of operation was an eight-mile stretch of the front centered on Merzig, held by the 3rd Cavalry Group. To the north was the 94th Infantry Division, and to the south the 26th Infantry Division.

The 3rd Cavalry Group assisted the operation by moving some of their real tanks about in an area known to be under German observation, and in general by increasing the amount of movement, fire, and activity in the area. At 1700 on 13 February, the 3rd Cavalry made a feint with one company of tanks roughly two miles to the north. This helped set the stage for the Germans to think the Allies were bringing in tanks. At some point during the operation, the cavalry also laid down a smoke screen to draw German attention.

On the night of 13 February, a sonic program was played near Mondorf between the hours of 2000 and 2245. Two sonic platoons were used to simulate two tank battalions moving into the area. Syracuse's 4th Platoon, as usual, provided security for the sonic cars. At 2300 the entire group returned to the bivouac area at Halstroff.

During the sonic program, the Germans fired an estimated eighty-five rounds from medium (81mm) mortars into that area. According to the intelligence summaries this was unusual, as the Germans were thought to be running short of ammunition and holding onto it for definite targets. Flares were also sent up by the Germans at regular intervals, illuminating the night.

The 3rd Cavalry Group intelligence report for the night of 13–14 February indicated "45 rounds of artillery and 109 of mortar fell throughout the sector, probably as a result of our harassing fire and demonstration. Flare activity and harassing machine-gun fire also increased over previous period, but vehicular movement was negligible."[2]

The following day, the next area of operations, east of Weiler, was reconnoitered. The security platoon secured the chosen positions at 1800 and two sonic platoons moved up twenty minutes later. A similar sonic program depicting two tank battalions moving up was played between 1930 and 2145. Afterward the group withdrew to the bivouac.

Again the Germans shelled the sonic demonstration area with fifty rounds of mortar fire and eight rounds of artillery. There were fewer flares this night, but now there were indications of German aerial reconnaissance. Enemy aircraft flew over the area at hourly intervals. Some, if not all of these, were probably reconnaissance aircraft that dropped flares to illuminate the ground for their photographs.

The report for the 3rd Cavalry Group for that night reads, "As a result of our demonstration for his benefit, the enemy showed his appreciation with stepped up harassing machine-gun fire, mortar fire and even artillery fire which has been noticeably absent or very scarce recently. 34 rounds artillery and 53 rounds mortar fell throughout the sector. Flare activity was normal and several unidentified planes held to be enemy were reported over the area during the hours of darkness. Six of those planes were reported simultaneously with the heavy vehicle movement in Besseringen and may have been air cover for the column."[3]

In comparison, the report for the following night of 15–16 February mentioned fifteen rounds of 20mm fire, four rounds of artillery, and only thirty-two rounds of mortar fire in the entire sector. Flare activity reportedly returned to normal over the next few days. On the afternoon of 16 February, the deception troops pulled out and returned to their home base in Briey.

Operation MERZIG certainly attracted German attention, as was shown by the increase in shelling and aerial reconnaissance of the area. The heavy concentration of German aircraft was unusual for this point in the war. The 23rd had been relying more heavily on special effects to fool ground agents due to the lack of German aircraft, rather than inflatable decoys to trick aerial reconnaissance. As Schroeder commented in his after-action report, "Rubber dummies could have been used effectively to simulate a combat command in march column on the road. This could have been done, due to local conditions, in that no civilians were in the vicinity."[4]

Intelligence reports from the XX Corps indicate that the 11th Panzer may have already been in the process of moving out of the area. There is no indication that Operation MERZIG effected the German plans, although a week later Field Marshal Model wanted to use his only two reserve panzer divisions (the 9th and 11th) together as a strong armored corps to repulse the American attack across the Roer River. According to the official U.S. Army history of the campaign, he was prevented from doing this because "not enough of the 11th Panzer Division had yet arrived from the Saar-Moselle triangle to justify that arrangement."[5] It is possible that the delay was partially caused by MERZIG, but it could also have stemmed from a simpler explanation, such as the difficulty in moving German troops in an area of strong Allied air superiority.

One possible side benefit of the operation was mentioned in the 23rd afteraction reports. Ten miles to the north, the 2nd Cavalry Group crossed the Moselle River on 21 February. They captured their objective of Wincheringen, along with eight hundred POWs, without much fighting. It was suggested that the Germans thought there were a large number of tanks across the river and gave up more easily than if they knew they were up against a lighter cavalry outfit.

Many of the operations of the 23rd had been taking place around the same area near Luxembourg. This posed somewhat of a risk, as the officers and men of the 23rd were sometimes seen wearing different insignias at different times. About this time, it became a problem for Lieutenant Syracuse of the 3132nd Security Platoon. He had a gregarious and memorable personality, and when he appeared in the area wearing the insignia of a different division each month some of his acquaintances began to question him. His quick-thinking response was to tell them that he really must be a screw-up as he kept getting bounced from unit to unit.

During February, the 23rd's staff developed a standing operating procedure for deception missions.[6] This utilized a code as a type of shorthand to indicate what kind of mission it was and how the troops were to be organized. As an example, the letter "A" indicated the simulation of one infantry combat team, while the letter "F" meant one armored combat command.

Colors were used to indicate what type of operation it was to be: GREEN meant radio, YELLOW indicated decoys, PURPLE meant sonic, and BLACK used special effects. Sonic programs were designated by a numeral: "1" indicated tank sounds, while "4" meant outboard motor sounds. A special "HEATER" code was used to indicate the exact type of sounds: "Q" was one tank, "AH" was tanks in a column. There is no evidence, however, despite all the work involved in developing these charts, that they were ever used.

Slightly more useful were plans for breaking the 23rd up into different detachments for a deception mission. This was very similar to how the unit had been split up for the previous missions, but having it down on paper was a good planning exercise. As an example, when the 23rd was portraying one infantry combat team, the notional service company would be played by the H&S company of the 603rd Engineers, while the notional 1st battalion would be composed of A/603rd, 3rd Platoon of the 406th Engineers, plus a seven truck detachment from the 23rd Signal Company. If the 23rd was simulating the division headquarters and two combat commands of an armored division, CCA would be portrayed by A&D/603rd, 3rd Platoon of the 406th, 3rd Platoon of the 3132nd, and a seven truck detachment from the 23rd Signal Company.

One standard assignment that was finally put down on paper was that Lieutenant George Daley's 1st Platoon of the 406th Engineer Company would normally be called upon to play the Military Police. Although they had no formal training in police work, the men of Daley's platoon had learned how to play the role of an MP so well that they could operate alongside genuine MPs without drawing any suspicion. It was an important lesson that the more a group played a specific role, the more convincing they became.

Chapter 24

Operation LOCHNIVAR
1–11 March 1945

For Operation LOCHNIVAR, the 23rd provided only radio support and advice to help cover the movement of a few divisions in the XX Corps sector on the Saar front.[1] The 26th Infantry Division was shifting to its left to take up the position of the 94th Infantry Division. The hole left by the 26th was to be filled by the 65th Infantry Division, which was new to combat.

When a unit first entered the front lines it was considered most susceptible to attack. In theory, if a new unit took a lot of casualties in its first combat experience, the morale of the unit might be permanently damaged. Therefore the main focus of LOCHNIVAR was to help the green 65th Division take on the appearance of the battle tested 94th. With luck, the Germans might think the 26th and 94th Divisions had simply exchanged sectors, which would give the new troops some breathing space until they had gained some experience on the front line.

The genuine 94th Infantry Division was moved behind the lines for a rest, with the 23rd advising on how to make sure this move was done without giving away its identity. Advice was also given to the 65th on how to assume the guise of the 94th Division (with bumper markings, signs, etc.). The fresh 65th troops relieved the 26th at night under blackout conditions (meaning no unit markings or shoulder patches). The 23rd took part in this aspect of the operation in an advisory role only.

Radio operators of the 23rd Signal Company had infiltrated the 94th Division radio net, and when the genuine units pulled back, the signalmen were to shift right into the notional new position of the 94th (played by the 65th Division). Unfortunately, when the 94th Division was roughly halfway through pulling its men out of the line, the Germans attacked.

The 10th Armored Division had just captured Trier. In reaction, the German 6th SS Mountain Division attacked the 94th Division sector in an

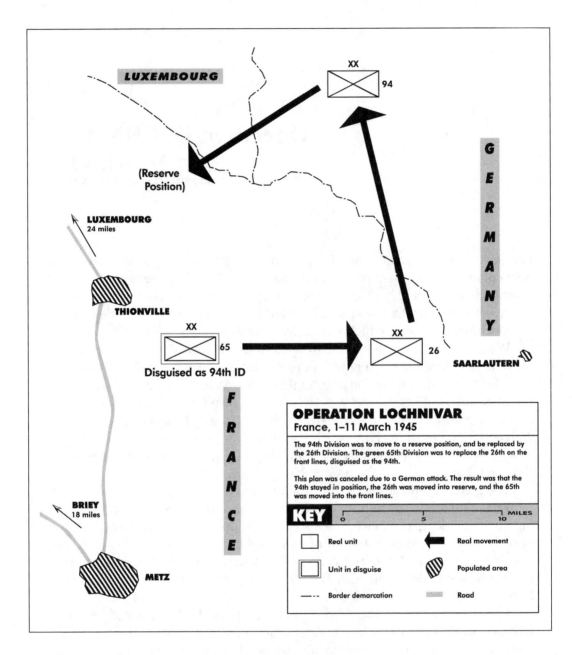

LUXEMBOURG

GERMANY

XX 94

(Reserve Position)

LUXEMBOURG
24 miles

THIONVILLE

XX 65
Disguised as 94th ID

XX 26

SAARLAUTERN

FRANCE

BRIEY
18 miles

METZ

OPERATION LOCHNIVAR
France, 1–11 March 1945

The 94th Division was to move to a reserve position, and be replaced by the 26th Division. The green 65th Division was to replace the 26th on the front lines, disguised as the 94th.

This plan was canceled due to a German attack. The result was that the 94th stayed in position, the 26th was moved into reserve, and the 65th was moved into the front lines.

KEY

| | MILES |
| 0 | 5 | 10 |

☐ Real unit

◀ Real movement

☐ Unit in disguise

⬟ Populated area

–·– Border demarcation

▨ Road

attempt to cut off the supplies of the armored advance. This German unit was the best trained and equipped in the area. They broke through the American lines to cut the highway leading south from Trier. It was actually part of a three-division attack with the German 2nd Mountain Division to the south and the 256th Volksgrenadier Division on the northern flank.[2]

What resulted was a very confusing situation in which some of the 23rd signalmen found themselves under fire. The official reports read that two radios were damaged by shellfire and another two radio teams were cut off behind enemy lines for forty-eight hours. There were rumors at the time that some of the radio teams had been shot up pretty badly, but no records have been located to substantiate this or detail what happened to them.

The largest cut-off unit was the 3rd Battalion of the 302nd Infantry Regiment. Under command of Lieutenant Colonel Otto B. Cloudt, this unit was surrounded, but held out under severe German attacks by the 11th SS Mountain Regiment. All American personnel, including cooks and drivers, were ordered into the lines. The battalion was awarded the Presidential Unit Citation for this action. Somewhere among this beleaguered unit was almost certainly one of the radio teams from the 23rd.

It took two days of counterattacks by the 94th to drive the Germans back and open supply routes to the surrounded men. The relief of the 26th Division then went on as planned, with the 65th entering the lines to the south. Lieutenant Fox later wrote of the operation, "The effects of this double-dealing ruse were never revealed, but if the enemy was half as confused as we were, LOCHNIVAR was a glorious success."[3]

★ ★ ★

In the early weeks of 1945, Colonel Reeder had been working on a plan to reorganize the 23rd. He had submitted it to the 12th Army Group, but had received no feedback. Operation LOCHNIVAR prompted him to renew his efforts and in his official report on the following operation, BOUZONVILLE, he made these comments:

"Through experience an SOP has been worked out for breaking down the unit to successfully simulate an infantry division complete or an armored division complete. However, it is felt that certain changes in organization would facilitate both tactical and administrative problems.

Under the present SOP procedure all organic units of this headquarters are divided into two or more forces and placed under the command of an appointed tactical officer not organically in the chain of command. This results in impractical administrative problems for the duration of an operation and prevents the tactical commander (who has command for the duration of the operation only) from correcting or improving any deficiencies after the completion of the operation. Further, it is not considered good policy to have personnel under one commander for training and another for operations. Attention is invited to the proposed T/O&E for a deception unit forwarded to the War Department by this headquarters 4 February 1945 which eliminated the above mentioned objections."[4]

Reeder had tried to reorganize the 23rd back in England without success, but gave it another try after the operations of 1944. This time he suggested a new plan for a deception unit of seventeen hundred men that mimicked a standard regiment with three battalions. The organization would have a headquarters of twenty-nine officers and one hundred and ninety-five enlisted men. A service company of nine officers, two warrant officers, and one hundred and thirty-three enlisted men would provide all support functions. Internal communications for the unit would be provided by a signals service company of eight officers and one hundred and sixty-two men. A detachment of three officers and thirty-six medics would take care of any medical needs.

The key to the new organization was to be a new type of unit called a "deception battalion." The 23rd would have three of these, and each would be composed of a headquarters company and three deception line companies. Each line company would have its own headquarters, maintenance section, special effects section, deceptive radio section, and three platoons. Each of these platoons would be composed of a headquarters, with one officer and thirteen men, and three squads, each containing one sergeant and eight enlisted men.

A key point for Reeder was that he felt such a unit should be commanded by a general officer. He thought that a high rank was necessary in order to work with other headquarters, and to attain the respect of units temporarily placed under his command. Reeder wrote, "Experience has demonstrated that rank is essential in time of war to secure officers with experience necessary to portray faithfully the units represented, and to maintain contacts with Army Groups, armies, corps and divisions with which operations are planned and conducted."[5]

A few of the officers in the 23rd thought that having a general about would only hamper deception operations. They felt there were enough nameless colonels in the army that no one paid them much regard, but if a general arrived people took notice and might ask questions about his unit. Both Lieutenant Colonel Truly (the executive officer) and Lieutenant Colonel Simenson (the S-3) refused to support his recommendation, much to Reeder's apparent fury.[6]

It had long been thought by men in the 23rd that Reeder resented having been assigned to the unit. A combat command was the best path to getting a general's star, and in the 23rd the issue of promotion seemed out of his hands. It did not help that Reeder's brother, William O. Reeder (West Point Class of 1917), had recently been promoted to major general in the Signal Corps, possibly stirring some sibling rivalry. The war was starting to run down, and Reeder may have felt that this was his last chance to get a star. The failure to support his commander's proposal was to have severe implications for Simenson.

At the end of LOCHNIVAR, Lieutenant Colonel Day, the antiaircraft officer, was transferred to the European Civil Affairs Division. The army was now deep into Germany and had discovered that they needed many more civil affairs officers to run the military governments set up in each occupied country. Colonel Simenson replaced him as antiaircraft officer, and in turn was replaced as S-3 of the unit by Major Bridges.

This was actually a demotion for Simenson. To be reduced from operations officer (S-3) to antiaircraft officer (when he was trained to be an infantryman) was a major reduction in authority. Simenson felt this was the direct result of his refusal to agree with Reeder's plan to reorganize the 23rd and to require a one-star general as commander. Major Bridges was a close friend of Reeder, but his promotion was seen as more of a way to punish Simenson than reward Bridges. Simenson realized that his time with the 23rd was rapidly coming to an end and began to look for an opportunity to transfer to another unit.[7]

Chapter 25

Operation BOUZONVILLE
11–13 March 1945

Operation BOUZONVILLE was the last mission in the XX Corps area, but the most costly in terms of casualties.[1] The task given to the 23rd was to draw attention away from the genuine build-up of forces between Saarburg and Trier. Instead, the Germans were to be shown a notional build-up in preparation for an attack to the south, opposite Saarlautern.

This would be done by the 23rd portraying the 80th Infantry Division assembling in a position to the rear of the genuine 65th Infantry Division. On the morning of the genuine attack in the north, the 65th Division would draw more attention to its own area with a limited ground attack. This feint would appear larger than it was through an artillery bombardment enlarged with artillery decoys and flash simulators.

The 23rd Signal Company detachments left Briey on 10 March for the locations of their notional units. At 1350 on 11 March, the notional 80th Division reported into the XX Corps command net. The 80th Division network began operating at 1500, and the artillery network at 1530. Transmissions were limited to periodic radio checks.

The rest of the 23rd once again broke down into the notional components of the division. Colonel Reeder was in command of the 80th Division Headquarters at Bouzonville; Colonel Simenson commanded the 317th Infantry Regiment at Filstroff; Major Raggio the 318th Infantry at Ittersdorf; and Captain Seale the 319th Infantry at Dalem. Captain Rebh ran the 305th Engineer Battalion at Brettnach, and Major Hooper the 80th Division Special Troops at Hestroff. Colonel Mayo commanded the detachment portraying the 80th Division Artillery Headquarters and the three divisional artillery battalions at Pickard, Germany.

The assigned detachments moved to their locations, and on the afternoon of 11 March began the standard program of special effects. Shoulder patches were worn, bumper markings displayed, trucks routed to supply points, and MPs patrolled the region.

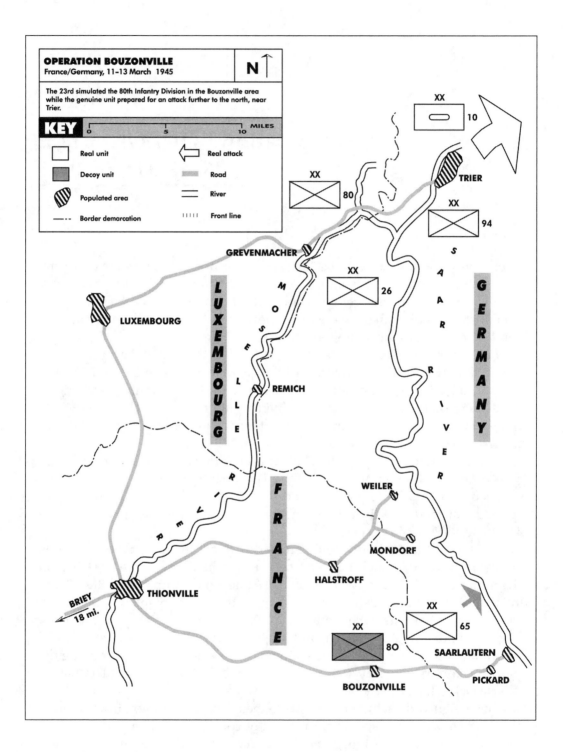

OPERATION BOUZONVILLE
France/Germany, 11–13 March 1945

The 23rd simulated the 80th Infantry Division in the Bouzonville area while the genuine unit prepared for an attack further to the north, near Trier.

KEY

☐ Real unit	⇦ Real attack
▨ Decoy unit	▭ Road
▨ Populated area	= River
–·–· Border demarcation	‖‖‖ Front line

MILES
0   5   10

N ↑

XX 10

XX 80

TRIER

XX 94

GREVENMACHER

XX 26

LUXEMBOURG

LUXEMBOURG

MOSELLE

REMICH

GERMANY

SAAR RIVER

WEILER

MONDORF

FRANCE

HALSTROFF

BRIEY 18 mi.

THIONVILLE

XX 65

XX 80

SAARLAUTERN

BOUZONVILLE

PICKARD

Decoy artillery positions were installed around Pickard, Germany. The three 105mm artillery battalions of the 80th Division (319th, 314th, and 905th Field Artillery Battalions) were placed so they could be used to support either the notional 80th Division, or an attack of the 65th Division. Flash simulators were used coinciding with the genuine fire of the 65th Division's artillery. The Germans did not attempt counter-battery fire at the decoy positions, but did increase the amount of harassing and interdiction fire in the area.

At noon on 12 March, German artillery struck near a group of 23rd men near Pickard. There was nothing special about this shelling, which appeared to be typical harassing fire. Nevertheless, Captain Thomas G. Wells, the 23rd Headquarters Company commander, and Staff Sergeant George C. Peddle, a radio platoon sergeant, were killed. Two other officers, Captain Raynor and Lieutenant Line (D/603rd), along with thirteen other enlisted men, were wounded. Lieutenant Adolphus Simpson took over as Headquarters Company commander the next day. This was the largest number of casualties suffered by the 23rd during the war.[2]

Pfc. Jacob Goldberg of the medical detachment ventured out into the artillery fire to help the wounded. For risking his own life to help others he was awarded the Bronze Star for valor. The 603rd Adjutant Gil Seltzer recalls working with Captain Raynor to assist the wounded men, only to finally notice that Raynor himself was wounded in the back with blood dripping down his field jacket.

On the night of 12 March, the 3132nd played a sonic program indicating a battalion of tanks moving up to the west bank of the Saar River, two miles north of Saarlautern. After they finished, the sonic cars withdrew. The spoof radio transmissions ceased at midnight on 12 March. All elements of the 23rd faded away during the night and returned to Briey by infiltration.

The genuine 80th Division attacked to the north on the morning of 13 March. They reported only light resistance. The XX Corps felt that complete tactical success had been achieved and were very pleased with the results.

Chapter 26

Operation VIERSEN
18 March–1 April 1945

Operation VIERSEN was by far the largest and most successful mission given to the 23rd Special Troops. It involved helping the Allies cross the final major obstacle before Germany: the Rhine River. Once the Allies had crossed the Rhine, there was nothing for the Germans to use as a natural defensive line, so they considered holding the river critical. The key to stopping an American crossing would be to find out, in advance, where the attempt was to be made, heavily defend the opposite bank, and have reinforcements close by for an immediate counterattack.

The 21st Army Group's Rhine crossing was given the code name PLUNDER. The two main aspects of PLUNDER were: a crossing in the north, coordinated with the airborne drop of two parachute divisions, named Operation VARSITY; and the Ninth Army's crossing farther to the south, code-named FLASHPOINT.

The deception aspect of FLASHPOINT was Operation EXPLOIT. The operation involved not just the 23rd, but the entire Ninth Army. This was the first time that the 23rd was able to plan for, and use, an entire army for a deception. Operation VIERSEN was the section of EXPLOIT that directly involved the 23rd, although the entire EXPLOIT deception was planned and executed with the assistance of the staff of the 23rd Special Troops. Lieutenant Colonel Truly, one of the liaison officers, was sent to Ninth Army Headquarters to oversee the operation on the army level.

EXPLOIT was designed to deceive the enemy as to the exact time and place of the Rhine River crossing. The plan was to make the enemy think that no part of the Ninth Army would be prepared to launch an offensive prior to 1 April 1945. The basic idea was to "conceal the genuine concentrations of troops and supplies in the XVI Corps area and build up a simulated attacking force in the XIII Corps zone."[1] The notional build-up of troops would be between Dusseldorf and the Erft River. Key to the plan was staging the build-

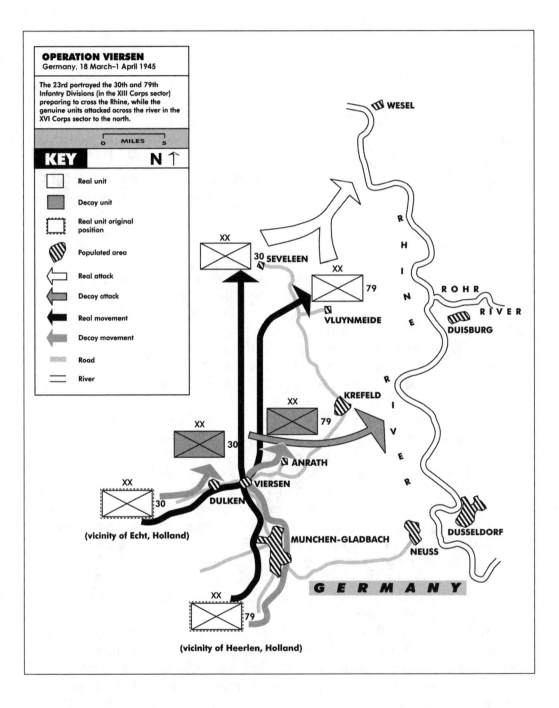

OPERATION VIERSEN
Germany, 18 March–1 April 1945

The 23rd portrayed the 30th and 79th Infantry Divisions (in the XIII Corps sector) preparing to cross the Rhine, while the genuine units attacked across the river in the XVI Corps sector to the north.

MILES
0   5

KEY   N ↑

Real unit

Decoy unit

Real unit original position

Populated area

Real attack

Decoy attack

Real movement

Decoy movement

Road

River

WESEL

SEVELEEN
30

79
VLUYNMEIDE

RHINE

ROHR
RIVER
DUISBURG

KREFELD

79

RIVER

ANRATH

30

VIERSEN

DULKEN

30

(vicinity of Echt, Holland)

MUNCHEN-GLADBACH

NEUSS

DUSSELDORF

GERMANY

79

(vicinity of Heerlen, Holland)

up in a way to appear that the Americans would not be ready to cross the Rhine before 1 April.

Captain Kelly, the intelligence officer of the 23rd, put together an estimate of German intelligence capabilities on 19 March 1945.[2] He found that the German Luftwaffe carried out daily reconnaissance flights throughout the area, weather permitting. Most of these flights were made by jets or fast fighters, which indicated that such reconnaissance relied upon aerial photography and not observations made by the pilots. Most of the flights were carried out in the early morning or late afternoon. The long shadows caused by the sun at these times made aerial photographs easier to interpret. Single aircraft also flew over the Allied lines at night and dropped flares to photograph the area below. This technique was considered very good for spotting road movements. Kelly warned, "German photo equipment is excellent and their photo interpreting methods are expected to be adequate."[3]

Ground agents, both civilian and military, were also known to be active throughout the Ninth Army's area. Not only military personnel in civilian clothes, but also women and children were to be considered potential agents. The Germans used ground agents to identify units by noting bumper markings, shoulder patches, signs, etc. Several incidents of tapped Allied telephone lines had been reported. Communication between such agents and the German Army was considered excellent, and there was evidence that there were telephone connections across the Rhine. In short, anything a German civilian observed or heard on the west bank would probably be swiftly communicated to the German Army on the east bank.

German radio intelligence was considered the most active and accurate aspect of German intelligence. Due to the seriousness of the military situation, Kelly felt that the Germans had probably intensified their radio interception efforts in the Ninth Army area in order to determine where the Americans would try to cross.

To counter German intelligence gathering, it was recommended that inflatable decoys be erected at night or under cover. Maintenance of these decoys had to be constant to prevent them from sagging, and any defective decoys had to be replaced at once. Tracks had to be made in the ground near decoys where appropriate, and decoy vehicles had to be shifted periodically so they did not appear to remain in place.

It was recommended that decoys were to be used only in areas that had been totally cleared of all civilians, and any unauthorized personnel later found in such areas were to be arrested and held until the actual crossing had taken place. This included anyone in an Allied military uniform who was acting suspiciously in a controlled zone. Added to this were the standard rules about not talking about the deception operation publicly, and making sure all indications of the genuine units (including addresses on mail) were kept hidden.

Lieutenant General William H. Simpson's Ninth Army was composed of three corps. From north to south they were the XVI Corps (the 35th and 75th Infantry Divisions and the 8th Armored Division), the XIX Corps (the 29th, 79th, and 83rd Infantry Divisions and the 2nd Armored Division), and the XIII Corps (the 30th, 84th, and 102nd Infantry Divisions and the 5th Armored Division). The terrain in the XVI Corps sector was the best for a crossing of the wide river, so the main assault would be made there. To strengthen the XVI Corps, the two most experienced units from the other two corps, the 30th and 79th Infantry Divisions, were to be shifted to the XVI Corps for the actual crossing.

To conceal the build-up for the assault, each of the three corps was directed to help in the deception. In the XVI Corps sector, the goal was to make everything look as though no attack was planned for that area. The 30th and 79th Divisions were to be moved in from their river crossing training area under strict security conditions. Artillery positions and engineer equipment parks were carefully camouflaged. The artillery units from the two southern corps that were sent to the XVI Corps to support the genuine crossing were required to fire their registration rounds mixed in with what appeared to be standard harassing fire so as not to draw any attention. These artillery units were to quietly leave their original positions in the XIX and XIII Corps at night, allowing decoy equipment to be installed in their place.

In the center, the XIX Corps was the least affected by the operation, but was instructed to keep activity in the front lines as close as possible to that seen in the other two corps sectors. Artillery units pulled from the XIX Corps to support the XVI Corps assault were instructed to leave their gun positions intact and camouflaged. The 83rd Infantry Division was pulled back to fill in the area left vacant by the 30th Division. Other than keeping up a similar appearance to the rest of the Ninth Army, this sector was relatively quiet during the operation.

Tank destroyers were considered very useful for a river crossing because they could be used to accurately fire at specific targets across the river. Emplacements for these vehicles were constructed on the bank of the river in the XVI Corps sector to support the genuine crossing. To make this activity seem normal, the same types of emplacements were constructed, at logical points, all along the army front. This was part of a pattern of having anything out of the ordinary that took place in the actual crossing area duplicated along the entire Ninth Army front.

Radio silence was ordered for all units not in contact with the enemy. The entire Ninth Army was told how during Operation GRENADE the positions of two divisions were disclosed to the enemy by the interception of individual tank-to-tank radio conversations. Radio silence was not just for the larger headquarters units, but was just as important for the short-range sets in the lower echelons. There were to be no radio transmissions unless a unit actually became involved in combat with the Germans.

Although the German air force was extremely weak, American antiaircraft units would play a major role in this deception. During Operation ELEPHANT it had been realized that almost as important as giving the Germans a decoy to look at was making them think the Americans did not want it observed by protecting it with antiaircraft guns. The attempt was made to continue the typical amount of antiaircraft defenses in the three corps areas, but make it appear that there was more to hide in the XIII Corps area.

The 19th Antiaircraft Group was in charge of air defenses in the XIII Corps. To beef up its presence, a notional 90mm battalion position was added through the use of decoys and dummy emplacements. Each of the lighter antiaircraft automatic weapons battalions constructed an additional two batteries worth of gun positions to inflate their strength. At random intervals during the night, the antiaircraft guns in the XIII Corps were to fire off barrages into the sky as if they thought a German aircraft was nearby. Such incidents were not uncommon and would point out to the Germans the areas the Americans were protecting.

Antiaircraft units also possessed searchlights to help locate planes at night. Such bright lights could also blind or disorient pilots caught in the beam. For the Rhine crossing, many searchlights were positioned along the riverbank. These lights created what was known as "artificial moonlight" by bouncing light off low clouds. This gave a diffuse dim light that allowed work, or patrolling, to continue on the ground. The searchlights were also to be used to harass the Germans on the east bank by blinding known enemy positions. They could also to be used to light up anything seen floating in the river (possibly a German patrol). These searchlight techniques were put into effect along the entire corps front so as not to attract undue attention to any one sector.

Air support from the XXIX Tactical Air Command was carefully balanced between the genuine and the notional crossing areas. The medical corps aided in the deceptive build-up by only installing one evacuation hospital in the genuine crossing sector, while moving more medical facilities into the notional crossing area.

Most of the actual deception work occurred in the XIII Corps sector. This was where the bulk of the 23rd ran Operation VIERSEN to simulate the notional 30th and 79th Divisions preparing for a river crossing. Engineer preparations for the genuine crossing, such as roads and bridge approaches constructed in the XVI Corps zone, were required to be matched or exceeded in the XIII Corps area. Patrolling was ordered to be at least one half greater in the XIII Corps area than in the XVI Corps area. The XVI Corps staff was daily required to inform their counterparts in the XIII Corps of the amount of patrolling in their sector so it could be matched or exceeded. Notional traffic control point radio networks in the XIII Corps sector were to broadcast reports of heavy vehicle movement.

General Simpson was very concerned about the security of the deception plan and issued the following order: "This information will be disseminated to the minimum number of subordinate commanders and staff officers to enable adequate implementation of this plan. A list of these individuals will be maintained at each Corps Headquarters."[4]

The plan for the XIII Corps consisted of five phases. Phase one, lasting from the middle of March until the genuine crossing in the north, consisted of a general build-up of engineer equipment and supply dumps, construction of approach roads for the notional crossing, constant patrolling, employment of artificial moonlight, and a build-up of artillery positions.

Phase two, taking place during the six days before the genuine crossing, involved the notional movement of two infantry divisions into the XIII Corps zone, and the protection of the area with genuine antiaircraft weapons. Antiaircraft barrages would be fired into the sky when no planes were in the vicinity so it would appear they were trying to protect something.

Phase three was to take place on the day of the XVI's crossing in the north.

Near Anrath a cluster of vehicles has been carefully positioned in a wooded area to appear as a poorly camouflaged unit. The inflatable decoys took a beating from the large amount of falling antiaircraft fragments in the area. Men from other units, including the 135th AAA Battalion, were used to help patch up the deflating decoys. They were told to never talk about what they had done.

Artillery within range would support the genuine crossing, including fire from tank destroyers, 90mm antiaircraft guns, and tanks on the riverbank. This would prevent any German movement along the river.

Phase four was to last until eights days after the XVI Corps crossing. This phase would see the final preparations for a notional crossing in the XIII Corps area. One (genuine) infantry division would move up to the Krefeld area and more artillery positions would be constructed. Much like Operation FORTITUDE, the Americans wanted the Germans to think the notional preparations were real and a second assault was coming.

The entire EXPLOIT plan would culminate eight days after the genuine crossing (expected to be 1 April) when the XIII Corps would conduct what would, hopefully, appear to be the preliminaries to a river crossing, including artillery preparatory fires and movement of troops to the riverbank. The 387th AA Automatic Weapons Battalion would rake the area across the river, in the vicinity of Ilverich, with its M-15 quadruple .50-caliber machine guns.

While the XVI Corps had to keep their preparations for the river crossing concealed, it was the XIII Corps that had to make it appear they were the unit chosen for the main assault. Four battalions of artillery (the 2nd, 787th, 608th, and 557th, the latter with 155mm guns) were quietly shifted north to take up new positions in the XVI Corps sector where they could fire support missions for the genuine crossing. Decoys, erected at night after the real weapons were removed, replaced the guns. The remaining genuine artillery units in the XIII Corps would continue to fire harassing missions at a consistent rate.

The engineer plan for EXPLOIT was quite impressive. The 1141st Engineer Combat Group, with two additional camouflage platoons (B/604th Engineer Camouflage Battalion and C/84th Engineer Camouflage Battalion), was in charge of the simulated engineer build-up in XIII Corps area. They set up both real and decoy supply dumps throughout the area. All the available captured German bridging equipment was utilized to create an impression of a large build-up of river crossing material. All civilians were evacuated from these areas and the supply dumps were put under 24-hour guard, not so much to prevent sabotage, but to keep any German agents from discovering that the space under some of the camouflage netting was empty or filled with decoy material.

The 604th Camouflage Engineer Battalion was no stranger to deception. Back in January and February 1944 they had constructed one hundred and fifty-one metal decoy landing craft in England as part of the build-up for FORTITUDE. Each decoy craft was welded from over fifty-two thousand parts. For working twenty-four-hour days and completing that mission ahead of schedule, the unit received a Meritorious Service Plaque.[5]

The 7th Engineer Light Pontoon Company was directed to bring its boats during daylight hours on 17 March to the engineer dump at Krefeld. It was followed the next day by the equipment of the 982nd Engineer Treadway

One of the decoy artillery positions designed to draw German attention to the notional crossing area. A line of expended shell casings helps to complete the image of a functioning gun pit.

Bridge Company. This equipment was then heavily camouflaged in a secure equipment depot, then at night quietly withdrawn to the rear. The next day it was brought up again in the daylight to the same dump. The units involved were ordered to repeat this as many times as possible before 1 April to portray a continual increase in the amount of bridging equipment arriving in the sector. Inside the Krefeld engineer dump, camouflage engineers set up a production line to construct decoy assault boats and pontoons out of canvas-covered frameworks.

All available engineer battalions with no other specific tasks were ordered to construct or improve roads leading to possible bridge or ferry sites centered on a crossing site at Uerdingen. This was to start on 17 April, and continue after the genuine assault in the north, by developing more roads, selecting and marking routes for assault boats to be brought up to the river, and by increased training in boat handling. Seven to eight days after the XVI Corps crossing in the north, the engineers of the XIII Corps were to begin bringing their boats and ferry components up to the river in anticipation of the notional river crossing scheduled for 1 April. Units were to begin assembling as much bridge equipment as possible, including any floating bridge sections that could be put together in sheltered harbors along the Rhine.

In addition to captured German equipment and any decoys that could be made, the engineers were provided with two hundred assault boats, four Bailey bridge rafts, one thousand feet of floating Bailey bridge, two hundred fifty-gallon drums, one thousand camouflage nets, and twenty-five outboard

242

motors as props. The genuine equipment might also prove useful for a fast crossing if the German defenses collapsed on the far bank.

Operation VIERSEN was the part of Operation EXPLOIT that involved the 23rd Special Troops simulating two infantry divisions (the 30th and the 79th) in the XIII Corps area. The genuine divisions had been involved in river-crossing training behind the lines on the Maas River. The 30th was training at Massey, and the 79th between Sittard and Aachen. There they should have drawn German attention because such training would certainly involve them in the forthcoming Rhine assault crossing. The two genuine divisions would move out, quietly at night, to secret locations in the XVI Corps area. There they would wait camouflaged, without any markings to identify them, until they would take place in the genuine 24 March crossing of the Rhine.

To fool the Germans as to the actual location of these two assault divisions, the 23rd was given the task of holding them in place at the Maas River training area in Holland. Then the 23rd would notionally move them into the XIII Corps area to prepare for the build-up to the 1 April notional crossing. The 23rd did not have enough men to adequately portray two entire divisions, so two rifle battalions from the 84th and 102nd Infantry Divisions, as well as the 430th Antiaircraft Weapons Battalion, were assigned to increase the number of troops visible in the deception. To increase security, the 23rd Special Troops was given the code name CANAL for this one specific operation. On 17 March, the 23rd divided into two groups at Sittard, Holland, to simulate both the 30th and 79th Infantry Divisions.

The notional 30th Infantry Division was under command of Lieutenant Colonel Schroeder. Assisting him were Lieutenant Colonel Watson (portraying the assistant division commander), Major David Haviland (chief of staff), Major Raggio (G-3), and Captains Hotchkiss (G-2), Dick (G-4), and Seale (G-5). The three notional combat teams were commanded by Captains Skelton (117th), Rebh (119th), and Comulada (120th). The division signal officer was portrayed by Lieutenant Wanerus. Bob Hiller of the 3132nd had the role of commander of the 823rd Tank Destroyer Battalion. For troops, Schroeder was given the bulk of the 23rd Headquarters, A&B/603rd Engineers, the 406th Engineers (less two platoons), half of the 23rd Signal Company, and the 1st and 2nd Platoons of the 3132nd.

To increase the number of men in the notional division, the entire 1st Battalion, 334th Infantry Regiment, 84th Infantry Division, and Batteries C&D of the 430th Antiaircraft Battalion were attached.[6] These additional troops were used to guard the area and help create the appearance of an actual division (normally about thirteen thousand men). The antiaircraft units were to not only make it appear that the Americans had something to hide, but to keep German reconnaissance aircraft at a high altitude where minor inconsistencies would not be noticed.

Schroeder's notional 30th Division began portraying the unit after it had

*The two aircraft are inflatable decoys, and marker panels have been set out to simu-
late a typical landing strip. The men setting up these airstrips had to be careful to
select ground that a plane could actually land on, in case a genuine aircraft spotted
the markings and tried to land.*

moved from the Maas River training area on 17 March 1945. The genuine 30th
Division moved to a secret location in the XVI Corps area under strict blackout conditions. Every vehicle was checked to be sure no unit markings or
patches were visible before they were allowed to enter the corps area. A new,
temporary code name for the division was authorized for the move, and all
troops were cautioned against letting anyone discover their true identity.

Starting on 18 March, the notional 30th Division sent advance parties and
billeting parties to the vicinity of Dulken, Germany. The genuine 30th
Division's route of march passed close by the 23rd assembly area at Sittard. As
the genuine unit convoys went past, the deception troops took on their identity. Notional traffic control points reported the progress of the deception
troops, while the genuine units were under strict radio silence. As the 30th
Division moved out of Echt, it was replaced in the river crossing training area
by the genuine 83rd Infantry Division (pulled back from XIX Corps).

Upon arriving at Dulken, Schroeder's men concentrated on simulating a
unit practicing river crossings on a local lake. The sonic troops were used to
play motorboat noises and other sounds of river crossing practice on the

nights of 20–22 March. The three notional combat teams of the 30th Division (the 117th, 119th, and 120th) were responsible for erecting decoys in their respective bivouac areas. In addition, the 119th was in charge of security for the lake area. The 117th was responsible for erecting camouflage netting at the edge of the lake to portray hidden boats and bridge equipment. A landing strip with two decoy liaison aircraft was set up in the division area, and each combat team commander was in charge of making sure genuine vehicles made fresh tracks around their installations. Observation aircraft were made available to the unit commanders to check their handiwork from the air.

Each notional division was given a large quantity of inflatable decoys and fifty-eight camouflage nets. The list of decoys for each division included: five liaison aircraft, twenty 105mm howitzers, twenty-three Stuart tanks, sixty-five Sherman tanks, one hundred and five 1-ton trailers, eighty-five 2½-ton trucks with top, and sixty 2½-ton trucks without tops.

To increase security, civilians were evacuated from the area and the word "authorized" was added to the password. The daily password and countersign used in the sector (such as " free" and "ransom") would become "free authorized" with the countersign "ransom" in the secure area. At first all mail was carefully handled so no envelopes bearing an incorrect unit designation would give away the game. All outgoing mail was to have the genuine return address of the 23rd added to the envelope only at the last minute in the orderly room and immediately placed in the outgoing mailbox. All incoming mail, which would bear the correct 23rd unit address, was to be read and then burned in the place of distribution. As the operation progressed, mail was eventually suspended. All medical problems, except emergencies, were to be handled within the deception unit so as few personnel as possible would be involved.

The full range of special effects was used. Shoulder patches were worn, over two hundred division signs were posted in the area, and properly marked vehicles were used to maintain the normal traffic circulation to supply and water points and corps headquarters. Military police painted the division insignia above the "MP" on their helmets. Radio nets and telephone wire circuits were set up connecting the 30th Division Headquarters to the divisional elements and the XIII Corps.

All officers playing roles in the notional division not only wore the correct 30th Division insignia, but also the rank of the position they were portraying. This led to one interesting situation with Captain Rebh. He wore colonel's eagles while playing the role of the commander of the 119th Infantry Regiment. Three different times, men who had been senior to him at West Point came to his command post looking for the genuine unit. Having last heard Rebh was a captain in an engineer unit, they just could not believe their eyes to find him now outranking them as a colonel commanding an infantry regiment. Rebh had to politely send them on their way without disclosing what was going on, but later was amused to find they all asked a sergeant on the way out, "What the hell happened with Rebh?" The quick-witted reply was, "Well sir, you know how it is in war, if you're at the right place at the right time . . ."[7]

On the night of 23–24 March, the notional 30th Division increased reconnaissance activity to the east, toward the Rhine. This was to indicate a future movement through the 84th Infantry Division sector to the Rhine River crossing areas. They did not actually move the units, but gave every indication they were preparing for the 1 April crossing.

After the operation, Schroeder wrote that in the future he would prefer to have the genuine unit move into the bivouac area, then slip out piecemeal as the deception troops took over. However, he did mention that the genuine 30th Division was very cooperative in the deceptive move. He also noted that the "attached infantry battalion and antiaircraft troops were extremely valuable and enthusiastically supported the operation."[8]

The notional "CRISIS CP" (Command Post of the 119th Infantry Regiment) was set up in this restaurant selling both Coca-Cola and Tivoli beer. The notional 119th Regiment was commanded by Captain George Rebh during Operation VIERSEN, who had a hard time explaining to passing West Point classmates why he was suddenly a full colonel commanding an infantry regiment.

The notional 79th Infantry Division was commanded by Lieutenant Colonel Simenson, with the assistance of Lieutenant Colonel Seaman (G-3), Majors Kelly (G-2) and Vincent (engineer officer), Captains Sidwell (CO 315th CT) and Cowardin (CO Division Artillery), and Lieutenants Seltzer (G-1) and Reeder (G-4). Simenson was given the H&S Company from the 603rd, C&D/603rd Engineers, the 2nd and 3rd platoons of the 406th Engineers, the other half of the 23rd Signal Company, and the 3132nd Signal Company (less two platoons). Attached to this group was the 2nd Battalion, 405th Infantry Regiment, 102nd Infantry Division (commanded by Lieutenant Colonel B. M. Byrant), and Batteries A&B of the 430th Antiaircraft Battalion under Captain Cameron.

The genuine 79th Division moved under strict blackout conditions to its destination in the XVI Corps area over the period of 18–22 March. Movement took place at a rate of approximately a regiment a day. The regiments' route of march passed within five miles of Simenson's men, who then assumed their identity. In turn, each notional detachment moved to the XIII Corps area, while their genuine counterparts went north to the XVI Corps. The notional division commander and an advance party had arrived first in the assigned area on 16 March to select billets for their men. They made sure they were seen examining the area and making certain it was evacuated of all civilians.

The remainder of the notional division arrived between 18 and 22 March. The sonic cars were used to play the sounds of truck columns at night, between 1930 and 2330, around the local villages. In the daytime, sonic programs of sawing, loading and unloading gas cans, jackhammers, engines, and bulldozers were played in the woods.

Enclosed farmyards were used to display decoys in the 313th and 314th Combat Team zones. The 315th was located in a leafless patch of trees. These locations provided some cover for the decoys from ground observation, but allowed them to be seen by aerial reconnaissance. The decoys were moved daily to prevent them from appearing too static, but in no case were they to be placed next to real vehicles in case the slight differences were noted. Tracks were made in the ground, but only after the area had been checked for mines. Men were to always be on duty at each site containing inflatable decoys, in case any began leaking air and needed to be immediately replaced. Liaison aircraft were used to check the view from the air, with the results being very satisfactory.

The typical special effects program of patches, signs, and markings were put into play. Civilians were evacuated from the region, and numerous telephone lines, both real and non-operational, were laid. It was assumed that eavesdroppers listened in on all conversations over phone lines, so the names of the genuine unit commanders were used in all conversations. The men from the 405th Infantry Regiment were used to visit local towns, after being carefully briefed on what they were allowed to say. Men from both notional divisions were trucked to the corps shower facility in Dulken.

The enclosed farmyards of Germany were perfect for setting up decoy installations. Such displays were hidden from ground view, and easy to guard against enemy agents. Genuine vehicles would be parked in locations visible to passing traffic. Note the large white stars and aerial recognition markers in use at this stage of the war, when the German Air Force could only observe, but not attack.

The notional Provost Marshall's office of the 79th Infantry Division was set up in the town of Anrath, allowing the German civilians a place to complain about the local American troops. It was known that the German Army had telephone communication with agents on the west bank of the Rhine, and they could not help but notice and report such offices.

The men acting as members of the combat division were encouraged to frequently do their laundry and hang it outside to dry, or air, in visible locations. The billets were in German buildings, so not only were the men cautioned not to loot civilian property but not to consume any food found on the premises in case it was spoiled or poisoned. Everyone was cautioned to avoid dropping trash, as a discarded piece of paper might contain just the information an enemy agent was looking for. The men were also issued insect powder (DDT) because of the fleas and lice found in several buildings.

Simenson's goal was to place genuine vehicles and weapons around the perimeter of his area, with the inflatable decoys and camouflaged positions at the center. Three real 57mm antitank guns from the 405th were shifted about the perimeter of the area in places where passing civilians would see them. The two batteries from the antiaircraft unit were positioned outside the secured zone. They not only fired at enemy aircraft, but also provided a few nighttime barrages to draw attention to the area.

Lieutenant Colonel Seaman was sent to the Ninth Army liaison officer's briefing to put in an appearance as a 79th Division representative in that sector. Each notional division kept one or two unmarked vehicles available for trips that would not normally be made by such a division.

On 23 and 24 March, reconnaissance parties were sent into the 11th Cavalry positions to scout for approaches to the Rhine River. Normally such identifiers as shoulder patches would have been removed by such parties, but in this case a few were conveniently left on to allow for easy identification of their division. Units from Combat Team 314 were to recon the northern half, CT 315 the southern half, and CT 313 the entire zone.

The radio aspect of VIERSEN was the most complex ever attempted by the 23rd. Radio communications were simulated for two separate divisions (and their links to corps headquarters), and for the radio traffic indicating the movement of the two units. On 14 March, the 23rd Signal Company was divided into three groups—two for each notional division and a third for the traffic control net.

With Lieutenant Colonel Truly overseeing things at Ninth Army Head-

A command post guard from the 79th Infantry Division is simulated outside Anrath. The sign shows the tactical marking of the division's 312th Field Artillery Battalion. This soldier has been issued the newer M43 field jacket and combat boots, to match that worn by the majority of the genuine division.

A detailed map of the routes of the notional 30th Division (headed to Anrath) and the 79th Division (headed to Dulken). Every aspect of this deceptive move was choreographed, but the men of the 23rd were encouraged to take advantage of local events, such as traffic accidents, to add more realism to their radio reports.

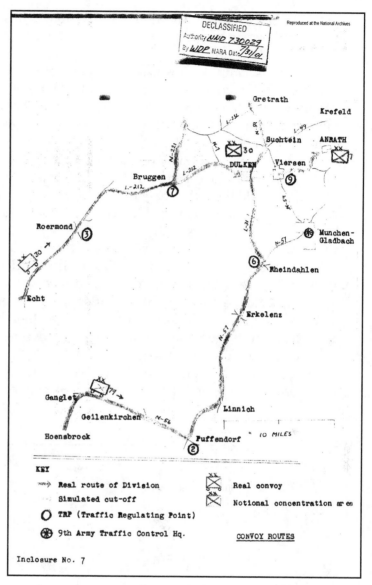

Inclosure No. 7

quarters, the radio teams had full cooperation in getting call signs and frequencies. Just as important, there was no problem having radio silence ordered for the entire XIII Corps area from 16–18 March. The German intercept units could not miss such a large unit suddenly going quiet and it would help draw their attention to this sector.

The two notional division radio detachments began transmitting in the Maas River training area under the guise of the 30th and 79th Divisions. Many of these messages were done in the clear or in the weak SLIDEX code. These messages were to give the appearance of a division in an assembly area preparing for a move. The notional division radios went quiet during the move, but began transmitting again when the two notional units arrived in the XIII Corps sector.

The traffic control net was strung along the route from the Maas training site to the XIII Corps. These posts kept the entire network informed of road conditions and the location of various convoys. This was a key aspect to convincing the Germans where the two divisions were going. Normally the Ninth Army was very good in terms of coding such transmissions. In this case, a chance was taken and much of the information was sent in the clear or with SLIDEX. Other armies had operated in this same way, so it was hoped that the Germans would think the change was due to poorly trained, or lax, operators.

The traffic control net broadcasted the actual times in which the convoys of the genuine units passed by checkpoints. If the Germans doubled-checked this information against enemy agents in that area, everything would match. When these real convoys reached the Traffic Regulating Points (TRPs) manned by the 23rd, they diverted to the north. No further transmissions were sent as to the location of the genuine units as they entered the XVI Corps sector. From then on, the 23rd radio teams used their knowledge of the length and speeds of the genuine columns to construct phony messages that fit into place with their local conditions.

To add an air of authenticity to the transmissions, no script was prepared in advance. Each operator was given a road map of the region showing the

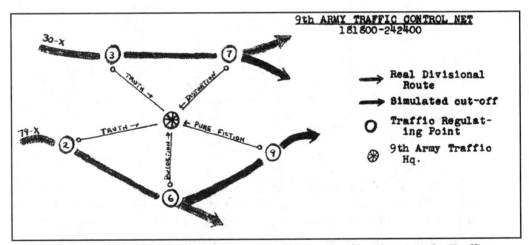

This is an original drawing from the Operation VIERSEN *files showing the Traffic Control Radio Network. The 30th and 79th Divisions traveled along the route until diverting to the north at traffic regulating points 6 and 7. Radio intelligence would indicate these units had continued to the west, where the decoy installations would offer confirmation.*

convoy routes, an information sheet (containing call signs, frequencies, SLIDEX keys, genuine convoy information, officer names, and even the convoy code numbers chalked onto the side of the genuine vehicles), and Ninth Army traffic movement forms.

Each day from 1030–1200, the crews of the TRPs made a reconnaissance of the area in which they operated. This helped ensure the transmissions would be as close to the truth as possible. The first two TRPs in the net (numbers 2 and 3) were along the route of the genuine convoys, so they broadcast accurate information. TRPs 6 and 7 were located where the genuine divisions broke off to the north, so they distorted their information to indicate more traffic heading east. TRP 9 and the Network Control Station (in Munchen-Gladbach) transmitted almost entirely phony information about the notional divisions heading east to their assembly areas. These last two stations were not only the most active in the network, but also closest to the German lines. It was hoped that these would then be the most likely to be monitored by the Germans.

Once in the assembly areas, the notional 30th and 79th Divisions began transmitting. Telephone wire teams from the 23rd went to great efforts to lay field wire for the two divisions' communications. Lieutenant Spellman's team eventually laid fifty-four miles of wire for the 79th Division, and Lieutenant Wanerus's team twenty-two miles. As an additional deception, the wire teams laid far more wire than was needed for their actual communications. Each run from divisional to regimental headquarters had six additional lines. If German agents examined the telephone lines they would find the standard amount had been laid.

Artillery radios of the notional 30th and 79th Divisions began transmitting from forward locations next to the 84th and 102nd Infantry Divisions—where they would logically be located to support a river crossing in that area. All radios went silent in the XIII Corps again from 22–24 March (just before the genuine XVI Corps attack). Decoy artillery guns were provided to the 84th and 102nd Divisions to create additional artillery positions in their areas.

The Germans obviously thought something was going on in the area, as they drastically increased air activity over the XIII Corps. The 19th Antiaircraft Artillery Group reported no German air activity in the area from 15–17 March. From 19–21 March, however, sixteen German aircraft were spotted over the XIII Corps. Air activity then decreased back to no aircraft, or just one a day. On 22 March a German jet was caught in the beams of a searchlight and crashed while attempting to escape its harsh glare. A number of aircraft flew over the XIII Corps sector on the night of the genuine crossing to the north, dropping flares to illuminate the ground below.[9]

On 25 March 1945, the XIII Corps Artillery estimated the number of German batteries that were capable of firing into each of the corps sectors of the Ninth Army:[10]

Located Opposite	Light Artillery	Antiaircraft Artillery	Medium Artillery	Heavy Artillery
XVI Corps	24 guns	12 guns	8 guns	-
XIX Corps	12 guns	12 guns	12 guns	-
XIII Corps	48 guns	60 guns	24 guns	6 guns
Total	84 guns	84 guns	44 guns	6 guns

Clearly, according to all available information on that date, the Germans had far more artillery positioned opposite the XIII Corps than at the genuine crossing site.

At midnight on 24 March 1945, the genuine assault divisions (30th and 79th) began moving up to the riverbank in the XVI Corps area. After an hour-long bombardment of the opposite side, the Americans crossed the river with only thirty-one casualties. British and Canadian troops of the Second British Army crossed the Rhine farther to the north at the same time.

The Germans' defense cracked wide open and the American forces moved inland without hitting much resistance. The German rationales for the poor defense were that the attack had hit a weakly held gap between two German corps; that the Germans were desperately short of trained solders; and that the Allied artillery barrage had overwhelmed them.[11] American casualties were light, and more than two thousand Germans were captured on the first day. It would not be until the night of the second day, when the German 116th Panzer Division moved into the area, that the Americans would face any serious resistance.

The attempt to portray a build-up in the XIII Corps sector continued for the next few days, in hopes of continuing to draw off German reserves. Operation EXPLOIT finally climaxed with the notional river crossing on 1 April (a highly appropriate day) between Dusseldorf and Uerlingen. After that one last effort the 23rd packed up, went back to Briey, and ended their deception careers in Europe.

The men of the 23rd were understandably proud of their achievement. One of the few suggestions for future operations was a recommendation that when there is an attempt to conceal a division by removing insignia, all other elements of the command should also be blacked out. Unless every unit in an area becomes anonymous, blacking out only one division tells the enemy a new unit has moved in, if not which one. With everyone anonymous, the only notice of a unit arriving in the area would be an increase in traffic.

Captain Kelly, the 23rd intelligence officer, compiled a summary of enemy activity in the XIII Corps sector from 15–27 March.[12] He noted that the opposite bank had been relatively quiet until some rear area movement was detected between 18–20 March, indicative of the arrival of reinforcements. German artillery fire was weak prior to 18 March, but built up to a peak on that day

This aerial photograph of the Viersen area was taken from the typical height of a German reconnaissance flight. At this scale details of individual equipment become lost, and such things as vehicles' tracks and shadows take on new importance. Antiaircraft fire was used to keep German aircraft from flying too low, and to make them think the Americans had something in the area to hide.

when five hundred and forty-nine incoming rounds were reported—many of them on the dummy gun positions. His information claimed that German air activity continued to increase with not only reconnaissance missions but also bombing and strafing. Starting 17 March, there was a noticeable increase in German ground defenses. Prior to that time, American patrols that crossed the Rhine ran into little opposition, but afterward the German defenses were suddenly manned with alert and aggressive troops.

Kelly expressed the opinion: "It is apparent that the increased scale of enemy activity, particularly in the air, indicated a growing concern over the activity in XIII Corps zone. The continued presence of 2 Parachute Division in the north of the Corps Zone after the crossing further north by XVI Corps on 24 March appears to indicate enemy concern over a possible crossing in the Mundel-Heim area. Road and rail movement in enemy rear area from 19 to 20 March indicated a possible movement of reserves into the area opposite XIII

Corps. Accurate and well coordinated enemy fires from 18 March on indicates that enemy intelligence agencies were functioning in a credible manner and considerable increase in air activity from 18 March to the close of the period is ample evidence of the increased enemy concern over this sector. Further evidence of this concern is shown by the increased ground activity and the general alertness of enemy outposts against our own patrols from 20 March to the close of this period."[13]

The 23rd after-action report claimed, "This operation was the most extensive and most satisfactory in which the 23rd Headquarters Special Troops has participated."[14] The crossing to the north was obviously very successful. Operation VIERSEN became the 23rd's first mission that the U.S. Army afterward analyzed to assess the effectiveness of the deception. Ninth Army intelligence collected information in an attempt to see just how much the deception troops had assisted in the Rhine crossing.

"Not one prisoner taken by this division (30th) in the attack across the Rhine, of the many interrogated, including battalion and regimental officers, expected an attack from the west. All agreed that they had been advised by higher commanders to expect and prepare for an attack from the north across the Lippe River and Canal. Evidence developed by G-2 of the 79th Division on our right confirmed this finding in his sector. A German order-of-battle map captured by the 79th Division showed all the US divisions west of the Rhine, north of Cologne, in their proper locations except for the 79th, which was shown considerably farther south than it actually was, and the 30th division, whose location was not shown anywhere."[15] The same report goes on to state, "So it is apparent that the extensive deception measures undertaken were highly successful and resulted in the attack of the XVI Corps being a complete surprise to the enemy with a consequence of saving American lives."[16] Various suggestions were made that VIERSEN saved an estimated division's worth of men (twelve thousand).

The Ninth Army G-2, Colonel H. D. Kehm, analyzed enemy reactions to the deception operation on 1 April 1945:

> 1. An evaluation of all available information indicates that the enemy, prior to the initiation of Operation FLASHPOINT, 24 March 1945, by XVI US Corps:
> a. Placed the boundary between XVI US Corps (on the north) and XIII US Corps (on the south) as being along the northeast-southeast line of the Fossa Eugeunua Canal, from west of LINTFORT (A12) to skirt Rheinberg (A22) on the east, thence north to the bank of the Rhine, east of Ossenberg (A23).
> b. Credited XVI US Corps with the 35th, 75th, 84th, 95th, Infantry and 8th Armored Divisions.
> c. Credited XIII US Corps with the 29th, 79th, 102nd Infantry and 5th Armored Divisions.

> d. Estimated that the Allies would make their main attack to cross the Rhine to the north of Wesel (A24) [in the British sector], with only a minor crossing south of Wesel; the later crossing to take place two or three days after the Rhine had been crossed to the north.
>
> e. Estimated that a crossing would be made in the Uerdengen (A20) area, and appear still to think so.
>
> 2. There is no doubt that Operation EXPLOIT materially assisted in deceiving the enemy with regard to the real dispositions and intentions of this Army, and thus contributed to the marked success of Operation FLASHPOINT.[17]

With all evidence pointing to the Rhine crossing being materially assisted by the deception, Lieutenant General W. H. Simpson of the Ninth Army sent the 23rd the following:[18]

HEADQUARTERS
NINTH UNITED STATES ARMY
Office of the Commanding General

APO
29 March 1945

SUBJECT: Commendation

TO   : Commanding Officer, 23d Headquarters Special Troops,
         Twelfth Army Group.
       THRU: Commanding General, Twelfth Army Group

1. 23d Headquarters Special Troops, Twelfth Army Group, was attached to NINTH UNITED STATES ARMY on 15 March 1945 to participate in the operation to cross the RHINE River.

2. The unit was engaged in a special project, which was an important part of the operation. The careful planning, minute attention to detail, and diligent execution of the tasks to be accomplished by the personnel of the organization reflect great credit on this unit.

3. I desire to commend the officers and men of the 23d Headquarters Special Troops, Twelfth Army Group, for their fine work and to express my appreciation for a job well done.

W. H. Simpson
W. H. SIMPSON,
Lieutenant General, U. S. Army,
Commanding.

Another period report from the Ninth Army claimed, "Unlike the majority of deception operations, the results in this case appear fairly obvious from the intelligence reports and from the low casualties suffered by the troops engaged in the real operation."[19] The question was, however, if the low casualty rates were due to the deception, or the poor status of the German defenders.

No one questioned the success of the deception operation until 1992, when Justin Eldridge published his study of Operation VIERSEN that looked further into the records of the Ninth Army.[20] Overall, he felt that the 23rd acted in a well-planned and professional manner, but his conclusion was that the outcome of the actual river crossing was not affected by the deception.

Eldridge felt that most of the claims of success stemmed from one captured map overlay (taken from a German officer, most probably from the 180th Infantry Division) which showed the notional American 79th Division placed in the XIII Corps. It did not, however, have a location for the 30th Division. This would appear to indicate that the Germans did not notice the notional 30th Division in the XIII Corps area.

Eldridge claimed that German intelligence lost touch with the Allied forces once they had been separated by the Rhine. He stated, "Their intelligence system was in disarray, which made tracking changes in U.S., Canadian, and British combat organizations nearly impossible. The system was so blind that they could not recognize the picture General Simpson wanted them to see."[21]

His evaluation of German intelligence estimates reveals a great deal of confusion. Two days before the assault, the Germans had the 30th and 79th still located at the Maas River training areas, but then on 24 March (the day of the genuine crossing) they placed the 30th in its real position in the XVI corps crossing zone. It was not until 26 March that the Germans placed the two divisions across the Rhine, and even then they were indicated as being ten miles farther south than they actually were.

An evaluation of postwar interviews with German officers shows that Field Marshal Albert Kesselring thought the Allied Rhine crossing would occur in the Wesel (British) area. Commander of Army Group H (General Johannes Blaskowitz) and the commander of his reserve Panzer Corps (General Heinrich von Luettwitz) both believed in addition that the Americans would cross near Wesel because it offered the best crossing sites and was near to the British assault area. General Alfred Schlemm (commander of the 1st Fallshirm Army) defending the river also felt the main assault would be at Wesel as he had no reports of crossing activity from the XIII Corps sector.

This would mean that the stepped-up activity in the XIII Corps area went unnoticed. In theory, the XIII Corps was to send more combat patrols across the Rhine than the XVI Corps, but this may not have been the actual case. Eldridge's evaluation of the records claims that the number of corps patrols barely matched. Between 18 and 23 March there were only eleven patrols in the XIII Corps area as opposed to fifteen in the genuine crossing sector of the XVI Corps.

According to Eldridge, the Germans knew a large Rhine assault was coming in the north in General Montgomery's 21st Army Group sector, because little had been done to hide the preparations. The Germans thus placed their best corps (under General Meindl) to defend against that crossing. The next most likely crossing location would be at Wesel (due to its extensive road network) and the obvious focus was the XVI Corps area just to the south of Wesel (because it had terrain perfectly suited for a large-scale crossing operation). A crossing further to the south, in the XIII Corps area, did not seem likely to the Germans because of the gap that would result between the British and American crossing points.

Eldridge has no problem with the ability of the 23rd to have fulfilled its role in the deception, but claims that the deception operation was doomed from the start because it was not tied into the large overall picture. Planning for the Rhine crossing started six months before, while the 23rd became involved less than a month before the actual crossing. He does suggest that planted documents and orders could have been used as part of the deception plan, except that the XIII's orders were so vague that even if captured they would have done little to help the deception. His main criticism is that there should have been a long-term build-up of forces far beyond the Ninth Army borders. This should have been a major coordinated Allied effort much like Operation FORTITUDE. Eldridge suggests that VIERSEN was treated as a tactical deception, when it should have been planned and executed as a strategic deception.

Eldridge does agree that the VIERSEN deception did mislead the Germans as to the location of the 79th Division, and that the Germans assumed it would be involved in only a feint and not a genuine crossing due to its location. On the whole, Eldridge feels that the Allies totally overestimated the German intelligence capabilities, which can be just as damaging as underestimating them. He makes the important point that before any deception can be planned, it is imperative to understand how an enemy intelligence agency collects, processes, and analyzes information.

Eldridge claims that, "An incomplete 21st Army Group deception plan meant that the Ninth Army's efforts were neither effective nor convincing enough to force the Germans to misallocate forces or delay their counterattack into the bridgehead."[22] There may be some validity to this; however, there is no doubt that the 23rd Special Troops had come a long way since their early experiments a year before. It would be a shame if all their carefully planned efforts were in vain because commanders at a higher level did not work the deception into the overall picture of the Western Front. If this was so, it is a valuable lesson that deception operations, even tactical ones, cannot operate in a vacuum.

Nothing in war is simple, and the efforts of the 23rd in the Rhine deception have to be figured in, at some level, to the success of the crossing operation. A full examination of the operation would have to include a study of all German unit records down to battalion level and an in-depth interview with each of the commanders as to exactly why they made their decisions.

An additional aspect to keep in mind is that even if the enemy does not fall for a deception, a well-executed deception operation will still tie up his resources (such as intelligence analysts, aerial reconnaissance, photo interpreters, and behind-the-lines agents). They have to spend time searching for, and examining the evidence that something is a deception, instead of focusing more productively on other projects. Tying up those enemy resources is a valuable contribution by deception units that generally cannot be measured.

However, if the Germans did not accept the notional XIII Corps crossing, the failure would be similar to the failure of Operation COCKADE in 1943. In that operation, the Germans did not believe the possibility of an Allied assault into France because they did not see enough troops for such an invasion. That failure led to the creation of the 23rd Special Troops, whose last mission may have been compromised because the high command once again focused on the operational aspects of a deception, without dealing with how appropriate it was, given the big picture.

It can be debated to what extent the 23rd's deception operation at the Rhine contributed to the crossing. However, it must be kept firmly in mind that the American troops in the XVI Corps sector, for whatever reason, made a highly successful combat crossing against German forces defending their homeland at their last natural boundary. What's more, they did so taking only a fraction of the expected casualties. Actions, it is said, speak louder than words.

Chapter 27

The 3133rd and the War in Italy

The 23rd was not the only American tactical deception unit in the ETO. After the 3132nd Signal Company shipped out from Pine Camp in May 1944, Colonel Railey lost no time in organizing a second sonic deception unit. The 3133rd Signal Service Company was authorized on 3 June and activated at Pine Camp on 21 June 1944.[1] This new unit was based around a small number of men retained from the 3132nd, as well as some of the staff of the Army Experimental Station (AES). At first it was authorized nine officers and one hundred and eighty-five enlisted men under command of Major John A. Williams.[2]

Training began immediately and was scheduled for nine hours a day, six days a week. The 3133rd began with only sixteen weeks of training allocated, but this amount quickly proved inadequate and eventually twenty-five weeks were allowed before the unit shipped out. Above the eight weeks of specialized sonic training were included twelve weeks of basic training, then another five weeks on tasks needed to prepare for overseas service (such as weapons training). The company was slightly reorganized under a new T/O&E on 10 October 1944 to ten officers and one hundred and ninety-two enlisted men. The unit formally completed its training on 9 December 1944. Throughout that time, work at the AES to promote sonic depiction continued.[3]

On 14 September 1944, Charles Yocum of the 23rd Special Troops (then in Europe) suggested some changes for future deception units.[4] His primary suggestion was to mount the sonic gear on a fully tracked vehicle rather than half-tracks. He also wanted all sonic vehicles equipped with the same type of speakers (the 3132nd actually had two different brands, which complicated matters). As to organization, he suggested the 4th Security Platoon be done away with and those men used to increase the number of sonic vehicles to nine per platoon (from five). He felt the size of the security platoon was too small to provide security for the company in operation, and that the job of security should be left to another, larger, detachment. In the 3133rd, the 4th Platoon would be known as the reconnaissance platoon.

With no modern armored vehicles available for the men of the 3133rd to train on, the army sent them a few obsolete M3 medium Grant tanks to practice with. A few were never equipped with sonic gear, but used only to train the Signal Corps crews to operate and maintain fully tracked vehicles. Colonel Railey is seen here in his tanker's jacket escorting an inspection party. PHOTO: FORT DRUM MUSEUM.

Various types of vehicles were tested for the new sonic unit.[5] Although it was possible to mount the equipment on the back of a truck, utilizing a fully tracked vehicle would lend some authenticity to the idea of tanks being in the area. No longer would the sonic unit have to borrow tanks to make tread-marks, and there would be a few actual armored vehicles to help round out the visual aspect of the deception. One of the vehicles examined was the small tracked M-29C commonly known as the "weasel," though it proved too small to hold the necessary equipment.

Colonel Railey initially wanted to use the T-41. This was a light tracked vehicle based on the M-18 tank destroyer chassis, but without a turret. The limited production run of T-41s, however, had already been guaranteed to tank destroyer units overseas, and Railey was unable to obtain any for the 3133rd. A number of 75mm M-8 motor carriages on the light M3 chassis (then surplus to the army's needs) were suggested by the War Department, as were the fully tracked amphibious LVT-4. The LVT-4 was not only too small for the sonic gear, but far too slow for what was expected of it. The M-8 looked promising, but the army suddenly decided those vehicles were needed elsewhere. Attempts were then made to obtain a supply of the brand-new M-18 tank destroyers (the turreted production version of the T-41). While the 3133rd had a priority level of A-2-B, units overseas in combat had a higher procurement level of A-1-B-1, and all M-18s were slated for overseas shipment.

The crew of SLUG 31 is shown leaping into action from their sonic tank. The former "coffee grinder" crank system, used to raise the speaker in the sonic half-tracks, had been improved with a counterweighted system that was easier to use. Note that the turret is still in the reversed position, allowing the driver access to his top hatch. One of the key design specifications for the sonic tanks was that when the speakers were lowered there would be nothing to indicate the vehicle had special equipment.

During the month of July 1944, the possibility of getting M-18s (or T-41s) went back and forth as the army and the manufacturer (the Buick Motor Car Company) shifted schedules and priorities. While the choice of vehicle was being decided, the 3133rd was issued twenty of the older M3A5 medium tanks (Grant) and ten M3A1 light tanks (Stuart) for training. These were deemed unfit for combat, but were used to teach the men how to drive and maintain tracked vehicles. It was not until 4 August 1944 that a number of M-10 tank destroyers were finally authorized for conversion to sonic vehicles.

The M-10 was a tank destroyer with an open topped turret and 3 inch gun. To convert these vehicles to sonic use entailed removing the barrel and breach assembly; installing the sonic equipment (including a redesigned counterweight mechanism to raise the speakers into position); installing a more powerful generator; and various other minor changes including redesigned storage, special shock mounts, and radios. The work on the twenty-four sonic cars was done by the New York Lock and Safe Company.

Without the need for a gun loader, only four crewmen (instead of the normal five) were needed for the sonic-modified tanks. These were driver, radio/sonic operator, vehicle commander, and assistant driver/gunner who

One of the sonic M-10 tank destroyers is shown passing in review during the demonstration given to General Lear. The M-10 generally traveled with the barrel pointed backwards, locked into a barrel clamp. This prevented wear on the gun mechanisms while moving on bumpy roads and allowed the driver to keep his hatch open.

This is the only known photograph showing the shortened dummy barrel of the 3133rd's M-10s. The entire gun mechanism was removed to make more room in the turret for sonic gear, and a short pipe was mounted on the front to give the appearance that it still had a gun. PHOTO: FORT DRUM MUSEUM.

manned a .50-caliber machine gun mounted on the turret for defense. A standard M-10 had a .30-caliber machine gun, but the heavier .50 was substituted to increase firepower. The crews quickly discovered that if this machine gun was fired, the concussive force of its loud sound would break the cardboard speaker cones.

An additional six sonic control cars were also converted from M-10s. These had additional communications equipment and were used by the officers as command vehicles. Due to the space needs of the new equipment, there was no room to carry water cans inside. Extra brackets had to be ordered for mounting two five-gallon water cans on the outside of the vehicle, a simple requisition that generated an amazing degree of additional paperwork.

To keep the outside appearance similar to a genuine M-10, a dummy gun was mounted on the turret. For weight reasons, these dummy guns were shorter than the M-10's standard barrel. This short barrel was the cause of some curiosity by genuine tank crews. The sonic crews soon learned to brush off any interest in their vehicles by casually saying it was an "assault gun," and changing the subject.

When not in combat, the M-10 was typically driven in "traveling position" with the turret pointed to the rear. A column of these sonic vehicles, covered with excess personal equipment and tarpaulins over the turret openings, would draw little attention from all but the most observant armored experts.

The half-tracks of the 3132nd were generally referred to as sonic cars, but the M-10s of the 3133rd were known by a different name. Each was referred to by the code name SLUG. Each SLUG was numbered from 1 to 6 in each of the three platoons. Thus the second platoon contained SLUG 21 through SLUG 26. The name SLUG was actually Colonel Railey's nickname from his days as a youthful boxer. Each M-10 had the two-digit SLUG number painted on the right front fender of the vehicle.

While the 3133rd was being trained, Railey continued his work to promote deception. In July 1944 the army held a conference to determine if there was a way to tell if sounds were real or recorded.[6] This was not only to see if the Germans might be able to spot the American deceptions, but also to see if there might be a way to detect possible German sonic deception. No conclusions on this subject were located, but the AES was already preparing for the day when they would have to develop countermeasures to enemy sonic deception.

Colonel Railey's enthusiasm ran headfirst into military bureaucracy when his calls to commit the 3133rd to a theater of operations, and organize a third sonic unit, were seemingly ignored by Washington. It appears that Railey had heard comments that the army was hesitant to use his sonic units in action in case the enemy might find out about them. Some high-ranking officers, it appeared, were more concerned with keeping the sonic troops a secret than with using them to help win the war. Colonel Railey became concerned about the future of not only the AES, but of deception itself.

On 16 August 1944, while the 3132nd were arriving in France, Colonel Railey wrote the following letter to Brigadier General J. V. Matejka, the chief of Signal Corps Personnel and Training Service. The letter was marked personal.

> Dear General Matejka,
>
> Uncertainty concerning the future of the Army Experimental Station presents increasingly so many problems that I feel I can no longer neglect at least an attempt at their solution. Since it does not appear expedient to raise this issue officially, at least for the present, I avail myself of the opportunity, and with appreciation of the privilege of addressing you informally and at some length.
>
> Immediately after the demonstration of our special equipment on May 12, General Meade told me that within a few days I should be ordered to Washington to participate in a conference on the future of the Army Experimental Station. It was my understanding that OPD, G-3, Joint Security Control, and the New Developments Division would be represented. As pioneer of both the Army's and the Navy's activities in this field I was led to believe my views would be thoroughly explored.

Although eventually I was not invited to attend—nor even present my convictions in memorandum—it was at such a conference, I believe, that the decision was made (a) to earmark our combat units for employment only by the highest levels of command in the Theaters, and (b) to activate but one additional unit until the 3132nd Signal Service Company had been committed and its performance appraised.

It is my belief, and without exception the belief of my 24 officers, that these decisions were myopic. Insofar as I am able to determine, presentation of the capabilities and limitations of our units to the Theater Commanders was inadequate for accomplishment of real understanding of their potential effectiveness. Consequently, with the exception of the European Theater, no requests were forthcoming. Even the unit now in training here remains uncommitted.

After more than two years of intense and costly effort, involving the expenditure of millions of dollars, the Navy has activated and committed nine units, trained under the direct supervision of the Office of the Commander-in-Chief, U.S. Fleet, without *advance* consultation with its Task Force commanders. Only two units—neither of them thus far committed—have been activated by the Army and notwithstanding the fact that it was the Army, not the Navy, which originated these activities.

When on my initiative the joint efforts of the Army and Navy were separated, it became the objective of the Army Experimental Station, by direction of the secret W.D. Planning Board, which had immediate jurisdiction under OPD, to attempt the development of weapons, which, if successful, could be adopted as organic by the Armored Force.

Although statistics prove that only one new weapon in 8,000 presented to the War Department ever reaches the blueprint stage, it has been officially acknowledged that the Army Experimental Station has demonstrated the development of several (3) weapons possessing three (in addition to the amphibious) tactical applications. Yet (a) on the score that these weapons should only be employed by the highest levels of command in the Theaters, where comprehension of their capabilities has not even been remotely achieved; and (b) on the score of security, the Armored Force, for whose use they were primarily developed, has not been permitted even to test their adoption.

It is the recently confirmed policy of the Navy to continue and extend its activities in the field. Hundreds of weapons are under procurement by the Navy. It is apparently the decision of the Army to remain on a stand-by basis until its first unit has been committed and thereafter to scrap its equipment and write off its investment of millions of dollars and its equity in the training of hundreds of specialists should the outcome of that commitment fail to be dramatically impressive.

To us—we who have done the job for the Army—that is the equivalent of concluding that because the performance of our tanks in North Africa proved tactically almost disastrous the Army would manufacture no more tanks.

In recent weeks I have been repeatedly and officially warned that the future of the Army Experimental Station is most uncertain. In letter and orally it has been indicated that everything we have tried to and have achieved is at stake in a single toss of the dice.

Should everything rest upon the outcome of the commitment of the first unit, is it not reasonable to ask what will happen if, in the increasingly fluid state of the campaign in France, that unit is never committed? That is certainly a possibility since, assuredly, the high command in France would not countenance commitment of our unit so long as the present pace of our forces is maintained.

On the basis of information informally provided we know that General Eisenhower's staff, on the Top Side, is enthusiastic over the capabilities of the 3132nd Signal Service Company. It is therefore logical to deduce that were they truly aware of its possibilities other Theatre Commanders, who up to now have been but indifferently circularized, might share that enthusiasm.

With the Navy our weapons are a *fait accompli*. With the Army, by whom our weapons have been officially acknowledged to have been *demonstrated as weapons*, utilization remains in doubt—and with even abandonment a neck-and-neck consideration.

I cannot refrain from the observation that having developed and demonstrated weapons which enable so few to accomplish so much—weapons which in combat enable one soldier in critical circumstances to replace fifty—a solemn obligation exists to extend the application of such weapons and to stabilize their future development.

From day to day it becomes increasingly evident that if the efficiency and dedication of my command are to be maintained on the high level which has been consistently characteristic of its efforts in the past, official clarification of the future is an urgent requirement. Even in war the strongest of men—and my people are both strong and mature—are demoralized by protracted uncertainty. It is impossible for me to conceal from my officers, and from many of my key enlisted men, that the fruits of their combined and arduous efforts may at any moment come to naught. Through their unshakable faith in our equipment many of them have sacrificed opportunities for combat command overseas. It is on the records that, deeply committed to this effort, I personally have forfeited three opportunities for duty overseas and with them promotion long ago to the grade of colonel.

I ask you to believe, sir, that in my own case, and without exception in the case of my officers, personal advancement is but a negligible consideration so long as we are able to feel that our efforts are constructive and not meaningless and are recognized as worthy of the utmost we can bring to bear in our collective output; and that our position is so recognized by our overlords.

There is an onset here of unavoidable suspicion that our ship is about to be scuttled. Within the hour I have (I hope) scotched such a rumor in a forthright address to the entire Station Detachment. Applications for transfer from both officers and enlisted men are multiplying.

When one's country is involved in global war, high minded men, their domestic lives and normal pursuits uprooted by the storm, would appear to deserve at least the consideration that their contribution to victory should be measurable.

I recommend:

(a) That the capabilities of weapons developed by the Army Experimental Station be brought to the attention of the recently appointed Joint Army and Navy Planning Commission which is empowered to determine what shall be done in the future, even in peace time, with new weapons developed in this war.

(b) That organic adoption of these weapons by the Armored Force be reconsidered, and that as the pioneer in their development I be given the opportunity to express my convictions.

(c) That General Henry be consulted in relation to (a) and (b)

Finally, Sir, most earnestly I ask you to believe that all of my officers and all of my men are aware of your personal faith and that therein their hope abides.

Faithfully Yours,

H.H. Railey
Lt. Col. Inf.
Commanding[7]

Colonel Railey is seen here during a demonstration of sonic warfare at Pine Camp. He never realized his dream of commanding a deception unit in combat, but it was only through his hard promotion that the 3132nd and 3133rd were able to prove their value. Of interest is that he is seen here in custom-made boots. According to veterans, most of his uniforms were tailor-made for him in New York City.

No response to Railey's letter was recorded, but slowly, as the 3133rd continued its training, some interest was finally taken in the sonic troops. Someone, possibly stirred on by Railey's efforts, considered sending a sonic unit to the Pacific. On 24 October the War Department sent Eisenhower's headquarters the following message, "Comments desired as to when the 3132 Signal Service Company can be considered available for transfer to Pacific Area. As soon as available, the War Department has received a request for such a unit."[8] The reply was sent back to Washington on 3 November 1944 over Eisenhower's name: "Release of 3132 is subject. Unit highly important factor in necessary deception operation. Present and future plans contemplate employment of unit in this role until cessation. Cannot concur in release of unit prior to this time."[9]

On 3 November 1944, Lieutenant General Ben Lear visited the 3133rd and observed a demonstration of it in action. Lear was the commander of the

Colonel Railey greats General Ben Lear, commander of the Army Ground Forces, during an historic demonstration of the potential of sonic warfare. With the army drastically short of manpower, Railey had to make a strong case to keep Lear from dismantling the AES and the 3133rd and using the men as replacements.

Army Ground Forces, which had the overall mission of providing ground forces units; properly organized, trained, and equipped for combat operations. He was a key individual to win over to the usefulness of sonic deception. Lear reportedly liked what he saw. He was very impressed with the nighttime demonstration of the unit and was quoted as saying, "Sonic warfare has infinite possibilities. Saving the lives of 200 men, it would pay for itself."[10]

In November 1944, the 3133rd was surrounded by rumors of its shipping out, but the priority rating assigned the 3133rd was not high enough to get a full compliment of equipment. At the time, the highest priority for equipment went to units overseas in combat. Until the company had its complete authorized load of equipment it could not officially be assigned overseas service. Eventually the needed material arrived, and on 27 December 1944, orders finally arrived for the 3133rd to leave for the San Francisco Port of Embarkation. This was the traditional place of departure for units heading to the Pacific.

With the movement orders came a problem for Major Williams. His 4th Platoon leader was not well liked, and the men did not want to serve in combat under him. They felt he did not understand their reconnaissance and security role, was too aggressive, and would go looking for trouble instead of defending the sonic unit. After presenting Major Williams with a petition calling for the officer's removal, everyone was called out in formation as Williams read them the Articles of War. A heavy emphasis on the punishment for mutiny put the fear of God into them and the men quietly backed down. Knowing his men were right, however, Williams quietly relieved the officer in question.

When the 3133rd finally boarded their troop train they hung a banner on the side of the train reading "Railey's Rodeo—192 clowns and 10 featured artists." The humor was appreciated, but it was declared a security risk and quickly removed. There was a great deal of confusion as to where they were actually heading, but eventually the men realized they were destined for the ETO when they arrived at Camp Patrick Henry, the embarkation camp for the port of Newport News, Virginia. The sonic tanks and equipment were shipped overseas separately, accompanied by an armed guard of fifteen men. This detachment stood guard over the shipment (two hours on, four hours off) during the trans-Atlantic voyage to prevent enemy spies from examining the sonic equipment. The rest of the 3133rd boarded the transport ship USS *General Brooke*, on 1 March 1945, for sunny Italy.

After a fourteen-day journey, the men landed at Naples. They soon discovered that all their equipment, vehicles included, had landed at Leghorn: a totally different port. Trucks were obtained to haul the men north to find their equipment. After drawing all equipment and supplies from the quartermaster in Leghorn, the 3133rd was billeted at an estate near Lucca (the Villa Mentuli).

About this time, the 3133rd had a platoon of British engineers attached to it. These men, from the 101st Royal Engineers, were specialized in the use of inflatable decoys. The 3133rd now had both sonic and visual means of deception (but not signal). To maintain the cover of the unit, the M-10s of the 3133rd were typically painted with unit markings of the 701st Tank Destroyer Battalion, a genuine M-10-equipped unit that was already serving in Italy. The use of the same designation as a genuine unit in the region was a good cover, but at times caused some problems with mistaken identity.

Italy was a perfect country for the Germans to defend. Mountain ranges and rivers ran east to west across the country, making natural lines of defense that caused the Allies to pay heavily for every mile on their drive north. From October 1944 to April 1945, the front line was essentially static at what was known as the "second winter line," just to the north of Florence. The Allies planned for a major offensive in April 1945 to break the German defensive position known as the Gothic Line.

The offensive was known as Operation CRAFTSMAN, and consisted of three phases. First, the 92nd Infantry Division, on the far left flank, would conduct a limited attack to draw off German reinforcements. Second, the British Eighth Army would attack on the far right flank of the Allied line and attempt to break through the German defenses. This would hopefully pin down the few remaining German reserves while the third phase, an attack in the central region by the American Fifth Army, would hopefully punch through the German lines, spurring a drive north to Bologna and the Po River. The 3133rd would take part in the first and third phase of this operation.

The limited attack of the 92nd Infantry Division was called Operation SECOND WIND. The all-black 92nd Division had, in the opinion of the theater commanders, not performed well in its first actions. For SECOND WIND the unit had been heavily reorganized. The best of the officers and men of the 92nd had been transferred to the 370th Infantry Regiment. The remaining two infantry regiments in the division (the 365th and 371st) were withdrawn from divisional command and put directly under control of the IV Corps to man the front line from the right flank of the 92nd over to the Brazilian Expeditionary Force and the American 10th Mountain Division.

To replace its lost regiments the 92nd was given the Japanese-American 442nd Infantry Regiment and the newly formed 473rd Infantry Regiment. The 473rd was an unusual outfit composed of white antiaircraft crews retrained as infantrymen, under command of the legendary paratroop officer Colonel William P. Yarborough. The Germans expected an attack in the 92nd Division sector, as they thought the Americans would use their amphibious capability to land a force on the western shore of Italy, then attempt to drive north along the coastal plain to link up with the beachhead. For this reason the area facing the American IV Corps was one of the most heavily defended of the Italian front.

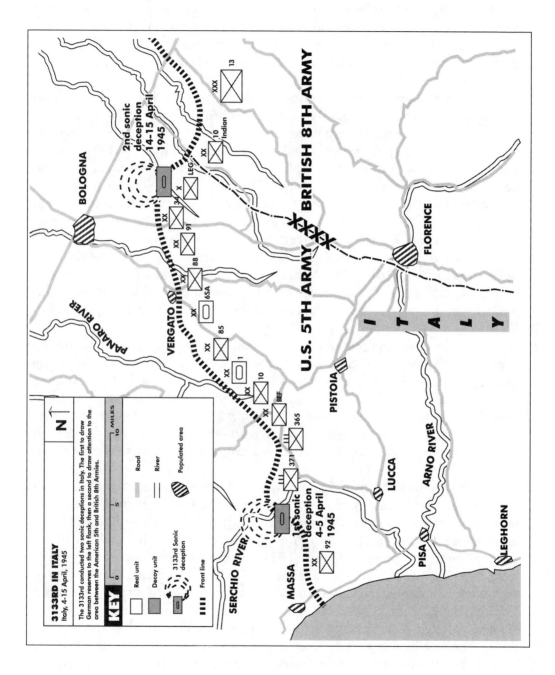

The 3133rd conducted two sonic deceptions in Italy. The first to draw German reserves to the left flank, then a second to draw attention to the area between the American 5th and British 8th Armies.

KEY

3133RD IN ITALY
Italy, 4–15 April, 1945

☐	Real unit
▨	Decoy unit
⌇	3133rd Sonic deception
▮▮▮▮	Front line

▬	Road
‖	River
▨	Populated area

N ↑

MILES
0   5   10

2nd sonic deception 14-15 April 1945

1st sonic deception 4-5 April 1945

BOLOGNA

PANARO RIVER

VERGATO

SERCHIO RIVER

MASSA

PISTOIA

LUCCA

PISA

LEGHORN

ARNO RIVER

FLORENCE

I T A L Y

U.S. 5TH ARMY

BRITISH 8TH ARMY

13
10 Indian
LEG
34
91
88
65A
85
1
10
BEF
365
371
92

As part of Operation SECOND WIND, the 371st Infantry, to the right of the 92nd Division, was scheduled to make a limited assault in the area of the Serchio Valley and the Cinquale Canal. 2/371st was to only make a deceptive attack towards the canal once the main attack started on 5 April, while the rest of the regiment attempted to capture locally important ground. The 3133rd performed a sonic deception mission to indicate a buildup of Allied armor in the area of the 2/371st.

The main German force in the Serchio River Valley was the 148th Grenadier Division commanded by General Fretter-Pico. After the war he was quoted as saying, "Initially, we were misled by the dummy armored division which you moved up the Serchio Valley from Bagni de Lucca to Barga on the night of 3rd and 4th of April 1945. I delayed moving reserve units from the Serchio Valley to the coastal area for two days, while waiting to see if an attack would be launched from that area."[11] Hearing an opposing commander admit he was fooled—and his plan of action influenced—by a deception is about as close to proving a deception operation was successful as possible.

Following on the heels of SECOND WIND, the British Eighth Army attacked in their sector on 9 April 1945. Although the experienced German defenders were well dug in, the Commonwealth forces, including Poles, Indians, South Africans, and troops from a number of other countries, began to push them back.

The 3133rd meanwhile shifted position to the far right flank of the American 5th Army, to a sector held by the Leganno Combat Group (Leganno Gruppo). This was a brigade-sized infantry unit of veteran Italian soldiers who had volunteered to fight against the Germans. The Leganno Combat Group was sandwiched between the American 34th Infantry Division on their left and the Indian 10th Infantry Division on their right. The American assault was to begin on 12 April, but was delayed until 15 April due to weather conditions.

While the exact nature of this second deception on the night of 14–15 April is not known, veterans recall it was similar to the first: portrayal of a decoy tank unit through sound and inflatable dummies. The genuine offensive entailed eight divisions attacking through an area only thirty miles wide to burst through the German defenses. The sonic troops were operating on the right flank, in the sector of an Italian unit of unknown quality. The sonic mission went as planned, but no evidence that it fooled the Germans has been located. The genuine assault, however, was a spectacular success.

The Allied assault quickly broke through the German lines and poured north. The result was greater than anyone had expected. The next natural defensive line was along the Po River and it was thought that the Germans would make a tough stand along its banks. A third sonic operation was planned to simulate a river crossing. Sounds of engineers preparing crossing sites, constructing bridges, and assembling assault boats would be played at night, and then under the cover of a smoke screen, to draw the defenders away from the genuine crossing sites.

The third operation, however, never took place because the German forces in Italy crumbled and the Po River was crossed at a number of different locations without much of a struggle on 22 and 23 April. At some points the Allies reached the Po before the retreating enemy, forcing many of the Germans to surrender.

German forces continued to fall back, until finally all German forces in Italy surrendered on 2 May 1945 (over a week before the total German surrender). The 3133rd had been in action only nineteen days. During that time they had suffered no casualties, but according to veterans, one of their sonic tanks had been damaged beyond recovery in a non-combat accident.

With the fighting over, the 3133rd was bivouacked at Lake Guarda, near Verona. There was no need for deception, so the men were given temporary signal corps–related assignments. A number were used as couriers for the Fifth Army. Orders were received for the 3133rd to be shipped back to Pine Camp in preparation for assignment to the Pacific. The unit packed up and moved to Rome, where it was temporarily bivouacked in a sports complex. Its shipping space to the States was shifted to a detachment of the 10th Mountain Division, which was desperately needed for the forthcoming invasion of Japan. While the 3133rd was waiting for more shipping space to become available, the A-bombs were dropped and the war was over.

The U.S. military had devised a system for returning men home from the war that gave precedence to men who had served overseas the longest. Points were awarded for time in the service, time overseas, for each campaign participated in, and for combat decorations. Men with high points had priority for returning home, while the most recent soldiers sent overseas (such as the 3133rd) were considered low-point men and would remain in Italy for some time. They were assigned piecemeal to take over jobs previously held by high-point men returned to the States.

At some point after the fighting, an unknown individual in the 3133rd decided that the unit needed a shoulder sleeve insignia. The army did not allow individual companies to wear their own unit patch, but this did not stop the 3133rd. They designed an insignia placing the nose-thumbing devil from the AES insignia over the triangle of the armored forces. Although the Italians made many different shoulder patches for American units, this design was sent back to the States and produced there by a private company. Enough were ordered for each man to be issued two patches; however, by the time they arrived many of the men had been sent off to other units and never received them.

The 3133rd moved to an Italian Army barracks near Caserta to assist with signal-related duties at the theater headquarters. The unit equipment was turned in to the quartermasters. The M-10s were stripped of the special sonic

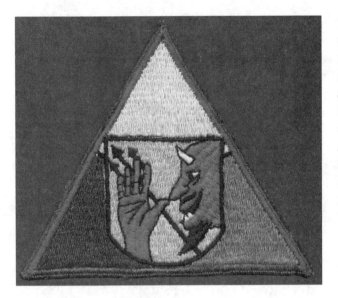

The 3133rd patch, consisting of the AES devil insignia super-imposed on an armored forces triangle, was designed at the end of the war. The small number of patches were actually made in the United States, but arrived in Italy too late for every man to receive one. This example was worn by George Stoffregen of the 3133rd's T&M platoon.

gear and handed over to the Ordnance Corps. The sonic equipment went into a signal supply depot. The three recording K-53 trucks and the M30 signal repair truck (plus the four K63 generator trailers) were kept intact due to the perception of a growing demand for sound recording.

More and more men were split off from the 3133rd and sent to other units. One group replaced high-point signalmen from the 88th Infantry Division based along the Yugoslavian border. Another detachment was sent to Greece in the spring of 1946 as part of the American Mission observing the Greek elections. Eventually the 3133rd was quietly—and unceremoniously—disbanded.

★ ★ ★

However, back at Pine Camp the German surrender did not stop Colonel Railey in his quest to develop tactical deception. As soon as the 3133rd had been activated, he had pressed for the formation of a third sonic company. This request was denied due to a massive shortage in manpower during 1945, but Railey was not discouraged. He attempted to form a new composite deception unit, encompassing all types of tactical deception. Many veterans felt it was his greatest wish to lead such a unit against the Japanese, but due to the manpower shortage Railey tried a different approach. He suggested that this unit be composed of men classified as not being fit for combat, and that it be used to travel the country demonstrating the various uses of deception. Possibly Railey felt that once his unit was organized it would be one step closer to overseas service, but his requests were denied and his composite deception unit was never authorized.

Experimental work at the AES continued, but with less enthusiasm than before. Decoy parachutists such as the British had used in Normandy were tested. The army sent a load of land mines to Pine Camp so tests could be run to see how effective they would be in frozen ground. On 28 August 1945, the men of the AES received the following letter of appreciation for their work from the head of the Signal Corps:

1. As a result of the successful termination of the war, orders have been released for the discontinuance of the activities so successfully conducted at the Army Experimental Station.

2. It is realized that the possession of special skills by the officers and enlisted men of the Army Experimental Station has thus far prevented the release of some of you for overseas service and in some cases has resulted in personnel being assigned to Army Experimental Station from units which were expected to go overseas in a short time. Only a greater military requirement for these special skills in this country could justify such an action.

3. Since many of you, therefore, have not yet had the opportunity of serving your country overseas, your pride in military achievement must rest in the knowledge of a mission well performed which permitted the forces in the theater to employ successfully a weapon developed by your skill and efforts. The new combat weapon developed at Army Experimental Station has been introduced in two theaters with a degree of success which warrants a feeling of pride in the heart of each officer and enlisted man who has been in any way connected with its development.

4. Accept my congratulations on the success of your mission, which was largely due to the untiring effort and faith in the ultimate value of this weapon so conclusively exhibited by each and every member of the staff of the Army Experimental Station.

(signed) H.C. Ingles, Major General, Chief Signal Officer[12]

Colonel Railey never achieved his desire to command a unit in a combat zone, but was awarded the Legion of Merit in September 1945 for exceptional foresight and outstanding leadership in the development of a project entirely new to the U.S. Army. The AES was finally closed down on 1 November 1945 and all its equipment sent to various supply depots for storage or for sale as surplus.

Everyone who came into contact with Colonel Railey recalled him as a man of vision, infectious enthusiasm, and great foresight. Sadly, most of his work in tactical deception was lost to the army, buried in mountains of classified paperwork. His one legacy at Pine Camp (now Fort Drum) is a street named Railey Road that runs by his one-time AES headquarters.

Chapter 28

War's End and DP Camps

In northern Europe, once the Rhine had been crossed it seemed like only a matter of time before Germany collapsed. The men of the 23rd began to hear rumors that they would be sent to fight the Japanese in the Pacific. In the meantime the unit performed a number of odd jobs. Part of the 23rd Signal Company was attached to the First Army to monitor radio communications. This kept them working in their field, and also provided them with valuable experience in how various types of military units appear through their radio transmissions. In this temporary job, the signalmen continued to move across Europe to the Czechoslovakian border.

Another radio section was sent to help out in the 12th Army Group code room. They were the ones who broke the news from Eisenhower that the war in Europe had officially ended. The wire platoon spent five weeks salvaging spiral-4 telephone wire that had been laid for Third Army military operations but was no longer needed. They recovered eight hundred miles of this wire, which was worth an estimated $400,000.

Having incurred the wrath of Colonel Reeder for not agreeing with his reorganization plan, Lieutenant Colonel Simenson was able to leave the unit to command a rifle battalion in the 75th Infantry Division. He arrived at his new unit, thrilled to finally have a combat command, two days before the war ended. He would be in a similar situation during the Korean War, when he took over command of the 14th Infantry Regiment only a few days before the fighting stopped. Paperwork finally caught up with Simenson informing him he had been awarded the Legion of Merit. Eventually he discovered the award did not originate with Reeder, but with the staff of the 12th Army Group who wanted to see his contributions recognized.

Once Germany was in a state of total collapse and Hitler was dead, the remnants of the German military finally surrendered. The fighting was over, but the Allies discovered a problem they had not anticipated. Literally millions of people had been uprooted from their homes and were now scattered across Europe. They were refugees from the fighting, prisoners of war, slave laborers, and even former Nazis attempting to flee from their past.

The army settled on the term "Displaced Persons," or DPs, to refer to these homeless individuals. DP camps were set up to temporarily house and feed them until they could be sorted out and sent home. Almost as important was to provide medical care to prevent the spread of disease. Possibly the most important thing the Allies did in postwar Europe was to prevent the spread of a growing typhus epidemic by chemically delousing as many people as possible.

The 23rd was transferred to the Fifteenth Army and given the job of running DP camps for an estimated one hundred thousand people.[1] Not only did they have to provide for basic needs such as shelter and food, but they also had to screen, process, and sort the DPs. One aspect of screening those in the camps was to prevent any possible German war criminals from hiding among the masses of refugees. No one in the unit had any experience or training in matters like this. In fact, the Allies were totally unprepared for handling the virtual flood of humanity caused by the war.

One soldier in the 23rd compared it to when he had helped refugees from a 1937 flood in Mississippi, but in that case everyone spoke the same language and the locals all wanted to help out. In Europe, however, the DPs spoke twenty-seven different languages (someone counted) and the local Germans wanted no part of assisting in their care. Some of the refugees wanted to go home, others wanted to move as far away from the Communists as possible, and many were in shock and just had no idea what to do with the rest of their lives.

The 23rd Headquarters staff moved into the Hotel Hermes in Idar-Oberstein, which also housed the staff of the XXIII Corps. The rest of the 23rd was given control of thirteen camps in the Saar-Palatine area. The 603rd Engineers ran camps in Bitburg, Wittlich, and Trier. The 406th Engineers were in charge of the Baumholder camp, and the 3132nd ran the DP camp at Liebach. Each unit also oversaw other, smaller camps in their sector.

To prevent riots among the different ethnicities in the camps, they were further broken down by nationality into thirteen sub-camps. The 603rd separated their camps into Italian, Polish, and Russian groups. The Italians proved by far the easiest to control. The Poles and Russians hated each other with a passion and every day brought word of men killed in fights.

DPs would escape from the camps and head to German homes to steal food. If a German civilian got in the way they were often killed without a thought. Upon return to the camp the Russian escapees would try to walk back through the front gate with their stolen loot. Even though it was always taken away from them and added to the main stores, they never seemed to understand that they should try to sneak back in if they wanted to keep the food for themselves. Some of the looting DPs caused enough problems that

In the Trier Displaced Persons Camp a large parade was held to celebrate May Day—the international Communist holiday. Of interest is that the portrait of Joseph Stalin on the reviewing stand is larger than those of Churchill and Truman. The Soviets had planned ahead for such events, while the Americans just wanted to get the war over with. PHOTO: GEORGE MARTIN

they had to be hunted down. There are rumors that a few 23rd men exchanged shots with some of these troublemakers, and were forced to kill them.

In the early stage, before the American Army was able to bring up food and basic supplies for the camps, the 603rd went to a local town mayor to tell him to collect a specific amount of food from the local citizens. The next day the mayor had only collected a tiny amount of food for the DPs and explained that the shortage was because they did not have enough food for themselves. Knowing full well the Germans had more food stored away, the Americans told the mayor politely that if he did not collect the specified amount of food by the next morning, the Americans would have no option but to release the Russians from their camp and let them fend for themselves. So terrified were the local Germans of these Russians that there was never again a problem getting anything needed for the camps.

One curious aspect of camp life was that the Russians not only volunteered but actually fought over the right to peel potatoes in the kitchen. Eventually it was discovered that this was because the peelings were highly valuable as a basis for making home-brewed vodka.

The Russian camps in particular were almost impossible to control. The Russians had previously been treated like animals by the Germans, and refused to cooperate in even the simplest things such as using sanitary facilities. Few Americans spoke Russian or could get the Russian DPs to understand them. One day a lone Russian junior lieutenant, sent by the United Nations Refugee and Rehabilitation Administration (UNRRA), showed up at the 603rd camp. He was not bothered at all by the tales of conditions in the Russian camp. He entered the camp, walked up onto a platform, and began speaking to his countrymen. No one knows what he said, or if he used threats, military authority, or if it was just the fact that he spoke Russian, but the DPs began to follow his instructions. The camp quickly began running smoothly under his command.

Captain Rebh's 406th Engineer Company left Briey on 12 April and assumed control of a DP camp at Neunkirchen the next day. Instead of the expected fifteen thousand DPs, there were only four Ukrainian girls living in the local bank. Within a few days the 406th was sent on to take over the DP camp at Balmholder. This contained sixteen thousand Russians, two thousand Poles, and two thousand assorted other nationalities. Roughly a quarter of that number were female, and a large percentage of those were pregnant.

Lieutenant Daley was given the task of feeding the camp. He used trucks from the 406th, the UNRRA, and a local French transport unit to scour the countryside for supplies. Lieutenant Robinson was put in charge of camp cleanliness and of keeping the inhabitants busy with work. Captain Rebh had proclaimed, "Idleness breeds trouble."[2] A medical staff was sent by the UNRRA, and a number of Russians with medical training volunteered to assist them.

With only his small company to operate the camp, Rebh decided he needed to set up an internal governmental structure among the occupants to help out. He called a meeting of representatives to work out the details, but the Poles simply would not allow the Russians to be in charge. After a meeting that went on long into the night, Rebh finally got the Polish contingent to agree to the Russians playing the major role in running the camp (they were, after all, a large majority). He promised the Poles that they could complain to him at any time if the Russians were abusing them. Major Rabovsky of the Soviet Army was made the head of the camp government.[3]

After a week, Rebh decided to send all non-Russians to the 3132nd-run camp at Liebach, in exchange for Russians in their camp. This helped lessen the friction between the nationalities. After the camp was running as smoothly as possible, the 406th was replaced by a full rifle battalion, and sent to take charge of a small 5,000-man DP camp at Wittlich.

At Wittlich, a former Polish soldier was shot, supposedly by accident, although it could have been by one of the Russian inmates. Rebh allowed the man a burial with full military honors. The historian of the 406th notes that when the 406th firing party at the graveside fired their rifles, it was the first time many of them had shot a weapon in the ETO.[4]

After a short time, new artillery units arrived in the XXIII Corps sector and took over control of the DP camps. Not before, as Lieutenant Fox was proud to point out in the unit history, the 23rd "demonstrated the uses of the latrine to 43,000 middle Europeans."[5] Along with the DP camps, the 23rd also oversaw German POWs being used as laborers in the area. When one group of former German soldiers was slowing down on a job loading heavy crates onto a train, a 23rd man quipped, "Come on lift them up, the Fuhrer says you are all supermen."[6] The Germans were not amused, but kept working.

By this time Lieutenant Colonel Simenson had left the 23rd for the 75th Infantry Division, and was later moved to the 90th Infantry Division. With all the changes being made in the army to prepare to send men to the Pacific, he was eventually transferred to the Theater Plans and Operations office in Frankfurt, where he took part in trying to provide the DP camps with food, clothing, and medical supplies.

In that position he received a telegram from Washington asking, "How many Polish officers are in your headquarters who are accredited to Warsaw?" In conjunction with the Foreign Liaison Officer, Anthony J. Drexel Biddle (a former ambassador to Poland), Simenson realized that if he were to name any of the Polish officers who had served with the Allies it would mean their forced return to Communist Poland (and possible execution). After the third request for this information, Simenson replied that there were none present. Needless to say, he had no problems afterward getting any assistance he needed from the local Poles.[7]

With the war in Europe winding down, there was an army-wide rush to turn in paperwork for awards and decorations. So many award recommendations were submitted by every unit in the ETO it became hard to get some passed through channels. Some awards, such as a unit citation for an entire division, were now expressly forbidden by the War Department (even though they had previously been authorized).

Some veterans of the 23rd have indicated they feel far too few medals were given out in their unit. Some blame Colonel Reeder for not approving award requests, while others feel it was due to the top-secret nature of the unit. In the 23rd's records there is a list of decorations awarded in the unit. Although this list is not complete (some Purple Hearts do not appear on it, nor do awards issued through the 12th Army Group Headquarters), it indicates that complaints about a lack of medals in the 23rd are unfounded. There was, however, a far greater awarding of decorations to senior officers in Reeder's headquarters than to the men in the engineer and signal units.

An interesting aspect to the awards in the 23rd is that a high proportion of them were Certificates of Merit. These were issued solely by authority of the commanding officer and did not have to be approved by a higher authority. This might indicate that Reeder wanted to keep the information about the awards inside the unit (for security purposes). It also could mean that as a former combat soldier Reeder probably did not feel that performing deception duties should earn the same medals as being in a frontline combat unit. As an example, during Operation BRITTANY, Staff Sergeant Tuttle was awarded a Bronze Star for his combat patrols in enemy held areas, while Sergeant Cogan received only a Certificate of Merit for traveling cross-country in enemy-infested territory, without maps or directions, to restore communications with headquarters.

During Operation MERZIG, Lieutenant Colonel Schroeder had recommended three men—Staff Sergeant Price, Sergeant Cattani, and Sergeant Sauro—for the Bronze Star for performing their guard duties under enemy observation and artillery fire. These decorations were downgraded to Certificates of Merit.[8]

There are two classifications of the Bronze Star: one for valor (in combat) and the other for meritorious service (non-combat). The 23rd lists twenty-seven Meritorious Bronze Stars compared to only four for valor. Three awards for valor were to Pfc. Jacob Goldberg (for his actions as a medic under fire at Pickard), Staff Sergeant Wendell B. Tuttle (for his leading combat patrols into enemy-held areas of Brittany), and Lieutenant William G. Aliapoulos (for service during Operation BRITTANY). It is interesting that half of the awards for heroism were awarded in one of the first operations. The third was given for an act of bravery (helping wounded men under fire), which easily fit the standards. The fourth such medal, however, was unusual.

Second Lieutenant Boyd F. Reeder from the 6th Armored Division was awarded a Bronze Star for heroic service during the period 27 March to 16 April 1945. Boyd was Reeder's nephew (the son of his brother, General William Reeder) serving as a tank platoon leader in the 6th Armored Division. Veterans could not recall why he would have been given an award from the 23rd; it was suggested, however, that he might have participated in the 23rd's portrayal of the 6th Armored during Operation BETTEMBOURG many months before. If this was the origin of his medal, it is confusing why it was awarded long after the fact, and why it was issued for heroic service. Reeder's son, Harry Jr., is listed in the West Point records as having been awarded a Bronze Star, but there is no mention of it in the 23rd's reports.

While rumors of classified medals, unit citations, and foreign decorations for the 23rd abound, there is no evidence in any of the unit records or files at the Institute of Heraldry that any were awarded. There is also no evidence that medals were withheld from the deception unit for security reasons. Military practice in these cases is to award the medal, but list as classified any details as to reason, place, or date.

What is odd is that the 23rd was not put in for a Meritorious Unit Plaque. This was the precursor to the Meritorious Unit Commendation (the non-combat equivalent to the Presidential Unit Citation), and was considered the equivalent to awarding all members of the unit a Legion of Merit. Certainly if the 604th Engineer Camouflage Battalion deserved this award for constructing decoy landing craft in England for the FORTITUDE deception (and the 604th actually received a second such award for later service in the ETO), the 23rd as a whole should have been considered for their participation in the Rhine crossing.

No paperwork has been located that would indicate the 23rd was ever put in for any unit award. Likewise, there are no records of any foreign award, even though after having spent so much time in Luxembourg it seems odd that the government of Luxembourg did not offer something.

The end of the fighting also brought more paperwork. The officers of the 23rd were asked to comment on how army doctrine and the Field Service Regulations should be altered to take advantage of the newly learned lessons of deception. It does not appear that many of their suggestions were incorporated into army literature. Possibly they were considered too secret to publish

The vehicles of the 23rd are seen here lined up for the final move to Le Havre and back to the United States. The men were careful to pack all their special equipment because they were sure they would need it for fighting in the Pacific. PHOTO: GEORGE MARTIN

or, more likely, the War Department lost their copies in the paperwork chaos at the end of the war.

By 28 April, the DP camps had been handed over to other units and the 23rd relieved of all responsibility for them. The men waited impatiently in the Idar-Oberstein area for orders. Late in May, the unit was told to prepare for the journey back to the United States, and after a three-day ride through France was moved to a staging area at Rouen.

The camps used for returning servicemen to America were all named after various brands of cigarettes. The 23rd arrived at Camp Twenty-Grand on 16 June. There paperwork was put in order and equipment turned in. Inspections were held frequently to make sure the men would be ready at a moment's notice to board a ship for home. Finally on 23 June 1945, the 23rd went to the Port of Le Havre, boarded the navy transport ship USS *General O.H. Ernst*, and sailed for home.

The voyage was pleasant, and concerns about being sent to the Pacific were lessened by knowing that each man would get a furlough of thirty days before he could be sent out of the States again. The ship's newspaper, the *Ernst Enquirer*, printed a short history of each unit having men on board. The 23rd was still classified, so in order to give the men something to tell their families of what they had done, Lieutenant Fox carefully wrote a history of the 23rd that said a lot, without giving away any details:

> The 23rd Headquarters Special Troops has probably been associated with more Armies and been to more places than any other unit aboard ship. Some of its members landed on D-day with the First Army. Later, part of the command participated in the British campaign with the Third Army. When Field Marshall Montgomery crossed the Rhine in March, the 23rd was attached to the Ninth Army. Finally, when the war was practically over, this versatile outfit took charge of 100,000 milling displaced persons for the Fifteenth Army.
>
> The itinerary of the 23rd sounds like a roll call of famous place names, although modest members of the unit will be the first to admit that they were not entirely responsible for publicizing those once-quiet little towns. They watched the liberation of Cherbourg, drove through the rubble of St. Lo, could have been cut off by the German counterattack at Mortain, helped put the squeeze on Von Ramcke at Brest,[9] took the cheers and kisses of frenzied Parisians, were second into Luxembourg after the 5th Armored Division, shared the cold snows south of Bastogne with the 4th Armored Division (but don't let a 23rder tell you we relieved the 101st Airborne!), hung around the dreary Saarland with XX Corps, and gaped as the 17th A/B flew over to secure a bridgehead on the lower Rhine. One detachment got as far as Pollwitz, a few miles from Czechoslovakia.
>
> Almost any man in this peripatetic unit can toast in six different lan-

guages, and talk knowingly of the ETO campaign from the beaches to the Elbe.

Naturally there have been some exciting moments. For instance, last summer one column was temporarily mislaid near Lorient; or when on 16 Dec. the cooks and KPs of the 4th Infantry Division held the Germans just east of Luxembourg's 23rd Hq; or when the displaced persons rioted at Trier because one nationality was borrowing its water while actually stealing its women.

After a month or so mouthing such sweet place names as Boston, New York, Denver, Phoenix, and Kalamazoo, the 23rd Hq Special Troops will possibly down a series of oriental sourballs including Chofu, Uchidonaria, Tomigusuku, Hakonegasaki and Fuchu. Igaga desu Ka![10]

The *General Ernst* docked in Newport News, Virginia, on 2 July. From there the men went to Camp Patrick Henry, where they were allowed to make telephone calls home. The weather was hot, but anyone who complained about it was immediately offered a trip back to cool, fascinating Germany. Beginning the very next day, men began their journey home for a thirty-day furlough, officially known as "temporary duty for recuperation, rehabilitation and recovery." They were cautioned not to talk about any of the secret activities of the 23rd.

While everyone was on leave, the 23rd was temporarily under the administrative command of Lieutenant William H. Murdock, of the 29th Headquarters and Headquarters Detachment. The unit had been moved to a new home at Pine Camp, New York. What better place for the home base of a deception unit than the birthplace of sonic deception. First to return from leave was Colonel Reeder and his son on 6 August; the following few days saw the return of the rest of the men.

It looked like it would be another long campaign against the Japanese. On 9 August orders were issued for the 23rd to begin preparations for movement to the Pacific. Everyone felt they would perform deception work for the invasion of Japan. A few days later, however, on 14 August, the A-bomb was dropped on Hiroshima and the war suddenly ended.

Most of the men felt they would soon be sent home, but the ways of the army are not always easily understood. The 23rd was kept on alert for movement to the Pacific, with an approximate date sometime in February 1946. It was not until 30 August that the Army Ground Forces officially decided to deactivate the 23rd as of 15 September 1945.

Slowly the men were discharged and sent home. Colonel Reeder left the unit on 23 August 1945 for a new position with the Second Army Headquarters in Tennessee. The final commander of the 23rd was technically Colonel Francis W. Crary, under administrative control of the 29th Headquarters at Pine Camp. The men immediately nicknamed him "Haircuts

The 406th Engineer Combat Company marches in the Watertown, New York, V-J Day parade outside Pine Camp. Captain Rebh was quite pleased with his men's precision; he knew many of them were hung over from celebrating the night before.
PHOTO: GEORGE REBH

Crary" for his insistence on a regulation appearance. Men with eighty points were discharged on 1 September. Anyone with less than forty-five points was transferred to the 95th Infantry Division at Camp Shelby under escort of Captain Seale.

The men were not just glad to have been spared the fighting in the Pacific; many were just happy to be out of the 23rd. Reading between the lines of the official records is evidence that some of the troops were near mutiny upon their arrival at Pine Camp. No good source of information on these troubles was located, but it appears that many of the deception troops were upset at what they considered second-class treatment by their commanders.

The rumors surrounding this problem indicate that Colonel Reeder had not been forthcoming with information on overall plans of action and the importance of the unit's mission. The more intelligent of the troops appear to have been angered at being kept in the dark, when they had proven themselves in combat and felt they could make valuable contributions to the unit's success. One AES document hints at the morale problems, saying that, "While training at Camp Forrest most of the officers and all of the men were denied knowledge of their mission on the decision of the CO."[11]

One junior officer mentioned that the subunits of the 23rd were issued orders from Reeder's headquarters, but were rarely kept informed of the actual situation. He also indicated that outside of his own group he knew few men in the other numbered organizations, and had only minor contact with the officers at headquarters. He painted a picture of each of the four subunits staying much to themselves, and many resented being ordered about by Reeder and his officers, whom they considered outsiders.

Veterans mentioned that some of the men were on the verge of mutiny and were asking to transfer out of the unit for something—*anything*—else rather than go overseas under Reeder again. Such actions are never taken lightly in the military, and if more than a handful of men were involved, the army would have been happy for any mention of these troubles to go unrecorded, so as not to encourage it in the future.

Some veterans claimed that complaints from the men reached the ears of AES commander Colonel Railey, who in turn made them known to the War Department. The indication is that the flamboyant Railey did not think an uncreative Regular Army officer such as Reeder should have commanded the deception unit. There are hints in unit records, which cannot be confirmed, that Reeder may have been in trouble over this matter by the time the war ended. A 23rd man recalled that one day Reeder just left the unit, without fanfare, a going away party, or a change of command ceremony.

According to the 406th unit historian, "A small revolt was stewing inside the unit's hierarchy. An inspecting general was sent up from Second Army Headquarters to investigate charges that the morale of the unit had been very bad overseas. Enlisted men from all the component units were picked at random to testify behind closed doors."[12] The history continues, "Whatever it was the IG discovered, the result was that Colonel Reeder was relieved of his command, and Lieutenant Colonel Snee given his post."[13]

In a letter to a former member of the AES, Major George Melvin (an AES liaison officer) wrote, "As you have probably heard, 3132 returned to the States in early July. Like I have probably told you, they had just completed a year under the most improper command—not their own but the next higher echelon. Colonel Railey managed to get the whole of 23d Headquarters up to Pine Camp and then after a long hard fight had its commanding officer, a full colonel in the Regular Army, and a few members of his staff relieved. This was rough because the Colonel had 30 years service behind him and was of the RA—you know what that means. It did much to boost the morale of the men of all the 23d Hq including 3132. They were plenty bitter."[14]

The actual charges and results cannot be known without access to Reeder's personnel file, however he did remain in the army until his death a few years later. The fate of Colonel Reeder is an important lesson for all nontraditional military units. Reeder had trained all his life for a combat command, and when denied one in order to run a deception unit it appears he was unable to mentally make the switch to this new type of warfare. It probably would have been better to allow Reeder to remain in the armored infantry, and give command of the 23rd to a different officer who not only wanted this command, but also was enthusiastic about deception. In trying to fit an old warhorse into a new type of warfare, the army destroyed one officer, and hindered the utilization of this unique unit. The commander of an experimental unit should not always be chosen for what he has done in the past, but for what he can do in the future.

Chapter 29

After the War

World War II was over, the deception equipment had been packed up in army warehouses, and the men had scattered back to their homes across the country. Interest in military deception, however, had not ended. Reports began to surface of Russian interest in the subject, and in the period of the Cold War arms race, deception was a topic about which the army appeared to be keeping quiet. The Russians actually had a specific term for military deception: *maskirovka*. This was a keenly studied topic in Soviet military schools and included the entire spectrum of deception: feints, simulations, decoys, camouflage, and the related topic of disinformation.

Although close-mouthed about deception operations during WWII, one of the most unusual Soviet deception missions became known through German sources. Operation SCHERHORN was a Russian attempt to draw vitally needed supplies, manpower, and attention to a nonexistent pocket of German soldiers trapped behind Russian lines.

In August 1944, the Germans received a radio message that roughly 2,500 Germans, commanded by Oberstleutnant Heinrich Scherhorn, had been cut off behind Russian lines in the forests north of Minsk. Every possible effort to support this group was made by the faltering German military. Radios and radio operators were parachuted into the pocket. Special SS groups were dispatched by air to help get them out. The great commando Otto Skorzeny was even told to plan a mission to evacuate them by air. Hitler was so impressed with the determination of these surrounded troops that he promoted Scherhorn to Oberst (Colonel) and awarded him the Knight's Cross. All officers mentioned by name in the few radio messages were also given promotions.

The final radio message was sent from Scherhorn's command on 4 April 1945, just before the Germans surrendered. After the war, German authorities discovered that the entire thing had been a ruse. There had indeed been a 1,500-man detachment trapped in the region after the Russian offensive in the summer of 1944, but it had been quickly overrun. Scherhorn and two hundred

German use of decoys, such as this wooden artillery piece, in WWII appears to have been limited to drawing enemy fire. So far no records have been located that indicate they had any comparable deception units to fool the Allies about their military plans.

men were taken prisoner, and agreed to send the false messages under duress.[1]

No evidence that the Germans had a similar tactical deception unit has been located. Wartime use of German decoys seems to have been limited to more standard uses. The following example of their use was provided in a 1944 wartime report: "Although German use of dummy tanks in France and Italy has not been extensive, such instances as have been reported make it clear that the enemy is capable of imaginative work along this line. For example, a typical enemy procedure is to site dummy tanks and real antitank guns in such a manner, with respect to the terrain, that Allied tanks maneuvering to engage the dummies will present enfilade targets to the German antitank guns."[2]

Due to Allied air superiority, it appears that the bulk of German deception involved camouflage and decoys designed to fool aircraft rather than influence ground battles. Airfields and factories would be painted to show extensive bomb damage so they would not attract further attacks. Near the vital oil-producing center of Ploesti, the Germans constructed a three-dimensional plywood duplicate of a refinery complex to draw off Allied bombers from the genuine target.

But it turned out that the Russians were the ones who were particularly interested in deception, as it allowed them to appear stronger than they actually were (not just in the military sphere, but also in science, politics, and economics). According to General Zhukov, the 1930s victory at Khalkin Gol had been achieved by appearing to be strictly on the defensive, then attacking when the Japanese were not expecting them.[3] The Russian attack on Japanese-held Manchuria in 1945 and the August 1943 offensive at Belgorod-Kharkov, among many other examples, relied heavily on deception to fool their enemies as to the location and strength of the Soviet forces.[4]

During WWII the Russians diluted German aerial attacks by constructing a large number of decoy airfields (called *imitatsiya*). They claimed that from July 1942 through May 1945 there were fifteen hundred attacks and five hundred tons of bombs were dropped on these dummy installations.[5] The Russians also may have experimented with sonic deception as early as 1942. According to one source, the Russians had planned an attack on a left flank, then constructed dummy tanks and artillery on the right flank to appear as a troop build-up. This was made more realistic with small explosives simulators and recordings of the sounds of tank motors.[6]

During the Cold War, *maskirovka* fooled the west about the capabilities of the Soviet military. During the 1955 Soviet Air Force Day celebration, every Bison Bomber that had been made was flown past the reviewing stand, then circled out of sight for a second pass to create the impression of a great force of these strategic bombers—roughly four times the number of B-52s in operation by the Americans. The large number of Soviet bombers seen during this event led to claims there was a gap in the number of strategic bombers held respectively by the West and the East (the so-called "Bomber Gap").[7]

It is almost certain that the American military was concerned with deception during this time, but seemingly not nearly as much as the Russians. The former equipment of the 23rd did, however, have a final use. It was used in the army's "Aggressor Force" training program. The Aggressor Force program was designed to give the army a hypothetical enemy to train against, without actually indicating they were preparing to fight the Communists. The Aggressor Force Army was a total construct bearing little relation to any actual military force in the world. Its men wore an unusual assortment of obsolete uniforms and attached square wooden blocks to their helmets to give them a foreign appearance. The army provided the Aggressor Force with an order of battle, tables of organization, its own ranks, and military doctrine.

Typically, genuine elements of the U.S. Army would fight against a unit of the Aggressor Army in a training exercise. To save on manpower and equipment needs for the Aggressors, the army pulled the old deception equipment

After the war, the deception equipment was utilized by the American Army "Aggressor Forces" as a training aid. The Aggressors, seen in their distinctive combed helmets, used the sonic equipment and inflatable decoys to increase their numbers on the battlefield and provide more realistic training with only a handful of men.

out of storage and made the small Aggressor forces appear stronger through the use of decoys, radio deception, and sonic deception.

Setting up inflatable decoys and putting on strange uniforms did not take much practice, but the army decided it needed a special unit to help coordinate the signals aspect. The Signal Company of the 23rd Special Troops was reactivated to help assist in these training maneuvers. In January 1947, the 23rd Signal Company was re-formed, but with a strength of only one officer and six men, at Fort Riley, Kansas. These seven men were obtained from the 1st Provisional Signal Detachment and included one captain as company commander, a chief radio operator, two radio operators, a chief radio repairman, and two radio repairmen. It was initially attached for administrative purposes to the 91st Cavalry Recon Squadron.

Although no proof has been found, it was probably during this time period that a round metal insignia for the 23rd Special Troops was designed. It was a small enameled emblem, referred to in the army as a "distinctive insignia." It was circular in shape and divided into three sections by three armored legs joined in the middle. Two of the sections were blue and one yellow, supposedly representing the two infantry and one armored divisions that the unit could simulate in WWII. Five fleurs-de-lis were placed around the edge to represent the five campaigns in the ETO. The motto "Deceive to Defeat" was placed at the bottom. This insignia was apparently never authorized by the army's Institute of Heraldry, and it is not known if any were actually manufactured for the small unit. At some point in the 1970s, however, a reproduction of this insignia was produced in Asia for the insignia collector's market.

The new 23rd Signal Company took part in Exercise SEMINOLE in Florida during late 1947. Later that year it took part in Exercise ASSEMBLY at Camp Campbell, Kentucky, and at some point was designated a "training reserve unit." The year 1949 saw the small detachment take part in a field exercise with the 82nd Airborne at Fort Bragg, and in 1950 the unit was sent to Hawaii for attachment to the 47th Engineer Camouflage Battalion and the Aggressor Headquarters during Exercise PORTEX. In the next few years it participated in Exercise SWARMER, followed by Exercise SOUTHERN PINE, Exercise TIMBERLINE, and Exercise FLEX 52. In 1952 the unit was at Pine Camp for Exercise SNOW FALL, followed by Exercise LONG HORN at Fort Hood, Texas. Coincidentally, its last major operation was Exercise SNOW STORM at Fort Drum (the former Pine Camp home of the AES) in 1953. The unit was deactivated on 26 March 1953.

The 603rd Camouflage Battalion was also reactivated after WWII. On 30 January 1947, it was redesignated the 590th Camouflage Battalion. The headquarters element was disbanded in June 1954 when Companies A, B, C, and D were redesignated the 609th, 631st, 632nd, and 634th Engineer Companies. In February 1956, the 603rd Headquarters and HQ detachment were again reactivated as one camouflage platoon (eighty-eight men total) and sent to White Sands Proving Grounds. This detachment was inactivated in March 1968. No information on whether these units performed deception tasks or standard camouflage tasks was located.

The 3132nd Signal Service Company was eventually re-formed in 1954 as the 123rd Signal Battalion, but with no deception capabilities. In 1966 it became the 509th Signal Battalion and was sent to Vietnam, where it was later redesignated the 523rd Signal Battalion.

There was apparently another peak in army interest in deception during the military build-up of the Reagan years. For a short period of time it appears there was actually an MOS (Military Occupational Specialty) for tactical deception. Efforts to track down current units involved with deception have not been successful. To an army outsider it appears that there is little interest in tactical deception, although rumors abound that the engineers continue to work on decoys, that there is interest at the Military Intelligence School, and that Psychological Operations (Psyops) units are involved.

Although technology has vastly changed since the days of wire recorders, deception continues to be used in the military world. During the campaign in

Bosnia, very expensive and complex American heat-seeking missiles were fooled into striking decoy targets by attracting them to heat sources in dummy vehicles. This simple tactic would certainly have pleased Colonel Railey, had one of his men thought it up.

The principals of deception do not change, but deception tactics and equipment need to keep up with changing technology. For every new military breakthrough there will be a way to turn it against the user through deception. Satellite imagery is not invulnerable to methods similar to those used against the Luftwaffe. An army that uses global positioning satellites can easily be tricked if one holds the key to the satellite software (which, thankfully, the United States government does). It takes only some creativity to gain the advantage through deception.

If there is one lesson that the deception veterans of WWII would like to pass on to today's military, it is that tactical deception can be a vital part of any battle plan. It can help achieve surprise, tie up enemy resources, or pin down reinforcements. Tactical deception may not always be suitable for every specific battle, but military commanders should know of its past, and be able to utilize it when appropriate.

The Correct Name of the 23rd

There is some confusion about the actual name of this deception unit. The question is whether the entire deception unit (headquarters and four component units) should be officially called the "23rd Headquarters" or the "23rd Special Troops."

In military terms, a headquarters is the command element of a unit. The term "special troops" specifically meant a subunit (generally of division or larger size) that supports the entire unit as a whole. Examples would be the military police platoon or maintenance company in a division. Both of these groups provide their services to the entire division, whereas an infantry regiment in a division does not provide any services outside its own regimental boundaries.[1]

Most wartime reports from the 23rd are headed "23rd Headquarters, Special Troops." Due to this it has been assumed that this was the unit's correct designation. Because most of the paperwork arising from the 23rd came from Reeder's headquarters element, it is not surprising that the word headquarters is found on the official reports. The question is: was the 23rd technically called the "23rd Headquarters" (with the "special troops" suffix indicating the four main component units as dictionary-defined elements supporting the entire unit), or was it the "23rd Special Troops" (with headquarters added in only when indicating Colonel Reeder's headquarters element)?

Normally the army is very good on matters of nomenclature such as this. In the case of the 23rd, however, the evidence remains confusing. The official records of the 23rd are cataloged in the National Archives (which is a continuation of the Pentagon's WWII cataloging system) as if it were a numbered headquarters unit. There were a handful of such headquarters units in WWII (such as the 19th Headquarters). These numbered headquarters units provided an easy way to put a number of nonrelated companies and battalions in a specific geographic location under a unified and coordinated command.

The organization of the 23rd Headquarters element bears a similarity to a corps headquarters. Each has specific branch sections (armor, engineer, antiaircraft, etc.). The 23rd was originally supposed to be able to portray a corps-sized unit, so it would make sense to pattern the 23rd Headquarters after a corps headquarters. Referring to a top-secret deception unit as a numbered headquarters would also add to the security of the unit's mission.

The U.S. Army's Unit Citation and Campaign Participation Credit Register, however, catalogs the unit as the "23rd Special Troops, Headquarters and Headquarters Company," followed by the "23rd Special Troops, Signal Company, Special."[2] The

244th Signal Company lost its numerical designation to become the permanently assigned signal company of the 23rd in January 1944.

While it would make no sense to refer to a secret unit by a name that would call attention to itself, the designation "Special Troops" was in such common use that no one would give it a second look. The anonymity and confusion the name would cause continues up to this day. Attempts to get a definitive answer from various departments of the U.S. Army (Institute of Heraldry and the Center for Military History) have been inconclusive.

Thus it appears that the correct terminology for the unit taken as a whole (the command element, the 244th Signal Company, 603rd Camouflage Battalion, 406th Engineer Combat Company, and 3132nd Signal Service Company) should be the "23rd Special Troops." To refer only to Colonel Reeder's command elements (and excluding the four previously mentioned units) the correct terminology should be "Headquarters, 23rd Special Troops."

That being said, a look at the official tables of organization (T/O) for the unit authorized on 4 April 1944 tells a different story. According to these, Reeder's command element is officially called "Headquarters and Headquarters Company, 23rd Headquarters, Special Troops." The signal company is "Signal Company, Special, 23rd Headquarters, Special Troops," and the 406th is called the "Engineer Combat Company, 23rd Headquarters, Special Troops." These T/Os put the word headquarters back into the name of the non-command elements. These tables of organization were drawn up in the unit and approved without comment by Washington. They then provide good evidence that, at the time, the men thought their official unit designation was "23rd Headquarters, Special Troops."

Another piece of evidence on the name is a series of reports requested from 12th Army Group on each operation, called "Report on operations involving Special Troops." These were requested in a letter from SHAEF (SHAEF/19006/Ops/B, 3 August 1944). In this request the words "Special Troops" are capitalized which would indicate that the 12th Army Group deception officers requesting the information thought of the unit as being called "Special Troops."

Although there is evidence to support both concepts, the final and official word on the subject must be the army's unit campaign register, indicating "23rd Special Troops." Therefore, until further evidence comes forth indicating otherwise, this should be considered the official name of the unit as a whole.

Officers of the 23rd Special Troops

Commanding Officer—Col. Harry L. Reeder, Inf.
Executive Officer—Lt. Col. Merrick H. Truly, USMA 1931, Inf.
S1 (Personnel)—W.O. Aldrich V. Cousins
S2 (Intelligence)—Maj. Joseph P. Kelly, Inf.
S3 (Operations)—Lt. Col. Clifford Simenson, USMA 1934, Inf.
    Asst S-3 Capt. Thomas L. Raggio, Inf.
S4 (Supply)—Capt. (later Maj.) David H. Bridges, FA
    Asst S-4 Capt. James Dick, Inf.
Adjutant—Maj. David Haviland, FA
Signal Officer—Maj. Charles H. Yocum, SC
Engineer Officer—Maj. Frederick D. Vincent, CE
    Asst. Engineer Officer—Capt. Imon M. Richardson, CE
Armored Officer—Lt. Col. James W. Snee, USMA 1934, Cav.
    Asst. Armored Officer—1st Lt. (later Capt.) Oscar M. Seale, Inf.
Antiaircraft Officer—Lt. Col. Frederick E. Day, USMA 1927, CAC
Field Artillery Officer—Lt. Col. John W. Mayo, FA
    Asst. Artillery Officer—Capt. Edward M. Cowardin, FA
    Asst. Artillery Officer—Capt. Joseph H. Sidwell, FA
Medical Officer—Maj. Burton E. E. Adams, MC
            (later Capt. Neil D. Elzey, MC after 1 Dec. 44)
    Asst. Medical Officer—Capt. Murphy P. Martin, MC
Dental Officer—Capt. Gerald N. Wagner, DC
Motor Transport Officer—1st Lt. Harry L. Reeder Jr. USMA 43, Inf.
Radio Traffic Analyst—1st Lt. Frederick E. Fox
Liaison Officers—   Lt. Col. John W. Watson, Cav.
                Lt. Col. Edgar W. Schroeder, USMA 1939, Cav.
                Lt. Col. Olen J. Seaman, USMA 1937, SC

23rd Headquarters Company
Capt. Thomas G. Wells, Inf.
XO 1st Lt. Adolphus C. Simpson, Inf.

23rd Signal Company, Special
Capt. Irwin C. Vander Heide, SC

3132nd Signal Service Company
Major Charlie Williams
XO—Capt. Robert Hiller
Supply Officer—Lt. John Walker
Technical & Maintenance Officer—Lt. Walter Manser
1st Platoon—Lt. Hartley, then John Walker
2nd Platoon—Lt. Harold Fasnacht
3rd Platoon—Lt. Leonard Davis
4th Platoon—Lt. Richard Syracuse

603rd Camouflage Bn.
Lt. Col. Otis Fitz, then Major Bill Hooper
XO—Major Bill Hooper
Adjutant—Lt. Gilbert Seltzer

A—Capt. Corriston
B—Capt. John R. Comulada
    1st Platoon—Lt. Albert B. Zintl
    2nd Platoon—Lt. Harold L. Skuldt
    3rd Platoon—Lt. John W. Stapp Jr.
C—Capt. Miller
D—Capt. Raynor

406th Engineer Combat Co
C.O.—Capt. George A. Rebh, USMA Jan. 1943, CE
HQ Platoon—Lt. Ted Kelker
1st Platoon—Lt. George Daley
2nd Platoon—Lt. Thomas Robinson
3rd Platoon—Lt. William Aliapoulos

Known Major Command Changes in 23rd Headquarters
Lt. Col. Truly becomes Liaison Officer, 30 Oct 44
Lt. Col. Snee becomes Exec. Officer, 30 Oct 44
Capt. Richardson transferred to 1135th Eng Gp., 1 Nov 44
Lt. Col. Frederick Day transferred to Civil Affairs Div., 6 Mar 45
Lt. Simpson becomes CO Hq Co., 13 Mar 45
Col. Simenson becomes AA Officer, 28 Mar 45
Maj. Bridges becomes S-3, 28 Mar 45
Capt. Dick becomes S-4, 28 Mar 45
Lt. Col. Truly transferred to 12th Army Group, 5 Apr 45

Branch of service:
Inf.—Infantry; Cav.—Cavalry; SC—Signal Corps;
MC—Medical Corps; FA—Field Artillery; CE—Corps of Engineers
CAC—Coastal Artillery Command (typically antiaircraft artillery in WWII)
USMA indicates year of graduation from the United States Military Academy at West Point.

Medals and Decorations Awarded in the 23rd Special Troops

Unit Awards

Campaign participation for: Normandy
Northern France
Central Europe
Ardennes–Alsace
Rhineland

Letter of Commendation, Ninth Army, 29 March 1945

Individual Awards

Legion of Merit
Lt. Col. James W. Snee, Task Force Commander
Lt. Col. Edgar W. Schroeder, Task Force Commander
Captain Oscar M. Seale, Task Force Commander
Lt. Col. Clifford Simenson (awarded through 12th Army Group)

Bronze Star for heroic service or achievement
*Lt. William G. Aliapoulos, Platoon Leader
Pfc. Jacob Goldberg, Medic
Lt. Boyd F. Reeder, Platoon Leader, tank battalion
*S/Sgt. Wendell B. Tuttle, Platoon Sgt.

Bronze Star (Meritorious Service)
*M/Sgt. Glenn M. Krantz, Communications Chief
*T/Sgt. Harold A. Hedrick, Communications Chief
Capt. Thomas G. Wells, Company Commander
Major Thomas L. Raggio, Staff Officer

Major David Haviland, Staff Officer (S-1)
S/Sgt. Victor E. Dowd, Platoon Sgt.
S/Sgt. Herbert T. Amborski, Platoon Sgt.
Major David H. Bridges, Staff Officer S-4)
Major Joseph P. Kelly, Staff Officer (S-2)
Lt. Orrie J. Holmen, Adjutant
Lt. Col. John W. Mayo, Staff Officer
Major William U. Hooper, Bn. Commander
Lt. Col. Olen J. Seaman, Staff Officer
Capt. Edward M. Cowardin, Staff Officer
Lt. Col. Merrick H. Truly, Staff Officer
Major Charles H. Yocum, Staff Officer
T/Sgt. Herman Schneider, Operations Sgt.
S/Sgt. Raymond A. Lawrence, Operations Sgt.
T/5 Alan Wood-Thomas, Camoufleuer
Lt. Bernard H. Mason, unlisted
1st Sgt. William L. German, unlisted
Capt. John R. Comulada, unlisted
Capt. William B. Skelton, unlisted
S/Sgt. William E. Senat, unlisted
Capt. Winfield F. Corriston, unlisted
Capt. Frederick E. Fox, unlisted
Capt. Wesley A. Davidson, unlisted

Certificate of Merit
*S/Sgt. Martin Cogan, Squad Leader
**Sgt. Carl N. Johnson, Squad Sgt.,
**S/Sgt. Joseph A. Taney, Platoon Sgt.
**Pfc. Charles A Gorman, Demolition Specialist
**T/Sgt. Jean L. Kunkle, Supply Sgt.
**Pfc. Nicholas L. Minutolo, Demolition Specialist
**T/5 Thomas Haney, Tool Room Keeper
**T/4 Otto M. Groeber, Radio Operator
**Cpl. Rolff E. Campbell, Construction Foreman
**Sgt. Stanley N. Kaufman, Camoufleuer
**T/5 Irving Stempel, Camoufleuer
**T/5 John F. Goring, Carpenter
**Pfc. William V. Hayes, Carpenter
**T/5 William B. Ormand, Camoufleuer
**Pvt. Albin S. Smolinsky, Basic
**Pfc. Martin J. Nicholson, Camoufleuer
Pfc. Robert J. Jackson, Basic
Pfc. Benjamin Schwartz, Camoufleuer
S/Sgt. Raymond A. Lawrence, Acting Sgt. Major
M/Sgt. James C. Taylor, Sgt. Major
CWO Aldrich V. Cousins, Personnel Officer
M/Sgt. Robert C. MacFarland, Sgt. Major

T/5 Augustine J. Creaghan, Mail Clerk
Sgt. John Cattani, Squad Sgt.
Sgt. Anthony R. Sauro, Squad Sgt.
1st Sgt. Fred C. Price, Platoon Sgt.
S/Sgt. Benjamin C. Nance, Platoon Sgt.
T/4 August J. Moorman, Chief Clerk
S/Sgt. Howard L. Hartzell, Platoon Sgt.
S/Sgt. M. Harry Johnson, Platoon Sgt.
S/Sgt. Allen Trumpower, Mess. Sgt.
Sgt. Christopher L. Lawless, Squad Sgt.
T/5 Walter T. Kadi, unlisted
T/5 Francis E. Paynton, unlisted
Sgt. Keith S. Williams, Camouflage Technician
S/Sgt. Raymond H. Green, Platoon Sgt.
T/Sgt. Joseph P. Endris, unlisted

Purple Heart
1st Sgt. William L. German
S/Sgt. Erasmus T. Beall
Sgt. Robert S. Danstadt
Sgt. William S. Enoch
T/4 Ralph L. Grindel
T/5 John Goring
Pfc George Epstein
T/4 John A Raparelli
T/4 Peter A. Shirk

Note: above Purple Hearts are all from shellings at Pickard on 13 March 1945. Some names of known casualties from other periods are not mentioned, Lt. Col. Day is known to have earned a Purple Heart during the Brittany operation as was T-5 Allison M. Severe, for burns received on 7 Jan 45.

* Awarded at Decoration Ceremony, 15 November 1944
** Awarded at Decoration Ceremony, 4 Jan 1945.

Appendix 4

Tables of Organization

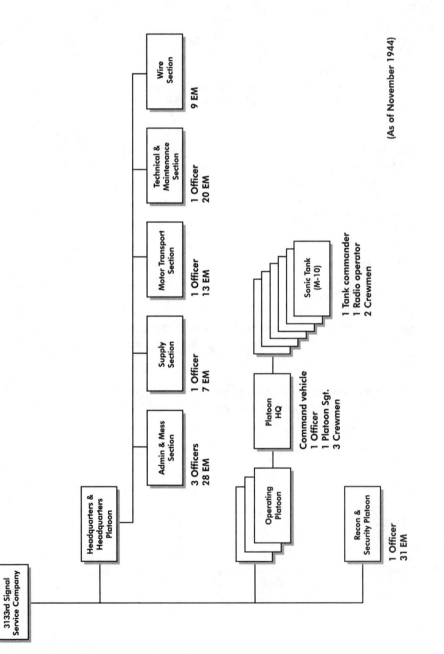

(As of November 1944)

Headquarters & Headquarters Platoon

Admin & Mess Section — 3 Officers / 28 EM

Supply Section — 1 Officer / 7 EM

Motor Transport Section — 1 Officer / 13 EM

Technical & Maintenance Section — 1 Officer / 20 EM

Wire Section — 9 EM

3133rd Signal Service Company

Operating Platoon

Platoon HQ — Command vehicle / 1 Officer / 1 Platoon Sgt. / 3 Crewmen

Sonic Tank (M-10) — 1 Tank commander / 1 Radio operator / 2 Crewmen

Recon & Security Platoon — 1 Officer / 31 EM

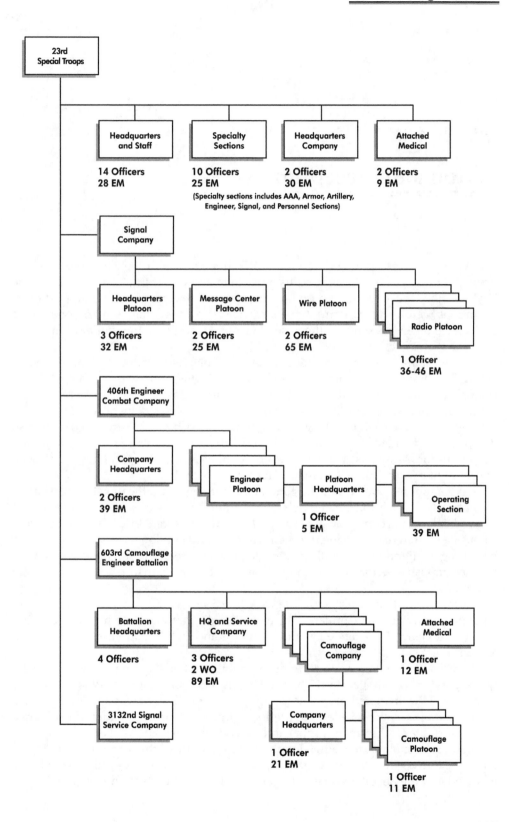

Appendix 5

Patton and Deception

While I was researching deception in WWII, an officer of the 23rd casually mentioned, "Patton's Third Army used us more than any other unit." He was right. The 23rd was the tactical deception unit for the entire 12th Army Group, but most of its operations were in Third Army territory. There is no way that so many operations could have taken place under the nose of General George Patton without him being aware of them.

There seems to be a continuing connection between Patton and deception in WWII. The first record of him involved with a deception plan was in 1943, when the rumor was spread that Patton was to be the replacement for General Wilson in the Mediterranean. As part of this operation he visited Cairo and spent some time with Dudley Clarke and A-Force. It was there that he first became introduced to British deception, and where he first met Noel Wild, who would later be running deception operations for D-day.[1] As an amateur historian himself, Patton must have been aware of past military deceptions and their value on the battlefield.

Contemporary portraits of the general indicate he had a theatrical and flamboyant nature (such as his lacquered helmet and trademark pistols). He might well have enjoyed taking part in such operations. Although referred to as "Old Blood and Guts," Patton felt that pressing the enemy hard would cut down casualties in the end by getting the fighting over with sooner. He may have realized deception would help him accomplish a victory faster, and with fewer casualties, than a brute force frontal assault.

In mid-1943, Patton played a role in A-Force's Operation BARCLAY. This was an attempt to convince the Germans that the Allies did not intend to invade Sicily, but rather that General Alexander would invade France while Patton invaded Corsica and Sardinia.

In Sicily, Patton was involved in the infamous soldier-slapping incident (actually two separate incidents) at the 15th and 93rd Evacuation Hospitals. When this story became widely circulated in the theater of operations, Eisenhower apparently told a number of reporters that he felt publication of this incident would hurt Allied morale and contribute to German propaganda.[2] The approximately sixty reporters at Eisenhower's headquarters agreed with him, as not one of them attempted to report on it. Patton was, however, asked to publicly apologize to not only the soldiers involved and the hospital staffs, but to every soldier in the Seventh Army. Thus confirming to a very large group, through public humiliation, that the incident had indeed taken place. The *New York Times* found out about it, but refused to print it for fear of breaking the wartime censorship code (which prohibited reporting incidents such as this which might hurt morale). The story then sat idle for three months.

Reporter Drew Pearson finally broke the story, feeling it was in the public's interest. Pearson first publicly mentioned the slapping incident on his Sunday night radio broadcast on 21 November 1943. The story had been shown to the Office of Censorship and the War Department and was approved, even though it seemed to violate the censorship regulations in the Code of Wartime Practices as it would hurt Allied morale and thus potentially aid the enemy cause.[3]

What is very interesting is that it was Pearson's lawyer, Ernest Cuneo, who initially brought the story to Pearson and advised him it would help make his career (as in fact it did). Actually releasing this story was a probable violation of the censorship regulations and it might well have destroyed Pearson's career, as well as sent him to jail. It turns out Cuneo, who pressed him to break the story, had a number of interesting ties to the army intelligence community. He had assisted the U.S. government as a liaison between the FBI, British Intelligence, and the Office of the Coordinator of Information.[4] So we have a man connected to the intelligence world advising one of his key clients to essentially break the law and possibly destroy his reputation as a reporter.

Pearson's broadcast script started with the line "General George Patton, nicknamed 'Blood and Guts,' will not be used in the European war theater anymore. He was a bit too bloody for the morale of the Army." The end of the script stated that, "He will not be used in important combat anymore."[5] The relief of Patton from a combat role was not true, but it is curious that this was stated in both the introduction and tag lines.

Although there were concerns over possible censorship violations, the script was approved on 14 November 1943 by government officials. However, Pearson did not use the story that week or the next. It was inserted into his Sunday night broadcast, at the last minute, two weeks later. The storm that erupted over the story certainly hurt Patton's public reputation, and many feel it greatly harmed his military career.

Why would it have been useful to put Patton in a bad light? Supposedly American public opinion was used as the excuse to move him, in disgrace, from Italy to England. It seems likely, however, that the Germans would look for a deeper reason for this transfer than just a soldier being slapped (which to the professional German officer must have seemed ludicrous). The obvious reason to the Germans might be that Patton was actually moved to England to command the forthcoming invasion of France, with the slapping excuse as a ruse to cover it. This would serve to reinforce the idea that Patton was actually sent to England to command the First U.S. Army Group for the main invasion of France. Of course, while the Germans thought they should keep their eye on Patton, Bradley, with the First Army, made the genuine assault.

After the slapping incident, but before being transferred "in disgrace" to England, Patton was sent on a trip around the Mediterranean, supposedly to attract German attention. His trip to Corsica was made with the specific intention of trying to convince the Germans he was preparing for an amphibious invasion in northern Italy behind their lines.[6] His trip was staged to appear as if he were inspecting locations for a buildup of troops prior to a forthcoming amphibious invasion—an example of Patton being used in a very specific deception role.

Patton's reputation was further tarnished in England by his supposed slight to the Russians at a speech given in Knutsford. Research into the Knutsford incident clearly shows that he was greatly misquoted. The army public relations staff does not seem to have worried much about correcting the error. The incident was manufactured into a major embarrassment to the general—either by error or on purpose.[7] This publicity would have allowed German intelligence to firmly place Patton in England, if they had not already discovered his whereabouts. This would be another clue that Patton was preparing for the invasion of France. It would also set the groundwork for yet another change in Patton's assignment.

In England, Patton took part in an unusual aspect of the FORTITUDE deception. The German General Hans Cramer was held as a POW in England. Due to illness he was being repatriated through the Red Cross. To help convince the Germans that southeast England was packed with material preparing to invade at Calais, Cramer was driven through the jam-packed southwest, but told it was the southeast area. He then had dinner with Patton, who was introduced as the commander of the First U.S. Army Group. Patton, supposedly, made a point of mentioning Calais. When Cramer arrived home it was certain he would be thoroughly debriefed on everything he had seen and heard.[8]

While Patton was acting as commander of the (notional) First U.S. Army Group (FUSAG), as part of Operation FORTITUDE, he was already aware he would be given command of the genuine Third Army once it was activated in France.[9] Since the Allies wanted to keep the Germans convinced that FUSAG remained a threat to the Calais area after the Normandy landings, thus pinning down the German troops at Calais, neither FUSAG, nor its high profile commander, could just disappear after D-day. To transfer Patton from an Army Group command to the lower Third Army command was clearly a demotion. It might spur German intelligence to take another look at FUSAG and why Patton was suddenly moved to a lesser command.

Two curious incidents occurred in the early days of the French campaign. First, the Public Relations Officer at Patton's headquarters briefed reporters on the secret plans for Operation COBRA. Patton, as the commanding officer, was blamed for this serious breach of security and reprimanded. Second, there was the case of two American soldiers who brought an English woman across the channel with them "for immoral purposes." Ridiculously, Patton was pummeled for this in the conservative American press. Their rationale was that the commanding officer was technically responsible for what his men did. Much like the slapping incident, blaming Patton for this in the media might also be construed as a violation of the wartime censorship regulations. This incident was used as one of the reasons to demote him to command of Third Army (which had been planned all along).

Some proof that Patton was genuinely in trouble with the Allied High Command over the many incidents is found in cables exchanged between Eisenhower and General Marshal in Washington discussing if Patton should continue in command. Of course, if Patton were being used in a deception operation, erroneous messages would have been sent in case the Germans were able to intercept them. In the same way that coded messages sent by the 23rd were always properly coded messages that fit the current situation, these cables could potentially be another link in the deception. Even if the code was not broken, an enemy agent with access to these telegrams might have discovered the information confirming Patton's situation.

Concern over the Germans intercepting Allied telegrams is not as far-fetched as it seems. Churchill and Roosevelt spoke on a transatlantic telephone line protected by an A-3 scrambler device. The Germans had not only been able to tap this line, but also to break the scrambler and listen in to these conversations starting in September 1941.[10] According to historian David Johnson, Churchill mentioned that Operation COCKADE was a deception during one of these calls, thus confirming German suspicions.[11] A new telephone scrambler, that the Germans were not able to break, was installed on the line in early 1944. There is no evidence that the Allies knew of the interception, but the new scrambler was put into place at an opportune time to deny the Germans any information on the Normandy invasion.

The same evaluation can be applied to material from Patton's diary and personal papers. If there was deception in play, Patton might have continued to play the game even in his personal writings. There would certainly be time after the war to explain it had all been part of a plan to fool the Germans and shorten the war. It was always possible that an enemy agent might catch a glimpse of his writing, intercept a letter, or steal the diary.

Once Patton was commanding the Third Army in France, his forces took part in a deception operation known as "Tactical Operation B" to trick the Germans into thinking a larger number of American troops were headed to Brittany than actually were. Part of this operation involved carefully planned reports sent to the Abwehr by the turned German agents in England working for the XX Committee. Also involved were the 23rd Special Troops notionally portraying some of Patton's forces moving west to Brittany. It is inconceivable he did not know of this operation, yet it is not mentioned in his writings.

All of the above remains conjecture until proven, but Patton's unsung personal role in deception is an interesting concept. It is quite possible that future investigation into Patton's wartime exploits may discover a further pattern of his connection with deception operations.

Appendix 6

Original Poop Sheets

During the war the 23rd visited as many different units as possible to take notes on their specific appearance. This information was distilled into information sheets, dubbed "poop sheets." At the end of the war they had records of most units in the ETO, unfortunately only a handful, presented here, have survived.

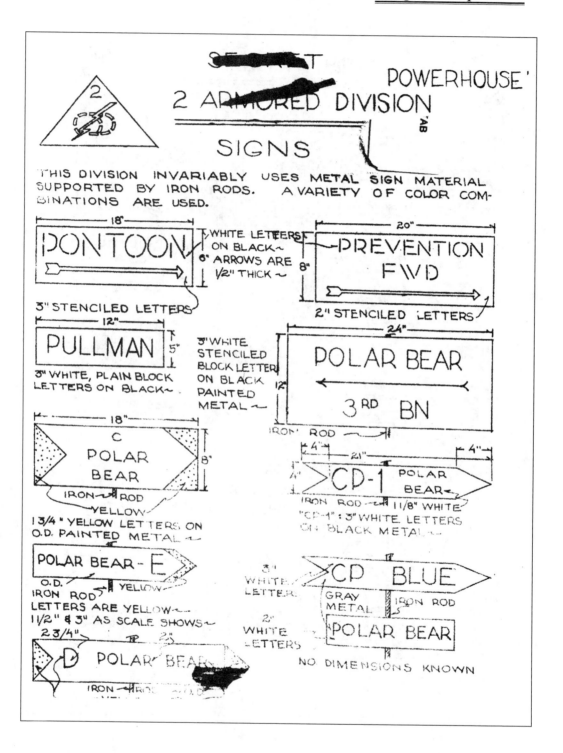

SECRET POWERHOUSE'

2 ARMORED DIVISION

SIGNS

THIS DIVISION INVARIABLY USES METAL SIGN MATERIAL SUPPORTED BY IRON RODS. A VARIETY OF COLOR COMBINATIONS ARE USED.

PONTOON
WHITE LETTERS ON BLACK~
6" ARROWS ARE 1/2" THICK~
3" STENCILED LETTERS

PREVENTION FWD
2" STENCILED LETTERS

PULLMAN
3" WHITE, PLAIN BLOCK LETTERS ON BLACK~

3" WHITE STENCILED BLOCK LETTER ON BLACK PAINTED METAL~

POLAR BEAR
3RD BN
IRON ROD~

C POLAR BEAR
IRON ROD
YELLOW
1 3/4" YELLOW LETTERS ON O.D. PAINTED METAL~

CD-1 POLAR BEAR
IRON ROD~ 1 1/8" WHITE
"CD-1" : 3" WHITE LETTERS ON BLACK METAL~

POLAR BEAR - E
O.D. IRON ROD~ YELLOW
LETTERS ARE YELLOW~
1 1/2" & 3" AS SCALE SHOWS~

CD BLUE
3" WHITE LETTER
GRAY METAL IRON ROD
2" WHITE LETTERS

POLAR BEAR
NO DIMENSIONS KNOWN

D POLAR BEAR
IRON ROD

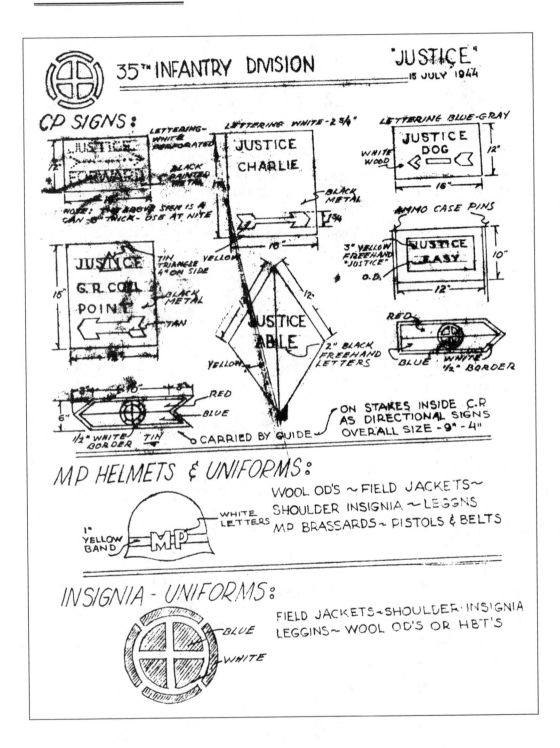

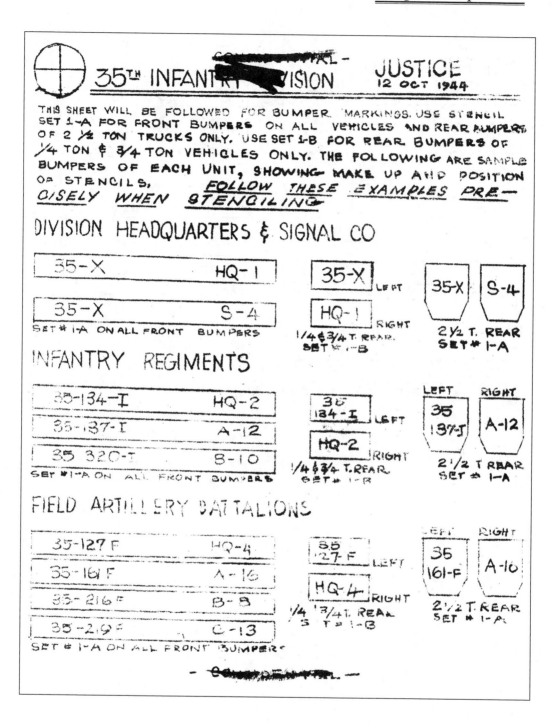

35TH INFANTRY DIVISION — JUSTICE
12 OCT 1944

THIS SHEET WILL BE FOLLOWED FOR BUMPER MARKINGS. USE STENCIL SET 1-A FOR FRONT BUMPERS ON ALL VEHICLES AND REAR BUMPERS OF 2 1/2 TON TRUCKS ONLY. USE SET 1-B FOR REAR BUMPERS OF 1/4 TON & 3/4 TON VEHICLES ONLY. THE FOLLOWING ARE SAMPLE BUMPERS OF EACH UNIT, SHOWING MAKE UP AND POSITION OF STENCILS. *FOLLOW THESE EXAMPLES PRECISELY WHEN STENCILING*

DIVISION HEADQUARTERS & SIGNAL CO

| 35-X | HQ-1 |
| 35-X | S-4 |

SET # 1-A ON ALL FRONT BUMPERS

35-X LEFT
HQ-1 RIGHT
1/4 & 3/4 T. REAR SET # 1-B

35-X | S-4
2 1/2 T. REAR SET # 1-A

INFANTRY REGIMENTS

35-134-I	HQ-2
35-137-I	A-12
35-320-I	B-10

SET #1-A ON ALL FRONT BUMPERS

35 134-I LEFT
HQ-2 RIGHT
1/4 & 3/4 T. REAR SET # 1-B

LEFT RIGHT
35 137-I | A-12
2 1/2 T. REAR SET # 1-A

FIELD ARTILLERY BATTALIONS

35-127 F	HQ-4
35-161 F	A-16
35-216 F	B-8
35-219 F	C-13

SET # 1-A ON ALL FRONT BUMPERS

35 127 F LEFT
HQ-4 RIGHT
1/4 & 3/4 T. REAR SET # 1-B

LEFT RIGHT
35 161-F | A-16
2 1/2 T. REAR SET # 1-A

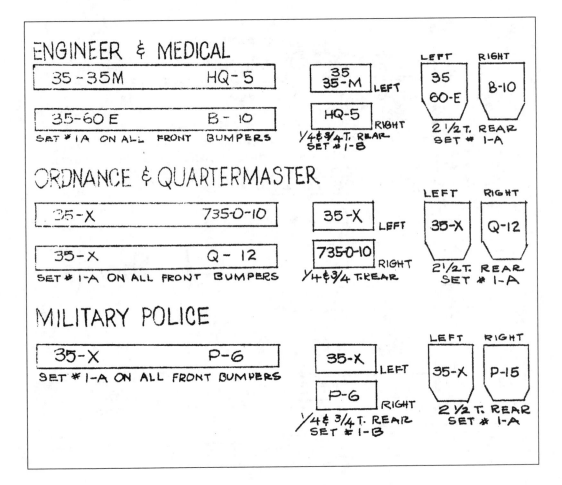

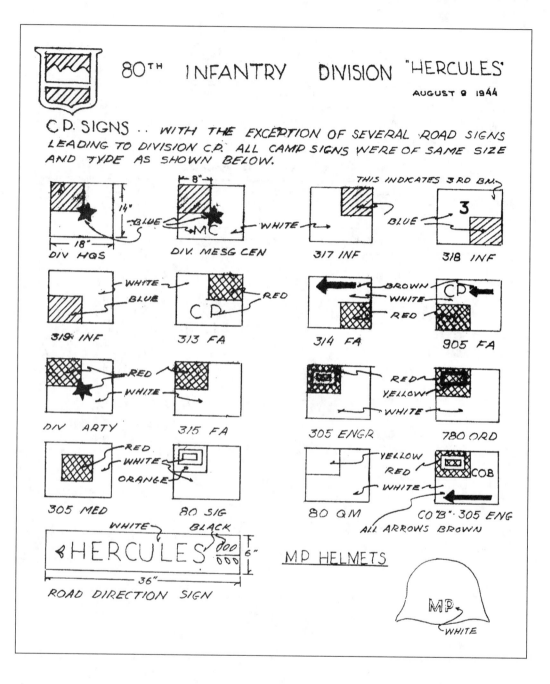

80TH INFANTRY DIVISION "HERCULES"

AUGUST 9 1944

C.P. SIGNS .. WITH THE EXCEPTION OF SEVERAL ROAD SIGNS LEADING TO DIVISION C.P. ALL CAMP SIGNS WERE OF SAME SIZE AND TYPE AS SHOWN BELOW.

DIV HQS
DIV. MESG CEN
317 INF
318 INF
319 INF
313 FA
314 FA
905 FA
DIV ARTY
315 FA
305 ENGR
780 ORD
305 MED
80 SIG
80 QM
CO "B" 305 ENG

ALL ARROWS BROWN

MP HELMETS

HERCULES

ROAD DIRECTION SIGN

315

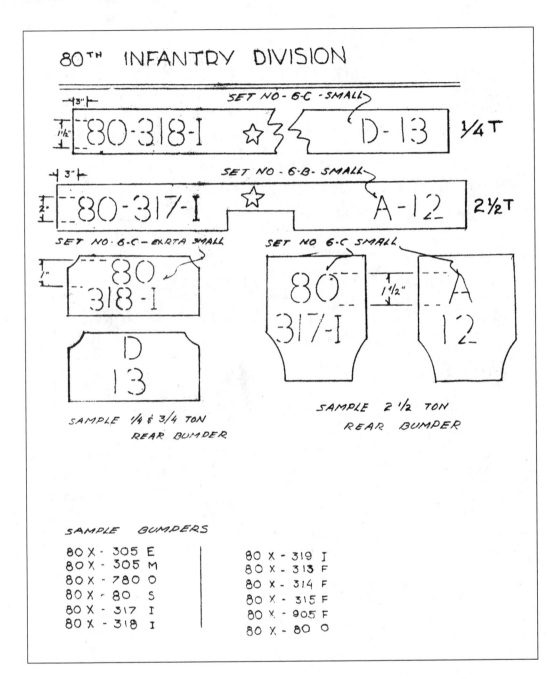

80ᵀᴴ INFANTRY DIVISION

SET NO - 6-C - SMALL

80-318-I ☆ D-13 ¼T

SET NO - 6-B- SMALL

80-317-I ☆ A-12 2½T

SET NO - 6-C - EXRTA SMALL

80 318-I

SET NO 6-C SMALL

80 317-I A 12

D 13

SAMPLE ¼ & ¾ TON REAR BUMDER

SAMPLE 2½ TON REAR BUMPER

SAMPLE BUMPERS

80 X - 305 E
80 X - 305 M
80 X - 780 O
80 X - 80 S
80 X - 317 I
80 X - 318 I

80 X - 319 I
80 X - 313 F
80 X - 314 F
80 X - 315 F
80 X - 905 F
80 X - 80 O

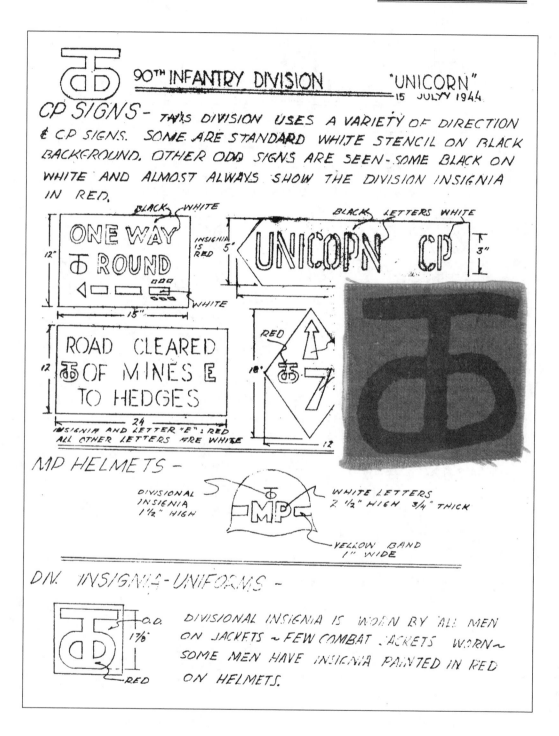

90ᵀᴴ INFANTRY DIVISION "UNICORN"
15 JULY 1944.

CP SIGNS – THIS DIVISION USES A VARIETY OF DIRECTION & C.P. SIGNS. SOME ARE STANDARD WHITE STENCIL ON BLACK BACKGROUND. OTHER ODD SIGNS ARE SEEN – SOME BLACK ON WHITE AND ALMOST ALWAYS SHOW THE DIVISION INSIGNIA IN RED.

BLACK — WHITE
ONE WAY
T5 ROUND
◄ ▭ □ □□□
12"
15"
WHITE

INSIGNIA IS RED
5"
BLACK LETTERS WHITE
UNICORN CP
3"

ROAD CLEARED
T5 OF MINES E
TO HEDGES
12"
24
INSIGNIA AND LETTER "E": RED
ALL OTHER LETTERS ARE WHITE

RED
↑
T5 7
18"
12

MP HELMETS –

DIVISIONAL
INSIGNIA
1½" HIGH

T5
MP

WHITE LETTERS
2½" HIGH ¾" THICK

YELLOW BAND
1" WIDE

DIV. INSIGNIA – UNIFORMS –

O.D.
1⅞"
RED

DIVISIONAL INSIGNIA IS WORN BY ALL MEN ON JACKETS ~ FEW COMBAT JACKETS WORN ~ SOME MEN HAVE INSIGNIA PAINTED IN RED ON HELMETS.

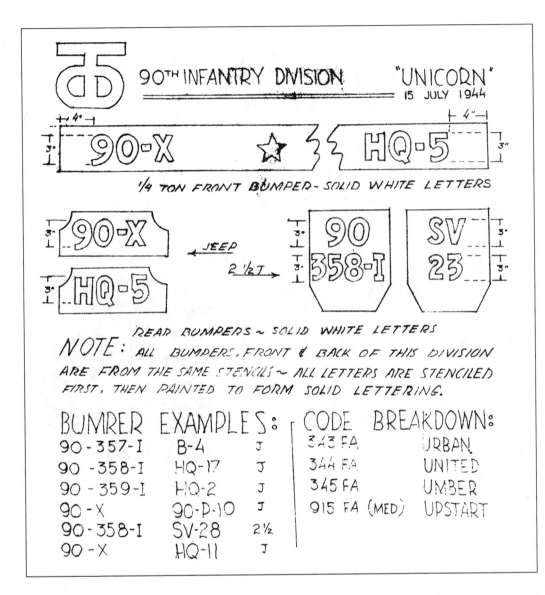

90TH INFANTRY DIVISION   "UNICORN"
15 JULY 1944

90-X   ☆   HQ-5

¼ TON FRONT BUMPER - SOLID WHITE LETTERS

90-X   JEEP   90   SV
HQ-5   2½T   358-I   23

REAR BUMPERS ~ SOLID WHITE LETTERS

NOTE: ALL BUMPERS, FRONT & BACK OF THIS DIVISION ARE FROM THE SAME STENCILS ~ ALL LETTERS ARE STENCILED FIRST, THEN PAINTED TO FORM SOLID LETTERING.

BUMPER EXAMPLES:				CODE BREAKDOWN:	
90 - 357 - I	B-4	J		343 FA	URBAN
90 - 358 - I	HQ-17	J		344 FA	UNITED
90 - 359 - I	HQ-2	J		345 FA	UMBER
90 - X	90-P-10	J		915 FA (MED)	UPSTART
90 - 358 - I	SV-28	2½			
90 - X	HQ-11	J			

Glossary

Military Units

HQ—Headquarters
Bn.—Battalion; an infantry battalion was about 850 men
Co.—Company; an infantry company was about 196 men
Regt.—Regiment; an infantry regiment was about 3,000 men
Div.—Division; an infantry division was about 14,000 men
Corps—Normally three or more divisions, plus support troops
Army—Two or more corps, plus support troops
Army Group—Two or more armies. In northern Europe the only American Army
   Group was Bradley's 12th. The British had the 21st Army Group under
   Montgomery.
CCA—Combat Command A—a main element of an armored division
CCB—Combat Command B— a main element of an armored division
CCR—Combat Command Reserve— a main element of an armored division
Group—A temporary collection of battalions, or other units, under one command
H&S Company—Headquarters and Support Company
Troop—The tank or cavalry equivalent to a company
Battery—The artillery equivalent to a company

Military Terms

T/O—Table of Organization
O/B—Order of Battle
FUSA—First U.S. Army
NCO—Non-Commissioned Officer
SOP—Standard Operating Procedure
EM—Enlisted men
FO—Field order
AES—Army Experimental Station
AFA—Armored Field Artillery; fully tracked self-propelled artillery pieces
BJ—Beach Jumpers; name of U.S. Navy deception units
BLARNEY—Code name of the 23rd Special Troops
CP—Command Post

CW—Carrier Wave, radio transmission sent my Morse code rather than spoken voice

ETO—European Theater of Operations

ETOUSA—Highest American headquarters in Europe, precursor to SHAEF

FDC—Fire Direction Center; the main control point for an artillery unit

FFI—French Forces of the Interior; Resistance fighters

Fist—The distinctive signature of a radio operator tapping out Morse code

Flash ranging—Locating enemy artillery batteries by observing their muzzle flashes

HEATER—Initial code name for the 3132nd Signal Company

MP—Military Police

Playfair—A cipher or code used by the Army

notional—A fictional appearance of a unit or position

SHAEF—Supreme Headquarters Allied Expeditionary Force

SLIDEX—A weak, but fast, cipher or code used by the army

SOI—Signal Operations Instructions; the standard operation procedure for a unit's communications

Sound ranging—locating enemy artillery batteries through the sound of their firing

Select Bibliography

Barkas, Geoffrey. *The Camouflage Story*. London: Cassell and Company, 1952.

Cruickshank, Charles. *Deception in World War II*. London: Oxford University Press, 1981.

Dailey, Brian. *Soviet Strategic Deception*. Lexington, MA: Lexington Books, 1987.

Dwyer, John. *Seaborne Deception: The History of U.S. Navy Beach Jumpers*. New York: Praeger Publishers, 1992.

Fairbanks Jr., Douglas. *A Hell of a War*. New York: St. Martins Press, 1993.

Fishel, Edwin. *The Secret War for the Union*. Boston: Houghton Mifflin, 1996.

Fisher, David. *The War Magician*. New York: Berkeley Books, 1983.

Fisher, Ernest J. *Cassino to the Alps*. Washington, DC: U.S. Army, 1977.

Gawne, Jonathan. *Battle for Brest*. Paris: Histoire et Collections, 2002.

Gawne, Jonathan. *Spearheading D-day*. Paris: Histoire et Collections, 1998.

Grennfield, Kent. *Command Decisions*. Washington, DC: U.S. Army, 1960.

Handel, Michael (ed.). *Strategic and Operational Deception in the Second World War*. London: Frank Cass, 1987.

Howard, Michael. *British Intelligence in the Second World War*, Vol 5: Strategic Deception. London: HMSO, 1990.

Johnson, David Alan. *Righteous Deception*. Westport, CT: Praeger Publishers, 2001.

Koch, Oscar. *G-2: Intelligence for Patton*. Atglen, PA: Schiffer Publishing, 1990.

Latimer, Jon. *Deception in War*. New York: Overlook Press, NY, 2001.

Mure, David. *Master of Deception*. London: William Kimber, 1980.

Railey, Hilton Howell. *Touch'd with Madness*. New York: Carrick & Evans, 1938.

Stanley, Roy. *To Fool a Glass Eye*. Washington, DC: Smithsonian Press, 1998.

Sweeney, Michael. *Secrets of Victory: the Office of Censorship and the American Press and Radio in World War II*. Chapel Hill: University of North Carolina Press, 2001.

Wilson, George. *If You Survive*. New York: Ivy Books, 1987.

Wolff, Perry. *Fortune Favored the Brave*. Mannheimer Grossdruckereie, Germany: 334th Infantry Regiment, 1945.

Zetterling, Niklas. *Normandy 1944*, Winnepeg: J. J. Fedorowicz Publishing, 2000.

Other Publications

Fox, Frederick, Unpublished Unit History, *Official History, 23rd Headquarters, Special Troops*. Located in Box 23270, RG 407, NARA.

Kronman, Mark, *The Deceptive Practices of the 23rd Headquarters, Special Troops During WW2*, Interim Note T-11, U.S. Army Material Systems Analysis Activity, Aberdeen, MD, 1978.

Tucker, Roy, *The Noisemakers*. Unpublished manuscript by 3133rd veteran.

Intelligence in the War of Independence. A monograph by the Central Intelligence Agency, Washington D.C., 1997.

U.S. Army Official Histories of WWII

Beck, Alfred M., *The Corps of Engineers: The War Against Germany*, Washington D.C., U.S. Army, 1988.

Blumenson, Martin, *Breakout and Pursuit*, Washington D.C., U.S. Army, 1984.

Cole, Hugh M., *The Ardennes: Battle of the Bulge*, Washington D.C., U.S. Army, 1965.

Cole, Hugh M., *The Lorraine Campaign*, Washington DC, U.S. Army, 1950.

Coll, Blanche D., *The Corps of Engineers: Troops and Equipment*, U.S. Army, Washington D.C., 1958.

McDonald, Charles B., *The Siegfried Line Campaign*, U.S. Army, Washington D.C., 1963.

Thompson, George R., *Signal Corps: the Outcome*, Washington D.C., U.S. Army, 1966.

Magazines and Journals

Eldridge, Justin L.C. "The Blarney Stone and the Rhine: 23rd Headquarters, Special Troops and the Rhine River Crossing, March 1945." *Intelligence and National Security* 7, no. 3 (Jul. 1992), p. 211-241.

Hundermark, Edwin, "Twelfth Army Group's Deception Team," *The Heralds Trumpet*, No. 19, Jan.-Feb. 1982.

Morgan, Roger, "The Man Who Almost Is," *After The Battle Magazine*, Issue #54, 1986.

Park, Edward, "A Phantom Division Played a Role in Germany's Defeat," *Smithsonian Magazine*, Apr. 1985, pp. 109–146.

Untitled period document on history of deception in SHAEF. p.3. Obtained from Cliff Simenson, who in turn obtained it from Ralph Ingersoll, who stated it was found in the SHAEF files in the National Archives. Handwritten note on the bottom indicating classification number 228.03. I was not able to locate the document in the Archives.

End Notes

Chapter 1

1. *Intelligence in the War of Independence*, Central Intelligence Agency Monograph.
2. Edwin C. Fishel, *Secret War for the Union*.
3. Michael Howard, *British Intelligence in the Second World War*, Vol. 5, p. 203.
4. David Mure, *Master of Deception*, p. 95. Also confirmed in Geoffrey Barakas, *The Camouflage Story*.
5. David Fisher, *The War Magician*. Sadly, this interesting book is a fictionalized account (see notes in book) and thus suspect as a source of information.
6. Howard, *British Intelligence*, p. 22.
7. Howard, *British Intelligence*, p. 37.
8. Charles Cruickshank, *Deception in World War II*, p. 222.
9. Cruickshank, *Deception in World War II*, p. 36.
10. Jonathan Gawne, *Spearheading D-day*, p. 221.
11. Very good reporting on this operation is found in *After The Battle Magazine*, which more recently has uncovered the identity of the corpse. Issue #54, 1986.
12. Howard, *British Intelligence*, p. 160.
13. Howard, *British Intelligence*, p. 163.
14. Cruickshank, *Deception in World War II*, p. 217.
15. Howard, *British Intelligence*, p. 218.
16. Howard, *British Intelligence*, p. 221.
17. Michael Handel, ed. Katherine Herbig, "American Strategic Deception in the Pacific," *Strategic and Operational Deception in the Second World War*, p. 274.
18. Handel, ed., Herbig, "American Strategic Deception in the Pacific," p. 287.
19. Mure, *Master of Deception*, p.142.
20. Howard, *British Intelligence*, p. 224.
21. David Johnson, *Righteous Deception*, p.10.
22. Roger Hesketh, *Operation Fortitude*.
23. Hesketh, *Operation Fortitude*.
24. Hesketh, *Operation Fortitude*, p. 38.
25. Johnson, *Righteous Deception*, p.19.
26. Johnson, *Righteous Deception*, p. 82.
27. Johnson, *Righteous Deception*, p. 212.
28. Records of the JSC, RG 218, Box 367, NARA.

Chapter 2

1. Cruickshank, *Deception in World War II*, p. 33.
2. John Campbell, "Operation Starkey 1943," *Strategic and Operational Deception in the Second World War*, ed. Michael Handel, p. 108.
3. Untitled period document on history of deception in SHAEF, p. 3. Obtained from Cliff Simenson, who had originally obtained it from Ralph Ingersoll, who stated it was found in the SHAEF files in the National Archives. A handwritten note on the bottom indicates classification number 228.03. I was not able to locate this document in the National Archives.
4. Untitled period document on history of deception in SHAEF, p. 3.
5. A great deal of information and interesting details on the 23rd are found in an unpublished and previously classified *Official History of the 23rd Headquarters, Special Troops*, written by Lt. Frederick Fox. Hereafter referred to as "Fox," a copy is located in Box 23270, RG 407, NARA. Lt. Fox was a natural writer and, as unit histories go, his is quite enjoyable to read.
6. Snee would later work on deception plans in Korea for the Eighth Army.
7. Organizational data on the 23rd is found in RG 407, Box 23270, NARA.
8. Interview with Simenson, Watertown, NY, 15 Sept 2000.
9. Telephone interview with Simenson, 12 July 2000.
10. Interview with Simenson, Watertown, NY, 15 Sept. 2000.
11. Telephone interview with Simenson, 12 July 2000.
12. Interview with Simenson, Watertown, NY, 15 Sept. 2000.
13. Blanche Coll, *The Corps of Engineers: Troops and Equipment*, p.85.
14. Desert Warfare Board Project No. 162-1 RG 337, Entry 40, Box 17, NARA.
15. Detailed information on the activities of the *406th Engineer Combat Company Special* are found in an unpublished unit history compiled during the war and kept by General Rebh. A few different men worked on it, but only one name, Rolff Campbell, is known. Much like the 23rd history, it is an amusing and enjoyable work. Hereafter referred to as "406th."
16. Interview with George Rebh, 22 January 2002.
17. SCR is sometimes erroneously referred to as "Signal Corps Radio." According to the official WWII list of Signal Corps abbreviations it actually means "Set, Complete, Radio," as every sub-component such as the transmitter, receiver, headphones, antenna, etc. had its own separate designation.
18. Letter from Simenson, 15 August 2001. Fox later went on to become a Congressional Minister in Ohio.
19. By coincidence Col. Railey, commander of the Army Experimental Station, also had his son transferred under his command.
20. Telephone interview with West Point classmate Bob Dwan, 12 December 2001.

Chapter 3

1. Mure, *Master of Deception*, p.82.
2. At this time it was technically known as the 1st U.S. Army Group, however that title was shifted to Patton's notional Army Group at the time of the invasion of France, and Bradley's army then took on the title of 12th Army Group.

3. Billy Harris was another up and coming officer. Graduating 20th in his class, he went on to command a number of units, including the 7th Cavalry in the Korean War in which he earned a number of medals, including the Distinguished Service Cross.
4. Mure, p. 65.
5. Mure, p. 120.
6. Orange was the branch color of the Signal Corps.
7. Proposed reorganization records are located in Box 23272, RG 407, NARA.
8. Records of the Thetford maneuvers are located in Box 23271, RG 407, NARA.
9. Records of Operation TROUTFLY are found in Box 23271, RG 407, NARA.

Chapter 4

1. The best records of this mission are found in the 406th history.
2. 406th, p. 47.
3. Records of Operation ELEPHANT are located in Box 23270, RG 407, NARA.
4. Letter from Cliff Simenson, 15 Aug. 2001.
5. Telephone interview with Gil Seltzer, 9 Dec. 2001.
6. Intelligence memo, Captain Joseph Kelly, Operation ELEPHANT, Box 23270, RG 407, NARA.
7. 406th, p. 51 (the men were Pvts. Ehiffen, Reuss, Ethier, and Rudes).
8. 406th, p. 57.
9. These cover the 2nd Armored Division, 35th, 80th, and 90th Infantry Divisions. Some of the 94th Division poop sheets have also been found in the files on Operation LOCHNIVAR.
10. Telephone interview with Cliff Simenson, 18 Dec. 2001
11. Memo from Col. Reeder dated 11 July 1944, Box 23270, RG 407, NARA.
12. Telephone interview with Gil Seltzer, 9 Dec. 2001.

Chapter 5

1. Michael Howard, *British Intelligence in the Second World War, Vol 5. Strategic Deception*, p. 38.
2. NRDB report # 4094, Office of Scientific Research and Development, N.R.D.C. RG 111-ET-319.1 Box 1073, NARA.
3. See Douglas Fairbanks's autobiography of his military career, *A Hell of a War*.
4. For an excellent history of the navy's deception units see *Seaborne Deception*, by John Dwyer.
5. Dwyer, *Seaborne Deception*, p. 16
6. No records of this facility were located. There is some evidence that these files were transferred to the CIA, which seems to have taken a great deal of interest in deception after WW II.
7. *Touch'd with Madness* is Railey's autobiography prior to WW2. He had planned a book dealing with the AES, called Top Secret, but it was never completed, and his family knows of no manuscript or notes.
8. Interview with Daniel Rippeteau, Watertown, NY, 15 Sept. 2000.
9. Memo on security from H. H. Railey, 14 March 1945. RG 111-OP-475, NARA.

10. Dwyer, *Seaborne Deception*, p. 16.
11. Memo on demolitions material, 18 May 1944, Box 2975, RG 111-OP-353.
12. Interview with Dick Syracuse, Watertown, NY, 15 Sept. 2000.
13. Memo, Major John M. Raleigh to Army Ground Forces. 15 Aug. 1944, RG 407, Box 23270, NARA.
14. Memo, Col. Railey to Chief Signal Officer, 11 July 1944, RG 111, Box 2975, NARA.

Chapter 6

1. Jonathan Gawne, *Battle for Brest*, p. 6.
2. Intelligence estimate, 8 Aug. 1944, Box 23270, RG 407, NARA.
3. Records of Operation BRITTANY are found in RG 407, Box 23270, NARA.
4. Johnson, *Righteous Deception*, p.203.
5. 406th, p. 79.
6. 406th, p. 87. (Cogan would be awarded the first Certificate of Merit in the 23rd for this action.)
7. 406th, p. 69. (The men were Pvts. Greenberg, Stopper and Wilson.)
8. S-2 Report and comments - Operation in Brittany, RG 407, Box 23270, NARA.
9. Report on Operation BRITTANY, H. L. Reeder. 5 Sept. 1944. RG 407, Box 23270, NARA.
10. Martin Blumenson, *Breakout and Pursuit*, p. 516.
11. 406th, p. 88.
12. Microfilm rolls, T-311-1 and T-311-2, NARA.
13. Martin Blumenson, "General Bradley's Decision at Argentan," in Kent Grennfield's, *Command Decisions*, p. 401.
14. Blumenson, "General Bradaley's" p. 407.
15. Omar Bradley, *A Soldier's Story*, p. 377.
16. These are the official U.S. Army estimates. For an interesting discussion of German casualties in Normandy, see Niklas Zetterling's *Normandy 1944*.

Chapter 7

1. Gawne, *Battle for Brest*, p. 6.
2. Records of Operation BREST are located in Box 23270, RG 407, NARA.
3. 406th, p. 93. Also verbally related by George Rebh.
4. Memo to 2nd Inf. Div. chief of staff, 24 Aug. 1944, Box 23270, RG 407, NARA.
5. Ibid.
6. 406th, p. 93.
7. Signal report on BREST operation, Box 23270, RG 407, NARA.
8. Report on Task Force Y, Col. John Mayo, 29 Aug. 1944, Box 23270, RG 407, NARA.
9. Report on deception operation at Brest, Col. Cyrus Searcy, VIII Corps, Box 23270, RG 407, NARA.
10. Ibid.
11. Ibid.
12. 406th, p. 106.

Chapter 8

1. Records for Operations TROYES and DIJON are located in Box 23270, RG 407, NARA.
2. Memo, Lt. Col. Simenson, 5 Aug. 1944, Box 23270, RG 407, NARA.
3. Records on Operation BETTEMBOURG are located in Box 23270, RG 407, NARA.
4. 15th Tank Bn., 9th Armored Infantry Bn., and 128th Armored Field Artillery Bn.
5. 68th Tank Bn., 50th Armored Infantry Bn., and 231st Armored Field Artillery Bn.
6. Signal Report on Operation BETTEMBOURG, 12 Oct. 1944, p. 2, Box 23270, RG 407, NARA.
7. Report of CCR, Operation BETTEMBOURG, Captain Oscar Seale, Box 23270, RG 407, NARA.
8. Interview with Cliff Simenson, 15 Sept. 2000, Watertown, NY.

Chapter 9

1. Files for Operation WILTZ are located in Box 23270, RG 407, NARA.
2. Consisting of 23rd HQ&HQ Co., 603rdEng.(-), 23rd Sig. Co. (-), 3132nd Sig.(-), 406th Eng.(-)
3. CCA Consisting of A/603rd Eng., D/603rd Eng.(-), 2nd plat C/406th Eng., 1st platoon plus ½ 3rd platoon 3132nd Sig., Det. 23rd Sig. Co. which was to portray the HQ CCA, 34th Tank Bn., 46th A.I. Bn., A/75th Med. Bn., A/127th Ord. Bn., A/22nd Arm. Eng. Bn.
4. Consisting of C/603rd Eng., 3rd and 4th plat D/603rd Eng., 3rd plat C/406th Eng, 2nd plat plus ½ 3rd platoon 3132nd, Det. 23rd Sig. Co. which was to portray HQ CCB, 81st Tank Bn., 15th A.I. Bn., B/75th Med. Bn., B/127th Ord. Bn., B/22nd Arm. Eng. Bn.
5. 406th, p. 138.
6. 406th, p. 140.
7. Report on Operation WILTZ, Lt. Col. Schroeder, 11 Oct 1944, Box 23270, RG 407, NARA.

Chapter 10

1. Files on these artillery operations are located in Box 23271, RG 407, NARA.
2. Report on artillery simulator mission, Captain Comulada, p. 3, Box 23271, RG 407, NARA.
3. Files on Operation VASELINE are found in BOX 23271, RG 407, NARA.
4. Operation VASELINE report, RG 407, Box 23271, NARA.
5. Files on these propaganda missions are located in Box 23271, RG407, NARA.
6. Operation VASELINE report, Box 23271, RG 407, NARA.
7. Report on propaganda missions, 28 Nov. 1944, Box 23271, RG 407, NARA.
8. Telephone interview with Gilbert Seltzer, 9 Dec. 2001.

End Notes to Chapter 11

Chapter 11

1. Records of Operation DALLAS are found in Box 23270, RG 407, NARA.
2. Report on Operation DALLAS, Lt. Col. Mayo, 11 Nov. 1944, Box 23270, RG 407, NARA.
3. Report on Operation DALLAS, Captain Sidwell, Box 23270, RG 407, NARA.

Chapter 12

1. Records of Operation ELSENBORN are found in Box 23270, RG 407, NARA.
2.. Operation ELSENBORN, Signals enclosure No.2, Box 23270, RG 407, NARA.
3. Ibid.
4. Signal Officer report of Operation ELSENBORN, 16 Nov. 1944, Box 23270, RG 407, NARA.
5. George Wilson, *If You Survive*, p. 131.
6. Fox, p. 19.
7. Fox, p. 131.
8. 406th, p. 147.

Chapter 13

1. Records of Operation CASANOVA are located in Box 23270, RG 407, NARA.
2. A description of this combat appears in Cole, Lorraine Campaign, p. 376.
3. 12th Army Group G-2 Periodic Report No. 158, 10 Nov. 1944, referenced in Report on Operation Casanova, Box 23270, RG 407, NARA.
4. 406th, p. 156.
5. 406th, p. 154.
6. Memo from Captain George Rebh, 406th Eng. C. Co., CASANOVA File, Box 23270, RG 407, NARA.
7. Attachment to Captain Rebh memo, 406th Eng C. Co., CASANOVA File, Box 23270, RG 407, NARA.
8. Ibid.

Chapter 14

1. Records of Operation KOBLENZ and TRIER are located in Box 23271, RG 407, NARA.
2. Operation KOBLENZ Counterintelligence Plan, VIII Corps, Box 23271, RG407, NARA.
3. Operation KOBLENZ, Special Effects Plan, Box 23271, RG 407, NARA.
4. History of 75th Division. Operation KOBLENZ files, Box 23271, RG407, NARA.
5. Enclosure #5, Radio plan for KOBLENZ, Box 23271, RG407, NARA.
6. Combat Team 289 commanded by Lt. Col. Truly and composed of the notional 289th Inf. Regt., 897th FA Bn., and A/275th Eng. C. Bn.
7. Combat Team 290 commanded by Lt. Col. Schroeder and composed of the notional 290th Inf. Regt., 898th FA Bn., and B/275th Eng. C. Bn. in the Altinster-Eschweiler area.

8. Combat Team 291 commanded by Captain Seale and composed of the notional 291st Inf. Regt., 899th FA Bn., and C/275th Eng. C. Bn. in the vicinity of Blaschette.
9. Commanded by Col. Reeder and simulating the 75th Division HQ.
10. 406th, p. 168, also interview with George Rebh, 22 January 2002.
11. Fox, p. 22.
12. After-action report, Operation KOBLENZ, Box 23271, RG 407, NARA.
13. 406th, p. 172.
14. Hugh Cole, *The Ardennes: Battle of the Bulge*, p. 73.
15. Cole, *Battle of the Bulge*, p. 71.
16. Memo, planning phase for Operation KOBLENZ, Box 23271, RG 407, NARA.
17. Fox, Annex, Historical Chronology 23rd Special Troops, Box 23270, RG 407, NARA.
18. Fox, p. 22.
19. Interview with Dick Syracuse, 15 Sept. 2000, Watertown, NY.

Chapter 15

1. Cole, *Battle of the Bulge*, p. 510.
2. Records of Operation KODAK are located in Box 23271, RG 407, NARA.
3. Enclosure 3, Operation KODAK, Box 23271, RG 407, NARA.
4. Cole, *Battle of the Bulge*, p. 512.
5. Cole, *Battle of the Bulge*, p. 510.
6. 406th, p. 23.
7. Ibid.

Chapter 16

1. Records of Operation METZ-I are located in Box 23271, RG 407, NARA.
2. Most of this information on the 3103rd comes from correspondence with 3103rd veteran Paul Sarber, November–December 2001.
3. Jon Latimer, *Deception in War*, 225.
4. Report of Operation METZ-I, Captain Seale, p. 1, Box 23271, RG 407, NARA.

Chapter 17

1. Records of METZ-II are located in Box 23271, RG 407, NARA.
2. 257 Infantry Regiment, 343rd FA Battalion, A/315th Medical Battalion.
3. 358th Inf. Regt., 344th FA Bn., B/315th Medical Bn.
4. 359th Inf. Regt., 915th FA Bn., and C/315th Medical Bn.
5. Report on Operation METZ-II, Box 23271, RG407, NARA.

Chapter 18

1. Records of Operation L'EGLISE are located in Box 23271, RG 407, NARA.
2. (A/603rd, 1st Platoon 3132nd, and 2nd Platoon 406th - portraying 10th Arm. Inf. Bn., 35th Tank Bn., 66th Arm. Arty. Bn., D/24th Recon, A/24th Arm. Eng. Bn.,

A/704th TD Bn., B/ 489th AAA Bn., A/46th Arm. Med. Bn., A/126th Arm. Ord. Bn.

3. B/603rd, 2nd Platoon 3132nd, 3rd Platoon 406th Eng. portraying 53rd AI Bn., 37th Tank Bn., 22nd Arm. Arty. Bn., C/25th Recon, B/24th Arm. Eng. Bn., B/704 TD Bn., A/ 489th AAA Bn., B/46th Arm. Med. Bn., B/ 126th Arm. Ord. Bn.

4. C/603rd, 3132nd less two platoons, 406th Eng. Co. less three platoons portraying 25th Cavalry Recon. less two platoons, C/704th TD Bn., 51st AI Bn., 8th Tank Bn., 94th Arm. Arty., 489th AAA Bn., 24th Arm. Eng. less two companies.

5. Telephone interview with Gilbert Seltzer, 9 Dec. 2001.

Chapter 19

1. Records of Operation FLAXWEILER are located in Box 23270, RG 407, NARA.
2. Operational Directive, Task Force Reed, 17 January 1945, Operation FLAXWEILER file, Box 23270, RG 407, NARA
3. Charles McDonald, *The Last Offensive*, p. 49.
4. 406th, p. 194.

Chapter 20

1. Records of Operation STEINSEL are found in Box 23271, RG 407, NARA.
2. Fox, p. 25.

Chapter 21

1. Records of Operation LANDONVILLERS are located in Box 23271, RG407, NARA.
2. CT 377 was composed of 377th Infantry Regiment, 920th FA Battalion, A/320th Engineer Battalion, A/20th Medical Battalion.
3. CT 378 was composed of 378th Infantry Regiment, 358 FA Battalion, B/320th Engineer Battalion, and B/320th Medical Battalion.
4. CT 379 was composed of the 379th Infantry Regiment, 335th FA Battalion, C/320th Engineer Battalion, and C/320th Medical Battalion.
5. Report on Operations Involving Special Troops, LANDONVILLERS, p. 2, Box 23271, RG 407, NARA.

Chapter 22

1. Records of Operation WHIPSAW are located in Box 23272, RG 407, NARA.
2. After Action Report, Operation WHIPSAW, p. 3, Box 23272, RG 407, NARA.

Chapter 23

1. Records of Operation MERZIG are located in Box 23271, RG 407, NARA.
2. Extracts, S-2 periodic reports, HQ 3rd Cavalry Group, Box 23271, RG 407, NARA.
3. Extracts, S-2 periodic reports, HQ 3rd Cavalry Group, Box 23271, RG 407, NARA.
4. Operation MERZIG, after-action report, Lt. Col. Schroeder, Box 23271, RG 407, NARA.

5. McDonald, *The Last Offensive*, p. 155.
6. SOP for Units of 23rd Headquarters Special Troops, 1 Feb. 1945, Box 23270, RG 407, NARA.

Chapter 24

1. Records of Operation LOCHNIVAR are located in Box 23271, RG 407, NARA.
2. McDonald, *The Last Offensive*, p. 242.
3. Fox, *Official History of the 23rd*, p.28.
4. Report on Operation Involving Special Troops: BOUZONVILLE, p. 2, Box 23270, RG 407, NARA.
5. Reorganization Plan, 4 Feb. 1945, Box 23273, RG 407, NARA.
6. Interview with Cliff Simenson, 15 Sept. 2000,Watertown, NY, and via telephone December 2001
7. Telephone interview with Simenson, Dec. 15, 2001.

Chapter 25

1. Records of Operation BOUZONVILLE are located in Box 23270, RG 407, NARA.
2. Most of the men were from the 603rd. Along with Sgt. Peddle, three of the wounded men were from the 23rd Signal Company.

Chapter 26

1. Report of Operation EXPLOIT, Ninth US Army, p. 1, Box 23272, RG 407, NARA.
2. Estimate of Enemy Intelligence Capabilities, Operational Memorandum No. 4, Box 23272, RG 407, NARA.
3. Estimate of Enemy Intelligence Capabilities, Operational Memorandum No. 4, p. 2, Box 23272, RG 407, NARA.
4. Cover plan, Operation FLASHPOINT. p. 2, Box 23272, RG 407, NARA.
5. Meritorious Unit Plaque Citation, File ENBN 604, RG 407, NARA.
6. The 334th Infantry Regiment unit history, *Fortune Favors the Brave*, does not mention this mission at all. It indicates the regiment was involved in garrison duties in Homberg and along the Rhine River, p. 101.
7. Interview with George Rebh, 22 January 2002.
8. Report of Operation VIERSEN - 30th Inf. Div. Phase, p. 2, Box 23272, RG 407, NARA.
9. Extracts from Para 3a, Situation Report, 19th AAA Group, Operation VIERSEN file, Box 23272, RG 407, NARA.
10. XIII Corps Artillery, Periodic Report, 25 March 1945, Operation VIERSEN file, Box 23272, RG 407, NARA.
11. MacDonald, *The Last Offensive*, p. 307.
12. Summary of Enemy Activity XIII Corps Sector, 5 April 1945, Box 23272, RG 407, NARA.
13. Summary of Enemy Activity XIII Corps Sector, 5 April 1945, p. 2, Box 23272, RG 407, NARA.
14. Report of Operation VIERSEN, p. 1, Box 23272, RG 407, NARA.

15. Annex #1 to G-2 Periodic Report No. 282, 30th Infantry Division, p. 2, 26 March 1945, Box 23272, RG 407, NARA.
16. Annex #1 to G-2 Periodic Report No. 282, 30th Infantry Division, p. 2, 26 March 1945, Box 23272, RG 407, NARA.
17. Analysis of Enemy Reactions to Operation EXPLOIT, 1 April 1945, Box 23272, RG 407, NARA.
18. Letter of commendation - 29 March 1945 NINTH U.S. Army. Box 23272, RG 407, NARA.
19. Report of Operation VIERSEN, p. 2, Box 23272, RG 407, NARA.
20. The Blarney Stone and the Rhine: 23rd Headquarters, Special Troops and the Rhine River Crossing, March 1945. Justin L.C. Eldridge, Intelligence and National Security, Vol. 7. No 3, 1992, p. 211-241.
21. Justin Eldridge, "The Blarney Stone and the Rhine," p. 222.
22. Eldridge, p. 233.

Chapter 27

1. Operation reports of the 3133rd are not in the RG 407 unit records in the National Archives. The best record of the 3133rd in WWII is from an unpublished manuscript by 3133rd veteran Col. Roy Tucker entitled *The Noisemakers*.
2. By coincidence both sonic units were commanded by a Major Williams (Mike–3132rd and John–3133rd).
3. Signal Corps unit survey branch report on 3133rd Box 480, file US 333.1, RG 111, NARA.
4. Capabilities and recommended changes of 3132nd Service Company, Special, Box 2975, RG 111-OP-353, NARA.
5. Vehicles for 3133rd Signal Service Company, 21 July 1944, Box 2975, RG 111-OP-353, NARA.
6. Box 2975, RG 111-OP-353, NARA.
7. Letter Col. Hilton Railey to Gen. J.V. Matejka, 16 August 1944, Box 2975, RG 111-OP-353, NARA.
8. Outgoing classified message—number WAR 51919, Classified Central Decimal files, Box 2975, RG 111-OP-353. NARA.
9. Incoming classified message—number E 59818, Classified Central Decimal files, Box 2975, RG 111-OP-353, NARA.
10. Report of inspection trip by Gen. Ben Lear, 30 Nov. 1944, Box 2975, RG 111-OP-353, NARA.
11. Roy Tucker, *The Noisemakers*, addendum p. 2. As quoted from *Fragment of Victory (92nd Infantry Division History)*, p. 187.
12. AES Letter of Appreciation, Box 2975, RG 111-OP-353, NARA.

Chapter 28

1. Camps supervised by the 23rd were at Idar-Oberstein, Wittlich, Baumholder, Lebach, Saarbrucken, Homburg, Zweibruken, Pirmasens, Gonsonheim, Neiderburg, Augusta, Daaden, three at Trier and two at Kaiserslautern.
2. 406th, p. 230.

3. Interview with George Rebh, 22 January 2002.
4. 406th, p. 239.
5. Fox, p. 33.
6. Story told at the 23rd Reunion, Watertown, NY, Sept. 2000.
7. Letter from Simenson, 14 Jan. 2002.
8. 406th, p. 203.
9. Ramcke actually did not use the aristocratic "Von." He had come from a typical farming family, and earned his commission on the battlefield during WWI.
10. *Ernst Enquirer*, 30 June 1945, reprinted from Fox, p. 34.
11. AES Report,12 July 1945, Box 2976, RG 111-OP-353, NARA.
12. 406th, p. 251.
13. 406th, p. 251.
14. Letter from Major George Melvin to Pfc. Robert Bloom, 11 Sept. 1945. Author's collection.

Chapter 29

1. Brian Dailey, *Soviet Strategic Deception*, p 10.
2. Intelligence Bulletin. Vol. III, NO. 4, December 1944, p. 75.
3. Dailey, *Soviet Strategic Deception*, p. 278.
4. David Glanz, "The Red Mask," *Strategic and Operational Deception in the Second World War*, ed. Michael Handel, p. 188
5. Dailey, *Soviet Strategic Deception*, p. 43.
6. Dailey, *Soviet Strategic Deception*, p. 47.
7. Dailey, *Soviet Strategic Deception*, p. 44.

Appendix 1

1. TM 20-205, *Dictionary of U.S. Military Terms.* 18 January 1944.
2. U.S. Army Unit Citation and Campaign Participation Credit Register, July 1961, p. 70.

Appendix 4

1. Mure, *Master of Deception*, p. 214.
2. Michael Sweeney, *Secrets of Victory: The Office of Censorship and the American Press and Radio in World War II*, p. 155.
3. Sweeney, *Secrets of Victory*, p. 155.
4. Sweeney, *Secrets of Victory*, p. 158.
5. Sweeney, *Secrets of Victory*, p. 158.
6. Oscar Koch, *G2: Intelligence for Patton*, p. 156.
7. Winston Ramsey, "Incident at Knutsford," *After the Battle Magazine*, p. 51.
8. Latimer, *Deception in War*, p. 229.
9. Koch, *G2*.
10. Johnson, *Righteous Deception*, p. 9
11. Johnson, *Righteous Deception*, p. 10.

Index